Recent immigrant Christians from India are changing the face of American Christianity. They introduce ancient Catholic Oriental rites, St. Thomas orthodoxy, the fruits of modern Protestant missions, and the outpouring of Pentecostal revivals. This book is the first comprehensive study of these Christians, their churches, and their adaptation.

Professor Williams describes migration patterns since 1965 and the growth of Indian Christian churches in the United States. The role of Christian nurses in creating immigration opportunities for their families affects gender relations, transition of generations, interpretations of migration, Indian Christian family values, and types of leadership.

Contemporary mobility and rapid communication create new transnational religious groups. Williams reveals some of the reverse effects on churches and institutions in India. He notes some successes and failures of mediating institutions in the United States – seminaries, denominational judicatories, ecumenical agencies, and interfaith organizations – in responding to new forms of Christianity brought by immigrants.

CAMBRIDGE STUDIES IN RELIGIOUS TRADITIONS

CHRISTIAN PLURALISM IN THE UNITED STATES

CAMBRIDGE STUDIES IN RELIGIOUS TRADITIONS

Edited by John Clayton (University of Lancaster), Steven Collins (University of Chicago), and Nicholas de Lange (University of Cambridge)

CHRISTIAN PLURALISM IN THE UNITED STATES

The Indian Immigrant Experience

RAYMOND BRADY WILLIAMS

LaFollette Distinguished Professor in the Humanities and Professor of Religion,
Wabash College, Crawfordville, Indiana

CAMBRIDGE
UNIVERSITY PRESS

Published by the Press Syndicate of the University of Cambridge
The Pitt Building, Trumpington Street, Cambridge CB2 1RP
40 West 20th Street, New York, NY 10011–4211, USA
10 Stamford Road, Oakleigh, Melbourne 3166, Australia

First published 1996

Printed in Great Britain at the University Press, Cambridge

A catalogue record for this book is available from the British Library

Library of Congress cataloguing in publication data
Williams, Raymond Brady.
Christian pluralism in the United States: the Indian immigrant experience /
by Raymond Brady Williams.
p.   cm. – (Cambridge studies in religious traditions: 9)
Includes bibliographical references and index.
ISBN 0 521 57016 6 (hardback)
1. East Indians – United States – Religion.   2. United States –
Church history – 20th century.   3. India – Emigration and
immigration – Religious aspects – Christianity.   4. United States –
Emigration and immigration – Religious aspects – Christianity.
I. Title.   II. Series.
BR563.E27W55   1996
277.3′082′089914–dc20   95-51450   CIP

ISBN 0 521 57016 6 hardback

Contents

Maps

Preface

America is the land of immigrants. The point is often made by new immigrants, and any college group of a dozen students can create from their family stories most of the history of immigration to America. My family once claimed Welsh ancestry, Williams being a good Welsh name, only to learn a few years ago that a German ancestor changed his name from Wilhelm. That discovery changed our whole personality, we say in jest. Our experience illustrates a contemporary interest in family histories, and the humor shows that we do not understand very clearly how we have been affected by our pasts. That we as individuals and as a nation have been greatly affected in ways of which we are not conscious is difficult to deny. Perhaps the renewed interest in genealogy and ethnicity arises in part from a renewing of the immigration stories of new immigrants. The stories look back, but they are also attempts to reveal who we are, how we situate ourselves, and what we shall become.

Stories of Christian immigrants from India arriving in the United States since 1965 are the focus of this book. They are often overlooked among adherents of several Indian religions both because they are fewer in number and because they appear less exotic than Hindus, Muslims, Sikhs, or Jains. They also take their place beside other new immigrant Christians – Korean Presbyterians, Vietnamese Catholics, Aladura Independent African Christians, and those from other churches and nations – in the work of reshaping American Christianity. Here the attempt is made to preserve the early history of the arrival and adaptation of Asian-Indian Christianity and to encourage reflection on their experience and the role of religion in migration.

Earlier research in India with Swaminarayan Hindus introduced me for the first time to Gujarati immigrants in the United States (Williams, 1984:193–200). "Do you know my cousin in Chicago," they would ask. The cousin brothers in the United States in turn directed my attention to other Hindu, Muslim, Jain, Sikh, and eventually to Christian, immigrants from India (Williams, 1988). Contacts with Christian immigrants established during that research led to participation in seven annual family conferences of Asian-Indian churches held in the United States during 1993–94. These conferences ranged in size from the few hundred Malankara Orthodox Christians gathering in Los Angeles in 1993 to the several thousand Malayalee Pentecostal Christians meeting in Chicago over the Fourth of July weekend in 1994. These annual conferences provided opportunities for conducting hundreds of interviews, eliciting 678 detailed questionnaire responses from participants, and observing both religious rituals and social interactions of thousands of participants. With the exception of one group, leaders cooperated, and the lay people were unfailingly gracious in offering assistance. They welcomed me to hundreds of homes, scores of congregations, worship services, and social gatherings across the country, and provided written materials and personal observations that provide the foundation of this work. A research trip to India in February–March 1994 afforded the opportunity to interview Christian bishops, pastors, and people, and to observe the work of churches, seminaries, and institutions, primarily in south India and Gujarat. Surveys of American seminaries and Bible colleges and questionnaires received from those students with family backgrounds in India provided additional information about people preparing for leadership in both India and the United States.

During previous research on Indian religious groups, I engaged in a modified participant–observer approach, observing ceremonies in temples, mosques, and homes and talking with leaders, participants, and families about their experiences, all the while preserving that sympathetic distance from ritual participation and affirmation that I thought appropriate to an academic researcher. I did not, for example, join in chants or songs, prostrate before gurus or priests, nor wave the arti lamp before images of deities. Undertaking this research on Christians, I thought it would be the same, but found out differently in Atlanta the first time a congregation asked me to offer the closing prayer. As an ordained member of the Christian Church (Disciples of Christ), I could not refuse and subsequently found myself participating in the Eucharist and occasionally delivering sermons in a variety of other congregations. I developed what anthropologists call an "observing participant" relationship with the Asian-Indian Christians. That stance affects my research in many ways, some of which I am unaware of, both in the access to people and materials and in subsequent observations. Three ways are obvious to me: (1) I am more critical at times in dealing with the

Christians than I would feel comfortable being as an outsider dealing with other religions; (2) I am more prescriptive than I normally would be bold enough to be, using at times the words "should" and "ought," especially in chapter 7; and (3) I include more explicit theological language from their comments and in analyses. Perhaps other evidences of observing participation will be more obvious to the reader than to the author.

A research leave in 1993–94 and support provided from Wabash College by its then-dean, Paul McKinney, and from the Louisville Institute for the Study of Protestantism and American Culture by its director, James W. Lewis, provided freedom from teaching and administrative duties for research and writing. Most of what I have learned comes from contacts with Asian-Indian Christians and their bishops, priests, and leaders, so profound gratitude goes to them for their assistance and Christian hospitality: *sine qua non*. That debt is to so many people that it is impossible to name them, but they will recognize their insights and comments in the text; I hope they will judge the results to be worth their efforts. The St. Ephram Ecumenical Research Institute in Kottayam, Kerala, was home during research in Kerala, and its director, the Revd. Dr. Jacob Thekeparambil, furnished important contacts and provided valuable information from his remarkable knowledge of Indian Christianity. Ms. Debbie Polly on the staff of Lilly Library at Wabash College expanded the library to research size and enhanced the research by her pleasant manner and efficient work in scouring many sources for reference materials. Mr. Christopher Runge was the student research assistant for this project and was especially helpful in recording field notes and results of surveys. Professor Charles Blaich assisted with analyses of the survey results.

My colleague, Professor William C. Placher, read early drafts of a few chapters. Mr. John John, a perceptive son of immigrants from India, and the Revd. Dr. Geevarghese Panicker, a leading figure among Keralite Christians, also read and commented on portions of this work. Mr. Christopher Coble, who was my research assistant during research on an earlier book on immigrants (1988), offered, from his now enlarged perspective as a student of American religious history, comments and questions that were enormously helpful. I am deeply grateful to them because their corrections saved me from errors of detail and interpretation, their comments provided additional insights, and their friendship enriches both research and life.

My first book published by Cambridge University Press is dedicated to my family, the second to colleagues in the religion department of Wabash College. It seems appropriate to dedicate this book to the church, specifically the First Christian Church of Crawfordsville, Indiana, which ministers to descendants of earlier immigrants from many lands and whose message of the essential unity of all Christians, forged from experience on the American frontier in the early nineteenth century, may serve us all well as we move toward new experiences and challenges as American Christians or Christian Americans.

Introduction

I want you to meet my neighbor, Mary Thomas. She is head nurse in the emergency room of our city hospital. She came to the United States in 1972 when the hospital was desperate to hire trained nurses, and then she went back to India four years later to marry her husband and brought him to join her in the United States. He now teaches computer science in the city junior college. They attend the St. Thomas Syrian Orthodox Church that meets in St. John's church hall. His brother, Father Matthew, recently came from Kerala to be priest for St. Thomas parish. Mary's children attend St. Xavier High School with my boys.

The composite introduction raises more questions than it answers because the presence of Christian immigrants from India confronts those living in the United States with new neighbors and new types of Christianity not previously a part of American Christianity or experience. Their presence exposes the ignorance most have of Indian history, and thus it requires some effort to make their acquaintance. Are many Christians in India? What is the Syrian Orthodox Church? How did it happen that Indian Christian churches are now established in the United States? Why don't they just join "our" churches; we are losing members and would welcome their participation? Do they know Arvin Patel, who runs the motel on Main Street? Are all the Christian women nurses? What's going to happen to their children; will they become Roman Catholics? Pentecostals?

Introductions are significant because they help lay groundwork for pleasant, effective, and harmonious relationships. They can also create false impressions, especially when they multiply into stereotypes. Not all Kanti Patels own motels; not all Gundar Singhs run taxi companies; not every Mary Thomas is a nurse; one is unlikely ever to meet a Muslim terrorist. Only careful, more complete introductions reveal the fuller complexity of groups of new neighbors. Even the individual neighbor discovers a clear identity in the context of associations with groups that develop in widening circles from the family to co-workers, religious group, acquaintances, and various kinds of social associations. Hence, any individual has to be situated in a nuanced set of associations before a neighbor can become acquainted; indeed, before the individual knows who he or she is. The set of associations is dynamic for new immigrants because migration initiates the formation and preservation of personal and group identities in new contexts.

It is no accident that in America becoming acquainted with new neighbors involves introduction to their religious affiliation, even though official government records are prohibited by law from including such information. Because most immigrant groups previously arriving in America have shaped their identities in their new homes by confessing a faith, by creating new religious groups, preserving boundaries based on religious affiliation, and negotiating both cultural and religious matters from relatively strong religious foundations, it follows that religious identity is an acceptable social marker in American society. Religious identification puts people in the correct pew, so to speak. "I am Catholic; she is Baptist; he is Jewish; I think they are Hindu." These are meaningful statements in the American context of freedom of religion and of voluntary association.

Mary Thomas is a St. Thomas Syrian Orthodox Christian from India, and, like everyone, is the product of social movements and forces that no individual controls. She and other Asian-Indian Christians in the United States are part of a massive movement from many countries made possible by dramatic changes in the United States Immigration Act of 1965. In the three decades from 1961 to 1991, some 17 million legal immigrants entered the United States – almost half a million coming directly from India – and the numbers exhibit a steady upward climb to almost 2 million immigrants in 1991 alone (INS, *Statistical Yearbook*, 1991: 27, 28, Tables 1 & 2). Even though Christians are a small minority both in India and among Indian immigrants, they are part of one of the significant migrations in modern times from east to west, from developing countries to the United States. Asian-Indian Christians are relatively anonymous among the representatives of the world's religions who are currently finding new homes in the United States. Spires and crosses on Asian-Indian Christian churches appear very much like those adorning other churches – unless one looks closely at the intricate decoration – but much different from the domes of mosques and temple towers that adorn the religious buildings of other recent immigrants from India. At the same time that these Christians are adjusting to American society, they are also forming new associations and engaging in negotiations with new immigrants of many faiths, some from Muslim mosques and Hindu temples down the street from where they grew up in India.

St. Thomas Christians from India join Christians arriving from many parts of the world with forms of Christianity burnished and winnowed by long residence in Asia, Africa, Eastern Europe, and the Caribbean. These immigrants precipitate changes in American Christianity as they develop transnational churches with manifestations in several countries where members and their families maintain associations at the same time as they negotiate new relationships with their American brothers and sisters in Christ. The new immigrants both reflect and create new dynamics in American Christianity and society that call into question dominant models of analysis. The two models of assimilation and pluralism seem inadequate to deal with the greater complexity of the new immigration. Analyses of the meaning of citizenship and ethnicity have not taken account of the transnational character of families and religious organizations. Denominationalism seems to be weakening in America at the same time as new immigrants are arriving who did not view themselves as members of denominations in the places of their birth. Hence, new immigration involves revision of the modes of analysis of American society and religion at the same time as it brings acquaintance with new faces and religious groups.

It is a startling realization that one could well teach about most of the living religions of the world by focusing on the religious institutions in any major American city. Students in Chicago, Houston, Atlanta, or other major cities could easily visit many types of religious institutions and talk with representatives of virtually all the world's religious communities. A walk through their hometowns would become a walk through the world's religions. That would not have been possible before 1965. Do you want to know about Nizari Ismaili Muslims, Swaminarayan Hindus, Punjabi Sikhs, Thai or Cambodian Buddhists, Caribbean Santaria, African Ogun devotees, Chinese Taoists, Iranian Zoroastrians or Indian Parsis? Become acquainted with your neighbors, observe the vitality of their home rituals and public celebrations, and explore the religious history they contribute to the American story. The same could be said about Vietnamese Catholics, Russian Orthodox Church members, Korean Presbyterians, African Aladura Praying Church members, Asian-Indian Baptists, and St. Thomas Christians. American society presents a moving kaleidoscope of living religions through which one can observe both the evolving shapes of American religion and the religious histories that all immigrants are contributing to the American story.

The goals of this study include providing a more complete introduction for Mary Thomas and other Christian immigrants from India by presenting clear and accurate information about the growth and development of the Asian-Indian Christian immigrant community and their religious institutions. These new neighbors provide a case study of contemporary experience of immigration with which one can compare and contrast earlier immigrants' experiences and those of contemporary immigrants carrying with them different religious traditions and commitments. Study of issues these Christians face in adjusting to American culture, the resources that sustain them in their adaptation, and the ways they respond to the issues reverberating in American religion can sharpen our perceptions of contemporary religious dynamics. Current changes in the transnational world in which immigrants move and in American society where they come to reside make it necessary to look at the effects the new immigrants are having on both American Christianity and Christianity in India.

Chapter 1 places the arrival of Christian immigrants from India in the context of the immigration history of the United States. The two mirror-image immigration initiatives of this century – that producing a lull in immigration starting in 1925 and that opening the doors in 1965 to those from previously excluded countries – together shape the major contours of twentieth-century religion in America. The Christians are situated in the larger migration from India to the United States, especially those from Kerala, who make up the majority of Asian-Indian Christians. The chapter attempts to answer the questions raised by the too-brief introduction of Mary Thomas. Who are they? When did they come? Where are they from? How did they get here? Why did they come? How are they doing now that they are in America? A statistical profile of the Asian-Indian Christians derived from questionnaires from 678 people attending annual Christian family conferences provides a profile against which one can compare the composite of Mary Thomas.

Asian-Indian Christians tell stories about the history of Christianity in India, to explain to their new neighbors, and to themselves, who they are. Chapter 2 provides an overview of these stories and relates them to the fuller narrative of that history prepared by historians. An array of collective memories, even though fragmentary, preserves in the United States a narrative of the long tenure and diversity of Christianity in

India. These stories are powerful agents in the formation and preservation of individual and group identities for immigrants. Three trajectories are traced through the main elements of the Christian story in India: (1) St. Thomas Syrian Christians: the first centuries; (2) the impact of Roman Catholic Christianity: sixteenth century to the present; and (3) the impact of Protestant missions: eighteenth century to the present. These constitute an adequate survey essential to understanding the Christian affiliations of immigrants from India. Analyses of linguistic, regional, and caste stratification supply material necessary to understanding the development and effects of early Protestant missions, evangelical churches, Pentecostal movements, and the ecumenical movement. The relation of the memory to the past is not so significant as the function it has in creating the present reality of immigrants as they sort themselves out and shape their relations to the larger society.

Chapters 3 and 4 focus on the adaptive strategies of Asian-Indian Christians and on the churches and institutions they are establishing in the United States. Transmission of religious tradition is always both a celebration and a quest because Christian immigrants from India constitute new communities in the United States, not identical to any found in India. Six trajectories or models of potential adaptive strategies are evident in both secular and religious organizations: individual, national, ecumenical, hierarchical, ethnic, and denominational. Variables in the process developing strategies of adaptation are: length of residence, population density, transition of generations, and majority/minority status. A survey of the development and current status of St. Thomas Christian groups – (1) the Syrian Orthodox Church, (2) the Knanaya Orthodox Diocese, (3) the Malankara Orthodox Syrian Church, and (4) the Mar Thoma Church – locates these Christians in their new contexts in America. Catholics from India are establishing themselves under three rites in the United States: Latin, Syro-Malabar, and Syro-Malankara. Each rite has priests assigned under American bishops through bilateral agreements with bishops in India; moreover, some Indian priests are permanent immigrants and serve as diocesan priests. Indian Catholic immigrants provide one perspective on dynamic changes in the American Catholic Church due both to modern migrations and to initiatives of Vatical II. An examination of the experience of Christians from several Protestant groups and their current status and programs illustrates the diversity of strategies of adaptation; these include: the Church of South India, Church of North India, Methodists, Brethren Assemblies (Plymouth Brethren), Pentecostals,

Church of the Brethren, Baptists, and language-based independent congregations. Chapters 3 and 4 provide information about all the types of Asian-Indian churches in the United States. Together they provide a road map for locating all these churches socially and religiously.

Chapter 5 presents three models or interpretive structures providing compelling symbols and images for relating to a present condition based on experiences of a past and the perceived potential of the future, compelling because Christian immigrants search for religious interpretations to help them to understand their experience. Movement of these immigrants is primarily social rather than geographical, so major issues involved in the formation and preservation of personal and group identity through the transmission of tradition are central to understanding their experience.

Major issues discussed in this chapter are:

(1) Transmission of tradition through rituals or words. Some trust that Christian traditions from India are best transmitted through participation in complex rituals and they try to instruct young people in the language, gestures, and meaning of rituals and to inspire them with their beauty and mystery. Others encourage study of texts and doctrines. The process of indigenization has an added dimension in America: what does it mean for Christianity to become more Indian in India and more American in the United States, especially for people caught in the middle? Styles of music in the churches are indicators of the strata of influences that shape the transmission of tradition.

(2) Gender differentiation. Christians form the only Asian-Indian community that comes to America on the shoulders of the women, which creates significant tensions in families and churches. Women have different economic and social status in America than they occupied in India. Each immigrant church is dealing with the issue of the role of women in the church. The reversal of gender roles in the immigration process may explain in part the tensions and politics in the congregations because the church is one of the few institutions in which males among recent immigrants are free, and have appropriate skills, to contest for leadership.

(3) Transition of generations and family. Virtually all Indian immigrants say the major contribution they can make in America is to demonstrate strong family ties and family values, yet it is precisely those that are most under attack by American culture. A result is strong tension between the two generations now making it in America. Immigrants fear they have made a Faustian bargain in which they gain the whole world

and lose their children. The major issues of debate and argument are: demands for traditional symbols of respect for parents; agony of children striving to live up to expectations of two cultures; desire of children to relate freely with their peers, even to dating; professional goals for the children; and different expectations regarding marriage arrangements and levels of endogamy. Part of the problem is that the parents are unaware of changes that have taken place in India over the past twenty-five years, so they carry a vision of the way the church and society was in India and try to replicate that situation in America, thereby being doubly removed from reality. A number of the resulting conflicts involve misunderstandings regarding friendship and family. Most of the first generation have primary social relations with family, so the role of the family is unrivaled. Because most social contacts are with members of the extended family, very few are with members of the majority society. Hence, much of what members of the first generation know about American families and lifestyles comes from distorted images presented in the public media. Their children grow up in a society that values friendship highly and they interact with friends in a way unfamiliar to the adults and have different insights into American families and lifestyles. Churches are loci of socialization for immigrants and their children and hence provide the forum for debate, conflict, compromise, and resolution of these issues.

(4) Leadership. Religious specialists are "intimate strangers" because they are separated to various degrees by dress, lifestyle, ethos, and ordination. Yet they are involved with the most intimate affairs of their people. Hence, they are able to be mediators between individuals, between the generations, between America and India, between the past and the future, even between earth and heaven. That mediation requires special skills and preparation, and bishops, pastors, and priests often feel they are ambushed in the middle inadequately prepared. Asian-Indian Christian churches struggle with different types of leadership and with diverse proposals about how to raise up new generations of leaders who will be effective in the United States.

Chapter 6 reflects on the differences between the experiences of recent immigrants and those of earlier generations and on the new transnational context in which migration occurs. Travel for European immigrants at the turn of the century was long and hard, so they rarely returned to their native land for visits. Communication was very slow and expensive, so a distinct separation occurred. One result is that subsequent studies focused attention on the immigrants and their effects on

America, with little attention paid to reverse effects immigrants had on Christianity and Judaism in Europe. Now travel and communication take only a few hours or just an instant, so bridges are maintained between the old country and the new, and studies of the reverse impact of immigrants on their native places are essential. The long-term impact of the brain-drain on parts of India and on its churches is yet to be noted. Much is made of the economic impact of hard currency, and, indeed, many areas of India now experience a building boom and some economic development from money transfers by non-resident Indians (NRIs). Beyond the secular economic impact, religious groups of all types are affecting religious developments in India. It creates an entirely different dynamic than the old foreign missionary model of effects of the West on Indian Christianity. It is part of the new globalization of religions that shapes the relations of expatriate Hindus, Muslims, Sikhs, and others with religion in India. A study of the relationships established between Indian Christians in America and their "mother churches" and institutions in India provides a case study of the reverse impact immigrants are having on financing religious institutions, in developing transnational families, on leadership transfer, in revising theology and practice, and on strategies of modernization.

The final chapter notes changes that mediating institutions in America are making or need to make to facilitate the entry of new Christian immigrants. American society is in the process of multiplying the social categories used to analyze, describe, and understand itself, analogous to adding new rooms onto a house. New ethnic groups, new religions, new nationalities, new forms of Christianity – all are building and thereby creating new networks (doorways) and boundaries (walls). Several groups are interacting with Asian-Indian Christians in creating rooms. Seminaries and theological schools have long welcomed and supported students from India, and many leading bishops and professors in India were students in the United States during the 1950s and early 1960s. Seminaries provided homes for pastors coming to serve the new Asian-Indian churches and training for some of the immigrants who entered the ministry after immigration in the 1970s and 1980s. A survey of all the seminaries and Bible colleges in the United States taken as part of this research reveals a current Asian-Indian student population of over 195 persons related to various Indian churches. Other ethnic groups, especially other Asian-American Christian groups, are positioning themselves beside the Asian Indians. Protestant denominations are just beginning to recognize new neighbors and to develop working relations with them. Ecumenical agencies and interfaith agencies have been heretofore more interested in dialogue with new immigrants from other religious traditions – Muslim, Hindu, Buddhist – but increasingly will have to take account of Christian immigrants from India who have experience living as minorities among Muslims and Hindus.

The conclusion traces elements of continuity and discontinuity with the experience of immigrants in the nineteenth and early twentieth centuries. The story of Asian-Indian Christian immigrants is an old tale with new twists. They adopt many of the same strategies of adaptation, assimilate easily in some areas but are blocked from full participation in others, experience disappointment when life in America does not meet high expectations, deal with tensions regarding how Americanized to become, agonize over the future of their children, and engage in conflicts regarding the authority of their clergy. Elements of a familiar story. However, a number of new twists are evident. As part of the brain-drain from developing countries to the United States, they constitute a different educational and professional population. They bring new strands of Christianity along with other Christians among the new ethnics resulting from changes in the 1965 immigration law. They bring many different faces of Christ to the United States to occupy spaces beside Sallman's *Head of Christ* on sanctuary walls.

The wish of the author is that those who read this book will be able to recognize the real Mary Thomas and other Asian-Indian Christians when they meet them and will quickly understand their backgrounds and experiences of immigration, thereby contributing to an ecumenical understanding of the church and to intercultural harmony.

CHAPTER I

Road to America

Go from your country and your kindred and your father's house to
the land I will show you.

Genesis 12:1

A pious mother kneels each morning during mass at St. Patrick's
Catholic Church in Bangalore to pray for her children scattered around
the world: a daughter working as an environmental scientist in
Indianapolis, an engineer son in California, a son in an accountancy
program in London, a physician son in Dublin, a daughter who is a computer specialist in Toronto, a son seeking admission to a graduate
program at Notre Dame in Indiana, and a daughter preparing for school
examinations that will determine her admission to an American university. The mother and many of her friends in Bangalore are part of
transnational families created by rapid emigration of highly skilled professionals from India to developed countries since the 1960s, a phenomenon that Elinor Kelly refers to as "transcontinental families" (Kelly,
1990). Each of her children struggles to make a place and a future – economic, social, and religious – in the adopted country. As matriarch she
binds the family together by her prayers and through regular telephone
conversations and visits. She plans to organize the family estates and
resources in India and move to North America to live with her children;
by then it is likely that no member of the family will still live in India.
Migration to America by this family and others like them was made possible by a dramatic change in immigration law, which reshaped this
woman's family and is changing the shape of American Christianity.

Although its significance is only now becoming evident, the United
States Immigration and Nationality Act of 1965 is the most important
law enacted by Congress in the last half of the twentieth century, pre-
cipitating fundamental cultural and religious changes in the United
States. New immigration creates patterns of pluralism different from

those of the old immigration, and much of both the cultural vitality and uncertainty in America as it approaches the turn of the century results from a new cultural situation shaped by the 1965 immigration law and the associated increase of immigrants, refugees, and illegal residents. The presence and dramatic growth in the number of Christians from India and their process of adaptation to American culture is an example of the impact of Asian immigrants, who, along with Muslims, Hindus, Jains, Sikhs, Taoists, and others from many countries, had previously been virtually excluded from immigration to the United States. Since 1965, doors to the United States have been opened to new immigrants, and the process of religious adaptation of these immigrants is changing the American religious landscape.

New temples, mosques, and gurdwaras enriching the landscape are symbols for religious identity of many of these new immigrants and of their adaptation to an adopted country. New Christian immigrants are building churches and creating space for themselves in existing denominational and congregational structures, and, although they are in many ways less exotic and hence less visible than other immigrants, they have as great an impact on the shape of American religion. Korean immigrants are a rare example of growth in mainline American Protestantism, especially in the Presbyterian Church, and Filipino immigrants join with those from Latin America in changing the face of American Catholicism. Christian immigrants from India represent well these changes brought about by immigrants arriving after 1965. It will be helpful to place their immigration in the larger context of immigration to the United States, to identify unique aspects of the Asian-Indian Christian experience, and to show how these new Christian immigrants are adapting to life in America.[1] This chapter addresses common questions about these immigrants: who are they? When did they come to America? Whence did they come? Where did they settle? What difference does it make?

CHRISTIAN IMMIGRANTS FROM INDIA

People are surprised when new immigrants from India and the rest of Asia identify themselves as Christians. It is assumed that they are Hindus, Muslims, or Buddhists, and, quite frankly, Christians from India become annoyed by the common questions: "When were you converted?" or "How did you get a Christian name?" or "Which missionaries saved you?" Americans have many popular misconceptions about the religious identities of people in immigrant groups, misconceptions that need correction. Korean immigrants are not necessarily Buddhists; half are Christian before they arrive, and another quarter become Christian in America. A large number of Hispanics are Pentecostal Protestants, not Roman Catholics. Most Irish Americans are Protestants, not Roman Catholics. Religious identities of new immigrants are far more complex than the general population is aware.

Christian immigrants from India come under the same provisions of the 1965 immigration law as other Asian Indians and occupy generally the same high educational and professional status. Many were students in American graduate schools in 1965 and accepted jobs and the offer of a "green card" to stay on. These student immigrants are often referred to as "the pioneers" because they have a longer residence in the United States than others and many hold prominent academic or professional positions. The early immigrants spread across the professional spectrum occupied by other immigrants from India: physicians, engineers, scientists, teachers, and technicians. They have been joined by relatives under the provisions of family reunification, now including in many families the grandparents, siblings, and children – what Meyer Fortes called "the living present" of any cultural group. They share with other Asian-Indian communities the problems of integrating the generations and the newly arriving family members, especially when the new immigrants do not have the same high educational, professional, and linguistic abilities. Christian immigrants come from many areas of India and form part of several regional–linguistic groups: Tamils, Telugus, Malayalees, Punjabis, Bengalis, etc., albeit in different ratios than Hindus, Sikhs, Muslims and other religious groups.

At a recent intercultural wedding, the father of the groom asked, "Why did they [the immigrants] come over here anyhow?" Christians share with others many of the same push/pull factors leading them to leave India (and other lands) for the United States. Education is the universal passport, especially in technical and scientific subjects. The English language is increasingly the universal language of science and commerce, and it is the one language used as a legal language throughout India and in ecumenical Christian affairs. Virtually all of the early immigrants were educated in English-medium schools in India and quickly adapted to American English. Wives and elderly parents brought from India for family reunification are in many cases not so fluent in English, which causes many difficulties of adjustment. Universal education in India results in a large number of people educated in Western sci-

entific subjects whom the stagnant economy in India is not able to profit-
ably employ or support, and they become part of the brain-drain. They
seek better opportunities for employment, more financial security,
freedom to pursue their research work with state-of-the-art equipment
unhindered by bureaucratic red tape, and a brighter future for their children. People from minorities flee social restrictions and discrimination to
a land that claims as its foundation that "all people are created equal."

Another factor pulling immigrants to the United States was the
upswing in the economy in the 1960s and 1970s that demanded specialists from developing countries. The military draft of physicians and
nurses for service related to the Viet Nam War closely coincided with the
beginning of Medicare and Medicaid, government programs to expand
medical coverage, thereby creating shortages of health specialists and
technicians. Indians became prime candidates for these positions
because the overlay of British customs, education, and language in India
enabled them to establish their professional credentials and adapt to the
American educational, business, and professional environments quickly.
Moreover, India has a very positive image for Americans as the world's
largest democracy and the home of Mahatma Gandhi, a hero and fore-
runner of the Civil Rights Movement. For many Indians, America
seemed to be the proverbial "pot of gold at the end of the rainbow,"
which they could enjoy for a while; then they could return to India with
wealth and status to assure a pleasant career and comfortable retirement. Most of the earliest immigrants expected to work for a few years in
America, save up a nest-egg to secure the financial future of their families, and then return to their native place in India. In fact, a reverse
movement has taken place as members of families – in many cases, the
entire family – come to the United States for permanent residence.
Indian Christians are drawn to America because they have heard stories
about America and its churches, presenting America as the Christian
nation *par excellence*. Defects in that picture leave a residue of many difficulties for Christian immigrants as they have struggled to save their children from what they perceive to be the threats of liberal American
Christian culture.

Christians share many of these characteristics with other immigrants
from India, but they, like every specialized group, are shaped by forces
that cause them to stand apart from the rest. Most Christian immigrants
come from the four states of south India where the majority of
Christians reside (see Table 1). Christians are not distributed uniformly
in states, so they come from specific regions in patterns shaped by the

Table 1 *Christian population in India by states*

	Christian population	% of state population	% change since 1971
India	16,165,447	12.43	16.77
Andhra Pradesh	1,433,327	2.68	(21.39)
Goa, Daman, & Diu	318,249	29.28	16.78
Gujarat	132,703	0.37	21.37
Kerala	5,233,865	20.56	16.46
Meghalaya	702,854	52.62	47.89
Nagaland	621,590	80.21	80.28
Tamil Nadu	2,798,048	5.78	18.71

Source: Adapted from the 1981 Census of India

push/pull forces of immigration. Hence, a large number of Christian immigrants are from a small area of central Kerala. Gujarat has a relatively small population of Christians, but, because so many Gujaratis have emigrated to the United States, a number of Gujarati Christians are in America. The Gujaratis have always been active in immigration, first to Bombay, which was the British seat of government for Gujarat, and then to East Africa and the industrialized West. Gujarat was also the location of American missions, both of the Methodist Episcopal Church and the Church of the Brethren, which provided contacts and resources for the immigration of Christians from those mission areas.

A unique, and the most important, aspect of the immigration of Christians from India is the role of Christian nurses. If one could choose the location to have a medical emergency, one of the best places apart from a hospital would be a gathering of Asian-Indian Christians because of the concentration of medical professionals in the Asian-Indian Christian community. In the mid-1980s before the influx of relatives for family reunification, it was common for pastors to report that between 70 percent and 90 percent of the women over 30 years of age in their congregations were nurses. The growth of the Malayalee Christian community of Dallas in the six-year period from 1973 to 1978 from 75 to 620 persons resulted from the immigration of nurses, who accounted for 50 percent of the employed adults (T. J. Thomas, 1978:30–1). Nurses are not explicitly mentioned in the Immigration and Nationality Act of 1965 in the third category, which states that "profession" shall include, but not be limited to, architects, engineers, lawyers, physicians, surgeons, and teachers of various types. The ascendancy of registered nurses to the third preference classification came about through case law ("Matter of Gutierrez in visa petition proceedings A-17653997, July 5, 1967" in *Administrative Decisions under Immigration and Nationality Laws of the United States*, XII, 418ff.)[2] The great shortage of nurses was created by the decline in women attending American nursing schools, in part because other career opportunities were open to them. Many schools of nursing closed or extended the curriculum from two to four years. These changes came at a time of increased demand for health-care workers created by Medicare and Medicaid. An uneven distribution of both physicians and nurses made the situation critical in some inner-city hospitals, which undertook recruiting campaigns reaching out to the Philippines and to India to attract physicians and nurses. In 1978 the National Council of State Boards of Nursing and the Commission on Graduates of Foreign Nursing Schools created tests of nursing and English-language competencies to be administered twice a year in cities around the globe, making it easier for nurses to get visas. Agents searched for nurses in India and made contracts with hospitals to provide foreign nursing graduates, and many Indian Christian nurses responded. One official in New York is quoted as saying, "During the evening shifts in the city hospitals the official language changes from English to Malayalam" (Badhwar, 1980:17).

Nurses gained entry in the preference category of "members of the professions" in the 1970s and early 1980s, but later they were in the category of "skilled workers or professionals holding baccalaureate degrees" or came with H-1 visas as temporary workers allowed to stay in the United States for five years.[3] The reason is that the quotas for immigrants from both the Philippines and India were filled with persons joining families, and fewer places were open for those in occupational preference categories. Some nurses came as temporary workers, hoping that their period of waiting for permanent residence would be completed during the five years. Between 1983 and 1989, about 32,000 foreign-educated nurses were licensed in the United States, constituting almost 7 percent of the total number entering nursing during that period.[4] An acute problem surfaced when the waiting period under national quotas stretched to between seven and fourteen years so that nurses on temporary visas faced the requirement that they go home, and some urban hospitals faced partial closure because of lack of nurses.

Congressional hearings revealed the reliance of some hospitals on foreign nurses. In Newark, New Jersey, close to half of the nurses in the emergency room, intensive care, and other critical care units worked with H-1 visas, and 10 percent of all positions were filled by foreign nurses. The crisis precipitated the Immigration Nursing Relief Act of 1989 (the Kennedy–Simpson Bill) which extended immigrant status to alien nurses currently employed and allowed 4,000 additional US-licensed, foreign-born nurses per year to obtain green cards outside the country quota system (*Congressional Record*, Senate, November 20, 1989:S16438–40; House, November 21, 1989:H9301–2).

Although Indian nurses had been numerous among those seeking permanent immigration, they were not prominent among holders of H-1 visas during the 1980s. Among the 9,151 nurses obtaining H-1 visas in 1988 (4,730 of whom were headed for hospitals in New York and New Jersey), only 69 were from India, while 6,239 were from the Philippines (Immigration Nursing Relief Act of 1989 Hearing, May 31, 1989, serial no. 13:63–7). The Asian-Indian community had accepted the reports that it was virtually impossible for nurses to enter, in spite of the influx of Filipino nurses. A major difference is that the Philippine government seems to encourage emigration by nurses, whereas the Indian government refuses permission for the Commission of Graduates of Foreign Nursing Schools examinations to be administered in India. Therefore, Indian nurses must travel abroad even to take the examinations, and agents of hospitals no longer seek them out for temporary appointments in the United States.

Virtually all of the immigrant nurses from India are Christians because until very recently nursing occupied a very low social status in India, much as was the case in the West prior to the example and influence of Florence Nightingale. Cultural perceptions of pollution and purity discouraged Hindu families from allowing their daughters to enter nursing, and religious sensitivities regarding purdah kept Muslim women out of the profession. The perception that physicians mistreated the nurses added to the stigma. Until almost mid-century nursing was universally regarded as menial work and many of the candidates were uneducated girls and widows. Those perceptions gradually broke down in the Christian community due to the influence of education and the medical work of missionaries, and Christian young women entered the profession in large numbers. The nurses respond to questions about why Christian girls entered nursing by saying, "We have the education, and we have the hospitals." Christian schools provided equal education for girls, and some eighty hospitals had training classes with an English-medium curriculum approved and examined by state boards in both north and south India. For many years, Indian Christians provided almost all candidates for the entire nursing profession in India. As late as the Second World War it was estimated that 90 percent of all the nurses in the country, male and female, were Christians, and that 80 percent of these had been trained in mission hospitals (Firth, 1960:202).

The special attraction of nursing for Christian women in India was that when young women moved out of the homes in the 1960s to seek jobs, nursing was one of the technical occupations open to women. It was accessible because it did not require a university education and the nursing school tuition fees were sufficiently low that families could afford to send their girls for training. Moreover, student nurses could earn money during the clinical part of their training. Nursing and medical technology were viewed as secure fields with steady demand and relatively good pay. The altruistic example of missionary nurses and Christian injunctions to "heal the sick" caused some women to choose nursing as part of their commitment to Christian service in a context where other ministerial activities were not open to them. It was a Christian vocation. Missionary teaching sisters would have been astonished to know that so many of their students would eventually serve in inner-city hospitals in America. Positions for training were plentiful in teaching hospitals throughout India as were jobs in India and abroad after graduation. Nurses from India served as temporary workers in hospitals in Europe and the Gulf states even before the special door for Christian nurses from India was opened to the United States.

The first to come to the United States were senior nurses invited to participate in specialized training through educational exchanges during the 1960s. A nurse who was a representative of the Nurses' Union at Osmania Hospital in Hyderabad entered the United States as an educational exchange student and upon return home encouraged other Telugu nurses to accept the invitation of the new immigration law. A little later a Tamil director of nursing at a Madras hospital was recruited by an American hospital. Now the entire extended families of both nurses are in America, many of them, both male and female, working in the health-care system. In the 1970s, agents commissioned by American hospitals actively recruited newly graduated nurses to immigrate. In some years nearly half of some graduating classes left almost immediately for the United States. In the 1980s, fewer nurses came, and those who did were sponsored by relatives. The period between application and sponsorship can be a decade, so during the interim some energetic applicants undertake training in the medical field that they believe will assure them secure employment soon after they arrive. In India, there are reports of cases of fraud by visitors from America who promise nurses that they will arrange visas, travel, and jobs in American hospitals – none of which ever materialize – in return for fees that disappear with the agent.

Nurses are the most important links in the chain of migration that shapes Indian Christianity in America. Those who arrive early reach back to India to help select those who will immigrate and then assist them to get settled in health-care occupations in American cities. Family, church, and school are the networks that mediate this selection and assistance. Young nurses go back to India for arranged marriages and sponsor their husbands to join them. The young nurses are sternly warned by their parents not to get married before they return to India to arrange a traditional marriage, and most heed the advice. Their return for marriage changes the marriage negotiation because the promise of a green card makes nurses, even those from modest families, prime candidates for marriage. Marriage advertisements and brokers place a premium on nurses and others with permanent resident status in the United States. Some of the nurses arriving early were already married prior to immigration and typically stayed in America for a year or so before they could send for their spouses and children. Later, nurses sponsored their siblings and parents for immigration. An Indian American Nurses' Association was established in New York in 1990 to look out for their interests. In a 1993 survey completed by 678 Indian Christians in the United States, 182 of the 256 identified as women listed nursing as their occupation. (See additional information regarding this survey on pages 42–6.)

The Christians are the only Asian-Indian group coming to America on the shoulders of the women. Gender roles in immigration are reversed for Christians from India compared to those of other Asian-Indian immigrants. In most families of immigrants from India, a man with high educational and professional qualifications either studied in America or was offered a job in a business or a position as a physician in a residency program. Then the man either went back to India to arrange for marriage and to bring a bride home to America or he sent for his spouse and children to join him. Even when the woman in the family is a professional person able to establish a career in the new home, the man is responsible for immigration and in the vast majority of cases earns the highest salary and provides for the family's financial security. Among Indian Christians, however, women gain permanent resident status, earn the higher salary, provide for family security – especially was this the case during the economic recession in the mid-1980s when many husbands lost their jobs as factory workers and engineers – and now enjoy secure professional status. The concentration of one immigrant group in a particular occupation is not a new phenomenon in American history because "occupational concentration has been a critical factor in creating and maintaining ethnicity" (A. Thomas and Thomas, 1984:109). However, the great impact on the formation of a specific religious group is distinctive. The most common response of Christian men to the question "How did you come to America?" is, "My wife is a nurse, and ..." The incongruence between gender roles in India, where the man is lord over the family, home, and church, and the claims Asian-Indian Christian women have to prominence creates tensions that require skillful and sometimes painful negotiation in both families and churches (see chapter 5).

Churches are part of the network for chain migration because nurses sponsor other nurses from their home communities and churches to join them. Membership in local churches in India (as elsewhere) consists of complex interrelated extended families, and some of these communities have lost many of their nurses through migration in India and abroad. A result is that many congregations in the United States consist of extended families who came with the support of aunts or elder sisters. The annual national family conferences of the church bodies are a combination of family reunions and school reunions.

Nurses in training at certain excellent teaching hospitals and schools established networks of friendships that led to a chain migration after one of the class established herself in America. Christian nurses traveled throughout India for training in teaching hospitals, and the alumnae associations for some of the programs, such as the Vellore Association in New York, are valuable in maintaining the networks in the United States and for providing financial and technical assistance to the institutions in India.

Physicians and nurses continued to be in demand in the early 1980s when the downturn in the economy cost others their jobs, thereby reinforcing the perception in the immigrant community that occupations in health-care are the most secure. Family members without professional qualifications undertook programs of training to enable them to join the physicians and nurses in hospitals. Some took menial jobs and worked their way up the hospital ladder. People in the marriage market sought out persons in India with training in the medical field. One young woman said that when she returned to India to find a husband, she did not want a doctor or an engineer, so she chose a pharmacist because that "is a secure occupation." A result of such decisions is that many Asian-

Indian Christians are employed in hospitals as technicians, pharmacists, administrators, and on staff. A surprising number of Asian-Indian pastors complete Clinical Pastoral Education and serve as chaplains and counselors in hospitals. They too have followed their wives into the hospitals. A survey of Asian-Indian Christians shows that 39 percent of those responding (which includes students, unemployed, and retired persons) are in health-related occupations.

Christians are also unique among Asian-Indian groups because they brought their religious specialists with them. Those priests and pastors who did not come as students in the 1960s came later with their spouses, most of whom were nurses. The wife of a Syrian Christian pastor estimates that four out of five of the wives of the more than fifty pastors in the United States are nurses. Nurses arranged for immigration of brothers who were pastors, including some Roman Catholic priests who joined American Catholic dioceses. The security of the nurse's income permitted the pastors in the early days to gather small congregations and nurture them into parishes, councils, dioceses, and denominations. The special category in immigration admitted certain ministers of religion, but few Christian ministers came early under that provision, and religious specialists of other religions – Hindu, Muslim, and Sikh – encountered difficulties supplying documents proving approved professional education and certification. The number of ministers of religion admitted is growing – from 777 in 1985 to 1,189 in 1991 – but few of these are Christian (INS,1991:36, Table 4). The relationship of physical healing and spiritual healing is close in the thinking of many Asian-Indian Christian families, so it seems appropriate that ministers of religion have spouses who are nurses.

Fewer nurses are arriving since the mid-1980s because the arrival and distribution of immigrants is more strictly regulated both by government policies and professional certification. Asian-Indian nurses are admitted or excluded from areas of the United States by state board certifying examinations, the rigor of which is variable. Hence, few nurses go to Massachusetts, where the examination is judged to be very difficult, and many more go to Texas, New York, New Jersey, and Florida. It has become increasingly difficult for graduates of foreign medical schools to come to America because they find it difficult to gain places in residency programs, even in urban hospitals. Although the argument was made in Congressional hearings that it was necessary to admit more nurses in 1989, a reduction in demand for H-1 visa nurses now makes it more difficult for them to gain entry. Some American nursing schools increased the numbers of graduates at the same time that there have been cuts in health-care dollars and a drastic reduction in hospital occupancy resulting in the closure of some hospitals. Fewer hospitals have a nursing vacancy rate of over 7 percent, which is necessary before they can import foreign nurses. Growth in the field relies on the demand for nurse practitioners, who assume physicians' duties, but very few Indian nurses have the graduate and clinical training necessary for certification as nurse practitioners. The role of health-care specialists in future immigration is difficult to predict. Families already present will continue to expand through new immigration and by birth, and their children will be encouraged to become physicians, but unanticipated results of health-care reform at the end of the century will almost certainly influence the shape of Asian-Indian Christianity into the new century.

Christians from India form a distinctive group as part of larger patterns of immigration to the United States. In order to gauge their special contributions to American religion, it is necessary to locate them in the stream of immigration to America and place them among other Asian-Indian immigrants.

REVIEW OF IMMIGRATION TO THE UNITED STATES

The most important factor in shaping American Christianity and in shaping the future of American religion is the changing pattern of immigration that through the centuries selected people from different countries with a variety of religious affiliations. New immigrants are aware that the United States is a country of immigrants with religious freedom and that it offers new immigrants citizenship along with economic opportunities, which make it especially attractive. Many Americans have a collective memory of immigration and of their families making their way in a strange new land and are therefore somewhat sympathetic to new immigrants, even though some nativists have responded negatively to increased immigration and have on occasion pitted immigrant groups against one another; or, so it seems to recent immigrants from India who do not face the strong nativist reaction and discrimination that some earlier immigrants experienced. Nor have they been pitted against other immigrant groups as were the Irish against the Italians or the Hispanics against the Haitians. (See Higham, 1955.) Previous waves of immigrants were diverse in their reasons for coming, in the regions from which they came, the religions they brought with them, and their strategies of adaptation. Each group brought significant

changes to the American experience. Factors in the economic and political situations that propelled people from different countries and that
attracted them to the United States create the diversity of peoples who
have entered throughout American history. Five distinct periods of
immigration shape American society: (1) the colonial period (1608–1775);
(2) the open door era (1776–1881), which ended when immigration came
under federal supervision through the first comprehensive federal law;
(3) the era of regulation (1882–1916); (4) the era of restriction
(1917–1964); and (5) the era of liberalization – 1965 to the present
(Bernard, 1980:486–95). The narrow door through which immigrants
have to pass has been constructed and reconstructed by articles of
immigration laws and their interpretation through bureaucratic regulations and court decisions.

The open-door policies that brought waves of immigrants from
Europe and a small number from China started to close toward the end
of the nineteenth century. Then the open door was pushed shut to
Asians by exclusionary laws passed toward the end of that century and
the beginning of the twentieth. Laws that restricted entry of Chinese
laborers culminated in the Chinese Exclusion Act of May 6, 1882,
further restricting entry and barring the Chinese from naturalization
(INS, 1991: Appendix 1, A.1.3). The Immigration Act of February 5,
1917, codified all previously enacted exclusion provisions and restricted
entry of Asian persons, including those from India, from what was called
the "Asiatic Barred Zone." Restrictions based on race culminated in the
Immigration Act of May 26, 1924, which placed the first permanent
limitation on immigration and established the "national origins" quota
system. It established quotas based on the number of foreign-born
persons of each nationality resident in the United States in 1890 (after
1927 to be based on the population in 1920). That law governed
American immigration policy until 1952 when the Immigration and
Nationality Act (McCarran–Walter Bill) made all races eligible for
naturalization – thus eliminating race as a bar in immigration – and permitted a minimum quota of 100 persons to enter from all countries, reaffirming a 1946 amendment that made a small number of Indians and
Filipinos eligible for immigration.

Immigrants arriving before the middle of the nineteenth century were
primarily Protestants from the British Isles and northern Europe – the
proverbial white, Anglo-Saxon, Protestants – who impressed a dominant
cultural image and a dominant Puritan ethos on America. They were
joined in the nineteenth and early twentieth centuries by those from

eastern and southern Europe, who were predominantly Roman Catholics and Jews, along with some Protestants of different denominations and nationalities, who together contributed to the perceived identity of American religion as "Protestant, Catholic, Jew." Although no religiously based restrictions existed, the national quota system assured that immigrants in the first half of the twentieth century would largely duplicate the national, racial, ethnic, and religious identity established by the earlier immigrants. The McCarran–Walter Act assured that more than 85 percent of the total annual quota served people from northern and western Europe.

The Immigration and Nationality Act of 1965, initiated by President John F. Kennedy and signed under the Statue of Liberty by President Lyndon Johnson, fundamentally changed patterns of immigration. The Act included several provisions: it (1) abolished the national origins quota system, eliminating national origin, race, or ancestry as a basis for immigration, but establishing a 20,000 per country limit; (2) established a seven-category preference system for family reunification and for persons with special occupational skills needed in the United States; (3) established two categories of immigrants not subject to numerical restrictions – immediate relatives of US citizens (spouses, children, parents), and special immigrants, including certain ministers of religion and certain foreign medical graduates; and (4) introduced a prerequisite that the Secretary of Labor affirm that a prospective alien worker would not replace, or adversely affect the wages of, a worker in the US (INS, 1991:Appendix 1, A.1.14–15).

The seven categories of preference in effect until the 1990 revision of the law were: first, unmarried sons and daughters of US citizens, and their children; second, spouses and unmarried sons and daughters of permanent resident aliens; third, members of the professions of exceptional ability and their spouses and children; fourth, married sons and daughters of US citizens, their spouses and children; fifth, brothers and sisters of US citizens (at least 21 years of age) and their spouses and children; sixth, workers in skilled or unskilled occupations in which laborers were in short supply in the United States, their spouses and children; and finally, nonpreference: other qualified applicants (INS, 1991: 17, Table A).

Principal changes made by the 1990 Act are increases in the numbers admitted and changes in the preference categories. The annual worldwide level for immigrants (exclusive of immediate relatives, special immigrants, and refugees) is increased to 700,000 for fiscal years

1992–94. Thereafter the maximum is reduced to 675,000. The exempt status of immediate relatives (spouse or minor child or parent of adult child of US citizen) is virtually unchanged, but a three-year annual allocation of 55,000 goes to family members of legalized aliens. The six former visa preferences for immigrants are substantially revised. The four family preferences in the former law are retained intact and grouped as first, second, third, and fourth preferences with a total allocation of 465,000, increased to 480,000 in fiscal year 1995. The preference categories of the current law perpetuate the bias of the old national origins quota system of 1925, insuring that the pool of legal entrants is dominated by Latin Americans and Asians from just a few countries: the Philippines, China, Korea, and India (Salins, 1993:14b). The former third and sixth preferences are replaced by three new preference categories, each including major subcategories, with a total visa allocation of no more than 140,000. The first employment-based preference category, designated as "priority workers," is allocated 40,000 visas, plus unused allocations of other preference groups. This preference includes aliens with extraordinary ability, outstanding professors and researchers, and certain multinational executives and managers. The second employment-based preference category, also allocated 40,000 visas, plus any unused visas from the first employment-based preference, includes aliens who are members of the professions holding advanced degrees or aliens of exceptional ability in the sciences, arts, or business. The third employment-based preference category, also allocated 40,000 visas, plus any unused visas from the first two employment-based preferences, includes skilled workers, professionals with baccalaureate degrees or other (unskilled) workers (Gordon and Mailman 1991:7–8).

Application of both forms of the law resulted in two principal ways for people from India to qualify for permanent resident status in the United States: (1) sponsorship by certain relatives who have status in the United States, or (2) sponsorship by an employer. Immediate relatives of US citizens (spouses, unmarried children under 21 years of age, and parents) are not subject to quotas or numerical limitations and normally gain entry in a few months. Other relatives of citizens can gain admission, but the period between application by a sponsor and the issue of a visa can be from two years for spouses of permanent residents to decades for siblings. One strategy is to sponsor parents who can then sponsor relatively quick entry for their children, which is one reason for the influx of retired parents. Several categories of people do not need individual work permits: nurses, physical therapists, certain ministers of religion, and persons of exceptional merit and ability in the arts and sciences. Non-immigrants coming for temporary residence are on student visas (F-1) and temporary worker visas (H-1), the H-1 visas stipulating a six-year limitation on H-1 status (Steel, 1993). Student visas are much sought after, and 16,128 students were admitted from India in 1991 (INS, 1991:100, Table 36).

Two groups of people enter the United States outside these categories: illegal aliens and refugees. Until recently, few people from India entered as refugees, only a handful of people claiming to flee communal conflicts in Kashmir and Punjab, but now people have learned that under current regulations simple application for asylum at an airport results in a granting of a work permit and a six-month delay in a formal hearing, permitting time for an immigrant to gain a foothold in the US or go underground. There were 743 Indian asylum cases pending at the beginning of fiscal year 1992, but the total grew to 3,591 cases pending by the end of the year. During the same fiscal year, 64 Indian asylum requests were granted and 87 denied (*News India–Times*, 1994 [March 11]:3). Illegal aliens remain largely invisible in the Asian-Indian community, but by 1991 there were 21,794 persons from India who applied for permanent resident status under the legalization program of the Immigration Reform and Control Act of 1986, indicating that illegal immigration is a factor. A total of 5,779 had entered illegally or over-stayed non-immigrant visas prior to 1982, and a surprising 17,946 requested permanent resident status as seasonal agricultural workers, which must represent a fairly large contingent of Punjabi farm workers in California (a state that accounted for over half of the agricultural workers seeking permanent status). The total number of immigrants admitted each year greatly exceeds the established annual quotas.

A review of committee hearings, Congressional debates, and public comments prior to passage of the immigration act of 1965 shows that none of those testifying anticipated the sea change in immigration precipitated by the legislation (R. Daniels, 1989:41). In 1991 some 1,827,167 persons were granted permanent resident status, the highest total ever recorded (INS, 1991:12, 18). Immigration shifted from Europe to Asia – in 1987 Europeans accounted for only 10 percent of immigrants, Asians 43 percent and those from Latin America and the Caribbean 41 percent – so that for the period of 1981–90 nearly 50 percent of the naturalized citizens were born in Asia. The United States is moving rapidly toward being what Ben Wattenburg termed "the first universal nation" (Wattenburg, 1991). Cultural and religious transformations are evident in all parts of the country, but especially in urban areas and a few specific states. Approximately 77 percent of all immigrants in 1991 intended to reside in six states: California, Texas, New York, Florida, Illinois, and New Jersey (INS, 1991:11). Religious diversity is revealed in an estimate by the Harvard Pluralism Project that 1,515 Buddhist temples, 1,139 mosques, and 412 Hindu temples now exist in the United States.

Immigration to the United States is part of a worldwide movement of populations. The World Bank estimates the number of international migrants of all kinds in 1992 at 100 million, and every demographic impetus toward migration promises to multiply over the next two or three decades as the combination of population pressures and economic imbalance seem likely to produce mass migration from poorer to richer countries. The relative decrease of heads of families on temporary work assignments and the increase of family members in the migrant flow transforms the immigrant profile in the United States, Europe, and Australia. Immigrant families are composed and recomposed in the process of migration, and immigration is the visible face of social change (UN Population Fund, 1993:6–7, 20, 29). This new immigration portends significant changes in both the religious identity of Americans and models of interpretation of American religion.

RELIGIOUS SIGNIFICANCE OF THE LULL IN IMMIGRATION
(1925–1965)

Reopening of the door to America in 1965 ended an important but unique lull in immigration that lasted from 1924 until well past mid-century. The number of immigrants in 1924 (706,896) was not reached again until the 1989 total of 1,090,924 (INS, 1991:27, Table 1). The restrictive legislation of 1924 had immediate results, cutting immigration to 294,314 in 1925, but the Great Depression and the Second World War had even more dramatic effects, so that the average annual immigration for the period from 1931 to 1945 was under 50,000. Indeed, during part of that period there was a gently receding wave of net loss as more people left the United States than immigrated – the years of net loss were: 1932, a loss of 67,719; 1933, a loss of 57,013; 1934, a loss of 10,301; 1935, a loss of 3,878 (Daniels, 1990:288, Table 11.1). With new immigration virtually ended, the second and third generations of immigrant families moved along in a stately procession, relatively uninfluenced by newly arrived immigrants, who had always followed and influenced earlier generations of immigrants as they adapted to their new home.

Immigration increased gradually following the Second World War so that by 1965 the total immigration to the US was 296,697, and it grew to 1,827,167 in 1991 (INS, 1991:27, Table 1). Hence, the religious development of the United States can be analyzed in three periods: (1) rapid immigration from Europe prior to 1924 – including a Protestant phase prior to 1790, a diversification phase in the first half of the nineteenth century, and the second wave of Jewish and Catholic immigration prior to the 1920s; (2) a lull in immigration between 1924 and the 1950s; and (3) renewed immigration from 1965 to the present.

Two classics on the interpretation of American religion serve as symbolic "book-ends" for the period of lull. H. Richard Niebuhr's *Social Sources of Denominationalism* describes the development of American religion through immigration from Europe and internal migration from east to west and south to north. His work sets the stage for understanding developments during the lull when the ethos of mainline Protestant denominations had reached maturity and was weakening with age, when the programs of assimilation through the ecumenical movement came to dominate the theology and life of those denominations, and when American Catholicism prepared for the Second Vatican Council, which came to a close just before the resurgence of immigration. Toward the end of the lull, Will Herberg's *Protestant, Catholic, Jew* surveyed the process of adaptation taking place during the lull, concluding that the process of adaptation is one of a triple melting-pot whereby people from a variety of ethnic and religious backgrounds assimilate in American society as Protestant, Catholic, Jew. A revival of religion in the United States after the Second World War seemed to strengthen the mainline Protestant denominations and other religious groups, such as Reform Judaism, that were willing to cooperate under an umbrella of benevolent assimilation. A relatively secularized, non-theological, homogeneous religious tradition strengthened elements of the "religion of the Republic" during the lull, a general religiosity captured in President Eisenhower's famous quip, "I don't care what you believe, as long as you believe." It may be, however, that neither that ethos of mainline denominations nor Herberg's thesis of assimilation is adequate for the new situation in which religious communalism results from new and constantly growing immigration.

A period of relative civic harmony flowered among earlier immigrants as cooperation between Protestants, Catholics, and Jews was worked out under the umbrella of what came to be called "the Judaeo-Christian tradition." This concept does not have a long history; rather, it

is an amalgamation of traditions that developed in the recent and sometimes tense negotiations between immigrants to determine how they
could live together in America as "one nation under God," the phrase
"under God" having been added to the American Pledge of Allegiance
in 1954. The God of this statement is the "God of Abraham, Isaac, and
Jacob" and "God and Father of our Lord Jesus Christ," with some elements of the Deists' divine being added on. The Judaeo-Christian tradition is thus not a universal concept, but is one that has a local meaning
and impact resulting from the immigration history in the United States.
Embracing "the Judaeo-Christian tradition" became in the third quarter
of the century a way of establishing a common cultural front in resistance to the perceived threat of communist ideology. The famous
Western Civilization Course developed at Columbia and instituted in
revised forms in many American colleges and universities enshrined the
best of the Judaeo-Christian learning in relation to other cultural and
intellectual traditions visible in American society. One result of renewed
immigration is controversy about the breakdown and inadequacy of the
old synthesis in the current social context both because the presence of
new ethnic and religious groups – including significant Jewish immigration from Russia – changes the nature of the negotiation between
Christians and Jews of the old immigration and because new immigrants representing different ethnic and religious traditions, primarily
from Asia, refuse to live comfortably under the old synthesis. The new
world order following the breakdown of the communist ideology will
inevitably result in new syntheses developed through tortuous negotiations in cultures throughout the world.

The 1960s saw the upheaval of the Civil Rights Movement led by
those who were not allowed to participate in the general assimilation of
immigrant generations, led by the Reverend Martin Luther King, Jr.,
and those who did not want to, led by Minister Malcolm X. Both wings
of the movement were reactions to cultural and religious developments
during the lull, from which African Americans were effectively excluded.
The religious and cultural homogeneity of mid-century did not include
them. The revival of ethnicity and religious pluralism begun in the Civil
Rights Movement continues apace, empowered and enhanced by the
new immigrants who began to arrive after 1965. As was the case with the
leaders of the Civil Rights Movement, new immigrants are finding religious identity to be fundamental to forming strong negotiating networks
and to establishing themselves in America.

Religion is ranked as very important or fairly important by 85 percent of the American population; 69 percent are members of churches or synagogues; and 41 percent of those surveyed in a recent Gallup Poll attended a church or synagogue in the past seven days. (The poll does not include temple, mosque, gurdwara, or shrine in the question about attendance, but surely will soon.) The percentages do not change significantly from year to year. Why this religiosity? One answer: because each immigrant group on arrival faces the daunting task of reshaping personal and group identities in the United States.

The period of the lull in immigration witnessed the flowering of a Christian ecumenical movement in America that erased distinctive barriers separating major mainline denominations evident until the 1950s and 1960s. One could argue that such homogenization of American liberal Protestantism is what is likely to happen whenever immigration to America diminishes as during the period of the lull. Sessions of Vatican Council II in the mid-1960s came at the end of the lull and permitted the American Catholic Church to become more like American Protestant churches, just at the time when those mainline churches were past the peak of their power and influence and were poised for rapid decline. The dramatic proposal for the union of the major Protestant denominations made by Eugene Carson Blake and James A. Pike on December 4, 1960, which resulted in the Consultation on Church Union (COCU), came in the last decade when such church union might be thought to be viable. The proposal involved assimilation by union as an ecumenical strategy different from the federation strategies undergirding the Federal Council of Churches (1906) and the National Council of Churches (1950). The enfeeblement of the ecumenical movement evidenced by the decrease in membership of the mainline denominations and by withdrawal of support for, and lack of influence exercised on American religion and culture by, ecumenical institutions, such as the National Council of Churches, results in part from renewed immigration and the breakdown of the synthesis produced by the lull.

Immigration and its cessation affects religion in America because religion is the sacred thread that weaves a transcendent cover for personal and group identity, a natural outgrowth of human character as a symbol-bearing creature. Such transcendence is potentially a powerful force both in the conservative stabilizing of a social world and in the transformative challenge to elements of a received tradition, the latter because religious commitment permits an individual to stand within a tradition involving transcendence with the power to call into question all traditions, including ultimately aspects of religion itself. Hence, it provides ties that enable immigrants to preserve their identities and adapt to new surroundings. Transmission of a tradition is always both a celebration and a quest. Religion is prominent at stages in the immigrant experience because in the midst of rapid social change it sustains memory that relates personal and group identity with the past. It validates those who are entrusted with transmitting and revising the sacred tradition, and it provides both social and ritual occasions in which personal identity is merged with group identity.

Immigration of religious persons from around the world and the accompanying revitalization of religions is one of the most important factors in the creation of the ethos of the United States. One may well expect that the advent of new immigrants will lead to a greater emphasis on religion in the future because religion will be a major element in negotiation of identity, but another component will be stress on diversity rather than unity.

IMMIGRATION OF ASIAN INDIANS

The children of the woman in Bangalore are now part of the Christian component of the new Asian-Indian ethnic group in the United States who contribute brand-new ethnic and religious voices to that negotiation because people from India were not present in significant numbers prior to 1965. From 1820 to 1960 a total of only 13,607 persons immigrated from India, and an unrecorded number of these departed (INS, 1982:2–4). The first discernable movement of Asian Indians into the United States was of Punjabi farmers who left British Columbia following a serious anti-oriental riot in Vancouver on September 7, 1907 (Jacoby, 1979:161). These Sikh farmers had great difficulty establishing themselves in California, and antagonism caused by the influx of numerous laborers from Asia at that time led to the restrictive legislation of 1917 mentioned above, which included India as part of the Asiatic Barred Zone. Even after the Second World War only a few Indians came to the United States, except for a growing number of graduate students in American universities, so that between 1951 and 1960 only 1,973 persons immigrated from India (INS, 1991:29f., Table 2).

Indians responded quickly after 1965 to the opportunity for permanent resident status. A provision in the law provided that for the first few years persons who had entered the United States with visitors' or students' visas could change their status to that of resident alien. Many students, including some Christian pastors attending American seminaries

Table 2 *Immigrants admitted by country of birth (India) in years from 1981 to 1991*

1981 (21,522)	1984 (24,964)	1987 (27,803)	1990 (30,667)
1982 (21,738)	1985 (26,026)	1988 (26,268)	1991 (45,064)
1983 (25,451)	1986 (27,227)	1989 (31,175)	

Source: Adapted from the 1991 *INS Statistical Yearbook*: 32, Table 3.

and graduate schools, elected to stay and were joined by young doctors, scientists, nurses, and other professional people. They were forerunners of a large new Asian community. From 1961 to 1991, a total of 484,816 immigrants listed India as their last place of residence (INS, 1991:29f., Table 2). The number of immigrants from India grew steadily during the 1980s. (See Table 2.)

This remarkable change in immigration is reflected in the growth in numbers of Asian Indians in the United States, first recognized as a distinct group in the 1980 census at the urging of groups representing immigrants from India. The 1980 census identified 361,531 Asian Indians, the number increasing by 125 percent in a decade to reach 815,447 in the 1990 census (CB, 1991, CB91–215, Table 1). Large numbers of Asian Indians congregate in larger states (see Table 3), but they have a special visibility across the country because they rank high in numbers among the foreign-born population in many states, ranking from first to fifth in Alabama, Delaware, Georgia, Illinois, Indiana, Mississippi, New Hampshire, New Jersey, North Carolina, Pennsylvania, South Carolina, Tennessee, Texas, and West Virginia (CPH-L-98:101ff., Table 16, "The foreign-born population of the United States, 1990"). This geographical spread results from the professional position of many of these immigrants which scatters them among the settled population in various service occupations such as medicine and motel management.

A majority of the immigrants until the mid-1980s entered under the third preference category, "Members of the professions of exceptional ability and their spouses and children," a part of the brain-drain from developing countries to the United States. President Johnson signed the new act under Emma Lazarus's lines: "Give me your tired, your poor, / Your huddled masses, yearning to breathe free... / Send these, the homeless tempest-tossed, to me" but those chosen by the new legislation for entrance were the doctors, engineers, professors, nurses, and technicians needed to spur the American economy in the 1970s.[5] It is common for Asian Indians still to speak of their community as having three main

Table 3 *Asian Indians in the United States in 1990*

Asian Indians 815,447 (1990)		361,531 (1980)		Percentage increase 125.6%	
Residence by state in 1990					
California	159,973	Massachusetts	19,719	Ohio	20,848
Florida	31,457	Michigan	23,845	Pennsylvania	28,396
Illinois	64,200	New Jersey	79,440	Texas	55,795
Maryland	28,330	New York	140,985	Virginia	20,494

occupation groups: physicians, engineers, and motel owners. Immigrants from India in the 1970s were among the best educated, most profession-ally advanced and successful of any immigrant group. Nine out of ten were high school graduates, and two out of three were college graduates. A survey of several hundred Asian Indians in New York recorded that more than half had postgraduate degrees at the master's level or above, 26 percent for the married women and 79 percent for their husbands (Saran, 1985:27). They quickly attained a high income consistent with their training, and the median household income for Asian Indians in 1979 ranked second highest among ethnic groups in the country at $25,644. (The median household income for the entire country was $16,841.) Although they came from several of the regional–linguistic ethnic groups of India, representing several religions, they occupy a rela-tively narrow range of the socio-economic scale of professionals. Their continued success is shown by the mean family income for foreign-born Asian Indians that, according to the 1990 census, was $65,381 while the per capita income was $17,777, whereas the mean family income for the total population was $43,803, and the per capita income was $14,420 (CP-3–5: 141, 153, Table 5).[6] These Asian Indians, especially those of the second generation, share with other Asians the burden of the "myth of Asian success" in which "all the parents are millionaires, all the children have genius IQs, and for a child not to become a physician or research sci-entist is to be a failure." In reality, many of the earlier immigrants had difficult times making it in the US, accepting positions below their qualifications, working hard for professional certification and accep-tance, forced to become self-employed, and running hard to flee the worst fate, that of returning home to India as failures. A common topic of conversation among Asian Indians is a desire to return to India upon retirement, but they are tied to their new homeland by their children so that few return for more than extended visits.[7]

Many of these immigrants are already westernized before they enter the United States, more so than one might immediately recognize. These physicians, engineers, computer specialists, scientists and their families are part of the intellectual elite, educated in curricula dominated by Western arts and sciences. Educational systems throughout the world, especially in India, have adopted Western models and are producing more intellectuals and scientists than the local societies can or are permitted to absorb. Moreover, many developing countries are modernizing so rapidly that many emigrants feel themselves disoriented when they go home, finding changes so dramatic that their nostalgic picture no longer comports with reality. As René Descartes observed, "When one spends too much time traveling, one becomes at last a stranger at home" (*Discourse on Method*, 1:6). Hence, recent massive migration changes the character of intercultural contact; no longer colonial or military-victor models of contact, but a much more healthy interchange of cultural traditions. India is no longer the distant Orient, but our neighbor, not in a metaphoric sense, but literally.

Entire families are moving to the United States under the family reunification provisions of the immigration laws. Once established, immigrants sponsor members of their families for immigration. Siblings and some others apply under the numerical quotas that impose a long delay before entry, whereas immigration of parents and children of citizens is unrestricted by the numerical quotas and therefore generally involves a relatively short delay. (See Table 4.) A major shift has taken place from the 1970s and early 1980s, when a majority of immigrants qualified by meeting professional and educational criteria, to the current situation when a large majority qualify for family reunification. Of the more than 45,064 persons of Indian origin admitted in 1991, over 35,000 were sponsored by members of their families already resident in or citizens of the United States (INS, 1991:40–45, Tables 6–8).[8]

The experience of immigration is very different for those who come to join families and networks already established. Tensions are created within the community between those already well-established early immigrants and those recent arrivals who occupy the first rung on the ladder to security and wealth. Stories of success are carried back to India along with expensive gifts for relatives and friends by Asian Indians vacationing in India, and those stories are validated by the arrival of new immigrants at the suburban homes or urban condominiums of the now middle-aged professionals. Although a few of these newer immigrants have professional and educational qualifications equal to those of their

Table 4 *Waiting period for Indian immigrant visa preference processing as of January, 1995*

Preference type	Date of application of those being processed in January, 1995
Family preferences	
1st Unmarried sons and daughters of US citizens	Current
2nd Spouses and unmarried children of permanent residents (2A)	Dec. 1, 1991
2nd Unmarried sons and daughters, 21 years of age or older, of permanent residents (2B)	Feb. 22, 1990
3rd Married sons and daughters of US citizens	July 2, 1982
4th Brothers and sisters of adult US citizens	July 1, 1983
Employment preferences	
All occupational categories	Current
Except 3rd Unskilled workers	Nov. 1, 1988

Source: Adapted from *News India–Times*, December 23, 1994, p. 58.

siblings and relatives, most who come for family reunification are not part of the elite brain-drain characteristic of the earlier immigration. Of the 14,310 persons of Indian origin admitted in 1971, more than half (a total of 7,543) were identified under the "Professional specialty and technical" category, whereas of the 45,064 admitted from India in 1991 only 5,188 were so identified and 3,761 were unemployed or retired (INS,1991:66, Table 20).

Some 3.5 million sponsored relatives are now waiting in line to enter the United States, and they will eventually be able to sponsor their direct relatives, so no visible limit to the number of legal entries is in sight. The 1990 revision of the immigration law attempts to adjust the imbalance between the family and occupational preferences by reserving 140,000 visas for employment-based immigrants (while maintaining 480,000 family-sponsored visas annually), assuring, nevertheless, that the vast majority of an increasing number of immigrants from India will for the foreseeable future be those sponsored by relatives. Even though they have assistance from relatives, it is much more difficult for these less well-trained immigrants to find quick success. Tensions are also present between the second-generation children brought up in the United States with little experience of Indian culture and discipline and the new immigrants, who are predominantly their grandparents and uncles.

Asian Indians in the United States are part of a global migration involving modernization and urbanization. Nevertheless, they constitute a distinct group not duplicated anywhere else in the world because of the particular selection processes of the preference categories – and hence are "Made in the USA" in ways that make them distinct from those in Canada, the United Kingdom, and even in the countries of south Asia. Immigrants cannot go home again, at least not to the same native place. They, their families, their religious groups, and their aspirations change during the process of immigration and adaptation so they view India differently. Indeed, society in India also is changing rapidly, albeit on a somewhat different trajectory. A frequent visitor remarked, "Every time I go back to India, it is a different place." It is possible to interpret immigration to the United States as part of modern urbanization, particularly the immigration of the modern technological elites to urban areas throughout the world. Many of the push/pull factors that caused the wave of response to the offer of residence in the United States are similar to those that move the elites in developing countries to the crowded urban areas. Many of the brightest and best, at least in modern science and technology, jumped at the opportunity to emigrate to America rather than to the cities of Asia – if not Bombay, Ahmedabad, or Madras for them, then New York, Chicago, Houston. Pico Iyer suggests that continued migration may make much of the world resemble Hong Kong, a stateless special economic zone full of expatriates and exiles linked by the lingua franca of English and the global marketplace and involved in service professions created by modern technocrats. Some people in urban studies already see the world as a grid of thirty or so highly advanced city-regions, or technopoles, all plugged into the same international circuit (*Time 1993*, Fall special issue: 87). Contemporary immigration from India is part of creating transnational families, businesses, social networks, and cultural and religious organizations that transform the negotiations and international communications and effects of these new immigrants.

Global migration is enormously disruptive as plausibility structures for both personal identity and group cohesiveness are threatened. Immigrants face the necessity of establishing networks and organizations that function to shepherd them through the transition and to aid in the formation and preservation of personal and group identity in the United States. The fact is that no group is transferred from India intact; groups are reconstituted after the disruption of emigration. They are formed by the selective process of immigration laws that bring a narrow range of the brightest and best and their families, by the individual decisions of persons who migrate, and by the reception given to those groups by what sociologists call the "host society." One cannot find in India social or religious groups identical to the Asian-Indian groups in the United States. Immigrants and their children have a past preserved by the slender thread of memory, and the process of formation and preservation of personal and group identity is the reformulation of that tradition. It is necessary, then, for immigrant groups to form and shape new identities, both group and individual.

The new identity is shaped in America by several layers of identity that immigrants bring with them from India. In spite of the fact that they represent a fairly narrow range of modern transnational professional families, they represent the diverse ethnic and social divisions in India – regional–linguistic groups, castes, political parties, and religions. Within India the major ethnic distinctions are those between regional–linguistic groups. The regional–linguistic composition of the people of the Indian subcontinent is extremely complex, partly because of the diversity of peoples brought into the modern nation state: Gujarati, Punjabi, Bengali, Tamil, Malayalee, and Sindhi are terms denoting ethnic affiliation, not tied to national boundaries. The ten Indo-European languages of the north and west and the four Dravidian languages of the south are the basis of divisions into cultural–linguistic regions, some of which have been recognized in state boundaries. The southern region from which most of the Christian Asian Indians come includes four major sub-cultures in four states: Tamil Nadu, where Tamil is the principal language; Kerala, where the language is Malayalam; Karnataka, where the language is Kannada, and Andhra Pradesh, where Telugu is spoken. (See Map 1.) A person is identified as a member of a regional–linguistic group – Malayalee, Telugu, Gujarati, and so forth – no matter what his or her place of residence. The designation refers not so much to a geographic residence as to the complex of language, culture, and social customs that provide the basis of identity. Asian Indians have nurtured various types of social organizations to serve them: caste-based associations; professional organizations of physicians, engineers, and other specialists; India-based political parties, and associations of alumni from educational institutions; and regional organizations, such as the Gujarat Samaj and the Tamil Sangam. These organizations reflect the diversity of the Asian-Indian community and different strategies of adaptation to America.

India is a land of many religions, several forms of which enter America along with Asian-Indian immigrants, adding new colors,

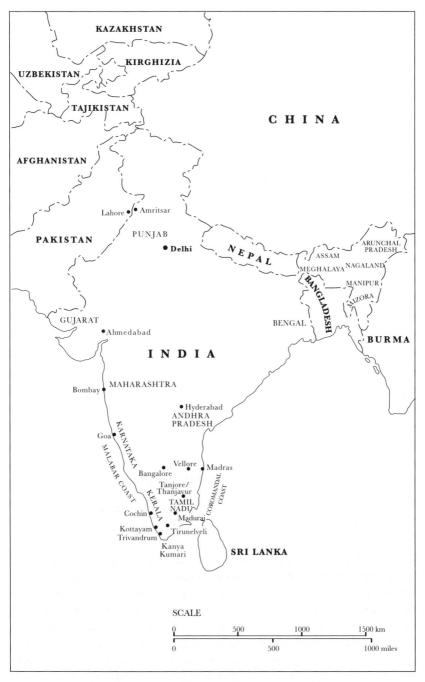

Map 1   India

shapes, and dimensions to the kaleidoscope of American religions. Gujarati Jains, many from Bombay, Parsis from Bombay, Muslims from the north, Hindus from across India, Christians from the south, and even a few Jews from Cochin and Bombay make their way to the United States. The individual religious groups are not uniform in language, customs, allegiances, or in their strategies of adaptation to the United States. (See Williams, 1988.) Indian religions are not distributed uniformly across the subcontinent, nor are they distributed uniformly across the United States. In some urban areas sufficient numbers are present for the ethnic and religious groups to subdivide, whereas in other areas the ethnic and religious groups must join larger more secure configurations. They face different challenges. Hindus leave India where they are the majority living in a culture heavily influenced by the ethos and mythology of Hinduism to live where Hindus are a small minority. Muslims from India are on a perpetual Hajj-like pilgrimage in which they are tossed together with Muslims from every country and ethnic group. Only in Mecca would Muslims come into immediate contact with so diverse a group of Muslims. Parsis in America are reunited with Zoroastrians from Iran from whom they were separated centuries ago by persecution, now to try to smooth over cultural and religious differences that developed during that separation. Christians join an ostensible religious majority of other Christians in a land that they had idealized as the "most Christian nation" and must work out their new identities amidst the tensions between Western secularism and American Christianity.

No reliable count or estimate of the religious affiliation of immigrants from the Indian subcontinent can be made now because a legal prohibition of keeping governmental records on religious affiliation has been in force since 1957. Nor are the records of the Immigration and Naturalization Service and the Census Bureau very helpful in establishing the numbers of persons in various Asian-Indian regional–linguistic ethnic groups. A couple of general conclusions can be advanced, however. First, for a variety of reasons, the percentages of immigrants from some areas of India – namely Gujarat, Punjab, and Kerala – are greater than from other parts. Gujaratis may make up as many as 40 percent of the immigrants, and Punjabis 20 percent. Second, persons who belong to religious minorities, especially Sikhs, Jains, and Christians, are represented by a larger percentage among immigrants than among the total population of India. Recent communal tensions in India and the emergence of a political party (BJP) stressing Hindu national culture cause minority families to search for secure anchors in other countries. Although a few immigrants bemoan the establishment of Indian temples, mosques, gurdwaras, and churches in the United States as both a waste of resources and seeds of a destructive communalism, immigrants from India have established impressive religious institutions and networks of all types to serve the community.

The Federation of Kerala Associations in the United States and Canada holds annual meetings attracting some 5,000 participants and claims affiliation of 120 organizations with 35,000 members. The best estimate is that over 100,000 Keralites now live in the United States. Well over three-quarters of the immigrants from Kerala are Christian. The best estimate of the number of Asian-Indian Christians in the United States at the beginning of 1995 is between 110,000 and 125,000.[9]

Each group brings its own particular resources to the project of forming and preserving personal and group identity and each faces distinct challenges posed by the host society. Christians from India constitute a good case-study of the process of adaptation because they come from several regional–linguistic ethnic groups, were constituted in the United States by a special occupational group, represent many strands of Christianity – Orthodox, Protestant, and Catholic – and exhibit different strategies of adaptation of American culture and religion.

SIGNIFICANCE OF KERALA IN IMMIGRATION OF CHRISTIANS

Chain migration is anchored in India in those areas having relatively large Christian populations, ones producing nurses and other technicians, and where the Christians have the education and linguistic ability in English to qualify for entry. The largest number of Christian immigrants are Keralites, Tamils, Telugu, Goans, and Gujaratis, with a smattering of representatives of other Indian regional–linguistic groups. The large majority, however, are from Kerala; indeed, most come from the fairly small central Travancore region. (See Map 2.)

Kerala is a small state on the southwestern coast of India, effectively isolated from the rest of India by the range of mountains to the east that complicates travel in that direction and to the north. By way of compensation, the Malabar coast has been since antiquity a center of trade with the countries to the west. Trade brought with it to this coast many cultural influences, including Christianity. Trade, farming, and fishing remain the staple occupations in a beautiful area and rural society. Its most important export is its people. Kerala is highly literate (228 university colleges) and over-crowded (population of 29 million or

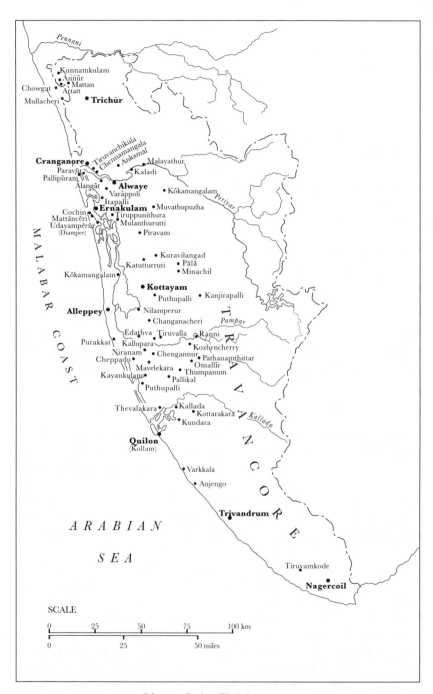

Pennani

Kunnamkulam
Aññūr
Mattan
Chowgat Artatt
Mullacheri
Trichūr

Cranganore
Paravūr
Pallipūram
Tiruvanchikula
Chennamangala
Ankamal
Malayathur
Kaladi

Alangāt
Varāppoli
Alwaye
Itapalli
Kōkamangalam
Periyar

Cochin
Mattāncēri
Ernakulam
Tiruppunithura
Muvathupuzha
Udayampērūr
(Diamper)
Mulanthurutti

Piravam

Kuravilangad
Katutturruti
Pālā
Kōkamangalam
Minachil

Kottayam
Puthupalli
Kanjirapalli

Alleppey
Nilamperur

Changanacheri
Pampar

Edathva Tiruvalla
Ranni

Purakkat
Kallupara
Kozhencherry
Niranam
Chengannur
Pathanamthittar
Cheppadu
Omallir
Mavelekara
Thumpanum
Kayankulam
Pallikal
Puthupalli

Thevalakara
Kallada
Kottarakara
Kundara
Kallada

Quilon
(Kollam)

Varkkala
Anjengo

Trivandrum

M A L A B A R

C O A S T

T R A V A N C O R E

A R A B I A N

S E A

Tiruvamkode

Nagercoil

SCALE

0   25   50   75   100 km

0   25   50 miles

Map 2   Syrian Christian centers

548 per sq. km.), but at the same time one of the least industrialized states in India. With 18 percent unemployment in a work force of 8 million, Keralites readily relocate in search of work (Nedungatt, 1989:15). Lack of an industrial base explains why, however, a smaller number of engineers and industrial technicians immigrated from Kerala than from Gujarat and other parts of India. If Kerala were a separate country, it would rank in economic standards as one of the poorest. Overpopulation and paucity of many industrial and scientific jobs force many Keralites to leave the state. One estimate is that 1.9 million Keralites live outside India, generating about one-tenth of India's foreign exchange, and about 5.2 million Keralites live in other parts of India (Thekkel, 1992:27).

The other side of the picture is that by some calculations Kerala is one of the most advanced areas in India. Even before Kerala became a state in 1957, the princely rulers had engaged in forms of land management that kept Keralites from being landless peasants. Having a strong state Marxist party and becoming in 1957 the first area to place a communist government in power through a democratic election produced policies that protected farmers and other smallholders from dispossession.[10] Kerala has little of the grinding poverty and hopelessness characteristic of some areas in developing countries. Kerala also has the largest Christian population and highest density of Christians of any state, which resulted in the establishment of many mission schools, colleges, and hospitals. Christians are not spread evenly up and down the state; rather, in the districts in what was the central Travancore area around Cochin and Kottayam they roughly equal in number the Hindu population. (See Table 5.)

Missionaries and indigenous Christian groups established schools throughout Kerala, but especially in the entral Travancore area. Keralites are proud that they have the highest literacy rate in India. In 1989 Kottayam became the first 100 percent literate town in the country (in the 6–60 age group), and in 1990 Ernakulam district was the first district to become 100 percent literate and Kottayam district claimed 99.6 percent literacy.[11] The quality-of-health index in Kottayam is well above that in the rest of India and parts of the United States. The infant mortality rate in India is 83 per thousand live births, while the figure for Kerala is 19.5 and for Kottayam it is 9.5. While the birth rate in India is 30 per thousand, it is 9.5 per thousand in Kottayam district, which is among the lowest in the country. Educational opportunities for women correlate with higher literacy, later marriage, and lower childbirth rate.

Table 5. *Christian population in Kerala*

	Christians	Hindus	Muslims
Kerala total	5,233,865	14,801,347	5,409,687
Kerala districts			
Cannanore	267,710		
Wayanad	135,504		
Kozhikode	107,711		
Malappuram	57,217		
Palghat	76,690		
Trichur	612,438		
Ernakulam (Cochin)	1,019,249	1,173,596	339,737
Idukki	419,288		
Kottayam	805,953	807,014	84,217
Alleppey	635,193	1,539,534	175,021
Quilon	637,516		
Trivandrum	459,396		

Source: Adapted from the 1981 census of India.

The areas from which many Christian immigrants come in Kerala and other states rank high in each of these categories. (See Table 6.)

High literacy, availability of education in English-medium schools, Christian teaching hospitals, and opportunities for young women combined with the overpopulation, lack of an industrial base, and unemployment are background conditions leading many Christian women and men to emigrate to the Gulf states, Europe, and the United States for better professional opportunities for themselves and their families. The demand in America for nurses and other highly trained technicians resulted in the establishment of transnational families with members moving between south India, the Gulf states, and America, in the extension of Indian churches abroad, and in members joining churches that had supported missionaries to India, thereby changing the dynamics of interchurch relations. The natural beauty of Kerala and other parts of south India causes expatriates to refer to it longingly as Eden, but they have moved west of Eden to make their new homes.

Most are well prepared to make the transition and are prospering in America. A survey with responses from 678 Asian-Indian Christians in 1993 and 1994, primarily at the annual family conferences of seven churches, reveals several aspects of a social portrait of the Christian immigrants who were selected by the push/pull forces of immigration to

Table 6 *Female literacy and marriage rates*

	Female literacy	First marriage, mean age
Total	22.3%	16.6
Gujarat	30.8	18.3
Kerala	64.8	19.1
Tamil Nadu	35.7	18.5

Proportion (percent) of married females aged 15–19 and 20–24 in 1981

	15–19 yrs.	20–24 yrs.
India	43.4%	84.5%
Gujarat	26.7	83
Kerala	14.1	57.9
Ernakulam	5.5	46.9
Kottayam	4.3	44.4
Nagaland	9.7	38.3
Tamil Nadu	22.8	75.5

Mean age at marriage by religion

All religions	16.7
Hindu	16.6
Muslims	16.8
Christians	19.4
Sikhs	19
Jains	18

Source: Adapted from: O.P. Sharma and Robert D. Retherford, *Effects of Literacy on Fertility in India.* Delhi: Office of the Registrar General and Census Commisioner, Govt. of India, 1990, p. 5, and Census of India 1981, *Female Age at Marriage: An Analysis of 1981 Census Data,* Occasional Paper 7, 1988, pp. 17, 33.

establish new Christian communities in America.[12] Those included in the survey are adults who are sufficiently active in various churches to assume leadership positions and attend the family conferences. It is a group unique to America, and no group like it exists anywhere else in India, Canada, the United Kingdom, the Gulf states, or in Africa. The most striking aspect and one most affecting the immigration and adaptation of the Christian immigrants is that of the 256 women in the survey – 178 list their occupation as nurse, and four men are nurses. The occupations of others in the survey are: 26 physicians (10 female and 16 male); 31 medical technicians; 83 engineers, applied scientists, computer scientists; 22 machinists; 68 in business; 33 in education; 6 in legal services; 10

homemakers; 38 students (but note that very few persons in the sample are under 18 years old); 16 retired; 17 unemployed; and 143 in other occupations. Among the 464 respondents who list an occupation in India prior to immigration, the largest groups are nurses (133), physicians and dentists (23), priests and pastors (25), teachers and professors (55), and students (40). Over 100 separate occupations are on the list of previous occupations, ranging from cook to evangelist.

Christians come already possessing or seeking high educational attainment; of the 643 who give their education, only 17 percent have only a high school education (female 25 percent and male 11 percent), 23 percent have some college (female 28 percent and male 21 percent), 24 percent graduated from college (female 27 percent and male 23 percent), and 34 percent have at least one graduate degree (female 18 percent and male 44 percent). Almost half of the 380 men in this sample have a graduate degree. Thus, significant gender variation exists in educational attainment. Although some immigrants are underemployed and have difficulty attaining economic security, those in this sample are relatively prosperous. Of the 615 persons providing information about total current annual family income, only 12 percent have incomes below $25,000 and an additional 26 percent are under $50,000. More than a quarter (24 percent) have incomes between $75,000 and $100,000. Incomes of between $100,000 and $250,000 account for 9 percent (54 respondents) and eight respondents earn more than that. Twelve of those in the top two income categories are physicians and eleven are engineers or computer scientists. Of the 182 nurses, 159 list family incomes between $25,000 and $100,000, about equal numbers in each category. Little variation in income level is evident in a comparison of data from the six church groups.

Only 11 people in the survey are over 65 years of age, reflecting the fact that few grandparents are present in the churches. Because the survey is aimed at adults, only 27 respondents are under 25 years old even though scores of children and young people were at the conferences. The median age is 45 and the mean age is 44, remarkably low for any adult Christian gathering in the United States. The group reflects the strong attachment to marriage and family cherished in the Indian Christian community. Of the 656 respondents, 87 percent are married and only 5 of them are divorced. Only 4 are widowed. A surprising 98 percent of the respondents were born in India and only 16 of them in the United States. Of the women, 40 percent are under 40 years of age, and over three-quarters of the 656 respondents have children: one child (58 respondents), two children (292), or three children (177). Of these, 370 report that they have children who were born in the United States. Only 103 have married children, whereas 524 do not yet have married children. That indicates the significance of both the rapidly approaching marriage cycle for shaping the future of the church groups and the large number in or approaching the age of fertility. The number of Asian-Indian Christians is likely to continue to increase through natural means as well as through continued immigration.

The survey sample is heavily weighted toward Keralites, and 609 of the 657 respondents regarding language report that Malayalam is their native language. A few are beginning to make the linguistic change to English, with 113 respondents reporting that English is the language they use most at home and an additional 175 indicating equal use of English and Malayalam.

Those in the sample evidence a remarkable stability in religious affiliation because 88 percent indicate that they participate in the same church group in the United States as they did in India. Some of the forty-two women who have changed affiliation may have done so at marriage. No evidence exists from this survey that Asian-Indian churches in America are stealing members from each other. Those attending family conferences are the immigrants least likely to have changed affiliation, so this percentage is not applicable to the immigrant population as a whole. Of the respondents, 70 percent indicate that they do not attend services of any church other than those of their own group, and no pattern is evident in the churches the others visit occasionally. Generally, immigrants become more active in religious affairs as they try to establish themselves and their families in a new location, and 60 percent of the respondents indicate that they are more active now than they were in India. Only 13 percent indicate that the level of their activity is less.

Thus, Asian-Indian Christians bring a wealth of talent and depth of commitment when they arrive. Their early professional and economic success enables them to establish strong networks and Christian organizations. The future holds great promise as families grow and encourage their young people to excel in their activities and to remain faithful to the Christian heritage families bring from India. New immigrants from India continually renew contacts with the Christian stories and practices in their homeland. The parents tell the stories and encourage participation in Christian activities in the hope that they will be able to build a firm foundation for their children before the cold biting winds of American culture threaten their families, their faith, and their identities. Out of that struggle new Christian groups are forming in America bearing the marks and telling the stories of the Indian Christ, his apostle, Thomas, and a great cloud of witnesses from Indian Christian history. The next chapter provides a selection of the Christian memories of the church in India that help shape the identities of the Asian-Indian church "Made in the USA."

CHAPTER 2

Christian stories about India

If ever I should forget thee, O Jerusalem...

Psalm 137:5

Asian-Indian Christians tell stories about their past in India to explain to their new neighbors and to themselves and their children who they are. "We are called St. Thomas Christians because the Apostle Thomas arrived in India in AD 52 to preach the gospel." "My mother was a devout member of the Mar Thoma Church, but a Pentecostal missionary prayed and healed my father when he was critically ill, so the entire family was baptized." "The genealogists trace my lineage to one of the families that came from Syria in the fourth century to revive the church in India, so we are contacting other Knanaya families to find a husband for our daughter." Every Christian immigrant has a collection of stories that places him or her in a specific social and religious place in India, just as the story that "my wife was a nurse and she got a job at St. Luke's and a green card in the United States so she could eventually sponsor me and our children" explains the presence of a new family in a particular neighborhood. Together these stories and hundreds like them provide insight into the diverse strands of Indian Christian traditions and background for understanding the dynamics that govern relationships between the various groups of Asian-Indian Christians in America.

These stories do not tell a complete story of Christianity in India, nor are they finely honed and joined. They are certainly not the story as developed by professional historians. They are more like the stories of the Bible, not just because they begin, like the Acts of the Apostles, in the first century with the story of the spread of the gospel "from Jerusalem...to the uttermost parts of the earth," but because the stories provide pictures of the past from the vantage point of the shaping and reshaping of a new religious community in a new promised land. These stories arrive in the United States in oral form in short narratives that

47

explain a name or activity, in songs at weddings and festivals, and in references in liturgical materials. Their situation in life (what biblical scholars call *Sitz im Leben*) is local and tribal, related to the religious identity and activity in a family or local area. A story that is told in several contexts appears in different, sometimes incongruent, forms. Elements of the sacred story are so tenuously related to the larger secular story that it is difficult to place them with precision in a modern historical work. Parts of the story have been adopted by disparate groups, revised to meet changing contexts, and on occasion created to establish a more general proposition.

The story results from the selective communal memory of the immigrants – and their structural amnesia. Those immigrants who share the same stories participate in the same churches and ethnic organizations, and those churches and groups that are social neighbors share significant elements of a common story. One can interpret the negotiations among religious groups, sometimes interpreted as political, as a process of story creation in which people who are drawn together through immigration and social contact join elements from their sometimes disparate pasts into a commonly accepted and projected story. The story provides also a basis for negotiation with both the Christian groups in the larger society and other Asian-Indian religious groups. John Fentress and Chris Wickham discuss the importance of such social memory:

In principle, we can usually regard social memory as an expression of collective experience: social memory identifies a group, giving it a sense of its past and defining its aspirations for the future. In doing so, social memory often makes factual claims about past events. Sometimes we are able to check these factual claims against documentary sources; sometimes we cannot. In either case, however, the question of whether *we* regard these memories as historically true will often turn out to be less important than whether *they* regard their memories as true...Social memory is a source of knowledge. This means that it does more than provide a set of categories through which, in an unselfconscious way, a group experiences its surroundings; it also provides the group with material for conscious reflection. This means that we must situate groups in relation to their own traditions, asking how they interpret their own "ghosts", and how they use them as a source of knowledge. (1992:25–6; see also Halbwachs, 1992)

The result of such collective memory among Christian immigrants is the preservation in the United States of a story that, even though fragmentary, reflects elements of the long tenure and diversity of Christianity in India. Christianity is very old in India, so the fragmentary story hangs on a twenty-century time-line, highlighting periods of new arrivals, conflicts resulting in divisions, and family and group associations. Stories are first of all local, told about and from the perspective of regional – linguistic groups from which the immigrants come, different in the north from the south and between the regions. Indian diversity is present in the immigrant community, and Indian Christian stories reflect local experiences. The immigrants' use of multiple adaptive strategies and creation of multivalent identities lead them to recount different stories in different contexts, depending upon which strategy or identity is stressed at the moment. Christians in America are able to learn from such stories a great deal about those parts of India where their new neighbors originated.

The stories provide significant information that cannot be ignored for two reasons. (1) The stories are not ahistorical. Even though Bishop Stephen Neill as a historian warned, regarding some of the most ancient traditions, "historical research cannot pronounce on the matter with a confidence equal to that which they [the story-tellers] entertain by faith," here as elsewhere the "historian cannot prove to them that they are mistaken in their belief" (Neill, 1984:49). Even though historical certainty cannot be assured – indeed, some legendary elements stretch modern belief past the breaking point – the stories bring alive historical events and contexts and clothe them with the flesh and blood of both the ancestors who preserved and transmitted them and their faithful descendants who receive the stories and reshape them for a newly formed community in America. (2) Religious traditions preserved and transformed in narratives, songs, and liturgy are powerful in establishing and preserving both personal and group identities among recent immigrants. Regardless of current ability to demonstrate by external sources the accuracy of portions of these stories, they provide the foundation for the existence of ethnic and denominational groups in both India and America. They provide the theoretic framework for the association of people in groups, and the sacred aspects of the stories anchor the identities and associations in a transcendent realm.

The story told in this chapter is a new creation, constructed by joining together fragments of stories told or hinted at in conversations with immigrants, relating these fragments with stories told by historians, and filling in the gaps to provide enough continuity to make it one story, even though no immigrant would construct the story in the same way. The narrative framework weaves together elements of selective communal memories with elements of research by professional historians, moving dialectically between the stories people tell and narratives of historians.

It is an outsider's story molded to help other outsiders enter the worlds of Indian Christianity sufficiently to appreciate the references and stories recounted by their new neighbors. Perhaps it will provide for those inside Indian Christianity insights into parts of the story forgotten and unfamiliar to them. The story deals with the basic details, colors, and material that will be used to decorate the unique India room in the house of American Christianity, but the shape of that room and its most appropriate decor is still undecided.

The shape of the Indian subcontinent resembles a funnel, and it is often said that nothing that is poured into India is ever completely lost. Beginning perhaps in the first century, forms of Christianity appeared in India in different centuries from different strands – Orthodox, Catholic, Protestant – and from different areas of the world – Syria, Persia, Europe, and the Americas. All remain parts of the story of Christianity in India, which developed its own character over the centuries while being in periodic contact with developments in the religious history of the West. A tour through the Christian regions of India is like a journey through the history of Christianity and a continuing conversation with apostles, patriarchs, reformers, popes, pastors, and preachers. Their voices still echo in the beautiful churches of India and influence the lives of Asian-Indian Christians trying to make a place for themselves in "Christian America."

Three trajectories lead one through the main elements of the Christian story in India: (1) St. Thomas Syrian Christianity from the earlier Christian centuries, (2) Roman Catholic Christianity resulting from missions after AD 1500, and (3) Protestant Christianity developing from the eighteenth century. These trajectories are increasingly interrelated into this century and resemble a swirl cake in which three layers of different colored and flavored batter have been poured and lightly swirled so that remnants of each layer appear in any section no matter how the cake is sliced. Perhaps that is what most history is like outside the books of professional historians. What follows is a sampling from the complex story of Christianity in India in the attempt to provide a background for understanding the commitments and resulting identities of Asian-Indian Christians in the United States because these immigrants are introducing new ingredients to American Christianity.[1]

Such sacred stories have been told by emigrants from ancient times to the present: "God said to our ancestor, Abraham, 'Go from your country, and from your kindred...to a land I will show you.'" "And Moses said to Pharaoh, 'Let my people go that they may serve me.'" "Jesus sent his disciple, Thomas, to preach the gospel in India." "Ida Scudder started a medical institution at Vellore, where my wife became a nurse, and now we have the opportunity to serve God in America by preaching for the Indian congregation and working in the inner-city hospital." "A great Pentecostal outpouring of the Spirit led to the founding of our Indian Pentecostal Church, which is now spreading throughout India and other parts of the world." All of these are elements of the Christian story told by Asian-Indian Christians – biblical stories and others like them – and those who tell them take on a role similar to the Deuteronomic historian.

CHRONOLOGY OF EVENTS

52	Date given for the arrival of the Apostle Thomas in India
72	Date given for the martyrdom of St. Thomas (July 3)
345	Date given for arrival of Thomas of Cana/Knai on Malabar coast with seventy-two families
1498	Vasco da Gama arrives at Calicut (Kozhikode) in Kerala (May 17)
1542	Xavier lands at Goa (May 6)
1543	Goa becomes administrative and diocesan center of Portuguese India
1599	Synod of Diamper convened by Alexis de Menezes
1653	Coonen Cross oath at Mattancheri (January 3)
1706	First Protestant missionaries arrive at Tanquebar
1793	William Carey arrives in Bengal
1802–03	Nadar conversions
1809	London Missionary Society establishes work in south Travancore state
1815	London Missionary Society enters Gujarat
1816	First Church Missionary Society missionary arrived in Kottayam in Travancore state
1827	Charter conferred on Serampore College by the King of Denmark
1830	Society for the Propagation of the Gospel enters Gujarat
1833	Plymouth Brethren missionary, Anthony N. Groves, arrives in Tinnevelli (Tirunelveli)
1834	Basel Mission enters north Travancore state
1836	Synod of Mavelikara reaffirmed supremacy of the Patriarch of Antioch
1836–40	Mar Thoma reformation under Abraham Malpan

1872	Methodist Episcopal Church missionaries arrive in Gujarat
1888	Evangelistic Association of the Mar Thoma Church established
1895	Church of the Brethren missionaries arrive at Bulsar in Gujarat
1909	Knanaya Orthodox establish a separate diocese in Kerala
1913	Independent Pentecostal missionary, Robert F. Cook, arrives in India
1920	Order of the Imitation of Christ (Bethany Ashram) founded by P. T. Geevarghese (Mar Ivanios)
1924	US Immigration Act established "national origins" quotas Indian Pentecostal Church founded by Pastor K. E. Abraham Servants of the Cross Society of the Syrian Orthodox Church established
1930	Mar Ivanios joins the Roman Catholic Church and leads a church union movement (September 20)
1932	Pope Pius XI authorizes the Syro-Malankara rite
1947	Church of South India formed (September 27)
1949	Mar Athanasius Yeshua Samuel arrives in New York as Archbishop of the Syrian Orthodox Church
1958	First Knanaya family arrives in the United States to start the "second migration"
1962	Indian Catholic University Federation formed for students
1965	US Immigration and Nationality Act opens door for immigrants from India
1970	Church of North India formed
1973	The Indian Christian Fellowship Church organized in Chicago
1974	National Service Team for Catholic Renewal in India formed
1975	Church of South India bishops authorize extraterritorial parishes in the United States
1977	First Mar Thoma Church parish recognized in the United States in New York Kerala Catholic Association formed in Chicago
1978	Commission on Graduates of Foreign Nursing Schools examinations created First Malayalee Brethren Family Conference held in Pennsylvania
1979	Malankara Orthodox Diocese of North America and Europe established

First full-time Mar Thoma priest appointed in the United States in New York

1980 Southern Asia National Caucus of the United Methodist Church recognized

1982 Knanaya Orthodox Family Conferences in the United States established
First Malayalee Pentecostal Conference in North America
Mar Thoma Zonal Council authorized
Mar Thoma Church signs formal agreement with the Episcopal Church in the United States

1983 Mar Thoma Family Conference in the United States established
Knanaya Catholic priest assigned to Chicago

1984 Dedication of the Nilakkal Ecumenical Church in Kerala
Malankara Catholic Mission of North America inaugurated
Brethren Gospel Mission India established

1985 Syro-Malabar Catholic Mission inaugurated in Chicago

1986 Pope John Paul constitutes the Syro-Malabar Church as a major archiepiscopal church

1988 Mar Thoma Diocese of North America established
Knanaya Orthodox Diocese of North America established by Mar Abraham Clemis

1990 US Immigration Act revises preference classifications

1993 Malankara Orthodox Diocese of North America and Europe divided into the Diocese of the United States and the Diocese of Canada, the United Kingdom, and Europe
Mar Thoma resident bishop appointed for North America
Indian Syrian Orthodox Church Diocese of North America authorized by the Patriarch of Antioch, and a new bishop is consecrated and appointed
Church of South India planning for a National Council in the United States
Knanaya (Catholic) Community Center dedicated in Chicago

ST. THOMAS SYRIAN CHRISTIANS: THE FIRST CENTURIES

The story

We are proud to be called "Thomas Christians" because the Apostle Thomas came to the Malabar coast in AD 52 to proclaim the gospel in India. He converted several families from the high-caste Nambudiri Brahmins, who were permitted to maintain their high status, so we who are Thomas Christians still enjoy a prominent place in south Indian society. St. Thomas planted seven churches in the Malabar region, one near my native place, and then he traveled to the eastern Coromandal coast, where he was martyred in AD 72. We commemorate the event every year on St. Thomas Day; once on that day I visited his burial place at the cathedral in Madras. Our Indian church has an ancient apostolic foundation; it has an ancient sanctity greater than the European churches.

Elaboration and context

Although not himself a Christian, Giani Zail Singh, a former President of India, quoted a common tripartite description of Thomas Christianity, "With deep roots in the soil, Indian Christianity has developed an independent personality of its own – Christian in religion, Oriental in worship, and Indian in culture" (*Syro-Malabar Catholic Chicago Souvenir*, 1988). Christianity is old enough in India to be an integral part of Indian culture, especially in the south. Two strands of tradition place the Apostle Thomas in India in the first century AD. The third-century *Acts of Thomas* preserve the conviction of Christians in Mesopotamia that Jesus sent St. Thomas to serve as carpenter for a King Gundaphorus, who was later identified as ruler of part of what is now Iran, Afghanistan, and areas of northwestern India from AD. 16 until at least AD 45 (Neill, 1984:28). A southern tradition, more popular among Indian Christians, is that St. Thomas arrived on the Malabar coast of southwest India in AD 52 and established seven churches in what is now Kerala – Cranganore, Quilon, Palayur, Pararur, Pallipuram, Niranam, and Nilakkal. The story continues to record his preaching to and conversion of high-caste Nambudiri Brahmins, who, it is claimed, continued after conversion to enjoy high-status in the eyes of the local population. After establishing the church on the west coast, he traveled to China to preach. He returned to the Malabar coast to organize the Christians there under leaders from prominent families and then moved eastward to the Coromandal coast near Madras where he was martyred on July 3, AD 72. In that early period little distinguished the Malayalee and Tamil languages. Thomas' service in Tamil country is now marked by a shrine on St. Thomas Mount, a cathedral in the Mylapore section of modern Madras marking the location of his burial, and a reliquary containing a finger bone of the saint, which is regularly carried in procession and shown to pilgrims. His death is marked by all Thomas Christians on St. Thomas' Day in the liturgical calendar. A Syrian tradition preserved in hymns of St. Ephream (d. AD 373) is that St. Thomas' body was moved from Mylapore near Madras to be reburied in Edessa (Moffett, 1992:46). The entire story serves to validate an apostolic tradition separate from those in the West even though there is little evidence of a continuity of clergy or bishops serving the Thomas Christians. It is plausible, however, that Christianity traveled to India in that early period prior to the rise of Islam because there is evidence of travel from Syria and Arabia to India, both to north India by the overland route that came to be known as the Old Silk Road and to south India by sea in ships carried on the monsoon winds to the Malabar coast. Christians point to five old Syrian crosses with Pahlavi (ancient Persian) inscriptions decorating Christian sites (four in Kerala and one at St. Thomas Mount) as material evidence of this intercourse.

The story
My parents carried identity cards identifying them as "Syrian Christians" because we are descendants from one of the seventy-two families that came to Cranganore on the Malabar coast with the merchant Thomas from greater Syria in AD 345. That is the reason we are called "Syrian Christians." Our ancestors came to settle and to purify the Christian beliefs and practices of the Thomas Christians and to renew ties with the Orthodox Catholicos of the East in Baghdad. Hence, Syrian bishops exercise legitimate authority over my church. When the merchant Thomas arrived, the ruler, Cheraman Perumal, gave high honors and gifts to him and his companions. Thomas came from a village called "Cana" or "Knai" so some descendants of families that came with him are Knanaya Christians and form a distinct hereditary group among Syrian Christians and maintain ethnic purity through intermarriage.

Elaboration and context
Considerable Western textual evidence places Christians in India in the early Christian centuries (Neill, 1984:36ff.). The earliest liturgical traditions of Malabar were in oral form, but were recorded in letters, narratives, and reports by the early Portuguese settlers. According to one tradition, the community converted by Thomas on the Coromandel coast migrated into Malabar and settled down at various places. The reports also testify to the early and close relation of the Indian Christians with eastern Syrian (Chaldean or Babylonian) Christianity in the area of the old Persian Empire with its center in Seleucia-Ctesiphon or Babylon. Hence, St. Thomas Christians often explain that the early Nambudiri Brahmin converts of St. Thomas merged with the Syrian immigrants in the fourth century to constitute the ancient Thomas or Syrian Christian community. The eastern Syrian forms of Christianity are distinguished

from those in the western Syrian parts of the Roman Empire, with its center in Antioch. The eastern Syrian churches came under the Catholicos of the East, whose relationship with the western patriarchs and bishops was complicated by both ecclesiastical and theological conflicts. He periodically sent bishops and priests to India. The eastern and western Syrian rites had both separate hierarchies and differences in the Syriac liturgy which still affect the Syrian Christians in Kerala, distinguished as western Syrian (Antiochene) and eastern Syrian (Babylonian). During the Christological controversies, the eastern church was branded as Nestorian, and even though the Nestorian church spread rapidly and widely to the east, it was effectively separated from Christians in the west by both political and theological factors.

Although some remnants of Nestorian doctrine may have appeared in Syriac texts in India, the St. Thomas Christians seem to have been little affected by the Christological controversies. From the third or fourth centuries the Malabar church used the eastern Syrian liturgy in Syriac – a language closely related to Aramaic – which became a major eastern commercial and liturgical language until the spread of Islam.[2] The eastern Syrian liturgy developed in Edessa in a church claiming its foundation from St. Thomas through two early missionaries, Agai and Mari, appointed by Thomas. The story of the removal of the remains of St. Thomas from India for reburial in Edessa is a testimony to that close connection.

Knanaya St. Thomas Christians form a distinct endogamous group among St. Thomas Christians and preserve a story of a migration of Syrians to Malabar in AD 345. The story begins with a dream vision experienced by the Metropolitan of Edessa, containing a revelation of the sad plight of the Malabar Christians. He reported the vision to the Catholicos of the East, who sent a merchant by the name of Thomas, first to investigate and report and then on a second journey to lead a group of 400 Syrian Christians in seventy-two families, including a bishop, priests, and deacons, from Jerusalem, Edessa, and Baghdad. They landed from seven ships at Cranganore where the ruler, Cheraman Perumal, is said to have welcomed these Christians by providing both land for settlement and honors that established them in a high social status at least equal to the Nambudiri Brahmin converts already present in Malabar who had been allowed by rulers and neighbors to maintain their symbols of status. Eventually they migrated south from Cranganore and established themselves in the central Travancore area around Kottayam.

"Knanaya" as the current designation for the endogamous descendants of these Syrian families relates to Thomas' origin either from
Cana of Galilee or from a village Knai in present-day Iraq. Origin in
either place supports the claim that the Knanaya are descendants of
Jewish Christians belonging to seven clans of a Davidic lineage who
came to Malabar via Babylon. The claim is that the Judeans did not
intermarry with the foreigners as did the northern tribes, and, moreover,
because the Babylonian Jews had been very observant in the matter of
preserving the purity of the genealogical lineage, the Jewish Christians
continued the Jewish endogamous practice both in Babylon and later in
India. Hence, Knanaya endogamy is said by insiders to have its roots in
the Jewish tradition and to have little to do with the Indian caste system
(Kollaparambil, 1992:109, 129). A study undertaken from a different perspective suggests that development of a Knanaya image, which refers to
a remote past, to high-caste privileges and sumptuous wedding feasts in
old Malabar, is a recent process, even though the group goes back a long
way in Kerala history. By claiming and preserving stories and wedding
songs from the Syrian tradition, they have won the right to behave like an
Indian social group, in effect as a caste with the blessing of outside hierarchies, and established themselves as a socio-economic upper class in
contemporary Kerala (Swiderski, 1988:7–8, 138).

Thus, the St. Thomas Christians divided into two ethnically distinct
communities known as Northists and Southists. The Northists are the
descendants of those who were evangelized by the Apostle Thomas and
later converts, while the Southists trace their origin back to Knai
Thomas and the Christian immigrants from Babylonia. The Knanaya
have no religion of their own; they follow the same liturgies and doctrines as other Thomas Christians. Nevertheless, they have maintained
an ethnic community through the vicissitudes of Indian Christianity.
The Knanaya remained united as one church under one ecclesiastical
order and one liturgy until the coming of the Portuguese. A bishop, who
was always an unmarried foreigner, and a married archdeacon from the
Pakalkomarram family in Malabar jointly administered the affairs of the
St. Thomas Syrian Church (Neill, 1984:206).

The two stories about men named Thomas with ties to Edessa provide
the ancient narrative background for the St. Thomas Syrian Christians
of Malabar. Until the Portuguese came, they were ecclesiastically, doctri-
nally, and ritually one church that had adapted to the social, religious,
and political culture of Malabar. Three types of isolation restricted
growth of Christianity: (1) the Malabar coast, while open to the west and

to the influences coming by sea, lacks easy access to the rest of south India because of the Western Ghat mountain range that in earlier times routed travel along the coastal areas of the southern tip of India and that today separates Kerala from Tamil Nadu; (2) this geographical isolation is reflected in political boundaries and antagonisms between ruling families; (3) the social isolation of Thomas Christians, claiming equality with high-caste Hindus and descent from honored Syrian immigrants, restricted both their desire and ability to gain converts from the range of social groups in Malabar. From the first to the sixteenth century, Malabar Christians did not actively engage in evangelism, which may have contributed to their peaceful relations with their Hindu neighbors. They continued a constant, if somewhat obscure, existence in Kerala and were present to welcome the array of visitors, merchants, and priests who washed up on the Malabar coast.

IMPACT OF ROMAN CATHOLIC CHRISTIANITY: SIXTEENTH
CENTURY TO THE PRESENT

Vimos buscare cristaos e especiaria

The story
A few of my acquaintances are Indian Catholics of the Latin rite, but they attend a separate Mass and have their own social organizations. The Portuguese came to India in search of Christians and spices and brought the Latin rite with them, but they were ignorant of the character of Indian Christianity. The Jesuits arrived in India in AD 1542 in the person of St. Xavier, who converted low-caste pearl-fishermen from the southern coast. Goa became a Portuguese settlement and a base for Jesuit missions to the East at the same time that St. Xavier and his fellow priests were attempting to bring the Indian church under the control of the Roman pope. Many converts since that time all over India follow the Latin rite.

Elaboration and context
Two narratives highlight Portuguese initiatives that shaped the history of the church in India during the sixteenth century, with results still in evidence: the arrival of Vasco da Gama under the Portuguese *Padroado* and the missionary work of St. Xavier. After Bartholomew Dias demonstrated that it was possible to sail south around Africa to the East, thereby making it possible for merchants to circumvent the spice trade routes controlled by Muslims, Vasco da Gama with three small ships arrived at Calicut (Kozhikode) on May 17, 1498, "in search of Christians and

spices," entering a territory already committed to the king of Portugal. Beginning in AD 1418, a succession of popes had delegated the right of patronage (*Padroado*) in conquered lands to the kings of Portugal. In 1493, Pope Alexander XI yielded to a petition of King Ferdinand and Queen Isabella of Spain by making a division: Spanish monarchs were assigned as patrons of conquered lands west of an imaginary line some 140 miles west of the Azores and Portuguese monarchs as patrons of lands eastward. Patronage included military, mercantile, and religious rights; the popes made the Portuguese kings their vicars with authority in the East to establish churches and monasteries, to ordain and discipline clergy, and to regulate religious affairs through the Order of Christ (de Melo, 1982:21–26). Thus began the latinization and division of the Indian church.

Vasco da Gama sought Christians and thought that he discovered in Calicut (Kozhikode) a shrine to the Virgin, although a careful reading of the report suggests that the sailors were in a Hindu temple dedicated to the goddess. Two years later a larger expedition under Pedro Alvares Cabral – including one vicar, eight secular priests, eight Franciscans, an organist, and one lay brother – reached Calicut, finally made contact with St. Thomas Christians, and established Cochin as the center of Portuguese trade (Neill, 1984:92, 114f.). When Vasco da Gama returned in AD 1502, St. Thomas Christians from Cranganore met him bearing gifts and asking for the assistance of the Portuguese king in their social and political relations. Although the early relations between the Portuguese and the Indian Christians were cordial, misunderstandings inherent in the meeting foreshadowed tensions and conflicts that later developed. The Portuguese were more than willing to become patrons of the some 30,000 Indian Christian families in both social and religious affairs and to protect them from their Hindu rulers and Muslim neighbors. The relationship worked to the material benefit of many Indian Christians. Although a poor minority seeking positive relations with a powerful ally, the Indian Christians, nevertheless, viewed their Christianity as in no way inferior to that of the Latins. They had their own bishops and priests, a venerable apostolic tradition, a liturgical language linked to that of Jesus and the Apostles, ties to the Chaldean patriarch that permitted considerable local autonomy, and a beautiful Syrian liturgy. In the joy of the first encounter, the Syrians underestimated both the determination of the Portuguese to bring the Indian church into union with the church in Rome and their belief that they had a divine right to bring the St. Thomas Christians into compliance. The

Portuguese underestimated the attachment of the Indian Christians to their Syriac language, songs, and liturgy and the authority the Chaldean patriarch exercised through the Syrian bishops consecrated by him for India. Tensions increased after Goa became the administrative and diocesan center for Portuguese India in 1534 and the first bishop was consecrated in 1538 (Neill, 1984:117).

The story of Francis Xavier (1506–52) takes pride of place in the early Catholic mission to the East even though he was neither the first missionary nor the most successful. He attracts attention as a missionary saint because of the winsome romance of his biography and because of the growing importance of the Society of Jesus in the decade between 1542 and 1552. Xavier met Ignatius Loyola at the University of Paris and took solemn vows in 1534 as one of the first six members of what was recognized as the Society of Jesus by the pope in 1540. Xavier accepted the call of the king of Portugal to serve in India and landed at Goa on May 6, 1542. Word had reached Goa of a Paravar community of fishermen in the extreme south of India that had sought the protection of the Portuguese from Muslim traders and their Hindu rulers in Madurai. Their traditional occupation was fishing and diving for pearls along the coast of Kanya Kumari (Cape Comorin). The whole community of some 20,000 people was converted and baptized, many taking Portuguese names. It was the first mass conversion of Indians and establishes a common pattern of communal conversions of entire villages, castes, and families from low-caste and untouchable groups (what are now called scheduled castes and tribes), but no provision had been made for spiritual care of the new Christians. Xavier spent four of his ten years of missionary activity on the Pearl Fishery Coast teaching, preaching, and establishing the church among these new converts and their neighbors. He was often away from the area extending the Jesuit mission to Malacca (in present-day Indonesia) and Japan, and for trips to Goa. While in Goa he attempted to ameliorate the growing conflict between the Portuguese and the St. Thomas Christians – even though he was not opposed in principle to the Inquisition – but he was not successful in resolving the conflicts or in avoiding the division between the Latins and the Syrians. His body is preserved in the Basilica of Bom Jesus in Goa as the patron saint of Goa.

The secular priests and Franciscans arriving on the annual fleet that sailed from Lisbon to Cochin and Goa had been active before Xavier arrived. Some served as chaplains to the Portuguese, but others were successful in attracting converts in the two territories, so successful that they requested the assistance of other religious orders. Franciscans were joined by Dominicans and Jesuits, who established churches, mission centers, colleges, and monasteries. The Latin dioceses were established in Goa (1534) and in Cochin (1558). It seems that the converts came primarily from those classes of people who were in close contact with the Portuguese: women and their children who lived with the Portuguese, merchants trading with them, and those of low caste who were drawn to the Portuguese and their lack of concern with Indian caste regulations. These new Christians provided the foundation of Latin Catholic Christianity in India upon which the Portuguese, operating under the *Padroado*, and other colonial powers helped build a significant Catholic presence. The three most prominent orders were joined by the Augustinians, Carmelites, Theatines, and the Oratorians, who, along with secular priests, expanded the mission work to other parts of India.

After a short period of cordial relations between the St. Thomas Christians and the Portuguese and between the bishops who came from eastern Syria and the missionary priests from Europe, tensions soon developed because of the project of latinization that the Portuguese viewed as part of their responsibility under *Padroado* and the view that the Syrian Christians had of themselves as part of a social and religious group superior to the new converts from communities of lower status, whom they called Latin Christians. Working-out of these tensions is an uneven tortuous process that still continues in contemporary Christian India and the United States.

Some of the missionaries treated the St. Thomas Christians as heretics required to recant and accept the Latin liturgy, orthodox doctrine, and the primacy of the pope, while other missionaries were more gentle in their ministrations. Latinization was evident in Cranganore and Quilon, where Thomas Christians lacked leadership of clergy. Everywhere the general tenor was to preserve new converts in Latin dioceses and to force Syrian Christians to conform to Latin patterns by removing several elements and practices offensive to the missionaries.

(1) Missionaries identified the Chaldean church as the Nestorian Church and by association came to view the Thomas Christians as infected with the Nestorian heresy. Although the Thomas Christians seem to be little influenced by Nestorian doctrines, some of their Syrian liturgical texts and hymns contained elements that the missionaries held suspect. Latin priests studied the texts and revised them to excise heretical passages, and some books were burned. The Syrians claim that the

Latins destroyed many of their ancient documents, thereby removing many proofs of their ancient and apostolic traditions.

(2) Charges of heresy led to objections to the eastern Syriac liturgy and to the use of the Syrian language. Hence, pressure to replace the Syriac language and rite with the Latin was an attempt to remove heresy by breaking the cultural and liturgical ties to Persia. Since Thomas Catholics did not know Latin and few missionaries knew Syriac, it was felt that a united church would need a common liturgical language and rite.

(3) Thomas Christians maintained their loyalty to the patriarch of Babylon and to the bishops and priests consecrated by him and ordained by his authority. The Thomas Christians welcomed Latin bishops and participated in Masses led by Latin priests, when their own priests were not available, but they gave primary allegiance to those in the Syrian tradition. The missionaries viewed this reserve as being rebellion against the primacy of the pope in Rome and ultimately against the unity of the church. Even though Mar Abuna Jacob, a revered Syrian bishop, gave in to considerable pressure from the Franciscans to affirm the authority of the Roman pontiff, he and his followers were treated as schismatics rather than as a sister church in communion with Rome. These were the major points of conflict.

A whole litany of minor differences increased tension and lengthened the list of issues.

(4) In accord with the eastern custom, married priests were ordained in the St. Thomas Syrian Church, even though the bishops remained unmarried and under monastic orders. The missionaries objected and refused to permit married men to perform the Mass in Latin churches. Hence, whereas Thomas Christians regularly communed with Latin priests, Latin Christians were prohibited from communing with the majority of Syrian priests.

(5) Thomas Christians rejected the use of images in their churches, whereas the Latins encouraged the use of images, leading some Syrians to accuse them of idolatry similar to that of their Hindu neighbors.

(6) The Syrian bishops refused to ordain priests trained in the Latin seminaries.

(7) The power of the archdeacon in the Indian church was both a religious and political problem for the Latins. The unmarried bishop from Syria exercised spiritual authority, whereas the archdeacon from the Pakalkomarram family in Kerala held considerable ecclesiastical and communal administrative authority. Negotiations between the

Portuguese officials, both religious and political, and the archdeacons were often fractious.

(8) From earliest times down to the twentieth century, Syrian priests were from prominent and relatively well-to-do families and they lived off the family inheritance. Their church income was from fees and gifts for performing baptisms, funerals, and other family rituals. Likewise, the main income of the bishops came from fees for ordination. The missionaries charged them with simony because they "sold" the sacraments and the means of grace. The Syrians protested that the Latins viewed any divergence in the eastern rite from the Latin rite as dangerous and probably heretical. Moreover, they argued that the disputes were fueled by the desire of the Portuguese to subject the Thomas Christians along with their spice trade and other enterprises to Western control (Verghese, 1973:79f.).

The primary strategies of latinization were twofold. (1) The Latin missionaries provided clergy to serve in locations where Syrian priests were lacking. In those locations they instituted the Latin rite and attempted to lead the people to submit to the authority of Rome and to participation in a Latin diocese. A dispute arose over whether Latin priests could baptize children in Thomas Christian families, a rite previously reserved to the Syrian bishops. The mission activity of Latin priests among Syrian churches is the reverse of the situation in modern independent India where the majority of missionary priests and religious are from the Syro-Malabar-rite church, who until recently, however, had to serve under the Latin rite. (2) Previously priests were trained in the traditional Indian gurukul system of living with the bishops and learning from them in "home seminaries" and under a "holy apprenticeship." The Latin missionaries recruited young men from the Thomas churches to be trained in the newly established seminaries where they were alienated from their Syriac traditions and indoctrinated in Latin rites and teaching. The seminary established by the Franciscans at Cranganore (Cranganur) became an important Latin center for training Syrian youth. Thomas bishops refused, however, to ordain priests trained in Latin seminaries, so most served in Latin churches. Even though unsuccessful in eradicating the Syrian rite, the program of latinization was successful in expanding the influence of the Latin dioceses, in revising elements of the Syriac liturgy, in weakening the authority of the Syrian bishops and their priests, and introducing into Syrian churches elements of Latin ritual and discipline. It also led to rebellion that divided the church in India and had profound effects on the future of Christianity there.

The story
Archbishop Alexis de Menezes was the worst and most aggressive proponent of latinization. He antagonized our Syrian Christian leaders by his misrepresentation of our doctrines and practices and he forced many of us to submit to the Latin rite and to Roman ecclesiastical authorities. The extreme example of his arrogance and intrusiveness was the Synod of Diamper (Udiyamperur) in 1599, which placed the Syrian Christians under the Latin archbishopric of Goa.

Elaboration and context
Thomas Christians tell this story of Alexis de Menezes, archbishop of Goa from 1595 to 1612, and portray him as the deceitful culprit attempting to destroy the Thomas church and identity, but Latin Christians tell the story differently, presenting him as a person of great integrity and winsomeness and as a staunch defender of the authority of Rome and Tridentine orthodoxy. He became archbishop and primate of the East in 1595 with a charge to investigate the Syrian bishop, Mar Abraham, who died soon thereafter in 1597 following a period of conflict with the Latin missionaries. That provided an opportunity to prevent his replacement by the Syrian patriarch and to force the Thomas Christians into compliance with Rome. Indeed, the archbishop decided that the separate existence of the ancient church must end and that the Indian church must accept the positions adopted in the Catholic Reformation in Europe. Menezes visited Cochin to establish his authority and convened the Synod of Diamper (Udiyamperur) in a village south of Cochin in 1599. There a new Syro-Malabar liturgy was imposed. Syriac was kept as the liturgical language, but portions identified as Nestorian and those commending church fathers judged by Rome to be heretical were omitted and new elements translated from the Latin were added. Two forms of the liturgy were now approved by the archbishop, the Latin rite and a Syro-Malabar rite, the latter based on an ancient eastern Syrian rite as modified under Latin influences. A major change in ecclesiastical structure allowed the archbishop in 1601 to consecrate a Latin bishop for the Thomas Christians and to place him as suffragan bishop under the diocese of Goa. Thereby the independence of the Thomas Christians ended, and they became part of the one universal Roman Catholic Church. Or so it seemed.

The story
Our Syrian Christian ancestors rebelled against the intrusions of Latin Christians by gathering in protest in the compound of the church in Mattancheri, south of Cochin. There, in 1653, they held ropes tied around the

leaning cross in the courtyard and took oaths renouncing their allegiance to the Latin archbishop and expressing their disdain for and rejection of the Jesuits. This act preserved Syrian Christianity in India, but split our Indian church into various Orthodox and Latin branches.

Elaboration and context

Resentment brewed under the surface only to break out a half-century later as told in the story of the Coonen Cross (the crooked cross) Oath. A new archdeacon of the Thomas Christians secretly contacted the Patriarch of Babylon, the Patriarch of Antioch, and the Coptic Patriarch of Egypt, hoping that a bishop might come from Mesopotamia to replace Mar Abraham. Into this scene of conflict appeared Mar Ahatalla, an Oriental bishop whose exact ecclesiastical authority is questioned. He arrived in Mylapore and styled himself "Ignatius, Patriarch of India and China." He was detained by the Jesuits and sent by ship to Goa for investigation by the Inquisition. Thinking that his prayers and petitions for a new bishop for the Thomas Christians had been answered, the archdeacon gathered 25,000 Syrian Christians at Cochin, demanding that the Portuguese release the bishop and establish him as prelate. The Portuguese captain rejected their request outright, and the ship sailed past Cochin without stopping. On January 3, 1653, disgruntled priests and people gathered at a church in Mattancheri and, touching ropes tied to a holy cross in the open courtyard, took an oath renouncing their allegiance to the Latin archbishop, and vowing not to be subject to the Jesuits. Thomas Christians passing by on the highway still point to the church and tell the story as a defining event of their history. Within a few months, the archdeacon was consecrated as bishop of the Thomas Christians, the ordination authorized in disputed letters purporting to come from Ahatalla. The Syrians and the Latins became two endogamous groups, with exceptions to endogamous marriage being very few. One group tells the Coonen Cross story as the restoration of the independence and purity of the ancient church of St. Thomas, the other as a schism from the one true church.

What follows is a period of confused negotiation and intrigue while archdeacon and archbishop maneuver to win the allegiance of the churches. Stephen Neill describes the situation: "To produce peace and order out of such a witch's cauldron of pride, self-seeking, duplicity and interested motives could not be an easy task. No one comes very well out of the story" (1984:322). A majority of the Thomas Christians wooed by Carmelite mediators remained in or returned to the archbishop's fold,

and the concession was made that one of their own would be consecrated as bishop, which happened in February 1663, less than a month
after the Dutch captured Cochin. Moreover, Thomas Christians continued to use the Syro-Malabar liturgy approved in the Synod of Diamper,
the same as that used by those who, with their new bishop, now named
Mar Thoma I, rejected the authority of the Latin prelates. As the story
develops, both a clear distinction between Syro-Malabar-rite Catholics
and Latin-rite Catholics and a split between St. Thomas Catholics and
St. Thomas Syrian Christians become so pronounced that the churches
remain separate in America today.

The story continues. Newly arrived bishops of the Antiochene rite
moved the Syrian Orthodox further from the Catholics by "restoring"
the Syrian rite, both by replacing the Chaldean rite as revised under
latinization with the Antiochene liturgy and by establishing the authority
of the Patriarch of Antioch over the churches of the East. Mar
Gregorios of Jerusalem was the first to arrive in 1665, and he was
restrained in making changes. He emphasized the antiquity and
attractiveness of the Syrian rite and persuaded Thomas Christians to
restore and maintain the Syrian traditions that had suffered through
latinization imposed by the Synod of Diamper. Two additional bishops,
Mar John from Mosul and Mar Basilius, arrived twenty years later, Mar
John with full credentials from the Patriarch of Antioch. A third delega-
tion landed in 1751, after Portuguese power had been replaced by the
more sympathetic Dutch Protestants. Although the process of adoption
or restoration of the Antiochene rite was not officially implemented until
1836, these bishops began a broadly based revision that continued for
two centuries. (1) They said the Mass, called the Holy Qurbana, in the
Syriac of the Antiochene liturgy. (2) They encouraged the marriage of
men who would be priests and deacons, while reserving the episcopal
office for monks according to their ancient custom. (3) They removed
crucifixes and images from churches and replaced them with pictures,
accusing Latin-rite Christians of idolatry. (4) They restored the old calendar and traditional vestments. (5) They replaced the eastern Chaldean
script of Syriac with the western Antiochene script. And, most importantly: (6) they affirmed the authority of the Patriarch of Antioch to consecrate bishops and to establish discipline for the Syrian Orthodox
Church. (7) They gradually replaced the eastern Syrian liturgy (Syro-
Malabar liturgy) with the western Syrian liturgy of St. James used in the
Antiochene liturgy. Hence, they are often called "Jacobites." Jacobite
apologists claim that St. Thomas Christians had an ancient relationship

with Antioch and these changes were simply the restoration of earlier loyalties and discipline. The transition was not complete, however, even when it was formally announced at the Synod of Mavelikara in 1836: "We the Syrian Jacobites, who are subject to the supreme power of the Antiochene Patriarch and who use the liturgy and rites instituted by the prelates sent by his authority, cannot deviate from such liturgies and rites and adopt a discipline contrary to them" (Cyril, 1973:83). The formal declaration and solidifying of positions were in part responses to the influence of Protestant missionaries who were encouraging changes in the liturgies, as much as they were responses to Latin pressures.

The story
The Syrian Orthodox Church suffered from a split between those loyal to the Patriarch in Baghdad and those loyal to the Catholicos in Kerala. A Malankara Orthodox priest, P. T. Geevarghese, founded the first Indian Orthodox religious order, the Order of the Imitation of Christ (popularly called the Bethany Ashram) and subsequently became bishop. He led a movement of reunion and joined the Catholic Church in 1930. The Pope responded by authorizing the Syro-Malankara rite as one of the Oriental rites of the church.

Elaboration and context
Unfortunately, the story of the Malabar church is filled with conflict and division. The Syrian Orthodox Church subsequently divided in dis-agreement about the authority of the patriarch of Antioch in the Indian church. In 1875 the Syrian Patriarch himself arrived in Travancore to quell disputes among the Syrians and between them and the British. He attempted to establish total control over the Jacobite church, divided Malabar into seven dioceses, and appointed a ruling Metropolitan. Tensions continued to mount so that when Patriarch Abdulla on a visit to India in 1911 demanded that Geevarghese Mar Dionysius pledge com-plete obedience to the patriarch, he was rebuffed. Whereupon, the patri-arch excommunicated Mar Dionysius, who then put forward a monk to be consecrated as Catholicos of the East by the former, then deposed, Patriarch of Antioch who arrived in India in 1912. The deposed patri-arch then conveyed to Indian bishops authority to elect monks as future Catholicoi. The office of Catholicos was new to India, but it was consid-ered a revival of one that had existed at Seleucia on the Tigris. A split developed between the Syrian Orthodox Church (the patriarch's supporters), which accepted both the spiritual and administrative authority of the Patriarch of Antioch, now in Damascus, and the Malankara Orthodox Syrian Church (the Catholicos' supporters),

which acceded to the spiritual authority of the patriarch but vested all ecclesiastical authority in India to the Catholicos. In 1909 the Knanaya Orthodox had been permitted to have a separate diocese and their own bishop under the patriarch of Antioch, and they continue to preserve their separate identity as an Antiochene-rite church under their current bishop, Mar Clemis Abraham, one of the senior Jacobite bishops. He resides at Mar Ephraem Seminary at Chingavanam a few kilometers from Kottayam. Approximately one-third of the Knanaya community is Jacobite and two-thirds Syro-Malabar-rite Catholic (Kuriakose Kunnasserry, personal communication, February 1994).

A series of tangled lawsuits and negotiations for reconciliation among Syrian Christians began in 1913 and are still unresolved. Lawsuits take a long time to resolve in India. One lawsuit ended in 1958 with a court judgment in favor of the authority of the Catholicos and a period of reconciliation. After twelve years a new suit was brought, however, and in 1990 a judgment again in favor of the Catholicos was handed down in the Kerala Supreme Court regarding control of institutions and property, a judgment that is currently under appeal in the Supreme Court of India. The current Patriarch of Antioch is Moran Mor Ignatius Zakka I, the Supreme Head of the Universal Syrian Orthodox Church, and his presiding bishop in Kerala is Mar Baselius Paulose II, residing at Muvatupuzha. The current Catholicos of the East of the Malankara Orthodox Syrian Church is Mar Thoma Mathews II. He resides at Devalokam in Kottayam and presides with 21 other bishops over 2.2 million Orthodox Christians in 21 dioceses (15 in Kerala, and 6 outside: Madras, Bombay, Calcutta, Delhi, North America, and the United Kingdom and Europe), and 1,200 priests, 70 cor-episcopas, 110 deacons, 180 monks, and 170 nuns. A Malankara Association made up of 1 priest and 2 laymen from each of the 1,000 or so parishes selects some 100 persons to constitute a management council. Among the institutions of the church are a seminary, 15 monasteries, 10 convents, 17 colleges, and 24 hospitals. The Syrian Orthodox Church loyal to the patriarch is about half this size.

A renewal movement within the Malankara Orthodox Syrian Church led to a movement of reunion and to a new rite within the Catholic Church. In 1920 a Malankara priest, P. T. Geevarghese, founded the first Indian Orthodox religious order, attempting to combine elements of Oriental Christian monasticism and Indian spirituality. His Order of the Imitation of Christ is popularly called the Bethany congregation of priests and sisters or the Bethany Ashram. He was consecrated as bishop,

Mar Ivanios, in 1925. Hoping to spark renewal and reunion of the church, he joined the Catholic Church on September 20, 1930, followed by all the Bethany sisters, most of the monks, some 35 diocesan priests and about 4,000 faithful. However, the majority of the Syrians did not follow Mar Ivanios. Nevertheless, Pope Pius XI issued an Apostolic Constitution, *Christo Pastorum Principi*, in 1932, establishing a Syro-Malankara rite, authorizing the continuation of the use of the western Syrian Antiochene liturgy, including that of St. James and the hymns and chants of St. Ephraem, and establishing a Syro-Malankara ecclesiastical province at Trivandrum (Kuriedath, 1989:14). Mar Ivanios was consecrated as the first Metropolitan Archbishop of Trivandrum in the newly constituted Syro-Malankara hierarchy.

Thus, the Catholic Church in India is divided into three rites, with distinct liturgies, dioceses, bishops, parishes, and institutions. The Syro-Malankara-rite Catholics started small in 1930, but have grown dramatically as their statistics attest: 3 dioceses (all in Kerala), 5 bishops, 267,290 lay people, 297 diocesan clergy, 71 religious clergy, 413 sisters, and 112 religious men (many of the religious from the Bethany congregations). The Syro-Malabar rite has had its own indigenous bishops since 1896 and is currently the largest Christian body in Kerala, where it has 12 dioceses, 2,128 priests, and 2,731,809 lay people (Nedungatt, 1989:14f.). The Knanaya Catholics participate in the Syro-Malabar rite and have their own bishop, Dr. Kuriokose Kunnasserry, in Kottayam. The vast majority of Catholics in these rites claim to be "old Christians" with ties to the Syrian ancestors and to St. Thomas. The 12,010,360 Catholics in India are in 119 dioceses served by 14,229 priests. The Oriental rites were largely restricted to Kerala, while the Latin rite outstripped both of the other rites in membership as it spread throughout India: Latin rite, 75.54 percent; Syro-Malabar rite, 23.31 percent; Syro-Malankara rite, 2.25 percent. Of the 119 dioceses, 96 are Latin rite, including 9 in Kerala with 1,279,809 lay people (Nedungatt, 1989:14). The Latin Christians are often called "new Christians" and generally come from the depressed classes, divided into different caste-based endogamous communities, and from the Anglo-Indians, all of whom are Christian descendants from marriages with Europeans. The Anglo-Indians suffer from serious economic problems and have little interaction with other Christian communities. Many in the Latin rite in Kerala are from fisherman castes along the southern coast. Several communities of the Latin rite in south India have no matrimonial relations with other communities of the same rite (Podipara, 1986:116).

Relations among these churches have not always been positive. Three issues caused tension. (1) The Oriental-rite priests were forbidden to evangelize outside Kerala except as Latins and on behalf of the Latin dioceses. That has the odor of the centuries-old Portuguese attempt to eliminate the Syro-Malabar ritual. The point is important because the two Oriental rites provide some 70 percent of the missionary personnel in India. About 2,000 priests and more than 8,000 religious sisters and brothers belonging to the Syro-Malabar rite work in mission dioceses outside of Kerala. Every year about 1,800 candidates are admitted to priestly studies and religious life. Of these about 700 join the Latin mission dioceses (Mundadan, 1984:105). Most have to discard their native rite and tradition, even in the 7 Latin dioceses where they out-number the Latin-rite priests. (2) The Latin-rite Catholics were per-mitted to establish dioceses and expand into areas of Kerala where the Oriental rites are established. A result is that some Syrian Catholics, including some of the lay leaders who worked with Mar Ivanios for reunion, face having their children and grandchildren baptized and trained in the Latin rite. (3) This seemed especially insulting when Oriental-rite Catholics outside Kerala were prohibited from being served by priests and bishops of the Oriental rites. Keralite Christians migrated throughout India in search of employment, so that in several cities the Syrian Catholics are more numerous than Latin Catholics.[3] As Keralites emigrated abroad to the Gulf states and to the United States, pressures developed to permit the extension of Syro-Malabar jurisdic-tion over those abroad. These pressures were stoutly resisted by the majority of those in the Catholic Bishops' Conference of India.

The story
The Second Vatican Council offered a ray of hope to Indian Christians, promising to give our Oriental rites, the Syro-Malabar and the Syro-Malankara, equal status with the Latin rite in the Catholic Church. Nevertheless, the last part of the century has seen a series of struggles of ancient Christian rites of India to establish equity with the Latin Church in India and abroad. Only now are we beginning to receive the recognition our ancient her-itage deserves.

Elaboration and context
The Second Vatican Council "opened the windows of the church" and led to negotiations within the Indian Catholic Church that still continue and exert influence on immigrants in America. The institution of ver-nacular languages requires the translation of all three rites into

Malayalam from Syriac and Latin. The institution of the first Mass in Malayalam in 1962 narrowed the separation of Oriental and Latin Catholics in Kerala, even though significant differences in the liturgy remained, but outside Kerala it established language-based churches so that the Keralite Christians increasingly pushed for parishes in which the Syro-Malabar rite in Malayalam could be used. The council document, "Decree on the Catholic Churches of the eastern Rite," affirmed the integrity of the Oriental rites in communion with the Roman church, which encouraged the Syrian-rite Catholics to hope for equal recognition in spite of opposition of the Latin bishops in India.[4] Increased worldwide emigrations since 1960, including those by Keralites, raised the issue of rites generally in the Catholic Church and especially in India. In 1978 Pope John Paul I appointed an Apostolic Visitor to study the situation of the Syro-Malabar Catholics in Latin dioceses outside Kerala. The Indian bishops accepted the theological equality of the rites, but argued that the council's teaching regarding the rights of individual churches would be difficult to implement in India. In 1986 the pope appointed a Pontifical Commission to study the issue and to submit a report. Progressive changes are still being implemented. A new Malayalam translation of the Syro-Malabar liturgy is being instituted which removes some of the Latin elements introduced by the missionaries and restores the liturgy to an eastern Syrian form. On December 16, 1992, Pope John Paul constituted "the Syro-Malabar Church as a Major Archiepiscopal Church under the title of Ernakulam-Angamaly, along with all the rights and duties incumbent on the same in terms of the Sacred Canons of the Oriental Churches" and Antony Cardinal Padiyara was installed on May 20, 1993 (*Mission India*, 1993:5). Greater freedom is given for the work of Oriental-rite dioceses and missions outside Kerala, both in the rest of India and abroad.

St. Thomas Christians were for many centuries a united and relatively autonomous church largely restricted to Kerala and the southern tip of India. Now they are in the process of becoming a group of transnational churches spread throughout India and abroad where Indian immigrants have located in the second half of the twentieth century. In the course of the centuries divisions developed over several issues that continue to divide them into several distinct groups. The Knanaya community remain divided and distinct as Syro-Malabar-rite Catholics and Antiochene-rite Orthodox followers of the Patriarch of Antioch, even though they practice ethnic endogamy across church boundaries. They once had a reputation as soldiers but now form a prosperous business community. The Syrian Orthodox Church continues a contentious division between those loyal to the Patriarch of Antioch and those loyal to the Catholicos of the East, even though they share the same liturgy and discipline. The Catholics maintain three separate rites with distinct liturgies and hierarchies, and the distinction between "old Christians" and "new Christians" previews caste discrimination that haunts Indian Christianity. The negotiations between the Latin-rite Catholics and the Oriental Catholics in India are similar to those made necessary in other places by pervasive, rapid modern migration.

In spite of past history, the St. Thomas Christians view themselves as relatives and join together in many good works. Intermarriage among them across church divisions is common, the woman generally moving to the church of her spouse. Ecumenical activities and consultations are common as several of the bishops are active in the World Council of Churches and other ecumenical bodies. Ecumenical cooperation among St. Thomas Christians is symbolized by the dedication of the Nilakkal Ecumenical Church in April 1984. Nilakkal is one of the seven churches believed to have been established by St. Thomas. It is near Sabirimala temple, a place of pilgrimage for devout Hindus. Attempts to rebuild the Nilakkal Church met with opposition, but a story of compromise and ecumenical harmony is recounted with pride:

The leaders of all the episcopal churches in Kerala met together and decided to accept another site at some distance from the original center with a view to respect the sentiments of the Hindu friends. The Government offered such a site in the thick forest and it was accepted by all concerned. For the first time in history a Church was built there by all denominations together. (Thoma, 1986:85)

Many hope that the Nilakkal Church will be a beacon for future cooperation among the churches.

IMPACT OF PROTESTANT MISSIONS: THE EIGHTEENTH CENTURY TO THE PRESENT

The story of Protestantism in India is one of bewildering diversity and occasional moves toward cooperation and unity. Diversity was fostered by both external and internal pressures. Several nations influenced affairs through travel, trade, and finally political control. The Portuguese were followed by Dutch Protestants who were in turn replaced by the British. French influence radiated from enclaves on both coasts. Each colonial administration had relations both with chaplains, who ministered to the administrators, merchants, and soldiers of the European community, and with missionaries, who sought to evangelize the Indians. When mission activity became well-developed in the nineteenth century, mission societies from different countries established churches, schools, and hospitals, which were served by their nationals and inculcated forms of Christianity with a distinct ethos for each area, and denominational mission boards established outposts throughout India.

Stratifications internal to India served to increase Christian diversity there. Governmental boundaries and political divisions were in constant flux, which affected where and when various mission groups could establish themselves. Many of these boundaries were related to geographic, linguistic, and cultural distinctions that influenced church development. Throughout the later seventeenth and the eighteenth centuries British control spread across India with the crumbling of the Mughal empire. Thus, distinguishing at any time both between territory under British control and that under other independent rulers and between territory under direct British control and the native states under indirect British control is important to an understanding of the development of Christianity in India. Some princes welcomed Christian missionaries and influence; others rejected and opposed them. Officers of the British East India Company were reticent about permitting Christian mission activity and pursued an "anti-missionary policy" in territory under their control. Hence, it was not until the evangelical awakening in Britain and a change in the company's charter in 1813 that British missionaries were permitted to work in territories directly under British control. South India was a "crazy quilt" of administrative divisions that influenced the development of Protestantism. For example, Cochin and Travancore were princely states, whereas the northern coastal area of Malabar came early under direct British rule as part of the Madras Presidency.

Ethnic regional–linguistic divisions were in place prior to Western influence and continue following independence to the present. Many current Indian state boundaries are based on language distinctions. Facility in an Indian language was essential for missionaries in their work of preaching, teaching, translating, and administration, so missionaries were largely confined to a single linguistic area. Hence, common references to Gujarati Methodist, Tamil Lutheran, Telugu Brethren, and Malayalee Anglican identify distinct denominational and linguistic groups resulting from this stratification. With increasing mobility and urbanization in the twentieth century, the large cities developed culturally diverse populations. Many of the ethnic-based churches followed their migrant members to the cities, thus creating a kaleidoscope of Christianity in urban India – and, eventually, in America as well.

A major Indian social stratification is based on caste or *jati*, which is itself localized. Already in the sixteenth century, as noted above, a distinction developed between the "old Christians" who claimed Syrian ties and the "new Christians" who were Latin-rite Christians, such as the converts on the Pearl Fishery Coast, and from the lower castes and untouchable groups in other areas of Portuguese control. The social structure in India dictated that most of the missions would work, or at least be successful, not only in a restricted geographical area, but also among a distinct caste community. With some notable exceptions, most Christian converts were from depressed classes and tribes. A number of mass movements similar to the early mass conversion to the Catholic Church on the fishery coast spread Christianity in other parts of India. "Mass movements" is the designation for "multi-individual mutually-interdependent conversion, which involves a joint decision by a number of individuals comprising a section of society which enables them to become Christian without social dislocation and leaves family and relations with other social groups largely intact" (McGavran, 1971:479f.). Conviction is buttressed by social cohesion in this case in a way not possible through individual conversion. Missionaries, mission executives, and church leaders have conflicting judgments about the validity and effectiveness of a mass movement strategy for church growth. One result in India is that the Christians adapted to the shape of the stratifications of society so that political, linguistic, caste, and regional boundaries marked and divided the Christian community.

Nevertheless, the story of the Protestant Christianity in India begins with cooperation and leads to union churches in the north and south of India. In July 1706 the first Protestant missionaries arrived at Tanquebar, a small Danish enclave in Tamil country about 150 miles south of Madras. Bartholomew Ziegenbalg and Henry Plütschau were German nationals influenced by Halle pietism, but they were sent and supported by the king of Denmark. Soon thereafter the Tanquebar mission spread into territory controlled by the British and the German Lutheran missionaries and gained support, beginning in 1732, from individual subscriptions raised by the Society for Promoting Christian Knowledge in London for the establishment of the Lutheran Church in south India. Protestant Christianity was established in five main centers – Tanquebar, Madras, Trichirapalli, Tanjore (Thanjavur), and Palayamkottai. The end of the eighteenth century (1797) saw a movement of mass conversion among the Nadar community of farmers and toddy-tappers in the Tinnevelly (Tirunelveli) district, annexed by the British in 1799, and the princely state of Travancore. Nadars were not considered polluting in Hindu custom, but they were of low caste and economically depressed. Between April 1802 and January 1803, 46 baptismal services were held and 5,629 persons were baptized (Neill, 1985:216). This success from cooperative efforts was exceptional, but cooperation continued under comity agreements between missionaries and agencies.

Comity is a term that loosely refers to all forms of agreement and cooperation on the mission field, but more strictly it refers to the mutual division of territory into spheres of mission work and to agreement not to interfere with converts or affairs of other missions. Its purpose was to prevent wasteful duplication, competition, and a confusing diversity in the presentation of the gospel, but it produced "denominationalism by geography" (Beaver, 1971:123a). It also increased the likelihood that individual missions would have *de facto* responsibility for a specific community or caste group even though such ethnic exclusiveness went against the better judgment of some missionaries. Even when missionaries expanded their activities to include people from different social classes, the result was often a dual structure that kept the converts separate, as, for example, in the Anglican mission in central Travancore. A number of Protestant groups, such as the Missouri Synod Lutherans and independent Baptists, resisted comity agreements. Moreover, comity agreements did not cover Indian cities with populations greater than 100,000. Nonetheless, comity agreements developed in India early in the nineteenth century and provided a structure of cooperation among Protestant churches that influenced twentieth-century ecumenical movements both in India and abroad. Increasing cooperation among Protestant agencies and independence and indigenization of Indian churches, inspired both by the worldwide ecumenical movement and missionary conferences, and by nationalism engendered by the Indian independence movement, resulted in the formation of a Church of South India (1947) and a Church of North India (1970).

Several Protestant initiatives in India in the nineteenth and twentieth centuries resulted in Indian churches that are currently sending to the United States members who will help shape American Christianity in the twenty-first century. A review of the complicated history of missions in India cannot touch on every group now represented in the United States, but some background about some of the larger or most distinctive groups is essential.

Protestant missions in the nineteenth century

The story

The missionaries first came to our part of India in the early nineteenth century. My native place is in the central Kerala diocese, where the Anglican missionaries of the Church Missionary Society served. They established a school and a medical clinic, and some of my family was converted. That is why we are sometimes called at home "CMS Christians," and our church is in full communion with the worldwide Anglican Church. Our missionaries cooperated with the Congregational missionaries of the London Missionary Society south of us and with the Basel Mission to our north. Together we have the best schools and hospitals in India.

Elaboration and context

Protestant mission work in central Travancore and Cochin (Church Mission Society), in southern Travancore and southern Tamil country (London Mission Society), and in Malabar (Basel Mission) contributed to the result that this area has the greatest concentration of Christians in India.[5] These missions encouraged changes among the St. Thomas Christians. A majority of the Indian Christian immigrants to the United States come from this relatively small territory, so it seems appropriate to continue with this story.

Early Anglican missionaries congregated in Cochin and central Travancore states where St. Thomas Christians were already established. One Syrian Orthodox priest explains that this area was more attractive than other parts of India because the climate and living conditions were more pleasant, people were more receptive because Christians were already present making it less difficult to gather a following, and the rulers were more cooperative. Another explained, "Kerala is like Hawaii, so the missionaries settled there in the most pleasant part of India." Anglicans tell a different story, one about a "mission of help" that was intended to help revive the ancient Indian church that had neglected its evangelistic mission. The first British Resident arrived in Travancore in 1799 and was succeeded in 1806 by Colonel John Monro, a devout Christian who encouraged missionary activity. Also in 1799, the Church Missionary Society (CMS) emerged from the evangelical movement in the Church of England, and the first CMS missionary arrived in Kottayam in Travancore state in 1816, having been diverted on his way to Ceylon (Sri Lanka). Stephen Neill remarks, "With the coming of the English the independent Thomas Christians emerged from the obscurity in which they had long been hidden" (1985:238).

The Anglican "mission of help" had several unanticipated results. (1) The Syrian Orthodox Church felt threatened by winds of change and by pressure to accept Protestant practices. It reacted in 1836 at the Synod of Mavelikara by reaffirming the supremacy of the Patriarch of Antioch and loyalty to the liturgies, ordinances, and prelates authorized by him. The synod agreed, "For this reason we do not follow any faith or teaching other than the orthodox faith of the Jacobite Syrian Christians." A brief Malankara Orthodox account states tersely, "The experiment of cooperation between the Syrian Church and the CMS of the Anglican Church was carried on, but it was found to be unsuccessful and was called off in 1836" (n.a., 1986:7). (2) Nevertheless, a split developed within the Syrian Orthodox Church leading to the establishment of a "Reformed Orthodoxy" in the Mar Thoma Syrian Church. (3) An Anglican community and eventually a diocese came into existence in Travancore. (4) Evangelism among members of backward classes was undertaken by the Anglicans, the Mar Thoma Church, and eventually by the Orthodox.

The story
A few years back we celebrated the sesquicentennial of the "protestant" reformation of the Orthodox Church in India under the influence of the Anglican missionaries. Abraham Malpan, our founder, left the Old Seminary in Kottayam and returned to his home at Maramon and led in reforming the church. Our annual convention at Maramon is the largest Christian conference in south Asia. We Mar Thoma Christians were the first of the Orthodox to use Malayalam in our liturgy, and we are the most progressive of the St. Thomas Christians.

Elaboration and context
The most prominent reformer was Abraham Malpan, who in 1840 left his teaching position in what is called "the Old Seminary" in Kottayam, that had been founded with the assistance of CMS missionaries in 1815 to replace the informal apprenticeship training of priests. He returned to his home church at Maramon. Although he did not nail theses on the church door, Abraham did institute a number of reforms that were influenced by his association with the Anglican missionaries. (1) The Holy Qurbana was observed in Malayalam. The missionaries had already translated the Bible and the Book of Common Prayer into Malayalam. (2) Sermons were preached on every Sunday, with emphasis on biblical preaching. (3) Priests were ordained only after proper seminary education. A new Mar Thoma seminary eventually came into existence in

Kottayam. (4) Auricular confession was discontinued. (5) Both bread and wine were distributed as holy elements of the Qurbana. (6) The Qurbana was not celebrated when none other than the priest was present to participate. (7) Elements of the liturgy suggesting that it was a sacrifice were removed. (8) Mediation of the saints and adoration of the Virgin Mary were removed from the liturgy. (9) Customs and practices introduced from the non-Christian culture, many thought to involve superstitions and witchcraft, were forbidden. (10) The marriage of deacons and priests was encouraged, even though the bishops must remain monks. The reform resulted in a church neither Protestant of the western type nor Orthodox of the eastern type, but one often described as "oriental in worship, autonomous in administration, and missionary in action" (Mathew, 1985:9).

The annual Maramon Convention sponsored by the Mar Thoma Church in the third week of February on the dry river bed at Maramon attracts as many as 150,000 people, making it one of the largest Christian gatherings in the world. People from many Christian denominations gather for a week of Bible study, preaching, praying, and fellowship. The convention established 100 years ago is a testimony to the growth, prominence, and importance of this third largest Christian group in Kerala (after the Catholics and the Syrian Orthodox). The church has 9 dioceses with 929 parishes of approximately 750,000 members who are served by 534 active priests and 72 retired priests (*1992 Directory, Malankara Mar Thoma Church Diocese of North America & UK*:5). The Mar Thoma Metropolitan is bishop of the headquarters city, Thiruvala, and is not superior to other bishops but is *primus inter pares*.

The Act of 1813 that renewed the charter of the East India Company stipulated that there be an Anglican bishop for India, and a bishop was established in Calcutta. Subsequently in 1833 a renewed charter added two suffragan bishops for Bombay and Madras. Some Anglican churches in the princely states of Cochin and Travancore were left independent by the establishment of the Mar Thoma Church, and they became the nucleus of an Anglican diocese. Missionaries had long conducted their own worship according to the Book of Common Prayer, and they were joined by some of the Syrians. Churches related to the Danish mission in Tamil country were transferred to the Anglicans, so the church was strong in the south. Part of the Anglican "mission of help" was establishment of schools and colleges, so Anglicans planted additional CMS schools during the rest of the nineteenth century. When in 1851 Christians were systematically counted for the first time,

Protestant Christians numbered 91,092 in India and were predominantly in areas of the CMS (24,613), the Society for the Propagation of the Gospel (SPG) Tinnevelly Mission (10,315), and the London Missionary Society (LMS) in south Travancore. The only other area with any considerable number of Christians was Bengal with 14,177, including 1,600 Baptists. Outside the Madras and Bengal Presidencies, only 2,739 Christians were numbered (G. Menachery, 1982:45a). Comity agreements largely restricted Anglican mission work in what is now Kerala to the central Travancore area of the Malabar coast, but the Anglican church grew throughout India. It became the leading church in movements toward union following Indian independence.

Comity agreements reserved southern Travancore for the London Missionary Society and Malabar to the north to the Basel Mission. The territorial division remained so pronounced that Protestants in Kerala still commonly refer to themselves as "Anglican Christians" or "CMS Christians," "Congregationalists," or "Basel Mission Christians." The London Missionary Society established work in Travancore in 1809. Although the mission was supported by evangelicals of many denominations, the LMS Christians were known as Congregationalists because most of their support and workers came from Congregational churches. They established a strong church in south Travancore that reached over into Tinnevelly district. This district (annexed by the British in 1799) had along its western border a common frontier with the Indian state of Travancore. For the greater part of this frontier the two regions are divided by the great barrier of the Western Ghats, but where the mountains break down toward the ocean there is no clear division between them. In the north and center of the state the people speak Malayalam; in the south they speak Tamil.

The Basel Mission began in 1815 as an ecumenical organization of evangelicals in Germany and Switzerland that originally provided missionaries for other societies, and in 1834 entered the Malabar coast in an area of 500 miles from Calicut north toward Bombay where there were no Protestant missions. A special initiative of the Basel Mission involved efforts to enable converts to earn their own living if conversion separated them from family or caste. A series of "cottage industries" developed, first agriculture, then a printing press and book binding, and finally a textile business noted for the excellence of its products and the efficiency of its administration. (The material called "calico" is said to be named from Calicut on the Malabar coast.) Thus, the three major missions in Cochin and Travancore states and in Malabar district won converts and established churches, supplying them with institutions that were very important for future developments within the Christian communities: schools, hospitals, and commercial outlets. These were of great importance to converts from the backward classes. The Basel Mission expanded its mission at an early stage to tribal people in the Nigiri Hills, and Basel missionaries encouraged, more than most, breaking down the caste and ethnic distinctions among their converts by making no provision either in the church or in the industries for caste divisions.

The story of Indian Christianity fragments dramatically during the second half of the nineteenth century and the first quarter of the twentieth, during the ascendancy of British control, when mission stations of various nationalities, types of missions, and denominations were established throughout India, with greatest success in the south. Thousands of stories about individual initiatives, personal and family conversions, local congregations, various denominations, and mission boards echo out of the depth of that turbulent history and the breadth of the country. The story of medical missions focuses on the life of Dr. Ida S. Scudder, of the Arcot Mission of the Reformed Church, USA, who founded the Vellore Christian Medical College and Hospital. She began what became the largest teaching hospital in Asia. Hundreds of Christian physicians and nurses studied there, including some who emigrated to America. A 1925 statistical analysis demonstrates the growth of institutions with a list of 110 mission societies with stations in India (British, 38; North American, 36; European, 10; Australian, 3; Indian, 23), with 45,448 Indian workers, and 6,705 organized churches. They claimed a membership of 2,157,154. Other missionaries followed the example of Dr. Scudder and started educational and medical institutions, which grew in number by 1925 to 36 colleges and universities, 89 theological and Bible institutes, and 244 hospitals served by 290 missionary physicians and 225 missionary nurses (Beach and Fahs, 1925). The number of Christian hospitals increased greatly following Indian independence. For example, in 1941 there were only four Catholic hospitals and 15 dispensaries in the whole of Kerala, but by 1972 the numbers increased to 142 hospitals and 94 dispensaries (Koiparampil, 1982:203). Although not all these were essential to the faith, education, and professional development of Christians who immigrated to the United States from India, some of these and others that developed later provided the base and the networks that led to immigration.

The Anglicans/Episcopalians and the British Wesleyan Methodists/ American Methodists developed the most widespread mission network and diocesan structures in India which were influential both in ecumenical negotiations in India and in the emigration of Indian Christians. Methodist churches grew to almost a million members by the mid twentieth century. Gujarat was a focus for several of these missions, important not so much for great numbers in India itself – 132,703 Christians numbered in the 1981 census (approximately one-third Catholic and the rest Protestant) – but because Gujaratis are prominent among immigrants. Anglicans entered Gujarat early, the LMS in 1815 and the SPG in 1830. The Methodist Episcopal Church of the USA entered Gujarat in 1872 and developed into a mass movement at the turn of the century resulting in a strong Methodist Church with close ties to American Methodism. Methodist missionaries instituted a program of setting up Christian colonies – types of housing cooperatives – which today results in areas of cities and villages heavily populated by Christians. For example, the Maninagar area of Ahmedabad has many churches and a high concentration of Christians. Methodists and Anglicans became numerous in both north and south India.

Other missions began in Gujarat near the turn of the century. The first missionary of the Church of the Brethren arrived at Bulsar in south Gujarat in 1895 and organized a church that now has members in a congregation in Naperville near the headquarters of the Church of the Brethren in Elgin, Illinois. The Church of the Brethren in Gujarat grew to 18,000, so that it was numerically the largest of the three churches from Gujarat uniting into the Church of North India in 1970. Irish Presbyterians, the Salvation Army, and the Methodist Church were already in south Gujarat. The Latin Catholic Gujarat mission began with German missionaries of the Society of Jesus in 1895 under the Archdiocese of Bombay. One of the novel features of the church in Gujarat after Indian independence was the migration to Gujarat of large numbers of Syrian Christians from Kerala. Among the earliest arrivals were nurses, who traveled to Gujarat to staff the newly established government and private hospitals. Christian nurses were in great demand because, as noted in chapter 1, until very recently few Hindu girls were prepared to take up nursing as a career. The Syrians use Malayalam in worship and are somewhat isolated from the Gujarati-speaking churches, so the Kerala churches are providing for the pastoral care of their members (Boyd, 1981:221, 235).

Evangelical churches

As in the United States, the established "mainline churches" in India are currently experiencing a much smaller rate of growth than the evangelical churches. The Brethren Assemblies and the various groups of Baptists and Pentecostals are growing rapidly. One of the largest concentrations of Baptist churches in the world (after the United States and areas of the former Soviet Union) is in a crescent extending along the shores of the Bay of Bengal from Andhra Pradesh in the south through the northeast, extending into southeastern Burma, and at the center is Serampore where William Carey served as the first Protestant missionary in India (Downs 1982:69). When he first arrived in Bengal in 1793, he was not permitted by the East India Company to evangelize, but he remained in India to work on a plantation, and eventually established in a Danish settlement both a ministry and Serampore College (which now grants all degrees for Protestant seminaries in India). Other Baptist missionaries and societies established churches in several states. Notable recent success is in the troubled northeast where, although still relatively small in numbers, the church grew dramatically in Meghalaya and Nagaland during the decade before 1981. (See Table 1, p. 14.) The majority of Baptists in India are in the northeast, and a majority come from the backward classes and tribal communities.

   The mission of an independent, separatist group of Plymouth Brethren began with the arrival of Anthony Norris Groves in Tinnevelly in 1833. He had offered himself for service with the CMS, but his Plymouth Brethren views were judged incompatible with positions taken by the agency.[6] He worked among missionaries of various denominations and societies for a number of years, which resulted in a movement of loosely connected congregations based on New Testament principles as the Plymouth Brethren interpreted them. They are anti-clerical and independent, so laymen lead the assemblies as elders without assistance from paid clergy or those with seminary training. They have a number of Bible schools to train leaders and they commission workers as evangelists if the individuals can gain the support of local assemblies. In 1950 they supported 200 assembly missionaries in India, but by 1983 only 50 remained. A number of the independent missionaries come from New Zealand. The Brethren claim 1,000 assemblies in India, the largest number in the south – most in Kerala, then Andhra Pradesh, Tamil Nadu, and Karnataka (Tatford, 1983:400f.). In Kerala they encouraged the St. Thomas Christians to repudiate all priests, bishops, and missionaries, and, in anticipation of Christ's Second Coming, to constitute themselves into independent local assemblies led by lay elders (Bayly, 1989:307). The most rapid current growth is among the Telugu-speaking people; as one commissioned worker explains, "They are very simple, and they do not emphasize education and materialism as much as in other areas." The Brethren do not cooperate with other denominations and do not allow other Christians to join them in the Lord's Supper. They refer to Christians in other churches as "nominal Christians," and much of their evangelism involves attempts to convert and rebaptize members of other churches. Hence, they are commonly accused of being "sheep stealers." They strongly discourage marriage outside the fellowship and they strongly emphasize the Hebrew scriptures, viewing them as the foundation of a patriarchal system. They gained many members in the early days from the Syrian churches in central Travancore and more recently from other churches. An elder in central Kerala reported that 30 Brethren Assemblies meet in Kottayam, some of them quite small. Bahkt Singh, a famous preacher and evangelist of contemporary India who was influenced by the Plymouth Brethren, established 300 congregations patterned after the Brethren that are entirely self-supporting, self-governing, and self-propagating. A special feature of his movement is the great Bible conferences attended by thousands of Indian Christians under tents or in the open air. He was very influential in Andhra Pradesh and Tamil Nadu. Among the strongest church groups in Andhra Pradesh are Methodists, the Church of South India, Baptists, Catholics, and Brethren Assemblies.

Pentecostal movements

The story
Our founder grew up as a "nominal Christian"; indeed, he became a pastor and teacher in the established church. Then he went through a religious conversion, being convicted by biblical truths and seeking immersion baptism as a believing adult, thereby separating himself from the dead wood of the past. He subsequently experienced the gift of the Holy Spirit, which authenticated both his ministry and the new spirit-led movement he founded. My father experienced healing from a serious illness in one of his large meetings in our town, and we are now Pentecostals.

Elaboration and context
The Pentecostal churches led the way in indigenization of the church in India, spurred both by the independent sponsorship of the early mis-

sionaries coming forth from the charismatic revivals in the early part of this century and by the local autonomy granted to Indian congregations and leaders. The Pentecostal movement continues to grow rapidly in India, especially in the south. The four largest Pentecostal groups are: Assemblies of God; Church of God of Cleveland, Tennessee; the Indian Pentecostal Church; and the Ceylon Pentecostal Mission. Pastor Robert F. Cook from Los Angeles, California, was the first Pentecostal independent missionary to India, landing in 1913 and settling in Bangalore. In 1920 he held a revival in Kerala at Kottayam and moved to Travancore state in 1922 and soon had 36 churches. J. H. Ingram visited India and explained the teachings of the Church of God to Cook and to the pastors of his church, whereupon all agreed to unite with the Church of God. The work of the Church of God is currently divided into six areas – Tamil Nadu (Madras), two in Kerala, Andhra Pradesh, central India, and north India – and includes 805 churches (300 in Kerala), 122 missions, 763 ministers, 4 Bible schools, and 51,059 members (LeRoy, n.d.:10–21). Many of the churches and 3 Bible schools were developed by Pastor T. M. Varguhese (1898–1985), a Syrian Orthodox Christian who was converted, rebaptized by immersion, and inspired by the Holy Spirit after he met Pastor Cook.

The Indian Pentecostal Church (IPC) is the largest and fastest-growing Pentecostal group in India, and its origin in Kerala is also associated with the work of Pastor Abraham. K. E. Abraham was a Syrian Orthodox Christian teacher in a Jacobite school. He was convinced by study of the New Testament that he should be baptized by immersion as an adult in 1916. He was filled with the Holy Spirit in 1924, an event remembered as the foundation of the Indian Pentecostal Church, even though he was associated with Pastor Cook until 1930. Pastor Abraham, perhaps influenced by the nationalist movement, believed that for evangelism to be effective, the churches of India must be indigenous and independent. Hence, the Indian Pentecostal Church has no direct affiliation with foreign societies or churches. The founder's son, Pastor T. S. Abraham, now serves as General Secretary from the church's headquarters at Kumbanad, a few miles south of Kottayam. The IPC claims 2,000 local churches throughout India (950 in Kerala) with an equal number of pastors trained in several Bible schools. They are occasionally called "Hebron Pentecostals" because of the Bible school at Hebron in Kerala.

The Assemblies of God, the Sharon Pentecostal Church, and many independent Pentecostal churches share the same basic doctrine and practice. They emphasize the biblical basis of faith and practice, baptize adults by immersion, rebaptize members from other Christian denominations, rely upon the revival of the gifts of the Holy Spirit, especially speaking in tongues, acts of healing, ecstatic expressions such as "slaying in the spirit," and enthusiastic worship and prayer. The numbers of Pentecostals are growing in Kerala, but a bishop reports that, although many of their members came early in the century from the Jacobites, Mar Thomas, and the Church of South India, they are not successful now in attracting Syrian Christians. Nevertheless, the Pentecostals are also accused of being "sheep stealers." As one priest described it, "They pluck fish from one bowl and douse them into another." Several of these churches cooperate both in India and in the United States in large revivals and conventions that draw thousands of participants from among Hindus and Christians of various denominations.

A group that preserves its separatist identity is known as the Ceylon Pentecostal Mission (recently renamed in India as The Pentecostal Mission or TPM to avoid association with the civil war involving Tamils in Sri Lanka). It was founded in Ceylon by Pastor P. Paul, a former catechist with the Church Missionary Society, but it quickly expanded into Travancore and Madras state (DeSilva, 1980:60). Pastor Paul (CPM) and Pastor Abraham (IPC) cooperated for a time, but a split developed that further separated the CPM from the other Pentecostal groups. Aspects that distinguish this group from other Pentecostals are these: pastors are unmarried and celibate (if married before conversion and ordination, they live in a platonic relationship), pastors "live by faith" without personal possessions, members place a stronger reliance on faith healing, and the community has distinctive interpretations of the Book of Revelation. Widows and unmarried women also serve in evangelism and the training of women and children. The world headquarters is now in Madras, where Pastor Ernest Paul is the chief pastor, overseeing a movement that is increasingly international, interracial, and multiethnic. Eight main centers are in Kerala, and Kottayam, one of the centers, has forty branches.[7] Groups of young men and women reside in the centers to be trained as pastors and church leaders, all dressed in white clothing – a mark of Pentecostal leaders in Kerala. They claim 5,000 dedicated workers in 600 churches in India. Large annual conventions are conducted at each center and a national convention is held in Madras. They are proud that collections of money are not taken at their conventions or in their worship services, but that all their activities are funded by tithes of their members.

Indian Catholics share in the Catholic Charismatic Movement through the National Service Team for Catholic Charismatic Renewal in India, which came into being in 1974. It is both a response to threats of "sheep stealing" by evangelistic and Pentecostal groups and a program of renewal and Bible study within the Catholic Church. The head of the Indian Catholic Charismatic Movement is a Jesuit priest who was formerly head of the International Catholic Charismatic Renewal with offices in the Vatican (1983–88). He indicates that the movement is strongest in Tamil Nadu, Karnataka, Kerala, and Goa. Approximately 100,000 Catholics are involved, with 60,000 to 70,000 in the three southern states.[8] The Catholic charismatics emphasize the Word of God, the charisma of healing, speaking in tongues, the interior healing of forgiveness, deep prayer, and "slaying in the Spirit." A Tamil priest, also a Jesuit, indicated that he held a prayer convention in January 1994 that attracted 13,000 people. A Catholic congregation in Bangalore signed up more than 400 parishioners to attend a charismatic retreat. Some excesses cause apprehension within the hierarchy and restraint among leaders. A couple of priests involved in the Charismatic Movement have been led astray from correct practice and became separated from the church. One priest indicated that the reason the bishops give tacit support for the movement, in spite of such excesses, is to keep their flock from being attracted to the Protestants. Another indicated that he is careful to preserve the union of sacrament and the "fruits of the Spirit" and avoids the designation of "charismatic" because of prejudice among Catholic priests regarding the Pentecostals. A youth in the Catholic Church in Bangalore attends the charismatic conventions and retreats because of the dramatic preaching, the lively singing, and the warm sense of fellowship. Charismatic Catholics contribute a vivid and colorful piece to the kaleidoscope of Indian Christianity.

Modern ecumenical movement in India since independence

The story
My church is a pioneer of the modern ecumenical movement because in 1947 my church united with others in the Church of South India. Our church is exemplary, and our bishops and theologians have been active in the World Council of Churches. Now the Church of North India is following our example. It has not been easy, but our church is a beacon to the Christian world as a united and uniting church. We are an early example of successful, modern, church union.

Elaboration and context

The trend-setting comity agreements begun in India prefigured the most dramatic story of church union in the Church of South India (CSI) on September 27, 1947, soon after Indian independence. This first united church that brought together non-episcopally ordained and episcopally ordained within the structure of an episcopal church inspired developments in the worldwide ecumenical movement. The union resulted from twenty-eight years of negotiations between the Anglican Church, the Methodist Church, and the various Presbyterian Churches in the four southern states of Tamil Nadu, Kerala, Karnataka, and Andhra Pradesh. Regional languages were preserved in the order of worship and local ecclesiastical affairs. When the CSI was formed in 1947, 6 of the diocesan bishops were Indians and 8 were British, including the great ecumenical leader Leslie Newbigin. Of the bishops, 7 were originally Anglicans, 3 were Congregationalists, 3 Methodists, and 1 Presbyterian. The CSI is now divided into 21 dioceses, with 1,345 presbyters serving 8,715 congregations and 1,718,265 baptized members. Synod offices are in Madras, and 88 colleges and 66 hospitals are spread throughout the synod. Since 1947 the CSI has engaged in conversations about cooperation with the Lutheran Churches, the Mar Thoma Church in Kerala, and the Baptists in Andhra Pradesh. It has a relationship of intercommunion with both the Mar Thoma Church and the Church of North India. In the founding constitution, Kerala was organized into three CSI dioceses, which roughly replicated the territories of the Basel Mission (North Kerala Diocese), the LMS (South Kerala Diocese), and the CMS (Madhya Kerala Diocese).[9] Recently the East Kerala Diocese was created, largely from territory of the Madhya Kerala Diocese. The Madhya Kerala Diocese is the central Travancore region and is one of the strongest dioceses of the CSI, with a membership of some 100,000 and over 128 pastorates within the diocese. The majority of the CSI immigrants in the United States come from the Madhya Kerala Diocese.

The Church of North India came into existence later, in November 1970, and is much smaller and less influential among immigrants to America than the CSI. Six churches joined the Church of North India – the Anglican Church with thirteen dioceses, the United Church of North India (itself a union of Congregationalists and Presbyterians dating from 1924), some Baptists, the Church of the Brethren, the Disciples of Christ, and the Methodist Church linked with Britain and Australia. After extensive negotiation, however, the larger Methodist

Church linked with American Methodists remained apart. Seven new bishops were consecrated by bishops from the Mar Thoma Church, the Church of South India, and a former Anglican bishop from the United Church of North India. The CNI is now divided into sixteen dioceses, each with its own bishop. Both the CNI and the CSI affirm their mission as uniting churches and look forward to a future union into the United Church of India that will incorporate many of the churches, but obstacles on the road to union are great.

The story of the church in India is one of unity, diversity and stratification, and partial reunions. The prism of Indian society refracts the image into a vivid display of diversity that evolves into different patterns through the centuries. Three sides of the prism are: geographical, separating Christians on regional, linguistic, and cultural lines; sectarian, stressing theological and ecclesiastical distinctions; and caste, creating boundaries along *jati*, occupational, and class lines. In religion, as in other affairs, William Blake's line, "But General Forms have their vitality in Particulars," is true, and Christians are never "Christians in General" but rather "Christians in Particular." A social location is essential, but, as H. Richard Niebuhr demonstrated regarding American religion, the social, theological, and regional aspects coalesce to make almost impermeable barriers (Niebuhr, 1929).

An ancient and significant barrier is raised by caste discrimination. Most Christians in India are from the lower castes. In Andhra Pradesh a majority come from untouchable groups and roughly 90 percent are from scheduled castes and tribes (groups designated for affirmative action for social advancement by the Indian government), and in Tamil Nadu the percentage is only slightly less.[10] In the Punjab, most of the Christians are originally from the sweeper group of Chuhras, and in the Madhya Pradesh and Bihar areas, where there have been many converts to Christianity and the movement is still strong, the converts are largely from among the tribal people (Wiebe, 1970:294). Converts from higher castes did not gain much in the social sphere from embracing Christianity but, prior to Indian independence, converts from backward classes had much to gain. They ceased to be Hindus and were no longer governed by caste rules or treated as untouchables. Moreover, Christian institutions brought about improvement in life through education, modern medicine, and occasionally employment (Alexander, 1972:54). More recently, conversion from a depressed-class community has involved losing rights to various affirmative action programs in education, housing, and employment, so a disincentive exists. Political debates about the reservation of seats for Christians in Christian colleges and medical schools remains a hot issue. In some regions of India, denominational church groups continue to be identified with distinct caste groups, so that church union negotiations are between social and regional groups in the guise of denominations. Many of the denominations are socially homogenous because members come from the same or closely related caste groups. Paul Wiebe noted, "A first general feature of Christianity in India is that it is largely contained within the lines of particular castes in particular areas" (Wiebe and John-Peter, 1977:297). Union agreements usually permit the continuation of regional – linguistic distinctions and previous cultural and social customs. Even within denominational groups distinctions exist between converts from different caste groups, usually between the few from the top and the many from near the bottom.

A clear distinction is made in Kerala between the Syrians (including Christian descendants of Nambudiri Brahmins), who are called "old Christians," and the converts from the Hindu depressed classes and their descendants, who are known as "new Christians." The Brahmins occupied the highest rank, and the Nairs and Syrian Christians were slightly lower. Castes like Pulayas and Parayas were placed at the lowest rung of the hierarchy. The latter two were bonded laborers, virtually agricultural slave castes. The toddy tappers (Nadars/Shanars and Izhavas) and the fishermen (Mukkavas) were important depressed classes, ranking between Nairs and the untouchables. We have seen that early Latin Catholic converts on the fishery coast were from low castes, and even among Latin Catholics caste distinctions were preserved.[11] Protestant missionaries served both the Syrian Christians and Hindu converts. The vast majority of depressed-class Christians are agricultural laborers who own no land of their own. Most of the LMS Christians in the south of Kerala came from depressed classes. The CMS dealt with large numbers of both Syrian and converted Christians, many of whom became part of the CSI. The Mar Thoma Church began mission work among depressed classes under the auspices of the Evangelistic Association founded in 1888. The Syrian Orthodox Church has a few thousand converts, resulting from the work of the Servants of the Cross Society, founded in 1924. Each of these groups maintained separate status for the new Christians, in some instances provided separate places of worship, and delayed ordination of priests from the depressed classes. The Anglican diocese in Kerala ordained three priests from the depressed classes for the first time in the 1930s, but they were appointed only to congregations of new Christians (Koshy,1968:45). Some of the Protestant groups in this century have been active among distinct caste groups. The Syrian Christian – depressed class conflict is minimal in some churches such as the Salvation Army, the Church of God, the Pentecostal groups, and the Lutherans because the membership of these churches is chiefly made up of the backward classes. Thus the Christians in Kerala are divided into various denominations and into various ethnic groups, based on caste background. Restrictions involve forms of endogamy and commensality. Denominational boundaries are weak compared with caste boundaries, so that marriages are frequent within caste groups and across denominational lines. Thus, marriage between Syrian Christians in various denominations is common, but inter-marriages between Latin and Syrian Catholics or between lower-caste and Syrian Mar Thoma Christians rarely takes place in the church (Alexander, 1977:53f.).

Opportunity to emigrate to America under the "brain-drain" provisions of the immigration laws depends upon the economic, educational, linguistic, and financial resources of Christian families in India. "Them that has, gets," as the saying goes, so those from the upper castes and classes were better prepared to take advantage of the opportunity, in spite of recent affirmative action in India by both church and government.[12] A majority of the immigrants are from the Syrian community in Kerala, and virtually all claim descent from the Syrians or other relatively high-ranking castes. When a person says, for example, that Mar Thoma Christians are proud to be part of that church, the undercurrent is that they are remembering a relatively high social status in Kerala. Of course, the experiences of caste have changed in Kerala and the rest of India in the three decades since many of these immigrants first arrived in America, even though memory tends to cast them in stone. Those changes are occasionally disconcerting when immigrants return to India for marriage negotiations. Moreover, the role of caste and class distinctions in the new setting of America is still in the process of negotiation and a major arena is that of marriage negotiations.

These stories of diversity and reunion provide material for the stories that Christian immigrants from India retell in the United States and for the new stories they create. The shape of Christianity emerging from these stories provides the contours of the networks – ethnic, denominational, professional, and geographical – that create the migratory patterns of immigrants. Immigrants reconfigure themselves as a new community in a new context and create a new identity and social location out of fragments of memory from the past. A story about what has become a sacred place with a crooked cross, stories about a great apostle, a charismatic preacher, an influential reformer – all now in some sense become sacred people – and stories about ancient or more recent events that mark sacred time in their memory all serve to include those who remember and tell the same stories in a sacred community and to exclude both those who do not know or value the stories and those who tell the stories in a different way. The stories are analogous to those in the Bible in these ways. Understanding the Christian lives and communities of the new immigrants requires that we listen to their stories.

The relation of the memories to the past is not so significant as the function they have in creating the present reality of the immigrants as they sort themselves out and discover their relations to the larger society. The memories are significant because they provide the foundation for the future. Immigrants tell stories about their past in India in order to remind themselves who they are and who they can become in their new homeland. In that process they enable others to know who the immigrants are and who they themselves will be in the future, because the stories of the immigrants will in due course be related in the story of us all. Hence, stories from the past are part of the strategies of negotiation that Christian immigrants develop in their adaptation in coming to America. Perhaps they provide a sufficient context to be able to listen with understanding to the recreation and retelling of the story by new Christian neighbors.

CHAPTER 3

Becoming what you are: St. Thomas Christians from Kerala

And I will bless you and make your name great, so that you will be a blessing.

Genesis 12:2

A progressive Indian bishop mediated a tense debate between parents and young people at a national family conference. Tensions had surfaced between his flock in America and leaders of the church in India and between the generations – parents raised to adulthood in India and their American children. He urged an understanding that, "We cannot replicate in America the church that exists in our memory of Kottayam." Immigrants relocate to America neither to stay the same as they were in India nor to lose their identities. Had they wished to remain more or less the same, they would have remained where they were. That's life! New contexts and experiences draw out the potentials brought to one's present by the experiences of the past. Stories of past experiences in India, even ones about events prior to the lifetime of an immigrant and those of shared corporate memory rather than those of individual experience, are statements of potentials in the present for new immigrants. As a Native American Indian wisdom saying indicates, "One who cannot remember before he [or she] was born is an orphan indeed."

Migration is enormously disruptive of individual and personal identity, so an essential task faced by immigrants is to "become what you are." That is, immigrants must gather and, as individuals and groups, adapt to both the potentials they carry with them from India and the potentials existing in American society, culture, and religion. Religion is only one aspect of such adaptation because religion is only part of a person's identity, but it is an especially important aspect because religion grounds identity and forms boundaries and passageways that are validated by transcendent sanctions. It provides ballast that enables immigrants to preserve their identities and adapt to new surroundings. The goals are moral coherence of the self (private) and establishing a harmonious relationship of communities (public). Transmission of a tradition is always both a celebration and a quest. To stay the same, to become something new, to try to do both is to try to reform heaven and earth. The process involves revising old stories about Indian Christianity and creating new ones as part of American Christianity that will support the immigrants in their various strategies of adaptation to the new context.

Adaptation is required because Christian immigrants from India constitute a new community in the United States, one not identical to any Christian community in India. The community is "Made in the USA" by the selection process of the Immigration and Naturalization Service, as directed by law, and by the networks linking India and the United States that encourage some immigrants and discourage others. The result is that people from a distinctive slice of Indian Christian society find themselves adapting together to American society. Christian immigrants from India seem to be less diverse than other religious groups among immigrants from India. A significant majority come from Kerala, and most of the immigrants from Kerala are Christian. They form a more homogeneous group than, for example, Hindus from Gujarat, even though most immigrants from Gujarat are in a general sense Vaishnava devotees of Krishna. Gujarati Jains constitute a larger portion of the immigrant population than do Kerala Hindus or Muslims. The Christians are firmly in the middle economic and professional class of immigrants from India, as a result of the prominence of nurses among the early immigrants and of a concentration of men in technical services in hospitals and similar skilled occupations. They tend to be more urbanized than Indian engineers and physicians, who have moved out in large numbers to smaller cities and towns. Indian Christians are concentrated near large metropolitan hospitals where the need for immigrant nurses is greatest.

They identify with different strands of Christian traditions in India – therefore, telling different stories – and arrive from different parishes of Indian states, cities, towns, and villages. No Christian group like this has previously existed in India or anywhere in the world. Immigration patterns to the Gulf states, East Africa, Malaysia, and Great Britain create Christian communities that are very different in professional status, economic and political prospects, and religious identity, to say nothing of the difference in the social context of the majority society in those places.

Hence, it is necessary for the immigrants to America to engage in delicate negotiations with their fellow immigrants to determine how they
will reconstitute themselves as a Christian community and identify
themselves as Christians. The process involves both group cooperation
and personal commitment.

Recent immigrants are not free agents adapting to America in any
way they would wish. They have to become in large measure what the
majority society allows. Religious identification is one of the markers
that is recognized and validated in American society. "I am a Southern
Baptist," or "He is a Roman Catholic," or even "She is Irish Catholic"
are statements readily understood, which place an individual in a clearly
defined religious group. However, what does "I am CSI," or "She is a
Syro-Malabar Catholic," or "He is a Gujarati Methodist" signify in
America? People have a general sense of what such designations mean
because the society preserves a structure for understanding and placing a
value on religious, geographical, and ethnic social locations, but exactly
what these specific statements mean is just now being worked out in a
complex negotiation. The political context of renewed attention to
ethnicity and minority groups places a different value on self-identification in those terms than was the case a half-century ago. A tension exists,
however, between the social value of identifying oneself as a member of
a distinct and immediately recognizable minority, "Asian-Indian," or a
part of the majority, "Christian." In India under both British and self-
rule, some Christians lost their rights under governmental affirmative
action when they or their ancestors converted to Christianity (Webster,
1992:168).[1] Although the United States government does not dis-
criminate against Christian immigrants, they must calculate the costs
and benefits of several potential self-identifications in various social contexts. Associations with other religious and ethnic groups among Asian-
Indian immigrants also determine the social location of Christians. A
person becomes what other people treat him or her as, so the range of
freedom an individual has is greatly restricted, even in a heterogeneous
society. Groups, however, are able to negotiate from a more powerful
and secure position than are individuals. That is why immigrants join in
groups in order to keep control, as far as possible, of their associations
with the larger society.

Naming is important because names establish identities and boundaries. Many Asian Indians are clearly identified by Christian names of
biblical figures or saints: Abraham, Sarah, Mary, Thomas, Mathew,
Rachel. Names give them a distinct social position in India, and they are

surprised and annoyed when new acquaintances in America ask them, "Where did you get a Christian name?" It is also significant which language and what accent is used in giving the name. Individuals have a large number of appropriate identifying names from which they can select in a given context: American, New Yorker, Christian, Disciple, and so on. These are generic in a way different from the roles one occupies as teacher, father, or scholar. Immigrants learn to use names wisely in appropriate social contexts to enhance their ability to adapt. The names are many: Christian, Indian Christian, Malayalee Christian, St. Thomas Christian, Pentecostal, Born-Again Christian. Each of these names represents a strategy of adaptation and each may be appropriate in a given context. Such adaptation is not only demanded by the future and hope; it is also permitted by the past and memory. The reason is the heterogeneity in tradition. Any developed society or culture has many diverse strands of tradition available to persons and groups within the society, and hence, also, several identities are available.

Moreover, names that people in the majority society give to the immigrants are significant in defining the social location they are permitted to occupy. Although the American government agencies are restricted in their overt power to define religious groups, they do exercise influence on the process of adaptation through a large number of regulations and procedures. For example, the government stipulates a precise procedure and requirements for a group to attain tax-exempt status or non-profit-organization status. Such procedures dictate how the religious organization will structure its legal officers and elements of its financial accounting. The government designates churches and religious groups in specific categories that determine their relations with governmental agencies. Established religious organizations of the majority society make requirements for adaptation to American structures in those groups that apply for assistance and/or membership. For example, one Asian-Indian church group contacted the National Council of Churches regarding application for membership. The bishop was informed of a requirement that the group be able to identify a membership of 10,000 persons before consideration of its application. The problem is that several Indian churches calculate membership and voting rights by household rather than by individuals. Hence, the immigrant church must change aspects of its structure to meet requirements of church agencies. Scholars are anxious to give names to new groups because names assist in understanding. However, names too quickly given may garble understanding and even distort the process of adaptation by establishing stereotypes and typologies that restrict the freedom of groups to develop along their own lines. How does one designate Asian-Indian Christian groups? As churches or sects, denominations or cults, ethnic or religious, or perhaps congregations or societies? The manner in which scholars designate new immigrant groups affects ways these groups coalesce and develop. Religious groups and individuals go by many names, and several segments of society have influence on what names are used and what they signify.

Names and designations imply a variety of strategies of adaptation that immigrant groups follow to construct their home and future in American society. One is reminded of a motion of an early New England School Board:

Resolution

We are going to build a new school;
We are going to build the new school on the site of the old school;
We are going to build the new school out of the materials of the old school;
We are going to carry on classes in the old school while the new school is being built.

Immigrants' resolution

We are going to create a new religious community;
We are going to create it in the New World;
We are going to build it out of materials from the old country;
We are going to carry on the religion in both worlds while the new community is being built.

This chapter focuses on the strategies of adaptation fabricated by Asian-Indian religious groups and the experience of Christian immigrants from India in establishing their religious groups and identities in the United States. It is therefore necessary to deal with the structured character of the traditions as repeated communicative acts shared by members of newly formed social and religious groups, and also with both the memory and reality of the continuing traditions in India. Each of the adaptive strategies is implicit in the traditions in India and is acceptable and recognized in the new American setting. It is also necessary to deal with the stories of migration and homesteading that record the early development of Asian-Indian Christian communities. Every individual, family, and church group tells an unfinished story that captures the excitement, frustration, hopes, and anxieties of Christians moving from India to that "shining light," that light of their imagining – Christian America.

STRATEGIES OF ADAPTATION

Six trajectories or models of adaptive strategies are evident in both secular and religious organizations that serve immigrant communities.[2] They are "ideal" types in the sense that they form a typlogy for analysis, but the types are rarely observed unmixed. Indeed, an individual or a group creates families of adaptive strategies that they can orchestrate for various contexts. Selection of strategies of adaptation by a group in a specific context is governed by both internal and external dynamics as complex and indeterminate as those governing the processes of selection in evolutionary theory. Elements of the theology, stories, organizational structure, and networks coming from the past collective experiences of the group as well as the social and political contexts in new settings direct the process of adaptation into identifiable streams along trajectories still marked by the actions of previous immigrants to America. The several adaptive strategies result in differences in selection of the language or languages used in programs, in types of religious leaders accepted and trained, in the general ethos of the community, in the cuisine and arts evident at meetings, and in the distinctive symbolic language – linguistic, gesture, and material – that governs communication in the group. An analysis of the six strategies of adaptation provides the background for a description in this chapter of the development of St. Thomas Christian organizations in the United States. The description of adaptive strate-gies of other Asian-Indian Christian groups continues in the following chapter. The six strategies are: individual, national, ecumenical, ethnic, hierarchical, and "denominational".

Individual

Christianity in India is intensely corporate in character, stressing the connectedness of the individual Christian in extended family, congrega-tion, and corporate identity. It is precisely that context of identity and related structures of plausibility that are disrupted by international migration. Most of the early immigrants arrived as individuals at a time before support structures of family, church, or ethnic group were estab-lished in even the large metropolitan areas. Many find themselves in locations relatively isolated from other Asian-Indian Christians. An early strategy of adaptation that is still viable for new immigrants stresses indi-vidual initiative and is reinforced by the individualism that Robert Bellah suggests dominates so much of American religion (Bellah,

Madsen, Sullivan, Swidler, and Tipton, 1985). In the first instance that means religious observances in private, continuing, perhaps, morning and evening prayers or developing a program of personal devotion. The Bible, a framed picture of the Madonna and Holy Child, or other objects of devotional attention brought from India occupy places of honor in a home shrine and serve to remind the individual of home and to inform visitors of a family's identity.

An individual strategy of adaptation can also involve a separation from or even a rejection of religion and a move toward secular commitments and identity. Migration removes individuals from social constraints and frees them to chart new paths that would not be viable for them in their previous residence. Some of the immigrants had already made a move in that direction after leaving home for university or during residence in the cities of India or in the Gulf states. It is virtually impossible to get information about those who have disappeared from the Christian community after arrival in the United States because no contexts exist in which they are comfortable in identifying themselves as lapsed Christians. While some Indian immigrants complain about the attempts to establish "little Indias" in America by spending so much of their resources on building temples, mosques, gurdwaras, and churches, no formal anti-religious Asian-Indian organization exists in the United States. No Asian Indian was identified in this research as having rejected a Christian confession to enter another religion, even though some persons of the majority society have become Muslims or Hindus, primarily as a result of marriage. Rather, for some immigrants, Christian identity is associated with India – and preserved for visits back to family and friends in India – and a secular identity is cultivated in America through a benign neglect of religion. A few persons who have returned to the church, usually after starting a family, refer to their backsliding as their "period of shame." Young people move into what Gandhi once identified as his experience in England of the "Sahara of atheism." They wish to exercise independence by making their own decision regarding religious affiliation or lack thereof. One goal given for active establishment of churches and prayer groups for Asian Indians is to prevent such backsliding and assimilation through secularization.

Another prominent form of individual adaptation is to join an already-established American congregation. Indian Catholics participate in parish churches; Pentecostals join charismatic prayer groups meeting in their neighborhoods; a Thomas Christian family sends their children to Vacation Bible School at the Baptist church; children from an Orthodox family join an interracial Jesus movement; a Gujarati Church of the Brethren family member seeks out a local congregation of that denomination. A large number of Christian immigrants regularly participate in local congregations of many denominations and some become active lay leaders, but no way exists to determine who, where, or exactly how many they are. Those who are relatively isolated from other Indian Christians often participate in local congregations and join together with Indian Christians on Sunday evenings, perhaps once a month, or on special festivals, such as St. Thomas' Day or at Christmas. Immigrants select congregations in which to participate for the same reasons other Americans do: programs for children, hospitality, denominational loyalty, pastoral leadership, location, and physical facilities. Excellence of programs for children and young people is the primary criterion for selection. Immigrants suffer the loss of virtually all assistance available to them in India for raising their children, the most demanding and terrifying of their experiences in America. Hence, Christian parents approach churches hoping for assistance in socializing their children and in providing a new American Christian identity. It is difficult for them to find congregations that can provide the form of Christian nurture they desire. Hospitality is the second criterion because immigrants read carefully the reaction of congregations to people from other cultures and races. Stories of racism, both overt and covert, come out of experiences of immigrants in search for church homes. Even the typical coolness of many American congregations is experienced painfully by immigrants as rejection and even racism. As with the majority population, denominational loyalty ranks low among the priorities in the search for a church home in a new location. One must question whether Indian churches are denominations, but, even if they are, most of the Christian immigrants from India do not have a natural denominational affiliation in America. Hence, their need to establish Indian Christian churches.

Pastors often immigrate as individuals, serve established congregations, and affiliate with American denominations – Episcopal, Methodist, Baptist, Pentecostal, Nazarene, and Disciple are ones encountered in this research. Even those denominations that keep careful records of ordained ministers with standing are unable to give an exact accounting of Asian-Indian ministers because their records include them in a larger category of Asians. Some serve independent congregations. A number of Catholic priests have gained permanent resident status under family reunification provisions of the immigration law as brothers of permanent residents and then serve established Roman Catholic parishes or as chaplains in Catholic institutions. Priests and ministers have come from India to the United States for graduate study since the 1950s, and many have stayed on after completing their education to answer calls from congregations and institutions. A common frustration comes when the pastor reaches a "glass ceiling" in moving from congregation to congregation or upward in denominational affairs. Nevertheless, it is common for students in all fields to want to remain in the United States after completing their schooling, but that was easier to do before the mid-1980s than it is currently. Still, students come for education and stay as individuals. Protestant pastors who are able to assimilate into American denominations are generally trained in American seminaries, fluent in English, and well-connected with an influential individual or a local congregation. Recent legislation permits entry of volunteer religious workers, a change made to permit nuns and monks to come to serve Catholic institutions facing the result of a lack of Americans drawn to religious vocations. That law will affect religious leadership of many types of institutions, but it is too soon to chart those changes.

National

A national strategy of adaptation is most evident in those organizations that unite Indians from different religions and ethnic groups in programs emphasizing Indian identity and allegiance to symbols, leaders, festivals, and cultural performance that have an all-India identity. Many of the secular organizations, such as the Indian Federations or Indian Community Centers, sponsor programs for the entire immigrant community. These generally value the secular stance of the Indian government, and Christians occupy leadership positions in some of these organizations. Much of the culture and arts, including some of the festivals sponsored by these organizations, are intimately associated with the Hindu past, however, which creates stumbling blocks to participation by some Christians. When does a dance, a song, food, or a festival associated with a Hindu deity cease to involve worship of that deity and become merely a remnant of ancient culture? It is a question similar to that faced by those who are not Christian when they decide to observe Christmas. Some Christians interpret participation in national cultural programs as a form of idolatry, while others think that they are merely harmless cultural performances.

Indian Christian Fellowships assume a national identity because they attempt to attract Christian immigrants originating from all parts of India and from several church groups. The welcome mat is out for all Christians from India. This strategy is particularly attractive at an early stage of settlement or in areas where there are few Indian Christians. These fellowship groups resemble community churches in their independence and eclectic character. These generally develop with lay leadership or under a minister educated in a liberal American seminary. Boundaries between various churches, traditions, and ethnic groups are muted through the use of English in liturgy, business, and fellowship, through emphasis on the Bible, and by resorting to a minimal creed similar to those of liberal American Protestantism. Local Indian Catholic Associations are all-Indian organizations in description because they attract Latin-rite Catholics from all parts of India, but some may view them as denominational. In any case, they provide social occasions primarily for Goans both because Goans constitute the largest number of Latin-rite Catholics and because their liturgical needs are met through the regular Latin-rite parishes in America.

No nation-wide inclusive organization of Indian Christians exists in the United States, such as an American Association of Christians from India. This statement itself points to the fact that analyses of immigrants involves two national social locations: in this case, India and the United States. Immigrants are able to emphasize identity as Indians or identity as Americans whenever one is more appropriate in a given context. Calls are regularly issued urging Christians from India to bring economic and political pressure to bear against Hindutva and the imposition of Hindu ethos and regulations as national policy in India. These calls have awakened leaders and congregations to action – in support of, for example, the *dalit* protest movement in 1990 – but they have not resulted in long-lived national organizations.

Hindus attempted in the 1970s to establish religious organizations that would include people from several Indian religions, but communal tensions and conflicts in the 1980s, between Hindus and other religious groups, including Sikhs and Muslims, which involve and enrage Asian Indians, make cooperation among the religious communities difficult. Indian Cultural Centers, which often house altars and shrines, are venues of political maneuvering, which restricts participation and repels many members of the community. Christians both in the United States and in India (especially in the south) tend to "keep their heads down" to avoid involvement in such communal conflicts. Moreover, Christians survived in India by establishing strong boundaries between themselves and other religious groups, and those boundaries have survived in America.

Ecumenical

Indian Christian Fellowships are ecumenical in character because they attempt to cross ethnic and church boundaries and create an inclusive fellowship. English is the common language of liturgy, business, and fellowship, and the worship service is informal and accessible. The major contribution of these ecumenical congregations is that they meet the need for worship and fellowship with other Indian Christians at a time and in locations where numbers of fellow Indian Christians are low. Such fellowships are generally both national and ecumenical. During early stages of immigration such churches meet a need for the first generation, but as soon as numbers grow in a location, other churches create opportunities for fellowship and identification along ethnic, linguistic, or denominational lines. Ecumenical groups could also provide a service for youth of the second and third generation who may identify themselves as Asian-Indian but who do not know the regional language of their parents and who may not be attracted by the Indian Christian traditions and practices loved by their parents. Ecumenical activities occur early in the process of adaptation (led by lay people), then wane when the community is growing rapidly and establishing congregations and institutions on other bases, and, perhaps, will be energized (led by pastors) when the community becomes larger and more diverse and is embarrassed by the resulting schisms in the body of Christ.

Most ecumenical initiatives are successful across narrow ranges of Indian Christianity. These groups are initiated by pastors who communicate with other pastors and encourage participation of their members. Thus, Pentecostals engage in partial ecumenical initiatives that bring together members of several Indian Pentecostal churches in annual family conferences, local gatherings of pastors, and evangelistic conferences. Thomas Christians, including Syro-Malabar- and Syro-Malankara-rite Catholics, sponsor ecumenical gatherings at Christmas and on other occasions. These occasions are both ecumenical and ethnic because they are organized by and for Keralites and the songs, dances, cuisine, and arts are from Kerala. It is ecumenism along linguistic lines, and the common language is Malayalam. Ecumenical initiatives move along structural lines, and some groups are formed by churches and pastors who are under episcopal control, referred to as "episcopal churches." These tend to have more in common historically and liturgically, and designation as an "episcopal church" group tends to exclude strongly evangelistic groups.

Several Indian churches are active in ecumenical affairs through the World Council of Churches (WCC) and have established ecumenical relations with other churches. Contributions of Indian Christians in WCC affairs have been extensive, a number of their leaders having been recipients of WCC scholarships for graduate study in the West and several occupying prominent positions. Indian immigrant churches do not find it necessary to be fully involved in programs of the National Council of Churches in America both because their churches are not large or well-organized and because the National Council of Churches has been so involved in internal conflicts and efforts to stay alive that it has not been able to reach out in any meaningful way to the immigrant churches. Individual churches have been more active. The Episcopal Church in the United States has been especially helpful to the Mar Thoma Church in arranging for visas for its pastors, by providing episcopal oversight before a resident bishop was appointed, and by arranging for Mar Thoma congregations to purchase abandoned Episcopal Church buildings. The two churches share eucharistic fellowship. A senior Mar Thoma bishop argued that the Mar Thoma congregations should merge into the Episcopal Church, but that has not happened. The Church of South India and the Church of North India are ecumenical in commitment and regional in design. Hence, it is difficult for leaders to know what to do with congregations in America. Some leaders urge an ecumenical approach by which immigrants of those churches would join their sister churches in America rather than starting their own congregations, but the pressure from immigrants for their own churches leads to establishment of separate congregations and dioceses. This is in spite of the fact that the CSI and CNI priests are episcopally ordained and the two moderators occupy positions in the worldwide synod of Anglican bishops.

These immigrant churches are forming at a time of the seeming demise of the ecumenical movement. It is too soon to predict what shape their ecumenical initiatives will take – indeed, too soon to know if the ecumenical strategies will be irrelevant to the Christian realities of the new century or whether the Indian Christians and Christian immigrants from other parts of the world, many of them from union churches, will bury, or breathe new life into, the ecumenical movement.

Ethnic

A pastor explains the diversity of Asian-Indian churches, "Where there is a language, there will be a church." He refers to the power of language in the transmission of religious traditions. The ethnic strategy of adaptation is attractive to new immigrants because all come from an ethnic background that embodies regional–linguistic distinctiveness. Christian worship is conducted in all the languages and dialects of India; each ethnic group has its own hymnal, catechism or Sunday School material, liturgical material, and preaching style. Moreover, people have a powerful emotional attachment to religious material in their ethnic language, especially hymns and prayers. At home in India the regional language is the medium of transmission of religion, and in the United States it becomes almost a sacred language for immigrants. One worshiper said, "I feel at home in God's house when I can pray and sing in my native language." This is true even for those who are fully fluent in English and educated from childhood in English-medium schools. Hence, language is the primary characteristic of the ethnic strategy of adaptation among Indian Christians.

It is not just language, however. Other means of communication in gesture and symbol are intimately tied to regional–linguistic identity. Regional cuisine takes on a character of sacred food for many participants. Regional cuisine is served at all dinners of the organizations, so that Keralite fish, Tamil *dosas* and *sambar*, and Gujarati *kitcheri* are signals of ethnic identification. Young people often gravitate, however, to separate tables set with "American food" at church fellowship dinners. One can gauge the power of the ethnic strategy by the use of the language and by marking the appeal of regional cuisine to the group as a whole and to segments within the group. Regional arts, culture, and festivals are valued by groups following an ethnic strategy. South Indian Bharata Natyam dance and Gujarati stick dances are examples of ethnic performances that preserve elements of regional cultures.

Churches of the Thomas tradition from Kerala are ethnic churches outside Kerala both in other parts of India and abroad. It is doubtful that a church or organization in Kerala should be identified as following an ethnic strategy, unless there is an endogamous component like that of the Knanaya. In the United States, however, most Keralite churches are ethnic because they distinguish themselves by language and culture from other Indian Christian immigrants. Malayalam is the language of worship, business, and fellowship in virtually all the meetings dominated by adults.

There are Telugu, Hindi, Gujarati, Tamil, and Malayalee congregations that attract people from different regions of the Indian states and from different churches in ethnic churches. These closely parallel secular organizations that are based on regional–linguistic identities, like the Gujarati Samaj or the Tamil Sangam. In some cases the regional organizations are natural outgrowths of the networks that made possible immigration and settlement in the first place. The language erects a strong boundary that discourages participation in programs, leadership of the organization, or appreciation of nuances of worship or cultural awareness by anyone not fluent in the language. Some of those deterred are, of course, children who are incompetent in the language and ignorant of much of the regional culture. Hence, much of the energy and resources of these groups must be expended to teach the language and celebrate the culture. An ethnic strategy of adaptation seems most effective among immigrants of the first generation who have a strong loyalty to memories of church and culture back home in India. It is possible that a weakened symbolic ethnicity will develop in the second and third generations, one that will value a few elements of ethnicity but ignore most of the original contexts in which the elements had meaning and power. "Asian Indian" could become a separate ethnic group because US governmental records and regulations will not value distinctive language groups or religious groups. The government values what is named in census documents for various forms of affirmative action, so perhaps "Asian Indian" will become a valued designation. Ultimately, definition of what that ethnic designation will mean culturally and religiously will be determined by people of the third generation awaiting birth.

Hierarchical

Christian groups are not so likely to adopt a hierarchical strategy as are those of some other religions. The chief characteristic of organizations adopting this strategy is loyalty to a living religious leader who provides a unity for the group beyond ethnic or national loyalties. The group preserves a specific tradition and set of rituals transmitted and authenticated by a hierarchy, and the current religious leader is the living symbol of the hierarchy who attracts personal loyalty and marshals resources for institutional development. Loyalty to a living authority figure often generates religious groups that include both immigrants and members of the established society from several ethnic, racial, national, educational, and economic class groups – breaking down social distinctions by focusing devotion on one person. Bishops, metropolitans, and popes exercise such authority for some Christians from India, and the authority of the pope as the successor of St. Peter authenticates a unity for Catholics that may transcend ethnic or national loyalties. Religion is thereby separated from ethnicity, at least officially. The strategy is, however, more central to groups of other Indian religions in which the guru tradition is strong – indeed, in which the guru is believed to be the embodiment or direct representative of a god.

Bishops are treated with great deference by members of their flocks both in India and in America. That empowers them to be effective mediators between past and present, between parents and children, and between forms of Christianity in India and their emerging counterparts in the United States. Bishops often have a unifying influence on emerging churches in the United States and become spokesmen for the churches in conversations with other American ecclesiastical and governmental agencies. Aspects of a hierarchical strategy seem to be involved in Christian sects that revolve around the personality, charisma, and authority of a recent founder or current leader. A famous preacher, a charismatic healer, or a powerful cult leader does attract a following, usually establishing an interracial and multiethnic community, and some Asian-Indian young people are attracted to such groups. The hierarchical strategy is, nevertheless, somewhat foreign to Christian groups and thought to be fraught with danger because in its pure form it attributes to the individual a status approaching that of deity. No Asian-Indian Christian leader has established a personality cult similar to the International Society of Krishna Consciousness or the Rajneesh Ashram. Establishment of organized churches with routinized leadership is one way parents attempt to "save" their children from following what they perceive to be dangerous sects and cults, both Christian and pagan.

"Denominational"

The title for this section is in quotation marks because, while it seems obvious that new religious groups would develop along denominational lines, reservations exist regarding the appropriateness of this term as a designation for new immigrant groups. The model is compelling because it is pervasive in both academic analyses and self-identification of American Christian groups. Denominationalism may be an American Protestant creation, resulting from experiences of adaptation of earlier immigrants. Hence, denominational adaptation is immediately available, understood by people in the society, and supported by some governmental agencies, which understand and are comfortable with denominational affiliation. Indeed, Allen Richardson suggests that Muslim, Hindu, and Sikh religious groups are moving toward denominational models (1988:126–53). These organizations may be influenced to move in that direction, but it seems premature to designate them as such. Naming by scholars may suggest a reality that does not yet exist.

The denominational model is pervasive in America, but it is becoming increasingly difficult to use it for new immigrants for three reasons. (1) Islam, Hinduism, Sikhism, and other religious groups do not so easily adapt to denominational stereotypes. (2) These groups, and even Christian immigrant groups, do not identify themselves as denominations in their places of origin. (3) Denomination as a category is defined as Max Weber's "church-type" in reference to mainline churches resulting from earlier immigration, whereas other Christian groups are called sects. Will these new Christian groups assimilate to American models by taking on the characteristics of denominations, or will they help transform the nature of church boundaries and structures in a context where denominations are becoming weaker? Breakdown of denominational loyalties, shrinking of mainline denominations, and proliferation of independent or loosely related Christian churches and institutions of the majority society cause one to question whether "denominational" continues to be a viable strategy of adaptation. Winthrop S. Hudson summarizes developments, "Since the common core of Protestantism had become so badly eroded, it is possible that 'Protestant denominationalism' may no longer be a viable term to indicate anything more than Protestant diversity" (1987:297a). He summarizes Martin Marty's point that "denomination" may serve only to designate existing ecclesiastical groupings that provide a "family tone" and clusters of memories and symbols that are invoked to sustain Christians in their daily lives (*ibid.*). Recent immigration of Christians from many countries not only adds new elements to American Christianity to be analyzed, but also may result in a confusing constellation of churches and church organizations that may require new categories of analysis. To name these new groups as denominations may be inaccurate and premature.

Having made that point, it is necessary to indicate the attraction of ties with American denominations. Missionaries sent by American denominational boards established institutions in India which they still support in part even though few foreign missionaries are currently allowed to work in India. Contact with these institutions provided networks that enabled immigration and assisted settlement in the United States. Many pastors are in America because of these networks, with education provided by scholarships and support given by congregations, dioceses, or conferences. A number of individuals and families seek out congregations – Methodists, Baptists, or Episcopal – with which their congregations and judicatories in India are affiliated. Some groups established by immigrants in America are formally affiliated as parishes or missions with regional or national synods and associations of these denominations. They thereby link their future with the denomination. Such linkage is usually more beneficial for clergy than for the congregation because affiliation generally assures a salary according to an established scale. Several congregations of immigrants refuse to affiliate because they are either unable or unwilling to provide a salary at the established scale or to submit to other regulations of the synod or association.

A denominational pattern of development for immigrant churches involves affiliation with an established American denomination, or the adoption of characteristics of denominations. It may be that the Mar Thoma Church or the CSI will eventually adapt to modified denominational forms; much will depend upon their success in preserving their youth for their churches. The nature of their negotiations with denominations and ecumenical organizations will be dictated by the health or enfeeblement of those institutions. It may well be that denominational designation is simply the name for constellations and amalgamations of adaptive strategies discussed above. H. Richard Niebuhr's thesis regarding the social sources of denominations suggests that denomination is only the designation of the results of several adaptive strategies that earlier immigrants used (1929). Will new immigrants create new denominations or will they create some other new type of church associations from their selection and experience of strategies of adaptation in America?

Process of adaptation

Strategies of adaptation are malleable because immigrants are able to stress several overlapping identities, depending upon the context.

Among family and friends the individual identity is named; in the political sphere, the national; socially among Asian Indians, the ethnic or even subethnic caste; in religious gatherings a church name is stressed. Thus a person can name herself or be named as "Marykutta," "Asian- Indian," "Malayalee," "Syrian," "Christian" or "Syro-Malabar Catholic." Indeed, for those who know intimate details of the social structure, a single name may reveal many aspects of a person's identity. Organizations are able to accommodate several overlapping strategies, such as ethnic and ecumenical or national and denominational. Moreover, strategies may change within a given organization as the immigrant group develops through time, and the strategies may differ in separate locations in the country. Immigrants contribute multicolored and many-shaped pieces to the kaleidoscope of American religion that is changing with disorienting speed. It is fascinating to observe how, when, and in what ways they will join and break apart in becoming part of the total picture.

Evolution and adaptation of Christian organizations for survival in a new cultural ecosystem is analogous to the processes geneticists envision in integrated theories of adaptation. A number of variables of social location influence selection of adaptive strategies, thus having a similar influence to environmentally directed effects in scientific models. Four variables influence both the selection of adaptive strategies and their viability: length of residence, population density, transition from the first to succeeding generations, and majority/minority status.

(1) The length of residence for Asian-Indian Christians is circum-scribed by changes in immigration law beginning in 1965 and continuing to the present. Growth of the Christian immigrant community from a few individual nurses to well-established churches and dioceses is dra-matic. Generally the length of residence can be marked in the few decades since 1965, but length of residence in given areas may differ greatly as immigrants move into new communities. The trajectory of development affected by length of residence becomes a progressive movement through strategies: individual, national, ecumenical (espe-cially by minorities), ethnic, hierarchical, and, perhaps, denominational.

(2) Population density of Asian Indians is closely allied with, but not identical to, length of residence. Population density cannot be placed on a time-line for several reasons. Urban areas did not experience growth of Asian-Indian Christian populations at the same time, and the size of the community is relatively small in some urban areas. Moreover, it is always volatile. The population in metropolitan areas has grown rapidly so it

appears the community is stable and growing, but in fact the community is unstable because new immigrants experience very high rates of mobility as they move from place to place to find an economically and socially secure home. Even within an urban area, immigrants move into new residential areas and establish new religious organizations. New immigrants arrive from India. Thus, the Asian-Indian population is in constant flux. As population density increases, the adaptive strategies develop through the pattern described above. At one stage a bifurcation takes place in development of regional or national centers that attract allegiance and participation of Asian Indians from a wide geographical area. For example, they may worship as individuals in an established American church near their home, but travel for several hundred miles to celebrate a festival or attend a convention sponsored by the Mar Thoma Church. Some ecumenical and national institutions disappear when the group reaches a size that can support ethnic and hierarchical ones.

(3) Transition of generations progresses in the immigrant community, arousing tensions and conflicts that affect strategies of adaptation. Religious organizations provide the primary forums in which the aspirations and fears of immigrants and the frustrations and desires of their children are expressed and encountered. First-generation immigrants are torn between strategies of adaptation, rooted in the Indian past, that are individual, national, and ethnic in character. They feel most "at home" when they are able to share the same ethnic language, food, dress, and customs. Such strategies are reinforced by what could be called the "late first-generation immigrants," those who arrived recently from Indian villages and cities. As a group they do not come from the educated, scientifically trained, professional elite, and they are more conservative socially and religiously. They provide a renewable continuity with religious organizations and traditions in India. Religious organizations come into existence when children of the second generation reach school-age and come under the strong influence of peer pressures outside the home. Development of new strategies or a combination of strategies often result from the attempt to meet the needs of both generations and to prepare for a third generation not yet formed.

(4) Majority/minority status is a complicated variable because it is always relative in degree, and every distinct religious group is an operative minority in some contexts, especially in a heterogeneous society. Both India and the United States are heterogeneous, and, due to regional variation, immigrants from India cannot be considered as each

leaving the same place regarding religious variations in the population. The relation existing among various religious groups, particularly in matters related to relative dominance and numerical superiority, depends on the area from which the immigrants come. Christians from some areas of India – from the central Travancore region or a Christian suburb of Ahmedabad, for example – come from an area where Christians are the largest group, if not a majority. Other Christians come from locations where Christians are a tiny minority. They perceive themselves in America as occupying various levels of minority status, and that affects relations with other Christian groups and with the larger society.

The formation of religious groups by immigrants and the strategies of adaptation that establish boundaries are not intended to separate individuals and groups from the rest of the population, but rather to provide the necessary basis on which the individual and group can negotiate effective relations with the majority population. Thus, that negotiation can be viewed as reaching out in concentric circles to form less stable, but more inclusive, social networks. The negotiation moves in general from individual to hierarchical to ethnic to ecumenical to national, and finally to the American national community. A Syro-Malabar Catholic joins with others loyal to the pope, then affiliates with other Keralites, then negotiates with other Christians, joins Asian-Indian organizations, and with all these supports speaks from a position of strength with other groups in American society. Groups adopt elements of more than one strategy, and any individual immigrant is a member of several groups stressing different strategies. These result from the need to preserve several identities within one unity and from the desire to be able to choose from several overlapping identities the most advantageous according to context. The concentric circles of negotiation are in evidence all around us, creating a variety of religious organizations that are increasingly visible and participating in a pluralism far more complex than a listing of major ethnic and religious groups. Within each group so designated great variation exists in types of adaptive strategies employed and in resulting religious structures.

ST. THOMAS CHRISTIANS IN THE UNITED STATES

This section focuses on the churches in the United States that have primary direct contacts with the St. Thomas tradition. As a group they are often called "Syrian" because of the influence of bishops and leaders from Syria who visited or settled in India through the centuries. They claim ancient hereditary descent either from the Brahmins said to have been converted by St. Thomas, from Syrian immigrants to India or from a few converts from the ruling class. As a family of churches, they share many common features as representatives of the Eastern Orthodox churches. Most of the people have family roots in Kerala, even if they migrated from other parts of India or after a period of residence in the Gulf states. Like families everywhere they quarrel with one another, split apart, recognize an affinity, share a common history, and occasionally rise above disputes to cooperate and support one another. In America, Thomas Christians often worshiped as one before increase in numbers encouraged establishment of separate churches. Chapter 4 deals with other churches from India that stand apart from the Eastern Orthodox family of churches.

The Syrian Orthodox Church in the United States and Canada

An archbishop dressed in Syrian garb, a metropolitan from India wearing a Ramban's (monk's) distinctive black pointed cap bearing thirteen white stars (representing Christ and the Apostles), and an Asian-Indian priest walked through the lobby of a Dallas hotel in 1993 on their way to perform the Holy Qurbana (Eucharist) at the local Syrian Orthodox Church. Vacationing families, oil workers, and business people observed this strange ecclesiastical procession with surprise, curiosity, and just a touch of hostility couched in humor. Most had never seen anything like it before. The day was virtually the last that the Syrian archbishop would exercise authority as representative of the Patriarch of Antioch over the Indian Syrian Orthodox Churches in the United States because the churches with ties in Kerala announced an agreement by the patriarch to establish a new diocese, thereby validating an ethnic strategy of adaptation.

Syrian Christianity came to America in the nineteenth century with immigrants from greater Syria, and by the 1920s approximately seventy-five Syrian churches – Melkite, Maronite, and Orthodox – were established in twenty-eight states. Prior to the Second World War, most Syrian immigrants were Christians from the Mt. Lebanon region (Naff, 1980: 132a), and still a majority of Syrians in the United States are Christians, not Muslims. The Patriarch of Antioch, now permanently residing in Damascus, established an American archdiocese and commissioned an archbishop, Mar Athanasius Yeshue Samuel, to serve as shepherd of the Syrian Orthodox Christians in the United States. Little did the observers in the Dallas hotel know his distinguished past. Before the establishment of Israel, Athanasius Mar Samuel was archbishop of Jerusalem. It was to him that the bedouin first brought sections of the Dead Sea Scrolls because they thought the manuscripts were liturgical documents in Syriac. When some Syrian Christians migrated from Israel, he took some of the Dead Sea Scrolls first to Damascus and then to New York in 1949, when he was installed in his archdiocese and took up residence in Lodi, New Jersey. He has resided in the United States since 1949.

Cooperation between Syrian and Indian Orthodox Christians was close in the early days of Indian immigration. Dr. K. M. Simon began worship services in Malayalam in a chapel of Union Theological Seminary in New York in 1965 and carried on an ecumenical mission under Mar Athanasius Yeshue Samuel for several years. A Malankara priest came to Chicago in 1971 when only about three Indian Syrian Orthodox families lived in Chicago. He first celebrated the Eastern liturgy in a side chapel of a Roman Catholic Church, but, when a Roman Catholic priest told him about a Syrian Orthodox church that served the Syrian community, he began to celebrate the first public Malankara service in St. John the Divine Orthodox Church. (Note that 1971 was the time when the Syrian Orthodox Church and the Malankara Orthodox Church in India had reached the end of a long period of union.)[3] When the Syrians did not have a resident priest, he celebrated the Qurbana for both communities. In 1976 the Indian community began to grow rapidly because of the influx of nurses. Currently they share the same building for services, with the Syrian service at 9.30 A.M. and the Malayalee service at 11.00. They share the St. James liturgy and similar patterns of personal and ecclesiastical discipline.

Yuhanon Mar Philoxinos, currently bishop of the Malabar diocese of the Syrian Orthodox Church in India, came to the United States in 1977 and gathered ten Syrian Orthodox families from India for meetings in the basement of Our Lady of Good Counsel Roman Catholic Church in Staten Island. He refers to that church as the "birth place of Malayalee Syrian Orthodox churches in the United States" and to himself as "the first vicar of the church in the United States." He gathered people for Saturday evening prayer services in their homes, because the Syrian Orthodox, like the Jews, begin the holy day at sundown with prayers. He engaged in individual evangelism by looking up identifiable names of Malayalee Orthodox families in the telephone books and calling on them with invitations to attend the services. He said, "We exploited their attachments to the mother tongue and the motherland to bring them together." They shared in a Malayalee feast following the service, "like the love-feasts in the first-century church." Mar Gregorios Syrian Orthodox Church of Staten Island became the first church owned and operated by the Indian Christian community. The community grew rapidly in other cities, and by 1984 seven more churches were established, one a year, in cities like Chicago, Dallas, Houston, and Detroit. Lay groups formed *ad hoc* administrative committees and organized prayer meetings, and a priest traveled to celebrate the Qurbana once a month or on special occasions. Priests were called from India to serve the newly established churches, and at that time they were able to get visas in about three months. All these groups had ties in Kerala, but their parishes were authorized by the Syrian archbishop and were under his ecclesiastical control. The founding priest returned to Kerala in 1984 to be consecrated as metropolitan of the Malabar diocese under the name Yuhanon Mar Philoxinos.

Priests came from India as immigrants on different paths: as students, as permanent professional immigrants, as temporary workers, and to join family members. Most eventually become permanent residents and call themselves "missionary priests" because they work at secular occupations and do not claim a salary from the church. A few are now wealthy, which conforms to the traditional pattern in Kerala where before Indian independence priests came from "aristocratic families" and were supported by family wealth without fixed income from the individual parishes into which they were ordained as a kind of "marriage for life." Several of the priests in America come from families that point with pride to ten or more generations of priests. The pattern of support changed in India after independence, so that now Syrian Orthodox priests are provided a salary and are under the jurisdiction of the bishop to be moved to different parishes. The change allows for priests to be sent to areas in north India and abroad where Malayalees congregate. The parishes in the United States are generally too small to support a priest, so their priests provide service without fixed stipend. Several are college professors, some are in real estate, several have very successful businesses, and a few serve as chaplains in hospitals or as certified counselors. Most of the priests in America are married men with secular jobs and families, so they face many of the problems and conflicts their lay people experience. The priests do receive gifts at ceremonies like baptism, marriage, and funerals – recalling those early accusations made by Westerners that they "sell the sacraments" out of ignorance that these gifts were their only income from the church. Arrival in

America of new priests as permanent residents often leads to splits when groups in the parish prefer one priest to another, thereby assuring that the congregations remain small.

The Syrian Orthodox Church in the United States continued as "one church but two communities." Like the Zoroastrians from Iran and the Parsis from India, they were merging two ethnic and national groups into one religious organization. (See Williams, 1988:121–4.) The Christians remained for a period administratively united under the Syrian archbishop as the representative of the Patriarch of Antioch in Damascus, but in growth patterns the Indians followed ethnic strategies of adaptation similar to those of the earlier Syrian immigrants. Tensions were inevitable. The Arab Syrians were more comfortable with the Syriac liturgy. Although the older immigrants had grown up in families using the Syrian language for worship and most could "understand and appreciate it," after the change from Syriac to Malayalam for the liturgy in Kerala they became more attached to the liturgy in their native language.

The Indian Syrian Orthodox Christians moved from Syriac to Malayalam, and now find themselves irresistibly drawn toward a move from Malayalam to English. Fortunately, the Syrian archbishop in 1967 approved a translation of the liturgy from Syriac into English for the second and third generation of Syrian immigrants, so a translation is available for use by future generations of new immigrants. The Indian Orthodox Christians sought direction from the synod and individual bishops in Kerala in ways that undermined the authority of the Syrian archbishop and threatened the unity of the church. Bishops and other Christian leaders came from India on unauthorized visits to churches to raise funds for projects in Kerala. Although the archbishop was said to be "very cooperative and outgoing," people from India desired a bishop for their churches who would "speak their language" and understand their backgrounds. It appeared for a time that the Indian Orthodox churches in America would become affiliated with separate dioceses and bishops from Kerala. One priest argued: "The Jacobites have to create separate churches to preserve their religious traditions and obligations. The Roman Catholics and Protestants can preserve their religious identity and fulfill their religious obligations in American churches, and participate in ethnic churches once a month or so as an 'over and above duty.'" As a result of conversations, without much rancor on either side, the Indian Syrian Orthodox churches in North America moved fully into an ethnic strategy of adaptation, uniting both their administrative and congregational strategies.

They celebrate the Holy Qurbana in Malayalam; only the words of institution and some words of Jesus are repeated in Syriac. The prayer book is divided, with one side Syriac and the other Malayalam. Many of the people understand the liturgical Syriac, but they are now more comfortable with Malayalam. Only very slowly are a few of the churches introducing services in English, although young men shift into English to read scripture or give announcements in the services. The Sunday Schools use materials published in English by American interdenominational presses – some churches use David B. Cooke Publishers' materials – but the Sunday School committee is working on a series of teaching materials "in good American English." The language of church business and fellowship is Malayalam. Both the style of leadership and the ethos of fellowship are Malayalee and these form boundaries that effectively discourage participation by non-Keralites. The Malayalee system of values, especially family values, is emphasized. Stress is placed on marriage within the Malayalee Christian community rather than upon marriage within the Syrian church. It becomes increasingly obvious that home is Kerala, not Syria, even though, ironically, the people are often called "Syrians" in Kerala.

The ecclesiastical structure for the Indian churches included a Delegates Committee, made up of a priest and two laymen from each parish, and a Council of Eleven, consisting of nine Keralites and two Syrians – the archbishop and the general secretary. On July 12, 1992, a Delegates Meeting in Nyack, New York, formally requested that a new diocese be established for the Keralite Syrian Orthodox community, asked that a new bishop be consecrated for the diocese, and elected Revd. P. G. Cherian as the person recommended to the patriarch and synod to become the new bishop. Six reasons were given for desiring a new diocese and bishop.

(1) The community was growing larger through both births and continued immigration, so the spiritual and administrative demands were greater than one person could meet.
(2) A bishop who knew the language and culture could deal more effectively with problems in families and parishes.
(3) The children and youth needed a younger bishop who could relate well with them so he could mediate between the cultures and between the generations.
(4) Someone was needed to protect the congregations from unauthorized visits by bishops from Kerala and unauthorized and disruptive action by newly arrived immigrant priests.

(5) A leader was needed to help organize the parishes and develop programs that would stop the drain of people leaving the parishes because they were so loosely organized.

(6) A younger bishop with more energy was needed to travel around the country establishing new parishes to take advantage of growth in the community.

The archbishop gave his seal of approval to the actions and recommended that a bishop be appointed. The Council elected four people to go to Damascus to talk with the patriarch.

By the time of the Delegates Meeting in July of 1993, the patriarch had agreed and issued a formal bull naming P. G. Cherian as bishop-elect, and indicated his intention to establish a new diocese in North America. Cherian was an unmarried priest at that time completing a doctorate at United Theological Seminary in Bangalore. He was relatively young at 38 and had to be consecrated as a Ramban (monk) at least one day before he could be consecrated as bishop. He had never traveled in the United States, even though he was fluent in English, but he had served on the youth and publication committees and was active in the Eastern Orthodox dialogue with the Roman Catholic Church. He was consecrated bishop and given the name Mar Nicholovos Zachariah late in 1993 and arrived in the United States in October to establish residence, begin a diocesan center in New York, and oversee 23 churches in North America, serving roughly 650 families of approximately 3,000 people. In his address, given in English, at the formal welcome ceremony at St. John the Baptist Syrian Orthodox Church in Chicago, he stressed the need for the unity of the church, speaking of division as "wounds on the body of · Christ." The Syrian Orthodox Church has an agreement with the Roman Catholic Church that, where members are isolated, they can participate jointly in the sacraments, and it is engaged in joint theological conversations on Christology with the office of the Presiding Bishop of the Protestant Episcopal Church in the United States.[4] The bishop's comments about ecumenical activities seem directed, however, more toward the St. Thomas Christians who as a united group could make a more effective impact in an alien culture. He said: "We are called here not to be what we were in another place, but what we are called to be here. A divine mission...Ours is not a glorious culture unless it confronts other cultures, contributes to other cultures, and receives from other cultures." That call marks out the challenge of the future of the ecumenical church.

Establishment of a new diocese with a new bishop necessitates a new constitution for the Syrian Orthodox Church in the United States and

Canada, and a committee is currently at work. Major issues involve relations between the bishop and the permanent-resident part-time priests
in his diocese. Will he have the authority and ability to move priests from
one parish to another? If not, are priests permanently assigned to a
parish? The constitution must establish appropriate relations between
the diocese and the synod in Kerala and with the patriarch's office in
Damascus. Much sentiment exists for placing the diocese directly under
the patriarch and not under the synod. It is proposed that the North
American bishop will be only an observer and not a full participant in
the synod in Kerala, but will report directly to the patriarch. The final
decision in this matter will greatly affect the authority of the bishop and
the power of priests in North America to direct their own affairs without
interference from Kerala. Work on the new constitution is important
because it will govern relations with the church in Kerala and with other
churches in America and thereby shape the strategies of adaptation that
are encouraged or permitted.

The archbishop, metropolitan, and priest arrived at St. Ignatius
Malankara Jacobite Syrian Church in a wealthy Dallas suburb to celebrate the Holy Qurbana according to the liturgy of St. James in the
western Syrian form as part of the national annual meeting. Men stood
on the left side facing the altar, and the women on the right. Incense
created a veil through which they observed the mysteries. The primary
language of the Holy Qurbana was Malayalam with a few phrases of
Syriac inserted. Traditional chants by priests and people were in patterns
developed in antiquity. At the end of the service the people filed by the
archbishop to kiss his hand as a symbol of respect for the episcopacy and
allegiance to the Patriarch of Antioch. Nevertheless, it was clearly a
Keralite congregation moving both locally and at a diocesan level
toward an ethnic strategy of adaptation. They seek to preserve both
their religious and ethnic identities in one institution.

Knanaya Orthodox

Knanaya mark the years of their "second migration" from the arrival of
one family in America in 1958. In both India and the United States the
Knanaya are a prosperous business and professional community that
seeks to maintain its identity through participation in an independent
Knanaya Orthodox diocese and through endogamy. The Jacobite
Knanaya have exactly the same liturgical practices, prayer books, and
discipline as the other Syrian Orthodox. They had a slightly different

immigration pattern because Knanaya women lagged behind other Keralite Christians in taking advantage of the opportunity nursing provided for immigration. Their administration is also different because a separate diocese was established for them in Kerala early in the twentieth century. Their churches in North America enjoy a separate diocese established in 1982 under the episcopal authority of Abraham Mar Clemis, the Valiya Metropolitan in residence at Mar Ephraem's Seminary in Chingavam near Kottayam. He is the third in the line of independent Knanaya bishops and presides over 64 churches with 68 priests and perhaps 100,000 Jacobite Knanaya in Kerala and the cities of India. Estimates of Orthodox Knanaya in North America are 500 families with 2250 individuals served by 11 priests and 3 deacons. There are 9 parishes (New York, New Jersey, Chicago, Philadelphia, Boston, Houston, Dallas, Edmonton, Toronto) of which 3 have their own buildings (St. Peter's Knanaya Church in Yonkers, NY, being the first with its own building; St. John's Knanaya Church in Houston; and St. Stephen's Knanaya Church in Boston). The community is scattered and the parishes are small; for example, the Boston congregation has only 35 families.

The small size of the community in the United States makes it difficult to preserve their separate ethnic identity. They face two immediate problems: (1) to interpret and justify endogamy both to their children and to the general public, and (2) to find appropriate partners for their children. They claim to be direct descendants of Jesus' family through Mary and identify themselves as descendants from families of Christian Jews. Betrothal is a binding ceremony, as it is for Jews, and the bishop is the only one who can release persons from betrothal vows. Resulting marriages within the community are very elaborate, with great pride taken in the wedding songs that are unique to the Knanaya. Young people question the rationale for maintaining such strict endogamy in America. Some believe that the claim to be "old Christians" and part of an aristocracy requiring endogamy is casteism at its worst that should not be imported to America. The response in religious terms is to apply to the Knanaya all the injunctions regarding exclusiveness found in some Hebrew texts and in sociological terms is to show that other groups practice *de facto* endogamy. Even if the young people are convinced, it is difficult to find appropriate partners.

Marriage to any person descending from one of the seventy-two Syrian families is acceptable, including Knanaya Catholics, but a detailed examination of family ties is made by the bishop before permission is given for marriage in the church. Formerly the expectation was

that an Orthodox Knanaya marrying a Knanaya Catholic would join
the Catholic community, or at least agree to raise the children as
Catholics. In 1994 the Syrian Orthodox bishops and the Syro-Malabar
Catholic bishops in Kerala reached an ecumenical agreement that individuals marrying from the two communities can keep their faith and
raise children according to the wishes of the parents. Knanaya youth in
America are just coming to the marriage age, so the issue evokes lively
debate. Parents prefer that their children return to India for marriage
within the community, but the youth look forward to marriage in the
United States. A person who marries outside the community is no longer
considered to be a practicing Knanaya, nor are the children enrolled.
That creates a great deal of resentment and misunderstanding. Already,
several young people have married out, some to other Syrian Christians
and some into other ethnic groups. That is a grave threat because the
very existence of the Knanaya depends on endogamy.

The Church is searching for strategies to help young people locate
appropriate candidates for marriage. An annual family conference
begun in 1982 is an occasion when families can establish networks for
marriage negotiations. The 1994 Knanaya conference attracted 250 participants. A youth convention preceding the conference provides an
opportunity for young people to become acquainted with potential partners. The Orthodox bishop suggests that the Church establish a graduate residence hall at a major university where Knanaya youth can meet
in a context that would encourage endogamy, following a familiar model
in India of funding student hostels.The search for a solution is a desperate quest.

Eleven Knanaya Orthodox priests are permanent residents in
America, which creates problems for the church in Kerala. It is a significant brain-drain from a relatively small pool of priests in India. Most
moved to America for graduate study, and several have doctoral degrees.
They also serve as volunteer priests and support themselves with secular
occupations. There is a need for full-time priests, but the community is
too small to support them. The bishop says that in the past when scholarships were readily available, he sent priests for study, but few were willing
to return to the diocese in Kerala where the salaries of priests are from
1,000 Indian rupees (Rs) per month (approximately US$35) for a young
priest to Rs 2,000 plus parsonage and allowances for a senior minister.
The bishop is himself one of the few who studied in the United States
and then returned to a parish in Kerala. Now the bishop rarely sends
priests for study even though he desperately wants training for his priests

in pastoral counseling. He fears the temptation to stay on is too great. Nevertheless, new priests arrive periodically under family reunification provisions of immigration laws.

The Revd. Dr. Abraham Thomas of Boston is cor-episcopa and administrator of the North American diocese in the absence of a resident bishop, and his story is instructive. His family is related to the bishop's family, and his ancestors donated land for the seminary. He is a twin in a family of fourteen children – seven brothers and seven sisters. The bishop visited his family in 1952 and explained a five-year plan to recruit priests. The family hoped that one of the twins would become a priest. Thomas was made a sub-deacon at the age of 18 and stayed at Mar Ephraem Seminary for a year. He received a master's in English at Madras Christian College and studied at Moore Theological College in Australia. After teaching English for two years, he received a Rockefeller Fellowship to study at Union Theological Seminary in New York in 1961–62. He entered Boston University for a doctoral degree in social ethics, which was awarded for a dissertation on "Christians in secular India" based on research in Bangalore. He was married while in India – he says people teased him by asking whether he returned to India to write a book or just to get married. He joined the faculty of a college near Boston and then was ordained in 1971. Five brothers and three sisters have now joined him and reside in America. One of his sisters is a member of the Orthodox Order of the Sisters of Magdalene and has established a convent with two other nuns in Waldham, Massachusetts.

Jacobite Knanaya Christians are struggling to follow one of the most restrictive ethnic strategies of any American church. They are small and endogamous like some branches of the Amish, but they live in the world, not separate from it, distributed in urban areas across the country. They wish to preserve ethnic ties even though they do not follow traditional occupations. Exclusion results from marrying out of the community even though, like the Parsis, the community is so small as to make it difficult to find marriage partners inside it. They prefer endogamy within the ethnic group to endogamy within the Church, although all recognized Knanaya are at least nominally Christians, albeit Orthodox and Catholic. It provides an interesting experiment in an ethnic strategy of adaptation. Members of the first generation value and pursue an ethnic purity that flies in the face of some contemporary American rhetoric and which leaves many young people uncertain about their individual prospects and the future of their distinctive community in America.

Malankara Orthodox Syrian Church

Two metropolitans stood before the assembled 1993 family conference at Los Angeles for the Saturday evening prayers of preparation for Holy Qurbana on Sunday. Thomas Mar Makarios was resplendent in the traditional silken purple robe of a bishop of the Syrian church. Hanging from his neck was the cross of gold, and on his finger was a bishop's ring. Tall, elegant, with groomed beard, the distinctive monk's cap with thirteen stars on his head, meticulously fluent in American English, he occupied the stage looking every inch a prince of the church. Mathews Mar Barnabas moved quietly around the platform wearing a simple saffron-colored robe made of homespun *khadi* cloth. Short of stature, wiry, bearing a scent of piety and prayer, he could easily be mistaken for a Indian sannyasin (a Hindu world-renouncer) except for the crude wooden cross on his chest and the monk's cap perched on his head. Two worlds revolving on one stage; two approaches to Christian life in America. Their sacred dance of movements on the platform and the wary deference with which they treated each other symbolized tensions rending the church regarding the path to be taken in adapting to American culture and shaping their place in American Christianity.

Each metropolitan is a person of integrity and devotion to the Malankara churches in America, but they are entangled in a controversy leading to lawsuits and, it seems, inevitably to a schism in the church. Meetings of congregations and annual national conferences are filled with emotion and sadness as priests and members take sides with one or other of the bishops. The synod in Kerala is concerned and unsure of what response to make regarding matters in dispute. It is too simplistic to frame the issue as a personality conflict, as it sometimes is in the heat of debate, between two bishops or even between two personal styles, one perceived as "too American" and the other as "too Keralite." The emotion and tension arise from uncertainty in the church, both among leaders in Kottayam and among priests and people in America, regarding what the shape and identity of Malankara churches and Christians will be in the United States in the twenty-first century. The problem transcends two individual bishops, although they are major figures in the dispute.

Thomas Mar Makarios is the founding metropolitan of the North American diocese of the Malankara Church. He was a student at the Orthodox Seminary in Kottayam and received a World Council of Churches fellowship to study at Lincoln College in England in 1958–59.

He also studied for a summer in Geneva at the World Council of Churches. He enjoyed the benefits of scholarships that were readily available in the 1950s and early 1960s for priests and deacons to study in Europe or America. He was then posted outside Kerala for eight years in charge of the parish in New Delhi and participated on the planning staff when the World Council of Churches' meeting was scheduled for New Delhi. At the WCC meeting, he became acquainted with the Episcopal Bishop of Buffalo, New York, who offered him a scholarship to study in America. He came in 1963 for a year at Nashotah House and received the Bachelor of Divinity degree. (The seminary in Kottayam was not a degree-granting institution when he was there.) He stayed on to receive a master's degree from Virginia Theological Seminary and a Th.D. degree from Union Theological Seminary in Virginia. He returned briefly to Kerala to teach at the Orthodox Seminary in Kottayam from 1972 to 1975 and then was consecrated and appointed as metropolitan of the Malankara diocese of Bombay, which at that time included northwest India, the Middle East, North America, the United Kingdom, and Europe. Four years later the North American diocese was recognized as a separate diocese, and he took up permanent residence as metropolitan in Buffalo, New York, with an office in Episcopal Diocesan House. For many years he has commuted from Buffalo to serve as a part-time adjunct professor at Alma College in Michigan.

Hence, when he stands before the community, he speaks with an authority of shared experience because, as he often says, he has been in America for thirty-two years and has spent most of that time associated on college or seminary campuses, first as a student and then as a faculty member. He is familiar with college-age youth, and is able to establish rapport with Malankara youth. His view of the church and its future in America is greatly influenced by his "view from Alma." He notes in his remarks to youth that he wears his ecclesiastical garb on campus as an indication that he is able to maintain his identity as a Malankara bishop while adjusting well to American society. He is proud that he adopted some American ways, like driving a car, owning a house, shopping and cooking for himself, and standing patiently in the food service line at the conference rather than being served, whereas bishops would be served in India. Although he is proud of the fact that he has lived and served outside Kerala for forty years, that exile may cause him to be insensitive to changes and the current situation in Kerala. All immigrants carry an imperfect picture of India created from their memory, but one wonders what picture of Kerala and the church in Kerala he carries with him.

The Catholicos of the East, Moran Mar Baselius Mar Thoma Mathews I, established the diocese on his first visit to the United States as the first separate diocese established in America by any Asian-Indian Christian group. Growth was rapid during the late 1970s and the early 1980s, and new parishes were recognized in urban areas across the country. That was also a time of immigration by many priests, some of whom were not authorized by the diocese. Nevertheless, the bishop said, "We make use of them." In fact, the influx of priests to reunite with families or to take secular employment led to divisions in the congregations as relatives and their friends in established parishes separated to form new parishes served by recently arrived priests. Even where the population is relatively small, three or four congregations compete for participation. The problem is exacerbated by the lack of an official clergy placement policy. Because priests are volunteer ministers, they are only loosely under the authority of the metropolitan; because they have businesses or employment where they have permanent residence, they are not mobile.

Mar Makarios continued until 1993 as metropolitan of the churches in North America, the United Kingdom, and Europe. Local tensions were then overshadowed by tensions in the diocese, and, it seems, by disputes about how the diocese should develop. Some of the priests complained to the Catholicos in Kottayam about the leadership of Mar Makarios, charging that he had himself become too Americanized and encouraged the young people too quickly to give up their Malayalee culture. A handful of churches claimed that they were "Catholicate Churches" directly under the Catholicos without allegiance to the metropolitan. In the midst of negotiations with the Catholicos and the synod in Kottayam, Mar Makarios resigned his position as metropolitan over the diocese. He was appointed and served for a brief period as personal secretary to the Catholicos in Kottayam, a position some in America incorrectly interpreted as leading to selection as Catholicos-designate.

The diocese came under the direct control of the new Catholicos, Moran Mar Baselius Mar Thoma Mathews II, and Mathews Mar Barnabas (1924–) traveled directly to New York from Kerala as the Catholicos' personal representative. His entire service in the church had been in Kerala, and he speaks with the authority of long involvement with the church's life there. He studied at Madras University and Osmania University and received a master's degree in botany and then a Bachelor of Divinity degree as an external candidate from Serampore Theological Seminary in India. He was ordained as a priest in 1951 and consecrated as a bishop in 1978. Thus, he and Mar Makarios are among the senior bishops of the Church. His was the common experience of becoming a Ramban (monk) just prior to consecration as bishop. He served as assistant bishop for four years in Ankamali and Kottayam dioceses, and has been for twelve years and continues to be metropolitan of the diocese in Idukki, a backward mountainous area on the border of Kerala and Tamil Nadu. He had already visited the American diocese once (in the summer of 1985) to gather funds for projects in the Idukki diocese. After Mar Barnabas was in America for a few months in 1992–93, the Catholicos and the synod decided that he should be officially designated as metropolitan of the diocese. They believed that because he is a very senior bishop and one known for his personal piety and humility, he would attract the allegiance of both priests and congregations and bring order to the diocese. As one metropolitan in Kerala said, "It requires great spirituality to deal with the problems in the United States." Thus, he serves at the same time as metropolitan of two dioceses: the poorest and the richest of the Malankara Orthodox Church. While priests and leaders praise his piety and devotion, they complain that he is "too much of Kottayam" and has little understanding of the experiences of immigrants and especially of the problems of young people. Thus, two metropolitans stand poles apart as symbols of potentials in the future of the church for becoming too American or too Indian. Tensions and conflict that swirl around these two figures are part of the awful agony of an immigrant church attempting to mark out its course for the future.

One future involves a strategy of rapid Americanization of the liturgical, administrative, and social aspects of the Church's life. The cry here is, "The church in America cannot be a carbon copy of the church in Kottayam." Leaders are conscious that a period of numerical growth such as the church in the United States is experiencing is a good time to institute changes. Priests and parents are greatly concerned about the future of their American children of the second generation, most of whom have little understanding of either the verbal, gestural, or symbolic language of the elaborate eastern liturgy. Efforts to shorten and streamline the liturgy are undertaken in order to maintain the interest of the young people. It is often argued that parents will have to accept the fact that their children will never return to India, so they must help them become good and effective American citizens. The youth say, "We are your best hope of having an Orthodox church in America, but you have to be willing to change." The use of English is encouraged in both liturgical and social activities. Popular westernized Christian choruses and hymns are played on guitars in non-liturgical meetings. Persons who are most fluent in American English, who are adept at moving in American society, who have leadership skills attuned to American patterns, and who represent what they want their children to emulate are valued and put forward for leadership positions. Calls for greater participation by women in official meetings of the parishes and dioceses meet with a sympathetic hearing. Children and youth are encouraged to participate in the social occasions of their peers, and parents are urged to trust their children as they move into wider social contexts. The administrative goal proposed by some is the independence of the American diocese to shape its future without the interference of leaders in Kottayam, perhaps leading to the formation of an administratively autonomous diocese that recognizes the spiritual leadership of the Catholicos but is not governed by the administrative structure of the management council or the synod of twenty-three in Kottayam. The diocese may continue to develop in a rather informal way, with little direct administration by the bishop, but with most power in the hands of individual priests and congregations. The priests are comfortable with part-time church assignments and full-time secular employment. A goal is often stated of enlisting priests from the second generation who have grown up in the United States and can be trained in American seminaries, priests who will be fully aware of American society and the experiences faced by immigrants. Perhaps that will lead to membership in the church and even the priesthood by people from the majority population.

A small group from the majority population already constitute a mission of the church in Spokane, Washington, and one white American is an ordained priest. The Revd. Fr. Michael Hatcher had been a student in a Roman Catholic seminary, but he met and married a Malayalee woman in Bombay, who was a Malankara Orthodox Christian. Through her he learned about the Orthodox tradition and contacted Mar Makarios in 1981 to discuss the possibility of ordination. He studied the liturgy with a cor-episcopa (a suffragan bishop, originally a rural bishop, who may be a married man) in Chicago and stayed for a few months at the Orthodox Seminary in Kottayam. He was ordained in 1985 (or 1986). He speaks very little Malayalam, but "does the Qurbana beautifully in English." He and his wife are well known among the churches, and he served as chaplain for one of the national family conferences in 1993. Does this intermarriage, conversion, Americanized clergy, and English liturgy foreshadow the future of the church? It is instructive that his name does not appear on Mar Barnabas' official list of priests of the diocese.

A second potential future involves a strategy of Indianization, at least stressing the strong ethnic and religious ties to Kerala. The cry is: "Do not give up the beautiful heritage you have for a 'mess of pottage.' Contribute the beauty and faith of your heritage to an American society that has become weak unto death." The appeal has more emotional power with members of the first generation than with youth of the second. Stress is upon the beauty of the ritual and symbolism of the ancient eastern ceremony performed in America as it has been for centuries in Kerala. Children are urged to learn Malayalam and traditional chants so they will be able to participate in the liturgy, just as Jewish young people have learned liturgical Hebrew in order to preserve their heritage. Much is made of traditional Keralite Christian values: the importance of family; the threat of divorce and the breakdown of marriage; a crowning of parents as priests of the home; regular family devotions each morning and evening; the status and authority of priests, metropolitans, and Catholicos; respect for the elderly; arranged marriages; and personal purity in sexual matters. The feeling is strong that their young people need protection from the vices and sins perceived to be rampant in American youth culture, even among Christian youth. This future leads toward a more formally organized diocese with close ties to the hierarchy in Kottayam. Leadership will be in the hands of those who are fluent in Malayalam and able to negotiate with authorities in Kerala. The argument is made that constitutional changes, such as those giving women a greater role, must be made in conjunction with the whole church and not just by a single diocese according to local circumstance. A goal is to have full-time priests trained in India and assigned by the Catholicos and synod from Kottayam as soon as the parishes in America are sufficiently strong to support them.

These two potential futures are sources of conflict not because they are represented by two metropolitans residing in the United States, but because they are strong attractions residing in the hearts of most of the adults and youth of the Malankara Orthodox Church. Both priests and lay people will speak from both sides of their hearts, stressing at one time aspirations for one future and then as the context changes stressing the other. The internal struggle is rending individuals, families, and congregations. The attractions and the dangers of both futures are great, and little Solomonic wisdom is present to dictate how the "child" is to be divided.

Shortly after Mathews Mar Barnabas arrived in America, Thomas Mar Makarios left his position as secretary to the Catholicos after another bishop was selected to be Catholicos-elect. Mar Makarios joked with a youth group in the midst of the American economic recession when many Indian families lost jobs, "I was laid off." The synod decided in July 1993 to divide the diocese and offered the new Diocese of Canada, the United Kingdom, and Europe to Mar Makarios. He accepted the appointment and serves the diocese from his office in Buffalo, while Mar Barnabas continues as metropolitan of the Diocese of the United States. It is an unequal division because Mar Makarios' diocese has only five or six congregations in Canada and three or four in England and Europe. A complication is that only three priests reside in Canada, and two priests travel from the United States to serve in Canada. The diocese in the United States consists of fifty-three recognized parishes served by sixty-one priests (all but one or two are also working in secular occupations, and all but two or three are married) and ten deacons. A majority of the priests are between 40 and 50 years old and are likely to serve the parishes well into the twenty-first century. It is unclear how the deacons will prepare themselves to serve as priests in the Malankara Church, either in India or in America. One is completing seminary studies at St. Vladamir's Orthodox Seminary in New York. Four or five young men in high schools and colleges are considering becoming priests, but they are not yet deacons.

The situation is fluid: some parishes divide; priests travel from their homes to various locations to organize and to minister to small groups of Malankara Orthodox not yet recognized as parishes; some small groups disband or change affiliation. New parishes develop, such as the parish in Oklahoma City which was started in 1981 and now claims 27 families with their own church building. Parishes in some urban areas divide and grow, such as in Chicago, which now has three separate parishes: St. Gregorios' with 130 families, St. Thomas' with 32 families, and St. Mary's with 25 families. The metropolitan can give no official estimate of total membership in the diocese. When Mar Barnabas contacted the National Council of Churches regarding membership, he was told that he must certify a membership of at least 10,000 persons in order to affiliate, but he is unable to establish the exact number. A long-time leader in the diocese estimated that 3,000 Malankara Orthodox families are in the United States, perhaps as many as 13,500 people. There are 56 parishes, of which 20 have their own buildings and 40 observe the Holy Qurbana every Sunday. A well-presented diocesan publication called *Malankara*

Light appeared for a few years, but is now discontinued due to financial problems. Mar Barnabas occupies a Diocesan Center in rented facilities in Bellerose, New York, and the plan is to purchase that property as a permanent residence for the bishop and center for the diocese. He has standardized relations with Kottayam by sending the appropriate reports and attending synod meetings. Because of turmoil existing before his arrival, he has been less successful in bringing peace to, and creating an inspiring vision for, the diocese. The conflict rages on.

Two developments brought the issue to a head: a lawsuit in New York and plans for two national family conferences each summer. The court case in Queens, New York, involves a congregation that prohibits Mar Barnabas from presiding in the church and refuses to install a priest appointed by him. The congregation officially changed its by-laws to affirm that the local congregation maintains absolute administrative control over its property, finances, and staff, and to designate Mar Makarios as spiritual leader, but not administrative leader, of the parish. Authority in parish affairs is denied to Mar Barnabas, the Catholicos, and the synod in India. The Catholicos has issued several directives in support of Mar Barnabas' authority. The legal response to his directives is that the parish is "an American corporation" and is under no obligation to abide by directives given from abroad. Mar Makarios indicates that he does not wish to exercise administrative authority over the parish but is willing to provide spiritual guidance if asked. A result of this first legal move is movement toward congregational autonomy in a classic American model of congregational polity of legally independent local corporations. Malankara congregations in Philadelphia and Brooklyn are in the process of amending their by-laws to the same effect, and others are awaiting with interest the precedent-setting judgment of the court.

The dispute affected the annual family conference planned for Los Angeles in July 1993. It was the first of the family conferences scheduled outside the northeast and was in the planning stages before it was clear that division threatened its success. Both metropolitans attended and participated in the conference in an amicable fashion, and the organizers saw to it that the dispute would not be raised publicly in the sessions; when one man started to speak about "politics in the church," he was immediately asked by the chair to desist. Issues of diocesan leadership and the relative strength of each metropolitan, as well as more important aspects of strategies of adaptation, were prevalent in private conversation because the effects of the dispute were obvious. Only about 200 people registered for the conference, and only 28 families from outside Los Angeles were present. Mar Makarios had authorized a rival annual family conference held a week earlier in New York, at the same time that Mar Barnabas was attending a synod meeting in Kottayam. The ostensible reason for the rival conference was the great traveling distance and huge expenses families from the East Coast, where most parishes are located, would have to endure in order to attend the conference in Los Angeles. That does help explain the larger attendance in New York of 800 registrants and some 2,000 people at the Holy Qurbana on Sunday. Nevertheless, an undercurrent of division was implicit in the two conferences. The practice developed of having two family conferences, attracting participants loyal to one or the other metropolitan. Each parish experiences internal division over the issue, and groups from individual parishes will attend different family conferences. Hence, the family conferences, which previously generated a sense of unity in the diocese, threaten to become occasions for decisions for both individuals and congregations about taking sides in an approaching division.

In an attempt to restore "peace and amity in the Diocese," the Catholicos sent a commission in 1995 to gather information and to make a report. The Holy Episcopal Synod made decisions based on the commission report in its meeting on February 21–25, 1995, which the Managing Committee confirmed in April. The Catholicos informed the parishes that "administration will be carried on entirely by the Diocesan Metropolitan H. G. Mathews Mar Barnabas" and that "H. G. Thomas Mar Makarios is designated the Senior Metropolitan of the American Diocese." Governance is thus to be by mutual consultation and concurrence of the two metropolitans, but the Catholicos reserves the right to make final decisions in matters on which they cannot agree. The Episcopal letter also directed "that both the Metropolitans together shall settle all matters of dispute in the Diocese including the settlement of court cases and their withdrawal."[5]

For the first time in its long history the Malankara Orthodox Church is faced in the late twentieth century with having a diocese with a resident metropolitan outside India. (Their churches in the Gulf states and in Malaysia are incorporated under dioceses in India.) It marks a major departure. The hierarchy in Kerala does not know how to deal with it, and leaders cannot assimilate the American church into their system. The disputes internal to the diocese and between those in the United States and leaders in India now have a life of their own, and it is difficult to predict how things will turn out. The diocese is clearly at a turning point. One possibility is that some churches will split in two, with each section following a different metropolitan. Some threaten to leave in disgust at the "politics in the church" and join other churches, thereby weakening an already small diocese. A middle way might satisfy a "silent majority" of priests and people who are unhappy with the way the church in Kerala is treating the parishes in the United States but who are unwilling to renounce their historic ties. Appointment of a new metropolitan with the ability to mediate a middle course between those represented by the two metropolitans and to attract the allegiance of the priests and people would be an auspicious event, if it were possible to find a person with such astounding ability. Another suggestion is that one or two bishops be appointed to assist Mar Makarios, but charged to administer the diocese in such a manner as to heal the "wounds on the body of Christ."

Healing is made difficult because attention is directed toward the two metropolitans who have come to represent distinct and conflicting strategies of adaptation rather than directly at the underlying issues facing the Malankara Orthodox and the other churches of Asian-Indian immigrants. Those issues have to do with cultural assimilation and the level of religious and ethnic particularity to be maintained by Christian immigrants. Metropolitans come and go, but the fundamental issues remain and their resolution determines the future shape of the Orthodox church in America and, more importantly, the future of the children in the second generation. Future generations will determine what it means to be a Malankara Orthodox Syrian Christian in America, if the Church survives to provide that opportunity.

An astute metropolitan in Kerala, Geevarghese Mar Osthathios, opposes emigration to the West because of the effects the "brain-drain" has on Kerala and the fatal attraction of the materialism of the West. He refers to the compulsion to emigrate as "the American disease" infecting Kerala. He is known as "the communist bishop" because of his attacks on the rich and his emphasis on social programs for the poor. He is familiar with life in the United States because he studied at Drew University for two years and for a year at Union Theological Seminary in New York and has since visited the churches several times. Despite his opposition to emigration, he is optimistic about the St. Thomas Christians in America and their mission. He claims they are gifted by their ancient heritage to make three major contributions in the West. (1) They can provide an example of family unity and solidarity, thereby giving meaning to the commonly bandied phrase "family values." (2) They can share the faith of the undivided early church based on the theology of the three truly ecumenical councils: Nicaea, Constantinople, and Ephesus. It is a faith based on but not limited to the Bible, one which values the tradition of the undivided church. (3) They have the experience to lead in the development of the global community of the twenty-first century, building a multilinguistic, multi-religious community beyond nationalism and, he hopes, beyond Western capitalism and materialism. He views that as the call of God for these immigrants and encourages a vision of mission now obscured by conflict.

Mar Thoma Church

The opening session for the 1993 Family Conference of the Malankara Mar Thoma Church Diocese of North America and UK was an elegant dinner served for 800 participants in the ballroom of the McLean Hilton in a suburb of Washington, DC. Small children welcomed Philipose Mar Chrysostom, bishop of the diocese and suffragan metropolitan of the Mar Thoma Church,[6] and his chief guests and clergy as they entered the hall in procession with a song in American rap style. After dinner a brief morality play highlighted the "betwixt and between" character of the immigrant experience. Two brothers, one dressed in the traditional Keralite wrap-around men's dress (*lungi*) and the other in Western garb of formal white shirt and bow tie, presented the *masala* of Indian and American elements in their experience as an immigrant church in a humorous mixture of Malayalam and English ("Malaylish"). The room rocked with laughter. The serious moral of the story, however, is the way to unite two cultures in one person – like a coconut, it is often remarked, brown on the outside and white inside! A male Indian barbershop chorus closed the entertainment with a rendition of "Golden Slippers." The theme for the conference was stated as "When Christ shall come...and take me home" without any explicit acknowledgment of a multivalence of meanings. Nevertheless, an overtone of *kairos* pervaded the conference because it celebrated the fortieth anniversary of the consecration of Mar Chrysostom as bishop, and marked his last conference as non-resident bishop of this diocese. It opened a second decade of family conferences – the first of which was held in 1983, now often called "mini-Maramon conventions" – and celebrated the fifth anniversary of the establishment of the diocese with the announcement that the new bishop of the diocese would be resident in the United States in a new diocesan center to be purchased on 4.5 acres of land in Richboro, Pennsylvania, a suburb of Philadelphia. It seemed a very auspicious occasion – a *kairos*.

The Mar Thoma Church is the strongest and best organized of the churches from the Syrian Orthodox tradition in the United States. The church is poised as a successful worshiping community searching for its mission as a witnessing community. The task was posed by the guest speaker at the banquet, the Revd. Richard C. Halverson, Chaplain of the United States Senate, under the title, "What does the Lord require of you?" Throughout its short history in America the Mar Thoma Church has moved between ecumenical, ethnic, and denominational strategies toward an unknown future. The lay people in America progressed more quickly than did the hierarchy in Kerala in the move toward an official organization. Most of the parishes grew out of small prayer groups meeting in homes during the early 1970s when immigration from Kerala began to pick up dramatically. These prayer groups meeting in homes were ecumenical, and most included Christians from several Indian ethnic and linguistic groups worshiping in English. Even a few Hindus participated in some meetings. As the community increased in numbers in urban centers, prayer groups divided into different ethnic groups; thus, Mar Thoma Christians met with other Malayalee Christians, especially with those having episcopal orders, for worship in their own language. Then the Mar Thoma Christians began to meet separately in rented halls and churches for the Eucharist according to their order in Malayalam and began to think of themselves as missions of the Mar Thoma Church.

Clerical assistance for these growing missions came from Mar Thoma priests studying in seminaries and graduate schools. They entered as exchange scholars (on J-1 visas) along with their families (on J-2 visas) and resided in seminary housing. Many of these priests became extremely busy and overworked as they responded to the needs of these prayer groups and missions by flying around the country on weekends to provide for regular worship and pastoral assistance. The Mar Thoma priest in Chicago completed a doctoral program on the Southside, ministered to a large and growing congregation of 350–400 persons meeting in Evanston north of Chicago, and oversaw fund-raising and construction of that congregation's new building in the northwestern suburb of Des Plaines. The students came on official assignment by the synod for graduate training and returned to India upon the completion of their studies, so a constant turnover and long periods without leadership characterized the 1970s. A popular bishop of the church, Geevarghese Mar Athanasius (1914–84), toured the United States to encourage both priests and people.

As Mar Thoma groups in the United States appealed for official recognition and for status as parishes in the Church, they met with some reluctance to establish separate institutions in America from bishops in the hierarchy. Some bishops, including Mar Chrysostom, preferred an ecumenical strategy that would lead Mar Thoma immigrants to unite with congregations of the Protestant Episcopal Church or other churches with recognized bishops instead of establishing their own separate parishes. Strong opposition existed to creating yet another denomination in America. Since Mar Thoma Christians have a long history of association with British Anglicans and their liturgy is similar to that of the Episcopal Church, it was thought that a distinctive mission could be established as the bridge-church between the Orthodox and Protestants. One suggestion was to provide Mar Thoma priests who could regularly visit Episcopal parishes to hold special services for the Asian-Indian Christians and, just as important, to help other members of Episcopal Churches to understand eastern Christianity. Hence, immigrants were encouraged to join established American churches, and many did, including a few priests who came independently and now serve Episcopal parishes.

Working against the theoretical commitment to ecumenical coopera-tion are very practical needs and experiences of the new immigrant community. The attractiveness of the liturgy in the mother-tongue and the lure of ethnic gatherings are very strong among new immigrants. Church gatherings are about the only places outside the home where Malayalees gather regularly and enjoy social intercourse, singing, and worship in Malayalam. Few other social opportunities proved to be as satisfying or as long-lasting as associations in the church, which for many immigrants had provided the primary social contacts and activities in India prior to immigration. Parents eagerly seek some assistance from the church in nurturing their children in ways that will provide systemic continuity between parents and children and preserve the children from the powerfully oppressive ethos of their American peer groups. Moreover, the immigrant community is relatively conservative in theol-ogy and social outlook, and a segment of Mar Thoma immigrants are repelled by the social elitism, liberal theology, and aspects of the social activism of the Protestant Episcopal Church. A number of the active Mar Thoma youth are influenced by conservative Christian groups on college and university campuses, such as Intervarsity Christian Fellowship and Youth for Christ, and their parents are influenced by tele-vision evangelists and evangelical congregations. The Episcopal Church appears to consist of a prototypical white Anglo-Saxon Protestant elite, and some immigrants just trying to establish themselves are not immediately comfortable in the parishes. Radical theological positions taken publicly by some Episcopal bishops are threatening to people who have a history of maintaining their Christian identity as a small minority. Recent actions in favor of ordaining women, which is not part of the Syrian tradition, in favor of ordaining homosexuals, and in support of sexual mores contrary to Indian patterns are troubling. The danger in the late 1970s was that Mar Thoma Christians would rather affiliate with other Malayalee churches if the synod in Kerala refused to authorize parishes. Indeed, the Pentecostal groups and Brethren assemblies began to actively recruit Mar Thoma members into their congregations. Sectarian conversion in America was a threat.

Mar Athanasius was persuasive in his argument to the synod in Kerala that in order to help Mar Thoma Christians to maintain contact with their episcopal traditions and to enable them eventually to take their appropriate place in ecumenical relations, it was necessary to approve institutional structures in America. Mar Chrysostom and the other bishops agreed, so Mar Thoma Christians took decisive steps toward becoming a transnational church. The Sabha Council and Synod is still wrestling with becoming the executive body of an international church and not just of a Kerala church. The first official parish was recognized in New York in 1977 and those in Chicago and Houston the next year. An annual national youth conference began in 1980 and was followed by the first family conference in 1983. After a great deal of pleading and persuasion, leaders in Kerala approved the organization of a zonal council of Mar Thoma Churches that became the prototype for the diocese recognized in 1988.

The long cordial relation with the Episcopal Church was evidenced by the presence of the Bishop of the Episcopal Diocese of Washington, Ronald H. Haines, as a chief guest at the opening ceremony of the 1993 family conference. He received a plaque bearing the seal of both churches as a sign of the close relation between the churches, of their intercommunion, and of the concrete assistance given to the Mar Thoma Church, including provision at a reasonable cost of a church building in the Washington diocese for the Mar Thoma parish. A formal agreement was signed between the two churches in 1982, providing that "When requested by the Metropolitan of the Mar Thoma Church, bishops of the Episcopal Church shall exercise episcopal oversight of clergy and laity of the Mar Thoma Church within the jurisdictions of this church [Episcopal]." Mar Thoma priests came under the discipline of the Episcopal bishops and also under their sheltering arms. Priests sent by the synod in Kerala applied for student visas authorized by the Episcopal Church, and the Episcopal Church granted licenses and ministerial standing. Under supplemental guidelines approved in 1984 the diocesan medical insurance plans were opened to Mar Thoma priests. Those agreements are still operative even though recent establishment of a diocese and appointment of a resident Mar Thoma bishop cause Episcopal leaders to suggest the need for renegotiation of the basic agreement.

The relative strength and unity of the Mar Thoma Church in America results from the high quality of the priests sent to America and from the pastoral rotation system of assigned priests. Mar Thoma priests accept ordination to the Church as a whole and not to a single parish, and both in India and America they participate in a regular rotation system that assigns them to a new location approximately every three years. Unconditional surrender to the church discipline means that no one is ordained for a particular parish, diocese or country (Samuel, 1993:7f.). Hence, Mar Thoma priests, unlike other Protestant clergy from India, are not permanent residents in the United States. They come on temporary visas for terms of three years and return to assignments in India. One priest wanted to stay on but was told that he would lose his ecclesiastical standing and therefore returned to Kerala. The first full-time priest came to the New York parish in 1979 and he was followed in 1980 by a priest sent to Houston (A. Thomas and Thomas, 1984:117). Students continued to serve missions and parishes throughout the 1980s, but now the parishes are requesting that priests be sent to serve full-time and not as students because the parishes have grown so large and the pastoral work is so demanding. Nevertheless, priests continue to apply for exchange scholar visas (J-1 and J-2 for students), which increasingly creates difficulties in obtaining entry for priests who are going to be primarily employed by the parish. Representatives of the Episcopal Church and the Mar Thoma Church, staff members of Senator Edward Kennedy, and the Immigration and Naturalization Service are discussing solutions to the visa problems of some priests and their families. No officially appointed Mar Thoma priest has yet failed to return to India when his appointment ended, so some resentment exists that Mar Thoma priests are treated like those who have used church appointments to attain permanent resident status.

Discipline within the Mar Thoma Church has the result that its par-

ishes in America are not divided by independent priests who are permanent residents. Two retired priests – one recently arriving with his wife to
live with his children in retirement – serve as volunteer assistants in
established parishes under the vicar or travel at the direction of the
bishop to serve isolated missions. No church fights or splits result from
loyalty or family ties to two or more priests. Hence, the parishes in urban
centers are larger, permitting stronger programs of worship, education,
and fellowship to support the families.[7] In most locations having several
Indian Christian churches, the Mar Thoma Church is the largest and
most active. Less divisiveness seems to be experienced in Mar Thoma
parishes, which can be attributed to the formal assignment of priests and
the discipline exercised over their appointment and return to India. Mar
Thoma lay people say with pride that their priests are servants of the
church and do not use the churches in America to make themselves
wealthy or to establish their families in America. More than fifty Mar
Thoma priests have served terms in America and returned to assignments in India. It is worth noting that all of their children born in the
United States possess the right to claim US citizenship when they
become 18 years old – a significant right of return – and it will be interesting to observe what effects that will have on both families of priests
and the church in a few years.

Although Mar Thoma priests are generally well educated and those
chosen for assignment in America are fluent in English, transitions from
an assignment in India to one in the United States and then to one back
in India are not without difficulty. An inevitable culture shock awaits the
priest and his family and, to a lesser degree, members of their parishes.
Mar Chrysostom indicated that criteria for selection of priests for
America are: (1) considerable pastoral experience; (2) good facility in
English; (3) an open and not rigid manner; and (4) good theological
understanding and the ability to communicate it. A lay leader recognized the superior qualities of the priests, but remarked: "Priests coming
from India are good for rituals, such as communion, baptism, marriage,
but they are not trained to make a contribution to be helpful to society.
They are not educated properly to understand American culture. By the
time they learn their way around here, it is time for them to go back. The
church is constantly 'baby sitting.'" Training for priests chosen for
assignment in the United States consists of a course in spoken American
English intended to help in the transition from British-based syntax and
Malayalee-influenced pronunciation to an American form and a two-
week orientation with priests who have served in America. There is a

recognition that the program is not sufficient. Two leaders recommended that, in addition to more preparation in India, the tenure of priests in the United States be lengthened to five years, the first year as a sabbatical for study in an American graduate school, which would provide an introduction to American culture and churches, and the second year as assistant in one of the parishes. They would then have three effective years as priests in the parishes. One reason for the appointment of a resident bishop is to give attention to the appropriate preparation of priests serving in his diocese.

The American diocese is the wealthiest in the church, and priests covet (if one may use the word) the opportunity to serve in it. Nevertheless, the relative economic status of the priests to the society is reversed in the move; in India the priests enjoy a position of high prestige and economic security, whereas in America they are poor in relation to members of their parishes. In addition to basic living expenses of house, car, utilities, and medical insurance, they receive US$1200 per month, which sounds in Kerala like more than it is in reality in America. Priests do receive extra income from significant gifts from members in the parish on special occasions and for performing family ceremonies. The perception of great opportunity and wealth creates some jealousy in priests serving in rural parishes in India who wonder why they do not have the same opportunities. That jealousy may be a reason for the practice of appointing the returning priests to village parishes in Kerala. Mar Chrysostom said that he is the second most senior bishop, so he asked to be appointed to the most rural diocese; so it is appropriate that returning priests should be appointed, if possible, to village parishes.

An older priest who is familiar with the situations both in Kerala and America responds harshly about the difficulty of priests adjusting when they return to Kerala: "Any priest who serves outside of India is totally ruined. They get used to the possessions and pleasures here and it is very difficult when they go back to India." It is more difficult for the children who are socialized in American schools and culture who upon returning to Kerala have to adjust to village life, to new school patterns, peer expectations, and even to their inability to speak Malayalam without an American accent. Indeed, some returning priests cannot be assigned in certain village areas because English-medium schools are not available for their children.

Legal entry from India to the United States has been relatively easy for Mar Thoma priests, but it is getting more difficult as entrance requirements and reviews are becoming more stringent. Three priests and the wife of another faced delays in getting visas in 1993. The immediate future of the Church in America depends on the regular pastoral rotation that has worked so well in the past. Threats to that rotation pose serious problems. Youths of the second generation regularly express the need for priests reared and educated in the United States who will understand them and their culture. The Mar Thoma Church has not yet ordained a person from the diocese, and the church constitution does not provide for special selection procedures for candidates from a particular diocese like this one. A thoughtful Mar Thoma scholar suggests a need for flexibility in the ordination of locally born Marthomites in North America because their assignment is essential for the stable growth of the Mar Thoma Church in this part of the world. He recommends the appointment of a theological education committee for the diocese, provision of a list of acceptable accredited seminaries or divinity schools in America for training of selected candidates, establishment of a scholarship fund for seminary education, establishment of a salary and fringe benefits scale comparable to that of other American Episcopal Churches, institution of a "diversified ministry," and procedures for intra-diocesan transfer of young ministers rather than transfers to India after a three-year tenure. The latter provision is important because it is impossible under current Indian government regulations for an American citizen to obtain a visa to serve as a priest in India. A long-range problem is provision for retirement of priests in the United States, because priests in Kerala do not own property except their ancestral homes. Appropriate preparation and support of priests for North America are pressing issues complicating the long-range future of the Church.

The Mar Thoma Church in the United States has grown rapidly since the official recognition of a zonal council in 1982. By 1993 the diocese had 37 parishes and 2 congregations and identified over 2,500 families and almost 10,000 members as active participants in parishes in the United States. (See Table 7 for data from 1991.) Members of the diocese are young, with approximately 3 percent over the age of 60, so parishes of the diocese in the United States are assured of rapid growth in the next decade through both natural means and new immigration, without depending upon evangelism among currently inactive or unreached people among immigrants from Kerala. Formal establishment of the new diocese in 1988 and the appointment of a resident bishop are responses to past growth, present strength, and future potential for growth. One layman from the diocese who appealed to the council and synod for the diocese and resident bishop said that he asked them this

Table 7 *Mar Thoma families and members (January 1991)*

Country	No. of families	Mother/father	Children	Total members
USA	2591	5058	+4618	= 9676
Canada	248	507	+ 434	= 941
UK	162	303	+ 240	= 543
Total	3001	5868	+5292	=11160

Source: From *Mar Thoma Messenger: A Publication of the Diocese of North America & UK* (October, 1993, p. 22).

question: "Do you want my children to grow up as Mar Thoma, or do you want to send evangelists to north India to convert Hindus?" He posed a false dichotomy, but the synod perceived the potential and approved the request of the parishes in America.

The Mar Thoma Pradhinidthi Mandalam met in special session in 1993 to elect three episcopal candidates. The Synod and Sabha Council met on July 22, 1993, and decided to give Ramban orders to the candidates on August 31, 1993, and to consecrate them as bishops on October 2, 1993. These three joined the metropolitan and six other bishops, providing the opportunity to appoint Zacharias Mar Theophilus as resident bishop of the diocese of North America and UK. He is familiar with American society and churches, because he was a student at Boston University in 1973–74 and served as a summer associate in a Presbyterian Church in Indianapolis. He was invited to participate in the 1986 annual conference in Chicago, celebrating the 150th anniversary of the Mar Thoma reformation in Kerala, because, as one of the younger bishops and one with experience in the United States, he could relate well with the young people. He is active and well known in ecumenical affairs as a member of the Central Committee and the Executive Committee of the World Council of Churches. Mar Thoma bishops are itinerant but generally stay in a diocese for from three to five years, so his arrival late in 1993 was greeted with great joy by his people.

A resident bishop in a diocesan center brings a significant new financial obligation for the parishes, but it opens opportunities for new initiatives. The property cost $368,799 and expenses of the bishop and his office will be significant. One result is that offerings to support dioceses and agencies in India are greatly reduced. Each parish has fourteen special offerings during the year to support the diocese and designated church agencies, such as the Kerala Evangelistic Association, the Youth

League, and the Women's Association. Now the diocesan offering will support the local diocese and other offerings will undoubtedly be reduced, at least in the short term. The bishop laid the foundation stone in late 1994 for a new Mar Thoma Center in Dallas that will eventually serve as both a worship center and Keralite community hall at a cost estimated at $1.5 million. Plans are underway for an educational center in Houston to provide educational materials and to support training of lay leaders of the education programs in the parishes. The parishes all now use Sunday School and Vacation Bible School material prepared by David B. Cooke Publishers because materials prepared in Kerala do not relate to the cultural setting and problems of the Americanized children in the parishes. On the other hand, the materials currently used do not speak to the bi-cultural situation of the young people living between Indian and American cultures and between Orthodox and Protestant Christian traditions.

At the *kairos* point in the life of this immigrant church expressed in the 1993 family conference, the people are a well-established, growing church in search of its mission in the future. One function of a bishop is to help form, embody, and articulate a vision of that mission. There is general agreement that the Mar Thoma Church has a current mission to serve first-generation immigrants and their families with parish programs of worship, education, counseling, and fellowship. Lay people urge increased attention to forms of worship accessible to the young people, counseling programs for youth and families undergoing the stress of adaptation to American culture, and planning of programs for the elderly as the community ages in the next decade. Now that the church is on a solid footing in America, discussion revolves around how to become a witnessing and serving church. The question is asked, "How can the Mar Thoma Church and the immigrants make significant contributions to American society?" Leaders urge congregations to change their focus from matters internal to the Church, which have necessarily occupied their attention, to the needs of society at large. The Mar Thoma Church has the reputation of being the evangelistic church of Syrian Christians, and parishes in America send support for evangelistic efforts in India, but it is unclear how that evangelistic ethos can be developed in America. The diocese could develop as a new American denomination and occupy a niche as an ethnic church. That possibility depends upon continuation of the open-door immigration policy permitting a constant renewal of loyalty to an Indian church by new immigrants. One leader said, "If the door closes, the Mar Thoma Church will not continue in America after the third generation." An ecumenical involvement is also clearly on the agenda, both in cooperation in social action and in matters of faith and order. Mar Chrysostom remarked: "An Indian Roman Catholic drug addict is no different than a Mar Thoma drug addict. We must join together to provide help for both." The future is uncertain, but a mission for this *kairos* is becoming clear. A prominent leader says that the Church will not be upset if, in the providence of God, this mission ends for the immigrant church and the Mar Thoma Church in America disappears to merge into the fabric of American Christianity.

CHAPTER 4

Becoming what you are : Catholics and Protestants from India

And in you all the families of the earth shall be blessed.

Genesis 12:3

Catholics from India join the largest religious group in the United States, and the one with the best developed infrastructure of parishes, schools, colleges, and social agencies ready to serve the new immigrants. Most Catholics move quickly into local parishes, place their children in parish Christian education programs, and enroll them in Catholic schools. Two factors retard the complete assimilation of Asian-Indian Catholics into American parishes. The first is the drive toward national and ethnic identity within the church as numbers of new immigrants increase to a level where separate organizations and missions can be sustained. The second is the desire to perpetuate the individuality of Oriental-rite churches within the Catholic Church as confirmed in the decrees of the Second Vatican Council. These decrees are being implemented in India as the Indian Catholic Church has been adjusting to the migration of Christians from the south of India throughout India and abroad. (See chapter 2.) These two factors influence the strategies of adaptation followed by Asian-Indian Catholics in relating to the church and its parishes in America.

CATHOLICS

The early process of delineation is best traced in the relatively large Indian Catholic population in Chicago. Even before the changes of the 1965 immigration act, a significant number of Catholic students from India studied in colleges and universities in Chicago. The Cross-Roads Student Center near the University of Chicago was the meeting place for some fifty students from Kerala in the early 1960s. (See Anthony,

1988, for the best report of this period; he was the founding president of the students' association.) In 1962 Catholic students from all parts of India formed the first national all-India Catholic organization in the United States, called India Catholic University Federation, which eventually developed into the India Catholic Association. Students continued to participate in liturgical activities of the diocesan parishes, but looked to the Indian associations for social activities and Indian support networks. Dramatic growth in numbers of immigrants in the late 1960s and the 1970s provided resources to support an ethnic strategy of adaptation. Keralite Catholics formed the largest Indian Christian group and met at Loyola University in 1977 to form the Kerala Catholic Association. The Loyola Jesuit community was its sponsor until the Association's move in 1983 to the Immaculate Heart of Mary Church in Chicago. The Association gave annual reports both to the Chicago diocesan chancellory and to Kerala bishops. Bishops from India visited occasionally and suggested that Catholics from Kerala form separate groups on the basis of rites, a suggestion that at first met with some resistance from the community. Events of 1983–84 demonstrated that the community had grown sufficiently large to adopt strategies of adaptation within the large Catholic community, based on the three rites of India: Syro-Malabar, Syro-Malankara, and Latin.

A similar pattern developed in New York. An India Catholic Association of America was informally organized in 1979 and then incorporated in 1980. The single organization served Indians of all three rites until 1982, when the Malankara Catholic Church was founded and the other groups began to meet separately. A rancorous dispute among members of rival India Catholic Associations was finally decided by the Supreme Court of the State of New York.[1]

Syro-Malabar Catholics

In the early 1980s the Kerala Catholic Association broke apart, both in New York and in Chicago, along lines of rite and ethnicity. The Syro-Malabar-rite Catholics began to hold a monthly Syro-Malabar Mass. In July 1983, Bishop Mar Gratian Mundadan on a visit to Chicago asked Anthony Kurialacherry, a Syro-Malabar priest retired in Chicago and serving as an assistant pastor at St. Bernadine Church in Forest Park, to help organize a ministry for Syro-Malabar Catholics. Fr. Kurialacherry had been in the United States from 1955 to 1962 for studies in education and economics at the University of Notre Dame and at Loyola University. These studies prepared him for a distinguished career in India, and, after his retirement, he became the founding director of the Syro-Malabar Mission in Chicago. He gathered the 150 Syro-Malabar Catholic (non-Knanaya) families in the Chicago area and in June 1985 gained the approval of the archdiocese of Chicago for a Syro-Malabar Mission. It was inaugurated on August 25, 1985, by Joseph Cardinal Bernardin of Chicago and Bishop Mar Joseph Pallikaparampil of the Palai diocese in Kerala, representing the Syro-Malabar Bishops' Conference. Three bishops of that conference constitute a Commission for Overseas Ministry that has liturgical responsibility for the mission; otherwise, the mission is under the archdiocese of Chicago even though its parishioners come from the three dioceses of Chicago, Rockford, and Joliet. The archdiocese provided a church building and small school in Bellwood for the Mar Thoma Sheelha Church of the Syro-Malabar Catholic Mission, where the first Mass was held in July 1988. The school was remodeled and dedicated in 1994 as all-purpose community center for the 350 families in the parish. That it is the first Syro-Malabar Catholic mission outside India to have its own building is a source of great pride. The church maintains a full range of ecclesiastical activities under the leadership of a full-time Syro-Malabar priest appointed by the bishops in Kerala and installed by the archbishop in Chicago. Some 500 people regularly attend the Sunday Mass, and a 4-day retreat each year – "like a Bible Convention" – attracts over 1,000 people.

Also in 1983, the 100 Syro-Malabar Catholic families of Dallas asked the bishop to provide a ministry in their eastern rite. The bishop permitted the assignment in his diocese of a priest from Kerala, who arrived in 1984 to start a monthly Mass in the Syro-Malabar rite for Keralite Catholics at Holy Trinity Catholic Church in Oak Lawn. The Dallas community now has its own church building. A third officially appointed Syro-Malabar priest serves in Detroit, but they continue to use a local church building until they can afford their own. These three are official missions, whereas the communities which have developed in New York, Los Angeles, and Florida are approved as associations, but not as separate missions. Houston supports two groups. One is officially recognized under the ministry of the priest from Dallas and has its own St. Thomas Community Hall. The other meets once a month in a local church for the Mass in the Syro-Malabar rite with a priest who serves a regular Latin-rite local parish near Houston. The bishop permits both groups to continue. No one in authority seems to know the exact number of priests of the Syro-Malabar rite currently in the United States. A number from the Palai diocese, which is known as the "mother of priests" because of the abundance of vocations in that diocese, now serve in parishes and institutions in the United States. The bishop of the Palai diocese was for a time chairperson of the Commission on Overseas Missions and sent some of his priests to the United States. The priest in Chicago remarked that on a recent St. Thomas' Day, twelve priests were present for the celebration and participated in the Syro-Malabar-rite Mass. Thirty priests from the Congregation of Mary Immaculate in Kerala serve in Latin parishes in the United States. Two parishes in Brooklyn and Lake Charles Parish, Louisana, are directly related to the order. Rules of this missionary order limit the number who can serve in first-world countries to 10 percent of its members. Plans are underway to began an annual national family life conference. Each local mission or association looks after its own affairs under the local bishop and the bishops' commission in Kerala. The Synod of Bishops of the Syro-Malabar Church has on its agenda the question of the pastoral care of Syro-Malabar Catholics in North America.

Virtually all the Knanaya Catholics follow the Syro-Malabar rite and have good relations with the Syro-Malabar dioceses. Nevertheless, they were the first Asian-Indian Catholics in Chicago to petition that a priest be sent by the Knanaya Bishop of Kottayam to care for the religious needs of the community. He assigned a priest in 1983, and the archdiocese approved the Knanaya mission. They establish ethnic rather than religious boundaries because their ritual and discipline are exactly the same as those of other Syro-Malabar Catholics. The Knanaya priest in Chicago is completely dedicated to organizing the Knanaya Catholic community and is director of the national conference and is the personal representative of the bishop in Kottayam. Of the 125,000 Knanaya in the Knanaya Catholic diocese of Kottayam, which was established as a separate jurisdiction in 1911, approximately 9,000 people in 2,000 registered families live in North America, primarily in Chicago (700 families), New York/New Jersey (650 families), and Los Angeles (200 families), which are the only associations that have resident priests (assigned by Bishop Kuriakose Kunnasserry). Other associations are in Houston (160 families), Washington (22 families), Philadelphia (35 families) Tampa (27 families), Miami (35 families), and Detroit (35 families). Fewer than 10 priests are in America, some of whom emigrated under family reunification provisions to serve in diocesan parishes, and a couple for study. Bishop Kunnasserry indicates that several associations regularly petition him to send priests, but he will do so only when the request is made by the local bishop. He plans to send priests for relatively short periods because, if they stay too long, they have a difficult time adjusting when they return to India. Bishop Kunnasserry studied at Boston College in 1962–64 for a master's degree in political science, and he has since visited his people in the United States several times.

The Knanaya Catholic community has now reached a size large enough to begin building an infrastructure. A building for a Knanaya Community Center was purchased in Chicago in 1993 for $600,000. Although it is not an official liturgical site – hence, the Mass for some 350 people is conducted on Saturday evening at the Immaculate Heart of Mary Church – it serves as the center for religious, social, and cultural affairs of the community. Fr. Cyriac Manthuruthil expresses the hope that it will be "the cradle of our development in America." The priest for New York arrived more recently and moves around to several churches to conduct Mass because the Knanaya Catholics are dispersed throughout the region. Agreement has been reached to place two priests in Houston and Los Angeles. The Knanaya Catholic Congress in North America organizes the family conferences held at three-year intervals, and the 1993 family conference held in New York attracted approximately 1,500 people from 500 families.

Two problems are of great concern. First, neither other Catholics nor their own children seem able to understand or appreciate their strong attachment to endogamy as the essential means for maintaining their ethnic identity. Until now most of the young people have returned to India for marriage so that, for example, only five or six marriages have been conducted in Chicago in the past five years. Those who return to India do not have sufficient time to select marriage partners and to have those selections ratified by the bishop according to the tradition. Societal pressures in America lead the young people toward intermarriage, which parents see as the greatest threat to their existence. Second, the strength of families is the bedrock for Knanaya identity, but that foundation is threatened by the absence of the extended family and by the economic and occupational pressures that occupy the parents and divide families. The bishop assigned a layman from Kerala for a tour of the associations in the United States to conduct premarital and family seminars to help the community to face these problems associated with the most narrowly defined ethnic strategy of adaptation of any Asian-Indian group.

Syro-Malankara Catholics

A problem Syro-Malankara Catholics face is that hardly any priests and only a minority of bishops in America are familiar with them as a distinct Oriental-rite church. Hence, the tendency is to recognize them as an ethnic group lumped together with the Syro-Malabar rather than as a separate rite. Nationally they come under the care of the Office for the Pastoral Care of Migrants and Refugees, whereas in Chicago they come under the Ethnic Ministries Office of the diocese, and in some dioceses the bishops believe that they can be appropriately served by Syro-Malabar-rite priests because both are from the same language group. There was a move begun in the Brooklyn diocese to place those of all three rites under a single Apostolate for Indian People that would follow the Syro-Malabar rite. Thus, they have a difficult time gaining recognition in some dioceses and have to instruct both priests and the hierarchy regarding their status as a distinct rite. In 1992 the president of the American bishops' conference investigated their claims and sent a letter to all the bishops indicating that the Malankara is a recognized rite.

The first Syro-Malankara celebrations in America for the new immigrants were held by Cyril Mar Baselius in 1970, attended by sixty Indian Christians, and then by a visiting bishop from Tiruvala, in New York and Philadelphia, in the summer of 1977.[2] The impetus for organization of prayer groups and eventually missions was given during visits in 1982 and 1984 by Benedict Mar Gregorios, the archbishop of Trivandrum and head of the Malankara Catholic hierarchy. He formally instituted the Malankara Catholic Mission of North America in 1984. Six missions gained official recognition in the mid-1980s in New York, Philadelphia, Chicago, Washington, Dallas, and Houston to serve approximately 500 registered Syro-Malankara families. There are 10 priests in America – 5 serving the missions and the rest in other positions. The first Indian Catholic ordained as a priest in America was ordained and celebrated his first Mass in the Syro-Malankara rite in May 1991 in New York and serves as a priest in the archdiocese of New York. The Malankara groups are relatively small, but growing. For example, in New York the liturgy has been celebrated weekly since 1982, but the Chicago mission until recently held Mass only twice a month (until 1992 for 36 families, but, beginning in 1994, every Sunday for 46 families). The archdiocese of Chicago, in June of 1995, reopened Ascension of Our Lord parish church in Evanston for use by the Syro-Malankara Catholics.

The mission in Chicago maintains close ties with the Order of

Imitation of Christ at Bethany Ashram in Kottayam. The current Superior General of the Congregation served the Chicago mission from 1989 until he was elected Superior General in 1992. The other priests serving American missions are secular priests of the Trivandrum and Tiruvella dioceses, who are requested by the Malankara Catholic Mission of North America, nominated by the head of the Malankara Catholic Church in Kerala, and appointed by the local ordinaries. Two nuns of the Bethany Ashram are also in New York, hoping to establish a house there.

Syro-Malankara Catholics will remain for some time the smallest minority among American Catholics, and their struggle is to preserve their distinctive Oriental rite of liturgy and discipline and to maintain their ties to the reunion church in India. If successful, they will place a bright but tiny spot in the stained-glass picture of American Catholicism as a separate rite beside the Latin rite. The fear is, however, that they may dissolve into the larger Syro-Malabar community even as both disappear into the huge American Latin Catholic Church. Much will depend upon the success of the papal initiatives affirming the rights of the several Oriental rites and the recognition and valuing of those rites by American Catholic leaders.

Latin Catholics

Although Latin Catholics outnumber those in Oriental rites in India, fewer Latin-rite Catholics have made their way from India to America. Because Latin-rite Catholics are so-called "new Christians" from the lower socio-economic strata, they lack the educational and professional opportunities that prepare people to grasp the opportunity to emigrate to America. They also reside in places in India where the networks that support immigration are much weaker or even non-existent. Those who do make it to America are less visible because they merge with other ethnic groups quickly and easily in the Latin-rite parishes. They come from several regions and language groups of India, so they must communicate among themselves in English just as they do with other ethnic groups in their local parishes. Hence, no special attraction of language or of a distinctive regional culture exists to bring them together. In those locations like Chicago, where Indian Catholic Associations were formed early – only to be reduced in size when the Keralite Catholics established their own associations – the surviving associations are primarily social organizations because the religious needs of the Latin Catholics are met in the churches, schools, and social institutions of the local parishes. The Indian Latin-rite Catholics do not constitute a community of sufficient size in any location to become a majority in any parish, so their adaptation must be different from both earlier and current Catholic immigrants, such as the Irish, Polish, or Hispanic immigrants. A number of Latin-rite priests have immigrated from India to the United States as permanent residents sponsored by sisters and brothers, and these gain positions in American dioceses. The Latin-rite bishop in Kottayam occasionally visits his six priests and his benefactors (institutions that support work in his diocese) in America, but he exercises no ecclesiastical control over their work.

The single distinctive group of Latin-rite immigrants from India are the Goan Catholics. The majority of immigrants from Goa are Latin-rite Catholics, so most members of Goan Associations in America are Catholics. Nevertheless, like the India Catholic Associations, the Goan organizations are primarily social rather than religious. They may function to preserve and strengthen regional ethnic identity through some association with religious authority, but both religious identity and commitment are maintained within the multiethnic context of local parishes. No reliable estimate of the number of Latin-rite Catholics from India in the United States is available. They are too widely dispersed and diverse in identification to be easily numbered. The future of Latin-rite Indian Catholics in America is bound up with the success or failure of American Catholicism in dealing with the new ethnic and racial diversity in local parishes of the church.

The charismatic renewal movement is strong in both India and America. Thus, Catholics from India join a large Catholic charismatic renewal movement in America, which provides wider associations across boundaries of ethnicity and rites in national and state conferences. Indian charismatic Catholics in America are not organized as a separate group with a national committee, in spite of the power of the charismatic movement in Indian Catholicism. A number of charismatic renewal retreats are sponsored by Asian-Indian Catholics. Each summer a group of charismatic leaders comes from a center of Indian Catholic charismatic renewal at Potta in Kerala to lead retreats sponsored by Indian Catholic missions and associations in America. These are extensions of the huge gatherings for retreats in India described in chapter 2. They attract participants from other Keralite Christian groups as well, even though people from the Pentecostal churches rarely join in these retreats. Another popular format is for a congregation to sponsor a weekend retreat, either for youth or for families, led by leaders of the Catholic renewal movement from other ethnic groups. Thus, viewed sociologically, the charismatic movement functions to lower barriers between ethnic groups within the Catholic Church, to establish contacts with other Indian churches, and to protect Catholics from the allure of the Pentecostal churches. Viewed theologically, the movement provides spiritual, emotional, and theological resources to support the individual and families through the trauma of immigration and adaptation in the new home.

PROTESTANTS

Uniting churches: Church of South India (CSI) and Church of North India (CNI)

Each of these churches is a territorial uniting church, so any concept of an extraterritorial diocese or the establishment of a separate denomination abroad is foreign to its genius and ethos. Nevertheless, members of both churches in America, especially of the larger CSI community, wish to maintain their identity and train their children within the context of language-based congregations. A son of a CSI bishop now attending an American Episcopal Church with his five siblings explains the dilemma (he calls it a "toss and turn mentality"): "If we go to American churches, we miss our native language and the special rituals of Indian Christianity. If we go to Indian churches, we become ghettoized and miss contact with other Christians." Leaders in India and their own ecumenical ethos push CSI immigrants toward assimilation into American Christianity, especially into churches that are constituents of the uniting churches or in full communion with them. The need to preserve a living memory and a secure identity in the midst of the trauma of migration pulls them toward pluralism in congregations and toward national organizations identified with Indian churches.

CSI congregations were not planted in America; they developed as volunteer growth. CSI members participated in prayer groups and ecumenical gatherings of Indian Christians in the early 1970s, but when the initial requests to establish parishes reached bishops in India, they responded with instructions that CSI Christians should affiliate with churches that were constituent parts of, or in full communion with, the CSI. Only in 1975 did the bishops accede to petitions to authorize American parishes. Even then there was clear indication that congregations should join existing churches and not attempt to establish a diocese or another denomination in America. An anti-denominational rhetoric accompanies the ecumenical commitment of the CSI, so that the CSI moderator told a family conference: "The CSI is a unique church, setting an example for the world church by uniting immediately after Indian independence as a second miracle after Pentecost. Hence, it is not a denomination but a movement and pilgrim church."

Nevertheless, the trajectory of development for CSI Christians in America has been from prayer groups to ecumenical congregations to language-based congregations to CSI Malayalam parishes to a national council. The moderator estimates that 95 percent of CSI immigrants claim a Syrian Christian background in the Madhya (Central) Kerala diocese of the CSI, which is the area of the old CMS Anglican mission. Hence, the congregations reflect the need of the first generation for a language- and region-based association. A close relationship with Bishop Mani of that diocese was developed by the 18 recognized Malayalee parishes serving an estimated 550 families and was maintained until his recent retirement. During his 12-year tenure as bishop, he traveled to visit the churches in America 10 times at the invitation of individual congregations. Following his retirement, the American churches came under the direct pastoral leadership of the moderator of the CSI. St. Thomas Church of South India of Houston with 175 members is the only parish outside India having its own building. A reticence to invest in buildings results from a suspicion that members of future generations will not attempt to maintain a separate church. A few Tamil, Telugu, and Kannada members are in America, but the only Tamil CSI church meets in New York. The others attend established American churches, primarily Episcopal and Methodist. In some cities Tamil CSI members get together three or four times a year for special services, but they do not go to the CSI churches regularly because those services are in Malayalam. CSI members led in founding some language-based Christian fellowships and remain active in them.

Because the churches were not planted in America, no official program exists for sending priests. The relatively large Woodhaven congregation in New York, of more than 100 families, asked the bishop of the Madhya Kerala diocese to supply full-time priests for three-year terms similar to the Mar Thoma arrangement. The parish has its own parsonage, but rents a church building for worship. He is the only full-time priest; the others work at secular jobs. Two patterns developed for supplying priests to lead the small congregations, both dependent upon provisions whereby siblings or spouses could sponsor persons for immigration. In some cases the wife of an ordained priest in India immigrated to America and then sponsored her husband and children. In addition to some secular occupation, often in a hospital, the priest serves a small congregation on the weekends. In other cases, persons who immigrated to join family members studied in Bible colleges or theological schools in the United States and presented themselves for ordination by CSI bishops. The pastoral board of the Madhya Kerala diocese recommended that the bishop ordain men abroad as priests. A few went back to Kerala for their first ordination as deacons and then were ordained priests in America. Twenty-two CSI priests are in the United States; a few serve as counselors in hospitals or in other ecumenical agencies. One serves a joint Episcopal and CSI parish, but when he attempted to unite the two halves great resistance came from the immigrants. The pastor is caught in the lonely middle between two cultures present in the congregation. Although the CSI has ordained thirty-six women as priests, none serve in the Madhya Kerala diocese or in the United States. The CSI maintains close, cordial ties with the Anglican churches, but has no formal arrangement with the Episcopal Church in America like that enjoyed by the Mar Thoma Church.

The recognized CSI parishes are in the initial stages of establishing a national council to oversee CSI programs in North America. At the 1993 family conference the moderator authorized an *ad hoc* committee to prepare a constitution for submission to the synod. One reason given for having a national council is to discipline and regularize the clergy. Several of the parishes have been divided because priests have encouraged their family members and friends to leave what are already small congregations to establish new ones. Because the congregations are too small to provide financial support for a minister, and all but one are settled in secular occupations, it is not possible to move priests regularly as is done in Kerala. Hence, priests do not leave, people do and establish splinter groups. As one bishop remarked, "It is a trait of Malayalees to argue and divide." Leaders also feel the need to regulate the visits of priests and bishops from India. A draft constitution calls for the creation of a council of priests and representatives from every authorized parish to provide discipline and assistance for the parishes and to establish cordial relations with other American churches. The parishes in America with their council will come directly under the authority of the moderator of the church. Opposition is raised, however, when powers of the national council or the moderator seem to conflict with the independence of the local congregations, as established by their legal status in the United States, or with the prerogatives of the already established priests. An earlier draft was rejected on these grounds. It is a delicate balance to give necessary powers to the council and moderator to maintain order and to define a clear identity as CSI Christians, while at the same time preserving rights of congregations and priests that will permit them to make their own way in the United States.

A thoughtful CSI member now active in another church reflects on both the short-term and long-term goals for this immigrant church. Short-term necessities are to reconstruct a compelling identity and to develop a sense of security; long-term goals are growth and holding fast to traditions. The CSI members do not share any recent history or stories with Christians in the United States, so they need to reconstruct a unique identity without creating boundaries that will isolate them from the majority population. Moreover, they must develop a sense of security and permanence in the United States. Until now the dominant ethos has been "It won't last." "Now," he says, "identity and permanence are the keys." As they move to greater financial security, a sense of security and permanence is essential. Over the long term, the community is likely to grow in numbers both through new immigration as individuals sponsor relatives and through births into relatively young families. Then it will be necessary to preserve the traditions by looking back to the rich Oriental traditions of India rather than to the West. He notes two rituals of importance: the hair-cutting ceremony and the last rites, two very Indian and even Hindu rituals that are common in Indian churches. His comments reveal an attachment to the first and last of the life-cycle rituals in the eastern tradition.

The Church of North India (CNI) has very few members in the United States – one bishop estimated fewer than 100 families. A majority of CNI Christians are from the *dalit* community and are not prepared to immigrate in large numbers to America. The CNI bishop of Gujarat traveled to visit Christians in the United States and in 1988 made a survey of Gujarati pastors there. Of the eighteen pastors in his survey, only one was from the CNI; seventeen were Gujarati Methodists. No American CNI congregation has been authorized; moreover, the synod is resistant to extraterritorial churches and hesitates to send pastors for study because, the bishop said, "Most people think that heaven is there, so when they get there they don't come back." A few CNI people have immigrated to join families and then obtained some theological training permitting them to start their own churches. Some of the language-based congregations – Gujarati, Hindi, and Punjabi – were established by CNI members. The few CNI Christians are widely dispersed and are divided into several language groups, so there is not a sufficient number or attraction to cause them to establish congregations. One of the two Gujarati Christian fellowships in Brooklyn has many members from CNI and wishes to be a CNI parish, but official permission to establish a congregation in North America is not forthcoming.

Territory-based uniting churches face significant difficulties in adjustment abroad. They do indeed have a "toss and turn mentality." They have common Christian traditions enabling them to join ecumenically with already established churches in America, and their claims to uniqueness as uniting churches force them in that direction. However, attachment to the "heavenly language" of India, especially Malayalam, calls them together in language-based CSI congregations or in language-based ecumenical fellowships. Leaders speak about a special temporary mission to people of the first generation who need the security of memories about and traditions from the church in India in order to help them to reconstruct a viable identity in America. Many are resigned to the idea that the mission will not be compelling for their children or future generations who will have to find new church homes. Still, they are not clear about a strategy that will help their children move from the churches now being established to other churches, or which churches will be most successful in ministering to future generations. The CSI was a pioneering church in 1947 leading the way toward church union; perhaps it will develop effective strategies to help the children of that church adapt to life and faith in America.

Brethren Assemblies

Brethren Assemblies gather in local Gospel Halls or Grace Chapels and claim to be Bible-based, lay-led, and locally governed. The tradition of local autonomy of conservative assemblies kept small by design and led by multiple elders creates relatively weak ethnic boundaries. More than half of the Indian immigrant Brethren (here to be distinguished from the Mennonite Brethren and the Church of the Brethren) worship in some of the 1,000 local assemblies made up predominantly of American white people. Many assemblies have only one or two Indian families. Some say that the Indians meet separately only to serve immigrants who do not know English very well, and predict that after the second generation separate Indian assemblies will not exist. The indication is that many Indian Brethren assimilate well into diverse congregations, and a mutual strengthening occurs. One leader said that the Indian immigrants infuse new life into many local assemblies and have kept several from dying. Some men serve as elders in dual ethnic assemblies, but a few reveal that they face some discrimination in assemblies where they form small minorities. Another remarks that other Brethren learn from the Indians about the strength of families, and the Indians in turn learn lessons about how to raise children in America. Indian Brethren exhibit a greater ability than most other Asian-Indian Christian immigrants in both singing and public speaking in Western styles, resulting from their participation in dual-ethnic assemblies. At one national gathering of Indian Brethren, the dramatic drop in participation in singing Malayalee hymns is so great that the youth chide their parents for speaking about Malayalam as "a heavenly language" but not being able to sing the Malayalee songs with skill and power.

Participation in assemblies of the majority population also places Indian Brethren in contact with variations among Brethren leading to different patterns of adaptation to the majority society. Indian Brethren tend to be a fairly conservative influence among Brethren in the United States. Those who go to conservative assemblies feel that the services and ethos are like those in India. Leaders claim that everywhere the doctrine is the same, but in some assemblies the application is lax. For example, everywhere it is said that women cannot partake of communion unless their heads are covered; in India leaders will not let them come bareheaded, but in America it is sometimes permitted. The assemblies experience tensions regarding the role of women; normally they are silent in the church and do not exercise leadership in any church forum where men are present. As one speaker explains, "The elders are keepers of the church; the sisters are the keepers of the home." One leader comments that some assemblies are "so tight that if you turn them, they will squeak," but others are open, by which he means that they welcome Christians other than Brethren at the communion table. Division is occurring in some assemblies over the introduction of musical instruments in the worship services, a dispute reminiscent of that between the Christian Churches and the Churches of Christ earlier in the twentieth century. At Indian Brethren conventions, the piano, organ, guitars, and drums are used in evening meetings, but singing at the Sunday service is without instrumental accompaniment. Such decisions are made by individual assemblies because no centralized authority can impose decisions on local assemblies.

Nevertheless, the conservative evangelical commitments of members create strong sectarian boundaries. A strong sense of insider/outsider boundaries is revealed in the operative terms of "saint", "brother," "sister," and "believer," placed in juxtaposition to "unbeliever," "nominal Christian," and "heathen." Outsiders are excluded from the pulpit, lectern, and communion table. The invitation to the Lord's Supper is to "those walking in fellowship with a local assembly." In the group rhetoric, identity as part of the Brethren movement is more important than ethnic identification. Hence, there is a strong emphasis upon endogamy within the religious group. "Be ye not unequally yoked together with unbelievers" (2 Cor 6:14) is the prohibition to the young people – or, as one speaker paraphrased, "Don't become a Siamese twin joined to a corpse." Leaders urge young people to avoid dating anyone outside the church fellowship so they will not be tempted to marry unbelievers or nominal Christians. No data is available to indicate how successful the prohibition is, but discussion among young people at conferences indicates that it is a hot topic. As a group with strong religious boundaries, the Brethren may provide a current test of Herberg's hypothesis that the third generation of immigrant families will tend to marry within the religious group but outside the ethnic group, but it is too early to tell.

Malayalee Brethren form a significant minority among the Brethren and engage in activities that maintain their ethnic identity in a few ethnic assemblies and in an annual conference. The best estimate is that between 900 and 950 Indian Brethren families are in the United States: about 3,500 people. More than 600 families are clearly identified on mailing lists of the conference; the rest are comfortable with associations limited to American Brethren assemblies or have assimilated in other American churches and are not identifiable in Brethren records. Only about 25 assemblies in America are made up totally of Indians, and all these are Malayalee except for 1 Hindi assembly in New York. Because the assemblies do not need financial resources for a paid clergy, some of the assemblies are small, consisting of fewer than 25 families and these are spread out in urban areas. The situation in Houston is a good example: approximately 50 Malayalee Brethren families support Indian Assemblies in four areas of the city, and 16 families attend dual-ethnic assemblies. A relatively large assembly in Sugarland has about 150 members, among whom are 6 Malayalee families. A few Brethren from Andhra Pradesh are in America, but they do not have separate assemblies nor do they gather in family conferences.

The major gathering of Malayalee Brethren is an annual conference
generally held on the campus of Mt. Vernon Nazarene College in Ohio.
It was the first annual family conference for Indian Christians in
America, started in 1978 by 200 participants at Greenwood Hills,
Pennsylvania, and it now attracts as many as 620 people for 4 days of
preaching, singing, youth meetings, Bible study, and fellowship. Many of
the leaders were influenced by the Fort Assembly in Bombay, the
"mother assembly" of the approximately 40 assemblies now meeting
there. During the introduction of families on the opening night of a
recent conference, so many indicated that their native place in India was
Ranni in Kerala that it became something of a joke – a majority from
Ranni against the rest. Many of the people identified themselves as children or grandchildren of the "founders," meaning in this case the people
who led the movement in India at the beginning of this century. Most
families are "converts" from various Syrian Christian groups; one
woman proudly displays a picture of her grandfather and identifies him
as the first person to receive communion as a Brethren member after
leaving the Mar Thoma Church. Such stories validate the claim to relatively high family status in Kerala.

Regional conferences of Brethren include people from dual-ethnic
assemblies, and the national Indian Brethren Family Conference is an
immersion in the Christian language and symbols of the group, both
Brethren and Malayalee Christian. Because so many of the people come
from the same region of Kerala – an indication of a strong localized
network bringing immigrants to America – the conferences are happy
occasions of reunion for families and friends. Speakers joke about
Malayalam being the language of Zion and about Ranni as Jerusalem.
Some families say that the conference is "just like going back to Kerala"
so in the four or five years between their visits to India they come to the
family conference. For those not in Indian Assemblies, the conference is
the only place they sing, pray, and give public addresses in Malayalam,
which explains the tentativeness early in the conference in the singing of
Malayalee hymns. "Be ye not unequally yoked together with unbelievers" as an injunction to endogamy is interpreted by parents as an
affirmation of the arranged marriage system. They fervently hope their
children will accept the marriage partners they select, most likely from
the Malayalee Brethren community, and, indeed, family conferences are
times for young people to become acquainted and for parents to initiate
marriage negotiations. Hebrew scriptures are used to support both the
pattern of arranged marriage and endogamy.

Some who have participated in the family conferences from the beginning suggest that the earlier conferences were more Malayalee in character than the current ones: more speakers from India, more pervasive use of Malayalam in both formal and informal portions of the conference, and use of Indian hymnody and music styles. More people on the platform now use English for their sermons and speeches; Western musical instruments and modes are commonly used; and more conversations are in English. Many of the young people are not fluent in Malayalam, and very few can read it. An Indian Assembly in Dallas was the first to adopt English for its entire program in order to reach the young people more effectively, which may foreshadow the future for Indian Assemblies.

Despite the intense local autonomy of Brethren assemblies and their anti-clericalism, some supra-congregational agencies are developing. They do not support clergy, but "commended workers" receive recognition from local assemblies and then engage in various types of mission work in the United States and in India. An Assemblies Ministry organization with headquarters in Wheaton, Illinois, supports the establishment of assemblies in the United States (but not abroad) and supports a couple of Indian commended workers. A Missionary Service Council is the counterpart in Canada. The Christian Missions in Many Lands is an agency related to all the Brethren Assemblies that supports commended workers in several countries, including India. In 1984 the Indian Brethren started the Gospel Mission India, which supports mission activities through organizations, assemblies, Bible schools, and orphanages in India. The fund-raising goal for the first year was $25,000, and in 1992 the Gospel Mission India raised $152,000. The by-laws stipulate that at least 90 percent of the income must go to India. The agency keeps a very low profile both in India and America so it will not arouse opposition from political forces. The mission has begun a small program of evangelism directed at Indian immigrants who are not Christian. *Victorious Living* is a publication of the Indian Brethren mailed to some 600 families. Publishing houses run by Brethren prepare pamphlets and educational material for the Brethren even though there are no standardized Sunday School curricula or uniform lessons. All these are independent agencies serving the Brethren assemblies.

Indian Brethren occupy a liturgical niche between the ritualism of the churches related to the Syrian traditions and the emotionalism of the Pentecostal churches, and they draw members from both and attempt to protect their own members from the allure of both. Of the nine Indian Brethren who indicated on a questionnaire that they joined the Brethren after coming to America, five were "converted" from Pentecostal churches and four from the Mar Thoma and Orthodox churches. The attraction of the emotionalism in the Pentecostal churches is perceived as a major threat to the Brethren, so much of their rhetoric is directed against the Pentecostals. A speaker distributes a tract he wrote to "expose" the claims of the Pentecostal movement, and he argues that the charismatics "lead God's people astray with the bedlam of Hell." In their rejection of both ritualism and emotionalism, the Brethren resemble the non-instrumental Churches of Christ in America, even though they do not have contact with one another because each is exclusive.

A surprising rhetoric of anti-intellectualism is a thread through some of the conference speeches – though more in those by white speakers from New Zealand and Canada than in those by Asian Indians, one must say. They portray too much education, materialism, and secularism as dangerous temptations. "The church is being spoiled by degrees," as one speaker argues. One wonders how the immigrants respond to such anti-intellectualism, much of which runs counter to their experience and their aspirations as Indian parents. The educational accomplishments of the Indian Brethren are virtually equal to those of other Christian immigrants from India and, one would estimate, greater than those of Brethren in America. Almost 80 percent have at least some college education, and 20 percent have graduate degrees, compared to 34 percent for all Indian Christian immigrants. Twenty-two of the thirty women at the family conference who completed the questionnaire identified themselves as nurses. The Indian Brethren report a relatively high family income equal to that of other Indian Christian groups, with 53 percent having incomes of between $50,000 and $100,000. The Indian parents push their children toward academic excellence and into professions that will provide economic security. A conflict of aspirations could be brewing here as the drive for education puts Indian youth in tension with the ideology of the church. The emphasis in discussions with youth is upon finding a "godly man or woman" juxtaposed to a "successful person" to marry. Will that mean the young people as "successful people" will have to "marry down" in the fellowship if they cannot find a well-educated spouse from an Indian family? The background and ethos of the immigrants from India, including Brethren immigrants, seems to run counter to the anti-intellectualism and to attacks on material security so prevalent in the rhetoric of some Brethren leaders. Indeed, three Indian Brethren are engaged in theological studies in America, one in an undergraduate Bible college, one in a conservative seminary, and the third in a Ph.D. program in theology. All three plan to return to India to engage in mission activity, so they may not have much impact on the outcome of this anti-intellectualism.

The Indian Brethren are an example of a low-church Protestant evangelical group following a dual strategy of existing within congregations of a larger, already existing church group in America and, at the same time, creating agencies and networks that enable them to maintain their identities as a distinct ethnic group of Malayalees within the larger whole. They are both a part of and apart from an international movement. Different strategies of adaptation are involved, as is demonstrated every time they come together for hymn singing. They have two options before them: to merge into the larger network of already existing Brethren assemblies or to continue maintaining separate Indian Brethren Assemblies, annual conference, and agencies. Much will depend upon the patterns of future immigration and upon the success or failure of the Brethren in maintaining the loyalty of their American-educated children. That is the struggle currently underway.

Pentecostals

When Asian-Indian Christians are asked about Pentecostal churches, they generally reply that there are twenty or so small Pentecostal churches in each of their cities and refer to them collectively, while denying that they know any of their pastors or much about their activities. The word is, however, that Pentecostals are the fastest-growing Christian groups both in India and among immigrants from India in America. That is difficult either to substantiate or to refute. The Pentecostal churches are small, highly mobile, given to fragmentation, and somewhat isolated from other Asian-Indian Christian groups. Although from the outside the Pentecostal churches appear to be alike both in doctrine and expression, internal distinctions are sufficiently pronounced to cause the continuation of sectarian divisions among them. The New Testament Church (NTC) – formerly known as the Ceylon Pentecostal Mission, and now known by different names in various countries: The Pentecostal Mission in India, the New Testament Church in the United States, Grace Covenant Church in Canada, and Universal Pentecostal Church in Britain – is the most distinctive of the Pentecostal groups. Other types of Pentecostal churches also serve Asian-Indian Christians – the Indian Pentecostal Church, the Sharon Pentecostal Church, the Assemblies of God, the Church of God of

Cleveland, Tennessee, and a large number of independent Pentecostal churches.

"Praise the Lord! This is the New Testament Church" is the telephone greeting from a pastor of the church known earlier as the Ceylon Pentecostal Mission. Although small, the NTC stands out from other Asian-Indian Christian groups because of the nature of its pastoral leadership and the multiethnic makeup of its participants. Approximately 2,500 people participate in 20 congregations. The size and ethnic makeup varies from congregation to congregation. The largest is in Washington with approximately 500 people attending, but less than 50 percent are Asian Indians; 200 participate in the congregation in Brooklyn where only 10–15 percent are Asian Indians; the Yonkers, New York, congregation has approximately 40 families, and all but 1 or 2 are Asian-Indian. (Note that participants are recorded by families in congregations where Asian Indians predominate, but by individuals where they do not, a significant cultural difference.) Most of the congregations are in the eastern part of the country, and a large majority of some 1,700 people attend the annual conference that generally meets for several days each summer on the campus of Ashland University in Ohio. The conferences, begun in 1988, are like great camp meeting revivals for the entire church – what one participant called "a great annual feast." They are small renditions of the huge annual conferences held in every center and area in India that attract as many as 50,000 participants.

Most of the 35–40 full-time consecrated workers and senior pastors are present for the conferences. The pastors are under strict discipline that requires that they live celibate lives and "live by faith," which means relying entirely on the church for maintenance without personal income or wealth. The pastors do not work at secular occupations. The leadership of this church in America is multiethnic; most are African-American or Caucasian, not Asian-Indian, and, thus, it represents a group where persons from the majority population or from other minorities provide religious leadership for a group of Asian-Indian immigrants, in much the same way as leaders of the International Society of Krishna Consciousness (ISKCON) in the early days provided religious leadership for some Hindu immigrants. One of the problems leaders identify is the lack of a sufficient number of full-time consecrated workers to meet the requests from small prayer groups across the country for pastoral leadership. Few Asian Indians are "called" to become pastors in America. They come to America for other reasons, or at least think they do. One African-American speaker contrasts their "brain power" with "spirit power" and "[their] will to come to the United States to make money and be comfortable with God's will" by saying: "You thought you came here to make a name for yourself. God brought you here for His purpose. Are you willing to give up cars, homes, comfort to serve Him? Are you still willing to shout, 'Hallelujah'?"

The main leaders of the conference exemplify the multiethnic character of the pastoral leadership. The acknowledged chief pastor, Ernest Paul, regularly travels from the world headquarters in Madras to attend the conference even though he is in his late sixties and in poor health. He has been active in the ministry since he was 20 years old. Pastor Don Spires, a Caucasian, is the chief pastor for the United States and administers the affairs of the church from New York. He has been associated with these churches since the early 1960s. (Note that would make the NTC the earliest Indian church to begin a ministry, even before the influx of immigrants from India, providing one reason for the multiethnic character to the church.) Before then Pastor Spires had been a non-denominational missionary in Argentina, working with the Assemblies of God and Christian Reformed churches. He returned to New York to work with David Wilkerson, an evangelist made famous in *The Cross and the Switchblade*. Then he met several Ceylon Pentecostal Mission people who arrived in New York from India – he calls them "missionaries" – and Spires has been associated with this group since that time. The NTC in America is tightly organized under Pastor Don, as he is popularly called, and he issues firm directives from the top to other pastors and to the congregations. He appoints and transfers the pastors and other workers. All pastors and congregations are accountable to him and ultimately to Pastor Paul in Madras. Pastor Don travels abroad a great deal to attend conferences in several countries where the church is established or has missions. An African-American pastor from the Chicago congregation is coordinator of the annual conference. A function of charismatic gifts is to authenticate an authoritarian hierarchical structure and break down ethnic barriers to leadership. The senior pastors preach, lead Bible study, pray for the sick and healing in private sessions, and counsel individuals and groups in the course of the conference. They oversee a dynamic charismatic movement, but one should note that their manner in leading public sessions in America is calm, deliberate, quiet, and without the exhibitionism associated with some revivals or charismatic meetings.

Women exercise positions of authority in this group, more so than in any other Asian-Indian religious group. Sister Joyce was converted from a Hindu family when she was 11 years old and became a medical doctor in India. She is now a prominent speaker and leader. Women have a special attachment to her and seek her ministry, but she teaches men and has their respect as well. Two women are pastors in charge of congregations: one a Caucasian who left the medical field to serve in Florida and the other a Jewish woman who left her job as a school principal to minister in Ohio. It is noteworthy that two people identified as former medical doctors are pastors in congregations that emphasize faith healing and view reliance on modern medicine as evidence of immaturity in faith.

Also at the conference are principals and teachers of the four schools run by the churches in Washington, Brooklyn, Chicago, and New Jersey. Each has under one hundred students and is closely related to the church ministry. All the teachers are identified as believers who have a call to teach the children. One principal stated with satisfaction, "Last year the Holy Spirit fell on all the children and they spoke in tongues and had visions."

Approximately 75 percent of the participants in the NTC in America are Asian Indians; the rest are African-American, Hispanic, Caucasian, and Caribbean. Many are recent immigrants who are attracted to the congregations in urban centers. No other Asian-Indian church has such a mixture of ethnic groups. Meetings at the annual conference appear to constitute a real "rainbow coalition." It seems that the charismatic ethos attracts people from several minority and recent immigrant groups and has the power to break down, or at least mute, the differences of gender, race, class, and education. Leaders speak about a "new Pentecost" that brings together in one church people from many countries and language groups, and they attribute that "miracle" to the work of the Holy Spirit. A lay volunteer helping with crowd control remarks to a friend that he could not assist with direction of traffic as a crossing guard because, he says, "I am not fluent in any language," and his friend interjects, "except speaking in tongues." Programs at the conference are conducted in English, but simultaneous translation is given to groups in reserved sections of the hall in Malayalam, Hindi, Tamil, French, and Spanish. It is a virtual Babel where the common language is speaking in tongues, and one wonders how the translators handle those portions of the speeches and songs that are in tongues. What do the people hear in translation?

The church does not encourage dating and encourages modesty in both dress and behavior in its members. The women wear clothing similar to that worn by some Muslim women, with long skirts and sleeves, with heads covered, but with uncovered faces. One leader reported that some parents from other traditions are adopting the Indian practice of arranged marriages, which is in tune with the church's emphasis upon the authority of the parents. He indicates that most of the parents prefer that their children marry within their ethnic group even though the church encourages cross-cultural marriages as a testimony to the Kingdom of God. Several interracial families were present at the conference. This is the only Asian-Indian-based church that encourages cross-cultural marriages. The church emphasizes preparation for, and the call to exemplify aspects of, the Kingdom of God as part of its preaching about the return of Christ and the Rapture. "This may be the last convention" is an oft-heard comment, and the fervent expectation of the Second Coming provides encouragement for evangelism and complete submission to Christ.

Praise programs at the conference are lively. Music is in a modern Western style, neither Indian music nor church hymns are common; rather, they sing gospel choruses in a manner to enliven and excite the congregation. A form of "holy aerobics" breaks out as people clap their hands, sway, and dance around in place to the rhythm of the music. Although senior pastors are remarkably calm and deliberate in their lectures, other speakers give testimonies that break into speaking in tongues. Praying for individual sick people and healing do not take place in public on the platform, but in smaller groups or in private when prayer and speaking in tongues are part of the ritual. People in the meetings greet one another as brothers and sisters across the rubble of racial and cultural barriers shattered by the intensity of the emotional experience of the Holy Spirit and the charismatic authority of the community.

The largest annual Asian-Indian Christian conference in America is held cooperatively by several Pentecostal churches – the Indian Pentecostal Church (IPC); the Church of God of Cleveland, Tennessee; the Assemblies of God; and independent churches. More than 3,500 Pentecostals from some 175 Malayalee Pentecostal churches across the country gathered in Chicago over the Fourth of July weekend in 1994 for the twelfth Malayalee Pentecostal Conference of North America. Initiatives to establish a national council of Indian Pentecostals have not yet been successful, but the annual conference continues as a witness to their common origins in India and to their early cooperation in founding churches in America. People at the conference report that their grandfathers worked together to found the Pentecostal churches in Kerala and that they joined naturally to establish the churches in America. They claim that no doctrinal differences separate the Keralite Pentecostal churches (with the exception of the NTC/CPM), only organizational differences. Hence, the first Keralite immigrants formed Pentecostal churches in the major cities to serve people from the various groups, and the annual conference grew out of that cooperation.

As the number of Keralite Pentecostals increases in urban areas, the congregations divide and reconstitute themselves, resulting in many relatively small congregations. Several leaders estimate that New York has over fifty Keralite Pentecostal churches. A factor contributing to divisiveness is that a larger number of pastors live in the United States than there are congregations. A wide range of preparation for ministry is found among the pastors. Some were certified pastors in India; others were "called" to the ministry in the United States. Some have graduate seminary degrees; others have only apprenticeship training or a few courses in Bible colleges. A few are full-time pastors; most work at secular jobs as well. All feel that they are called to ministry and have the charismatic authorization. Not having easy access to leadership of congregations outside their ethnic group, they establish new Keralite Pentecostal congregations by attracting members from existing churches. In the early stages of immigration, these Pentecostals followed an ethnic strategy of adaptation modified by an ecumenical strategy within the Pentecostal movement. As numbers grow in urban areas, the tendency is to establish congregations affiliated in various ways with the specific churches. Several congregations typically develop out of one founding congregation in each metropolitan area.

Of the Pentecostal churches, the IPC has the largest number of churches in both India (over 2,000) and the United States (approximately 55, with 60 to 75 pastors), and these large churches exercise the greatest influence upon the annual conferences, which were begun by a brother of the General Secretary of the IPC, who at that time was a pastor in Chicago and now lives in Dallas. Members of other Pentecostal churches regularly join the IPC churches because so few of the other congregations are readily accessible. Members of the Sharon Pentecostal Church immigrate to America, but no separate congregations of that church exist, so members join other congregations. The Assemblies of God of Springfield, Missouri, have approximately 20 Asian-Indian congregations and 40 pastors in America. The pastors enjoy options of maintaining their ordination in Kerala or transferring their ordination to a state district of the Assemblies of God, so organizational affiliation is diffuse. A few were ordained by American churches before immigrants established their congregations and procedures for ordination. The Church of God of Cleveland, Tennessee, recognizes 22 Keralite congregations and approximately 32 pastors. The Church of God of Anderson, Indiana, has mission work in south India from which a few individuals immigrate, but no separate Asian-Indian churches exist in America.

Many independent Pentecostal congregations attract members from various groups and exhibit elements of the sectarian affiliation of the pastor or of the majority of members. For example, an independent church in Yonkers, New York, serves 54 families, most with IPC backgrounds, eight each from the Church of God and the Assemblies of God, and a few from the Sharon Church. Some congregations identify with more than one group. Four reasons are given for establishing and maintaining congregations independent from the established groups: (1) members from the various groups unite in places where, and at times when, each denominational group is too small to support a separate congregation; (2) pastors desire to remain independent from interference by either Indian or American denominational leaders; (3) no doctrinal differences separate the members of the congregation; and (4) they desire to avoid political disputes. No one knows the exact number of Asian-Indian Pentecostal churches in America. Anecdotal evidence suggests that only a relatively few members are assimilated into non-Keralite churches, while most prefer to preserve their ethnic religious identity.

Boundaries between the Keralite Pentecostal groups are relatively weak, but language and ethnic boundaries set them apart from other Pentecostals. Malayalam is the common language that brings these Pentecostals together and continues to be the dominant language of worship and conversation. A distinctive form of Keralite Pentecostal culture is evident in speeches in Malayalam, in strictures regarding the dress and adornment of the women, in separation of men and women in services, and in many other gestures. Parents initiate marriage negotiations at the conference because their first preference is for Keralite Pentecostal partners for their children, while the second preference is for Malayalee Syrian Christians. A great deal of movement takes place across the weak boundaries between Keralite Pentecostal groups. A man ordained by one group serves as a pastor for another. Intermarriage links families across sectarian lines. Members affiliate with the congregation nearest their homes regardless of affiliation. Malayalam-speaking Pentecostal believers are clearly insiders; others are welcomed guests.

In contrast to the NTC/CPM, these Pentecostals do not break down ethnic barriers with charisma, but support ethnic barriers through their religious participation. Hence, little contact is maintained with Tamil-, Telugu-, or Hindi-speaking Pentecostals who maintain a few language-based congregations. A great majority of Keralite Pentecostals claim descent from the ancient Thomas and Syrian Christians, so a tendency exists to look down upon more recent converts. Ethnic identification is a strategy of inculcating the parents' values on the children. One speaker to youth indicated that, in a desperate attempt to maintain ethnic purity, their parents give a confused message, sometimes seeming to proclaim that: "speaking Malayalam is better than speaking in tongues; wearing a sari is more important than wearing the armor of God; and eating curry is preferred to the fruits of the Spirit." The youth are caught in the middle trying to live out their Christian commitment. They do not have the Malayalee skills to witness to the adults, but when they try to reach out to witness to peers in the majority society, they face restraints from parents who see that as a threat to ethnic identity, wanting them, therefore, to "stay within the four walls of our community." A great deal of effort in the churches and conferences is expended in maintaining the disciplines of ethnic identity according to Keralite Pentecostal teachings.

Two threats to unity within that ethnic identity surface in the annual conferences. The first is the bifurcation of the annual meeting into concurrent Malayalam and English sessions that results from strong representations by the young people at the conference in 1989. In the early days the sessions were entirely in Malayalam and later the speeches were translated into English; now there are separate sessions. The Malayalam sessions in 1994 met in a huge tent seating 2,200 people in the parking lot of the conference center; the English sessions met in the grand ballroom seating 1,250 people. Since the changes in 1989, an increasing percentage of conference participants attends the English sessions, including many older adults. The Malayalam sessions exhibit more visible exuberance, speaking in tongues, public healings, Keralite hymns, Keralite disciplines of separate seating for men and women and head cover for women. The English sessions are more restrained, have more mixed seating (unless the ushers or speakers insist on separation), sing English choruses, and listen to university-educated speakers employing a different speaking style. A mixed message is given through selection of main speakers for the conference, typically a renowned speaker from south India who exhibits an Indian form of Pentecostalism and a white church executive who exhibits an American form of Pentecostalism, neither of whom faces the biculturalism of the immigrants. Nor can they be of much help to the young people in what one leader called "the second stage of Americanization." The "fresh off of the boat preachers" are not, one young person said, "much help to us in our daily lives." Parents and recent immigrants face the anxiety of "the threat of non-being," fearing that if they begin to give up aspects of their culture they will lose their identity. Nevertheless, most of the local congregations are beginning to conduct their services in a mixture of Malayalam and English "for the sake of the young people." The speed of change depends upon the percentage of teenagers and their parents in the congregations and the number of American trained pastors, who seem to be less threatened by the requirement to minister in English. Some leaders predict that in a few years, if the annual conferences continue, the larger sessions will be in English and not Malayalam and the speakers will be Asian Indians who have made a successful Christian adjustment to life in America.

Another threat to the unity and viability of the annual conferences is the developing tendency of subgroups to form their own councils, organizations, and conferences that may take precedence. The North American National Council of Indian Pentecostal Churches holds an annual conference and pastors' meeting and is related to regional organizations in the northeast, midwest, and west. These churches and pastors are, nevertheless, relatively independent, but still claim authorization from the IPC headquarters in India. The IPC heavily influences the annual conference because approximately 45 percent of those attending are IPC members. A popular speaker notes that he is introduced as coming from the IPC even though his ordination is from the Assemblies of God in America. The Assemblies of God congregations are in the process of forming an Indian Assemblies of God Conference that will be directly affiliated with the church in India even though some of their pastors and churches are related to the state organizations of Assemblies of God. The Assemblies of God Fellowship in the Northeast has a regional conference in New York that in 1994 attracted 400 people from 12 churches the week before the larger conference in Chicago. The congregations and pastors of the Church of God are assigned to the State, Metro, or Territorial Overseer and share in the Cross Cultural Ministry administered from the world headquarters in Cleveland, Tennessee. Pastors are certified by the headquarters at three levels: exhorters (10 percent of the Asian-Indian pastors); licensed pastors (40 percent); and ordained pastors (50 percent). The executive of the Cross

Cultural Ministry oversees 26 different language groups in the United
States. Leaders of the Church of God headquarters in Tennessee recognize that it is difficult for members of the dominant culture to understand the dynamics of the immigrant churches and are considering the
appointment of an Asian Indian as the National Coordinator for the
Keralite churches. Each of these initiatives establishes new hierarchies
that provide opportunity for immigrants to gain status, ego satisfaction,
and provide service. An undercurrent at the annual conference is political negotiation regarding the formation, staffing, and make-up of these
new organizations.

   These Pentecostals share social, economic, and immigration patterns
with other Christian immigrants from India. When a speaker in the
tent meeting called upon people in several professions to stand as part
of a fund-raising effort, a few men identified themselves as businessmen, then a handful of doctors, but when he called for nurses, several
hundred stood in the women's section. There are 60 percent of the
Pentecostal women who completed the survey (and one man) who identify themselves as nurses. Three physicians and eleven medical technicians are among the group. These are surprising statistics because early
Pentecostal leaders in India preached reliance on faith healing, causing
Pentecostals to refrain from establishing hospitals. The men identify
themselves primarily as businessmen, medical technicians, or machinists. Graduate degrees are held by 36 percent of the Pentecostals, and
another 30 percent have a college degree. Five of the eight people in
the total survey reporting family incomes of over $250,000 are
Pentecostals. As a whole they must rank among the best-educated and
most wealthy members of Pentecostal churches in America. Their children exhibit a rate of success and professional aspirations similar to
other second-generation Asian Indians. A leader indicated that 90
percent of the young people do not understand Malayalam and yet live
in two worlds. He concludes with a hard question: "These young
people are not experiencing just the normal rebellion and rejection of
youth but are rebelling against being forced to live in two worlds. In a
few years they are going to be in key positions in society – their brains
and hard work will accomplish that – but where will they be culturally
and spiritually?" The Pentecostal churches stand at a crucial point in
their development in America, and the tensions and strategies of
adaptation evident in the annual conference witness to the struggle for
survival and faithfulness.

Methodists

American Methodist missionaries established churches in India that remained separate from the uniting churches and that now send both members and pastors as immigrants to the United States. Hence, the immigrants are able to establish relationships at both the local and national levels with the quintessential American denomination. A number of Asian-Indian Methodists, including pastors, follow a strategy of individual adaptation by merging into local Methodist congregations or, in the case of pastors, by accepting appointments to pastorates or staff positions without responsibilities for immigrants from India. If the individual is willing to limit Asian-Indian Christian socialization to family influences, or if the pastor already has the educational and ecclesiastical certification before immigration, or is able to earn them in the United States, this mode of adaptation is fairly straightforward and simple. However, if an attempt is made to maintain separate ethnic identity, the process is much more complicated.

Two local congregations in the Chicago area affiliated with the Methodist Church illustrate two models of immigrant church development: the India Mission Telugu United Methodist Church in Oak Park and the Emmanuel United Methodist Church in Evanston. The first started as an ecumenical fellowship and developed into an ethnic mission; the second started as an ethnic fellowship under the wing of an established Methodist congregation and now forms the majority of that church.

The India Mission developed from the initiative of families who opened their apartments for Christian fellowship meetings of prayer, scripture reading, and hymns. In 1968 a famous preacher from India, Bhakt Singh, came to Chicago to speak in a Chinese home, and several Asian-Indian Christian families went to hear him. At his urging they began to meet each week in different homes for fellowship. When attendance outgrew the homes, they received permission to use the building of the United Church at the Medical Center, a church near Cook County Hospital affiliated with both the Methodist Church and the Presbyterian Church. By 1973 the fellowship had registered as an ecumenical church named the India Christian Fellowship Church, having grown to about 300 members speaking several Indian regional languages: Tamil, Malayalam, Hindi, and Urdu. As the number of immigrants increased dramatically in the early and mid-1970s, this ecumenical strategy began to disintegrate with the departure of several regional groups. In 1976 the Telugu Christians separated and formed the India Christian Telugu Church. Students from seminaries and Bible colleges provided leadership for both the ecumenical and the ethnic groups.

The bishop of the Northern Illinois United Methodist Conferences in 1978 recognized the Telugu group, and it began to worship on Sunday evenings at the Willard Memorial United Methodist Church in Oak Park. The congregation included Telugu-speaking people from many denominational backgrounds, but they affiliated with the Methodist Church as an official Telugu mission. Because of difficulty in obtaining pastoral leadership, one of the early leaders, who had immigrated as the spouse of a nurse and who worked for twenty-four years as an X-ray technician in Cook County Hospital, undertook in 1983 a five-year program of studies at Garrett Theological Seminary. He was first a volunteer lay-preacher and then was ordained by the Methodists. After meeting in the church in Oak Park for fifteen years, in 1993 the Telugu congregation purchased the building for $300,000, and the pastor took early retirement from his position at the hospital to serve as full-time pastor for 150 members from 46 families. The pastor reports that he once prepared a genealogical chart showing that virtually all of the members are part of one large extended family. The church as family is characteristic of many Asian-Indian churches, as it is also among many other churches in America. The other Telugu churches in the Chicago area are a Brethren Assembly, two Baptist churches, and one fellowship within a Methodist Church, but none of those has a full-time pastor. It is very difficult for small congregations to become a fully recognized Methodist congregation because they cannot afford to provide the remuneration and fringe benefits stipulated for Methodist ministers and the regular apportionment payments. Hence, the India Mission Telugu United Methodist Church remains a mission. One member remarked that members are from many denominations, so the designation is a convenience. Nevertheless, the congregation is following a Telugu ethnic strategy of adaptation as a part of the Methodist Church. The natural relationships of this congregation with other Christian groups follow an ethnic network of other Telugu congregations, a weakening ecumenical network of other Asian-Indian churches, an "Indian denominational" network of other Indian Methodist groups, and an "American denominational" network reaching tentatively into the Methodist Church nationwide.

The Emmanuel United Methodist Church in Evanston, a congregation with a long history as a union of Swedish and Norwegian immigrants, now exhibits a different model of development by becoming primarily an Asian-Indian congregation. A young Gujarati man accompanied his bishop to a Methodist meeting in Chicago in 1976, and he stayed on for a college and a seminary education sponsored by his sister, who is a nurse. In 1977 he visited Emmanuel Church seeking funds for his home church in India, and the Caucasian pastor invited him to start a Gujarati fellowship, which met for its first service in 1978 and then began weekly services in 1982. Methodist bishops in India encouraged the formation of churches in America, hoping these new churches would maintain strong ties with the church in India (Das, 1991:25). A Hindi fellowship also started to meet in another location in 1977, led by an Indian pastor who immigrated to join his wife, also a nurse. His father had been a Methodist pastor in India, but he was ordained in the Reformed Presbyterian Church and served for twenty-five years as a pastor and evangelist in India. The Hindi fellowship met in homes and at an Assembly of God Church until a chance meeting with the Gujarati leader led to an invitation to meet in Emmanuel Church in 1981. The Gujarati leader subsequently graduated from seminary, was ordained in the Methodist Conference, and was appointed first as full-time associate pastor in 1984 and then as senior pastor in 1985. The Methodist Conference provides some funding to support the work among Asian-Indian immigrants. One of the immigrant leaders complains that some of the members operate for too long on "the old missionary concept – let the whites do it."

When the Hindi leader died suddenly in 1985, the Gujarati pastor's brother became assistant pastor with responsibility for the Hindi fellowship while he attends North Park Theological Seminary. He also travels regularly to the western suburb of Bolingbrook to minister to a Gujarati fellowship spinning off from Emmanuel Church. A large majority of the members of Emmanuel Church are now Asian Indians – 140 Gujarati members, 45 Hindi, 15 non-Asian-Indian members, and 25 Gujarati members in Bolingbrook. It is a multiethnic congregation with members from Jamaica, Guyana, Trinidad, India, Pakistan, and Puerto Rico, but it appears that a significant "white flight" has taken place in the last fifteen years, so that very few remain as members. A majority of the Asian-Indian members are second- or third-generation Christians from India, and in most cases their families were converted in American or European missions. A result is that Emmanuel Church (along with the India Telugu Mission and other Asian Indian Protestant churches) preserves a strong evangelistic ethos. The primary outreach ministry to

Asian Indians is a radio ministry each week in Hindi and Gujarati. Several variations on these two models of development lead to many different types of organization, but these two are typical. They also demonstrate the significance of both the nursing occupation of many pastors' spouses and the role of American seminaries in preparing immigrants for Methodist ministry.

No exact record of the number of Asian-Indian Methodist pastors in the United States is available because pastors are officially identified as part of the larger category of Asian Americans, which is not further defined. One reliable estimate is that between sixty and seventy-five Asian-Indian Methodist pastors are serving in the United States, and that five or six women from the Indian subcontinent are ordained. Several were educated at Leonard Theological Seminary at Jabalpur in north India (Das, 1991:25). A majority of those who come to the United States for graduate studies do not return to India, and, as we have seen, some come as immigrants with their spouses who are nurses or are sponsored by siblings. Most of the Asian-Indian pastors serve Methodist congregations that have few, if any, members from India. The pastor of the Willard Memorial United Methodist Church (that hosted and later sold its building to the Telugu Mission) is an Asian Indian who moved with his congregation to a new location. Thus, an Indian immigrant pastor of a Caucasian congregation handed over the keys for that building to an Indian immigrant pastor of a Telugu congregation. Eight ministers are enrolled in the Northern Illinois Conference, and only two serve Asian-Indian congregations. A few serve on college and seminary faculties throughout the United States; others receive appointments from the conferences. A perception exists that Asian-Indian pastors face some discrimination in the appointment process.

Overcoming the perceived discrimination and encouraging outreach among the immigrants are reasons given for the existence of the Southern Asian National Caucus of the United Methodism (SANCUM), which gained formal recognition in 1980 and attracted about 100 participants from eleven states to its second convocation in Nashville, Tennessee, in 1993 (McAnally, 1993:1–2). The caucus owes its existence indirectly to African-American Methodists who first formed a caucus and to Japanese Methodists who followed that example. The caucus is open to individuals, both clergy and lay people, from Bangladesh, Burma, India, Indonesia, Malaysia, Nepal, Pakistan, Singapore, Sri Lanka, and Thailand, but the participants in the annual convocation are all Asian Indians. The caucus is integrated into the administrative structure of the Methodist Church as part of the National Federation of Asian American United Methodists under the Commission on Religion and Race (Chang, 1991:135). The Asian-Indian caucus is much younger and smaller than the Japanese, Korean, and Filipino caucuses and is searching for its niche in the Church. An observer at the convocation says, "The pastors attend for political reasons; the people come for fellowship." They support the language ministries of the Methodist Church, decry continuing discrimination in the church, and seek empowerment in its political structure. Hence, both at the local and national level, Asian Indians are becoming more visible and active.

Church of the Brethren

The year 1995 is the centennial of the mission work of the Church of the Brethren in Bulsar, Gujarat, approximately 125 miles north of Bombay. It was begun by the Revd. Wilbur Stover, who was a member of the Naperville Church of the Brethren in Illinois. Now half of the Naperville congregation is from Bulsar. A road recently dedicated in Bulsar to honor his ministry – Bishop Dr. Wilber B. Stover Road – ironically leads several families back to Naperville. Two granddaughters of a Brahmin convert immigrated as nurses in 1976 and began a process of relocating family members in the Chicago area, thereby providing Gujarati members for the Naperville church. By 1983 eight family units were participating as active members, and in 1987 they began to meet separately on the first Sunday evening of each month as the Gujarati fellowship. The father of the first two immigrants, after his arrival in 1980, was ordained by the Church of the Brethren and serves the Gujarati fellowship. On Sunday mornings Gujaratis constitute half of the eighty-person congregation and sit on the lectern side of the sanctuary. At their Sunday evening meetings conducted in Gujarati, they occupy the pulpit side. The fellowship is an extended family group and provides an illustration of the narrow networks of chain migration that support recent Christian immigration.

Although the Churches of the Brethren in Gujarat entered the Church of North India in 1970, the Bulsar congregation and several others separated from the CNI in November 1978. The Gujarati fellowship intervenes on behalf of the separating group with leaders at the Brethren headquarters in Elgin, Illinois, but without much success. Some thirty-three court cases are pending in India over division of mission properties, because the dissident group is challenging the CNI as the legal successor. The group in Naperville maintains a close relationship with the churches and institutions in south Gujarat. The Naperville Church of the Brethren has declined in overall membership and participation since 1978, experiencing some difficulties and conflicts, but the Gujarati fellowship remain significant and loyal participants. The model of development is similar to that of Emmanuel United Methodist Church in Evanston, but many fewer Gujarati Brethren than Methodists are available to support a church.

Baptists

The independence and local autonomy of Baptist churches is attractive to some Asian Indians, and many small Asian-Indian Baptist churches have come into existence. These small congregations are affiliated with several Baptist groups, and raise up preachers – ordained, licensed, students, and lay – in a variety of ways. Some Baptist churches are started by students from India studying in American colleges and seminaries. It is impossible to number these congregations, but several exist in most urban areas. Few Baptists have immigrated from India, so the congregations are made up of immigrants from other churches and converts from other religions. The strategy of development of congregations by the Baptist Convention of the State of Georgia of the Southern Baptist Convention is instructive.

An Asian-Indian woman, Norma George, works as "Catalytic Minister" for Asian Indians in the Language Division of Ethnic Ministries of the Home Mission Board in Georgia. National Consultants serve in the Language Division for many ethnic groups, but currently Asian Indians do not have a National Consultant. A Catalytic Minister of the Southern Baptist Church serves as a church planter, leadership trainer, and consultant to the churches in starting ministries with special groups. She was a teacher in Christian mission schools in north India for twenty years, where she worked primarily with American Presbyterian missionaries and their children, before she came to Drew University in 1977 to study for a master's degree. Thereafter, she obtained a green card, and her family joined her as immigrants. For two years she worked as a volunteer, and in 1983 began to work with the Baptist Convention of the State of Georgia to help establish Asian-Indian churches.

She says that "ministry with Indians is very, very slow." In the early days she gathered names from telephone directories for the Atlanta area, from listings at Indian grocery stores – that were then prime locations of Asian-Indian public announcements – and then from the membership list of the India Cultural Association. She visited Christian families, wrote letters, established Bible classes, organized Vacation Bible Schools, taught Hindi language classes, and gathered members of her family and friends. Networks of family, language group, friendship, and occupation led her to additional prospects. Three Telugu families from Hyderabad moved from Tennessee, and she made contacts for them with a local Baptist Church. Most of these contacts were people from other Christian groups in India, but many responded to the invitation to join Baptist fellowships. She also contacted immigrants from other religions to interest them in the Christian church. In 1986 she started a weekly radio program in a mixture of Hindi and Urdu, which helped her locate many people, both Christian and non-Christian. A great deal of media attention developed on the radio, on television, and in the newspapers, regarding the growing Asian-Indian population in Atlanta. Those outlets publicize the Christian groups along with those of other religions, and the exposure greatly expanded the contacts and accelerated growth. She worked through local Baptist churches that opened their doors to meetings of Asian Indians.

Three small new Baptist churches "nest" in established churches, which means that they have an agreement to use the building for their services. The First Asian Indian Baptist Church of Marietta, the Asian Indian Baptist Church of Riverdale, and the First India Baptist Church of Claremont Hills each meets regularly with an attendance of under a hundred. It is difficult to arrange pastoral leadership, but all three called part-time ministers in 1992. One of the ministers had attended a Baptist church for ten years and received a ministerial license to become pastor of the church. Another was a pastor in Pakistan whose family was in Atlanta. He came to preach for the church at Christmas in 1991, and it called him to return as pastor. The third had been involved with a charismatic group in Macon, but joined the church and became leader. None has a degree from a seminary or any formal theological training. In addition to these three churches, a Bengali fellowship has formed, and a Tamil fellowship is at the initial stages of gathering for prayer meetings and worship.

The Catalytic Minister serves under the Home Mission Board, but she says it is generally best to avoid the designation as a missionary. The term "turns the Hindus off" and implies an element of condescension to Christians from India, some of whom claim a long tradition of

Christianity and all of whom believe their faith has been tested in the fire of living as a small minority in hostile environments. Home missions are often shaped by what is called "the hinterland approach" to foreign missions, as though they were serving culturally deprived people (Chang, 1991:136). Both Christian immigrants and those belonging to other religions resent the implication that they constitute a mission field. The manner of establishing the relationships both between nascent immigrant church groups and established congregations of the majority population and between the national and state structures of American churches and the immigrant Christians is fraught with the danger of misunderstanding and perceptions of power inequities that make it difficult for immigrant Christians to claim their place in American Christianity.

Innumerable independent congregations exist in cities across the country, developing out of the individual initiative of a lay person, a family, or a pastor. Some are affiliated with an existing church structure: a Nazarene Church here, a Disciple fellowship there, a Mennonite Brethren prayer group in another place. Most of the independent congregations are meetings of people from the same language group: a Gujarati fellowship, a Telugu prayer group, a Tamil congregation sharing a building with a Presbyterian Church and a Korean fellowship. Each is a vital location for the immigrant Christians as they seek a place under "the everlasting arms" to shape a new identity, coherent with their past, that can enable them to be faithful in their new circumstance and to hope for the future.

National ecumenical organizations

No comprehensive national association of Asian-Indian Christians exists even though Asian-Indian pastors meet occasionally in ecumenical gatherings in most metropolitan areas and discuss initiatives to start such associations. A Federation of Indo-American Christians was organized in reaction to the perceived threat to Christianity posed by the so-called Freedom of Religion Bill before the Indian parliament (Lok Sabha) in 1978. The proposed bill was a response to mass conversions to Christianity in the northeastern area of India, an area that now sends several people for education in the United States. These converts were primarily persons from the *dalit* and *adivasi* communities, and leaders charged Christianity with "buying converts." The bill included a "prohibition of conversion from one religion to another by the use of force or inducement or by fraudulent means and for matters incidental thereto."

Christians feared that the true intention of the bill was to make conversion to Christianity impossible. The Federation organized rallies and protest marches to Indian consulates in America to protest the bill. After the bill was defeated and the election defeat of the government of Prime Minister Desai, the Federation weakened and died. The Hindutva movement in India in the 1990s has not yet aroused a similar response.

Three groups held their first "annual" conventions in the summer of 1993 and form nascent movements toward a national Christian identity with two foci: India and North America. The North American Consultation of South Asian Christians met at the Billy Graham Center at Wheaton College and seems to represent the conservative evangelical section of the Asian-Indian Christian population. The coordinating office for this consultation is in Canada. The Fellowship of South Asian Christians in Texas is a similar evangelical ecumenical movement on the state level that held its first convention at a Methodist Church in Dallas in 1993. The National Association of Asian-Indian Christians in the USA met at Hofstra University in New York. Each of these groups gathers several hundred participants for a weekend of meetings, but they do not yet have the level of commitment and participation or the infrastructure that would identify them as national associations of Asian-Indian Christians. The Christian immigrants are in the process of establishing many levels of Christian institutions segmented by diverse strategies of adaptation, and it is not clear if or when they will be prepared to attend to national Asian-Indian Christian associations.

STRATEGIES OF ADAPTATION REVISITED

The first part of chapter 3 presents a typology of six strategies of adaptation employed by Asian-Indian Christians. The reality displayed among the religious groups portrayed in the intervening pages is much more complex and dynamic as individuals and groups mix and match various strategies to meet different situations by manifesting first one and then another aspect of their evolving identities. Strategies of adaptation are malleable to meet the diverse needs of a growing population. Which strategy or elements are dominant in a particular group depends on many things: on the tradition, history, and theology of the religion; on vagaries of the current situation in the United States; and on the conscious decision of members and leaders of the group regarding both their own future and that of their children. One should not underestimate the role of individual initiative, creativity, and leadership in this process. The result is a rapidly changing kaleidoscope of strategies creating many distinct Asian-Indian Christian groups and institutions.

The six strategies discussed above nevertheless represent parameters that define the process of adaptation of Asian-Indian groups which was introduced in chapters 3 and 4. Together they provide a road map of intersecting lines along which it is possible to locate at any given time most of the Asian-Indian religious groups both socially and religiously. It seems clear that the directions in which the adaptation of the new immigrants is going will not result in a reprise of "the melting pot" or "the triple melting pot" described as typical for earlier immigrants (see p. 27). Adaptation of elements of these strategies, even those with the most narrowly conceived ethnic or denominational boundaries, does not function primarily to separate persons from the rest of the population, but to form the gate through which the immigrants can enter more effectively into the society and to enable their descendants to be good citizens of both the Kingdom of God and the United States of America. In chapter 5 the basic challenges that these strategies are marshaled to meet are raised topically, and then chapters 6 and 7 explore the effects these Christian immigrants and their families are having on the church in both America and India.

Wilderness, exile or promised land: experience and interpretations of migration

How shall we sing the Lord's song in a foreign land?

Psalm 137:4

An Asian-Indian doctoral student in an evangelical seminary explains that his calling is to go back to New Delhi to be an evangelist because the city resembles Corinth in the first century in which migrants from all over the world gathered. There old patterns of life were broken and old associations, customs of the extended families, and previously dominant institutions were in disarray. That type of situation provides, he argues, the best context for preaching the gospel. His fellow student perceptively interjects that the same could be said of American cities that now exhibit a similar diversity and also shelter people who are attempting to create new homes, spiritual as well as physical, in urban settings, out of the shards of their diverse pasts. Such reorientation spawns theological reflection.

Migration is for Christians from India both a disorienting and a theologizing experience as they attempt to preserve, reshape, and create anew personal and group identities in the face of competing claims and pressures. Timothy L. Smith notes that immigration to the United States has throughout its history produced significant alterations in theologizing about the immigration experience and in the relationship of religious commitment to ethnic identity (1978:1161–65). As immigrants are forced to determine how to act in relation to their customary behavior, the ethos of the dominant culture, and the shape of many competing subcultures, they have in all periods of American history interpreted behavior and experience in religious terms. Smith indicates that migration causes redefinition of identity through three initiatives. First, a redefinition of peoplehood, usually in religious terms, creates new boundaries that create solidarity with a newly formed group not identical in its shape or in its goals with any group previously existing either in the old or new location. Second, immigrants experience an intensification of the psychological basis of theological reflection and ethno-religious commitment. Uprooting and resettlement are moving emotional experiences – separation, loss, trepidation, fear, disorientation – that for many immigrants result in strong religious commitments. That may explain why a majority of the immigrants from India belonging to various religions report that they are more active in religious affairs in the United States than they were in India. (See data on religious activity on page 45 and Williams, 1988:177.) Third, the new context revitalizes the conviction, at least of those with a biblical foundation, that the goal of history is the creation of a common humanity. Smith indicates that the last two initiatives create a strong dialectic between ethnicity and religion so that the goal of the unity of humanity is juxtaposed to intensified religious commitment and to sharply drawn boundaries (1978:1161).

Similarity to the cultural setting of the Mediterranean world of the first century is striking. A new world-order and increased mobility involved a breakdown of city states and princely states and the creation of a new expanded world view. The old mediating institutions were weakened or thrust aside, resulting in new emphases on individualism and on universality. Establishment of individual freedom, personal identity, and meaning of life in the new ecumenical ("in one house") setting of today provides both an opportunity and a burden. Creating a corporate identity within a group that provides the basis for individual expression, group loyalty, and ecumenical commitment is now the challenge for every immigrant group. Ultimately it requires communication and compromises among the various groups reconstituted through migration to establish new working relationships within the civic order. It is common for commentators on the first century to refer to this challenge as the *preparatio evangelia*, similar to the struggle of the Jewish people throughout their migrations to create their identity as a people of God. Immigrant churches serve as mediating institutions in the dialectic between the diversity that holds the seed of a common humanity and the need for corporate construction of a defined community of faith and values.

Migration is enormously disruptive and creates special strains on the preservation and transmission of religious traditions. (1) It creates new minority groups through voluntary association in new locations that posit a presumed common cultural descent. (2) New communities take shape governed both by impersonal push/pull factors that determine who is selected to migrate and by personal decisions about what religious alternatives to pursue in the new context. (3) Affiliation to newly formed groups involves a reshaping of personal and group identities. (4) The religion carried by the immigrant and its religious symbols are transformed and have new meanings and contexts, so that the Christianity of Asian Indians is "assembled in the USA" from materials mainly processed in India. (5) Religious specialists perform different functions and "enjoy" a different array of status positions than in India. (6) Religion helps shape both minority identity and the negotiations with the majority community regarding status, identity, and opportunity. Smith overstated the case when he argued that what Marcus Lee Hansen called "immigrant Puritanism" owed virtually nothing to colonial New England, but was rather a predictable reaction to the ethical and behavioral disorientation that affects immigrants (1978:1176). Nevertheless, the demonstrated need for most immigrants to give expression to their experience in religious terms and to attempt to shape their future in religious communities does provide a recognizable Puritan cast to immigrant religions that is revitalized by the arrival of new immigrants.

MODELS OF INTERPRETATION

Much of the preaching and teaching in Asian-Indian congregations is exposition of the Bible, so the Bible acts as the template onto which the immigrants project their experiences and which brings coherence to their very different journeys. Such exposition both interprets the experience and at the same time shapes it, so that a circular hermeneutic of experience develops. Three important experiences from the Bible are prototypical models for interpretation of migration: the Exodus with Moses wandering around the wilderness, the Exile with Daniel striving to be faithful in the lion's den, and the Promised Land of every pilgrim trying to reach Zion.

"Let my people go!" is the primary text for Jewish and Christian theological reflection on the experience of exodus from oppression. Every migrant leaves some form of security of home and established patterns to venture into the unknown, but the security left by modern immigrants may not be that of the shackles of tyranny and slavery nor the voyage a search for democracy or freedom. Many earlier migrants and others who experienced deprivation or discrimination adopted the symbols of exodus to picture their oppression under the Pharaohs, both ancient and modern, and to express their divine right to freedom and security. A strong theological movement in India shapes a form of liberation theology, called "*dalit* theology" out of the experience of untouchables and low-caste Christians (Webster, 1992). "New Christians" converted from the *dalit* and *adivasi* communities make up a majority of the Christians in India, but they live in real hardship and face discrimination from both the "old Christians," who claim descent from Syrian immigrants to India or from Brahmins, and the majority society, which excludes them from compensatory preferments established by law. A majority of the theological students in Indian seminaries are from the oppressed communities (some 40 percent in the prestigious United Theological College in Bangalore), and a form of liberation theology influenced by Marxist thought finds expression in contemporary Indian theological debates and writings.

Elements of liberation theology appear in the rhetoric of immigrants, especially in the early stages after arrival when many must struggle not with any oppression in India but with the feelings that they are unsettled, facing an insecure future, and harassed by antagonistic neighbors whose territory they approach. They sing about being tempted to return to the "fleshpots" of security and pleasure they left and about moving forward in the great struggle to make a place for themselves in a new land. Marxist-based liberation theology does not provide, however, the dominant model for interpreting Asian-Indian experience for two reasons. First, the development of *dalit* theology in India occurred in the absence of the immigrants. They left India before *dalit* theology became a widespread interpretation of Christianity in India, and now the basic shape of that theological movement is weakened by recent events in Europe with the breakup of the Soviet Union, and in China. Hence, the *dalit* theology movement is in a process of reorientation in India. Even if Asian Indians in America wished to become involved in that rethinking, they would not be permitted to do so. From the perspective of Indian liberation theologians, the immigrants are those who have taken the advantages they gained from educational and professional opportunities provided by the Indian government and have sold out to capitalism, consumerism, and materialism by emigrating to America. It is as though Joseph's descendants had retained their lofty positions and then left the rest of the Hebrew slaves in Egypt so they could enjoy prosperity and the good life in the Promised Land. As one theologian explained: "We lose our right to speak about Indian theology when we come to the United States. It would be different if I had become a missionary teacher in another developing country."

The second reason that liberation theology does not work for most of these immigrants is that they do not come from the *dalit* or *adivasi* communities. Most of them claim a relation to the Syrian Christians or higher-caste associations and they come from families with at least sufficient status and wealth to provide for them the educational and professional advantages that enabled them to immigrate. Liberation theology is contextualized in India and is rooted in social class. Hence, it is not readily available to explain the experience of immigrants. They are part of the elite brain-drain, not "your tired, your poor, or your huddled masses." Indeed, some of the rhetoric about their status both in India and in America is tinged with class and caste consciousness. This is especially so when they plan for marriages. The new immigration to America seems to call for a different model of theological interpretation from that of much European immigration because the status of these contemporary elite immigrants is so different both in India and in the United States.

The call to sing a song of Zion in the midst of an alien culture brings forth the lament, "How shall we sing the Lord's song in a foreign land?" It captures the sense of exile, living among people who worship other gods and who cannot understand the language or the melodies of Zion. Although the Indian immigrants thought they came to a Christian country, they experience moving from their homeland, where the church was often a dominant force in their families and social groups, to exile where Christian values and symbols are muted and ignored. Christian immigrants feel under siege in an alien culture made all the more threatening because it appears as a "false friend" wearing some familiar trappings of Christianity. Different churches, indeed, individual congregations have various experiences of relation to the culture, somewhat on the lines of Niebuhr's "Christ in culture," "Christ over culture," and "Christ against culture," but many of the immigrants feel that their Christian identity and that of their children are profoundly threatened by the alien culture in which they live (Niebuhr, 1975). This experience is heightened because Asian-Indian churches are urban churches, and many members live at least for their first few years in America in the midst of urban decay – having moved from the villages of Kerala to New York or Chicago. The families feel beset like the children of Israel in exile in the fiery furnace of Babylon. Many find themselves living a sect-like existence, going out from the shelter of the community only for work – as one immigrant said, "like the Brahmins back home in India." Thinking that their Indian Christian culture is better than American culture, they are tempted to adopt some of the rhetoric of the Christian right, but in this case the longing for the "good old days" has a geographical location in India.

Indeed, they share the feeling, with many conservative Christians, that they are excluded from the cultural mainstream because aspects of both exclusion and exclusiveness characterize the community. Even though very successful in many areas, they experience exclusion from some social and religious affairs. One of the reasons that new immigrants start ethnic churches is because they feel excluded from the local congregations. One faculty member in a theological seminary recalled his treatment when he and his family attended the local congregation of the church of which he was a minister in India: "We were always treated as guests and not as members of the family. You cannot survive as a guest in a church." Therefore, he and his family attend services at the university chapel because, he said, "Even if people don't say, 'hello,' you don't think anything about it." A layman said that he has been a member of a local congregation for five years, but he will never become an elder because he is "brown." Many such stories of exclusion are told with real sadness by Christian immigrants. Many Asian-Indian Christians struggle with that challenge of living as exiles in an alien culture.

As protection from elements of the alien society, the immigrants erect exclusive boundaries in the attempt to protect themselves and their families from threats from assimilation. The nature of the exclusiveness depends upon which of the potential adaptive strategies dominates. One approach is for India, and especially Kerala, to assume in the rhetoric the character of a sacred homeland. The church is viewed by many of the adults as the means by which the children are to be socialized in traditional Indian ways by sacralizing Malayalam as the sacred language, Kerala as a sacred land, and the extended family as divinely instituted. One university professor explained the attraction of the language: "If I worship with Indians, I want to worship in Telugu; it is no fun to worship with Telugus in English." Here, ethnic boundaries define both the religious community and the social circle. It requires a strong counter-pressure to break those ethnic ties in those locations where the population is sufficiently large to sustain ethnic churches. Such strength to break down ethnic barriers is attributed to the power of the Holy Spirit in some charismatic churches. Indeed, being "born again" breaks many previous allegiances and establishes new criteria for leadership, new patterns of behavior, new rituals, and a new community. The power of the Holy Spirit breaks down dividing walls, but it also establishes new boundaries that include "brothers and sisters" and exclude the alien world. Every Indian Christian group is in the process of boundary creation and maintenance, and most try to maintain a delicate balance by creating sturdy boundaries that will assist in establishing personal and group identity and that are at the same time sufficiently porous to permit sufficient freedom and effective relations within the dominant culture.

America is viewed by many modern immigrants as the Promised Land "flowing with milk and honey." As one Gujarati bishop remarked, "Most of my people think that heaven is there." America is etched on the minds of many Christians in India as "the city set on a hill," as *the* Christian nation. Missionaries and other visitors to India extolled the civic virtues of the United States and the Judaeo-Christian ethos undergirding those virtues. Indeed, many immigrants adapt well into elements of American society – church, school, profession – and are at peace with the combination of public secularity and private religiosity. One person expressed this by noting that when he landed in the United States virtually everything was foreign and bewildering, but he recognized the steeples of the churches that made him feel immediately at home. The individual religious freedom and voluntary association that mark American religion provide the opportunity for new initiatives in Christian faithfulness, whether that means establishing new forms of Indian Christianity or merging by various paths into the Christian body politic.

Immigrants often remark that their relatives in India believe that the streets in America are "paved with gold." Indeed, immigrants from India do not come to escape oppression or to gain religious freedom, but to take advantage of economic and professional opportunities. Even though some have fallen through the cracks in the midst of economic recession, so that they can neither stay comfortably in America nor return without shame to India, most of the immigrants have been immensely successful, prospering beyond the wildest dreams of their friends and relatives in India. American incomes take on unreal proportions when translated into a rupee economy. The immigrants generally came from economically secure strata of society, but in America they are *nouveau riche*. One of the challenges for the new immigrants once they are well settled is to deal with the new affluence. "I've been poor, I've been rich, and rich is better" reads the sign on the office wall of a new immigrant, but that disguises the difficulty of the transition and the necessity of giving meaning to wealth and interpretations to the opportunity wealth provides.

As the ancient Israelites discovered, it is almost as difficult to live and be faithful in the Promised Land as it is in the Wilderness or in Exile. Several injunctions can be heard regularly in the churches: "Your parents have sacrificed to provide for you the opportunities available in America, work hard to take the best advantage of them." "You have achieved great wealth, so you should contribute to the poor and needy in India through your churches." "We have the most beautiful tradition of family values that we must exemplify for others to emulate." "We have to stop being so self-centered and contribute more to the society here." "We must stop taking so much and giving so little to our new homeland." "We must preserve Oriental forms of Christianity as part of American Christianity." These injunctions do not, however, constitute a compelling theological statement of mission for the Asian-Indian churches. The people have been so busy establishing their families and then their church institutions that they have not had time for adequate theological reflection, nor have the churches raised up theologians capable of providing serious analysis of their current situation and guidance in the quest for meaning. The theological reflection on contemporary immigration to America remains a task for the immigrants themselves, one most likely to be completed by their children.

One pastor spoke about a concept of a "Holy Homelessness" as a model for theological reflection on the experience of the first-generation immigrants. It incorporates aspects of pilgrimage that are common in many sacred stories. The homelessness that new immigrants experience is geographic, social, and spiritual. They are unlikely to be completely at home in America no matter how successful they may become, and they are not able to go home again to take up their lives in India. They are indeed caught in the marginal state and are forced to make sense of their existence without the theoretic structures taken for granted elsewhere. One professor said, "People like me have become so bi-cultural we are not at home anywhere, but it does bring a certain kind of critical perspective." It is precisely in such marginal states that, in analogy to the biological ecosystem, the most creativity takes place. The new immigrants since 1965 may be prototypical of a new transnational world-order characterized by increased mobility and rapid communication that will place much of the world's population in marginal states seeking for a theoretical framework, perhaps a theological interpretation, for discovering meaning in their holy homelessness. Reflections of Asian-Indian Christian theologians about their experiences could have a more universal application.

For now, however, Asian-Indian churches face immediate problems of adapting to life in America, and they do so by facing real challenges of self-definition that they meet by making concrete decisions about issues that face the church. A Jacobite bishop tells a story to illustrate the situation: "When the new rains come and the rivers of Kerala are rushing with new color and fresh sediment, the fish are very active and enjoy the fresh water without thinking about the future drought. America is like a new stream for the Indian people, and they are caring for themselves without a clear vision of what is coming." Whatever theological statement arises from their experience will be contextualized in the tensions and conflicts that develop in the process of forming congregations, building churches, establishing dioceses and institutions, and trying to remain faithful to the gospel as learned in the past and envisioned for the future. The issues are many, here summarized under four topics: transmission of tradition through ritual and words, gender differentiation, transition of generations, and leadership.

TRANSMISSION OF TRADITION THROUGH RITUALS AND WORDS

A young man who came from India with his parents as a small child is no longer able to converse in an Indian language, but he stands watching a video tape of himself at 5 years of age speaking to his parents in a language he has now forgotten. Such amnesia is at the heart of the process of forgetting and remembering that is the transmission and reformulation of tradition in immigrant communities. Each of us recognizes that the image of the baby one observes in a carefully preserved family album is both oneself and not oneself in ways too deep for words. Yet the continuity and discontinuity between the past and the present provides the fragile basis on which people project and attempt to weave a future. It is no less so for Christian immigrants from India as they face the difficulty of preserving a living tradition for themselves and transmitting it to their children. Nothing is static, not the individuals, the tradition, the community, nor the life stage; rather, the process is a complex stream of associations moving through time. Remembering and forgetting in many groups by thousands of people gives shape and substance to the stream. No one can step into the same stream again, it has been said, and, given modern technology, all can imagine viewing themselves speaking a language they no longer know. Nevertheless, the transmission of tradition is the most central of human activities. Robert Petty explained:

[Life is] a relay race of generations. It requires that things, which in themselves are insignificant, are passed, at times rather desperately, from one generation to the next. At the least, it is the transfer of a tool, a skill, a craft; at its grandest and most dangerous because most vulnerable, it is a way of seeing the world – a world that goes on and on, seen from a life that is once and only. (Petty, 1985:30)

Parents and leaders grapple with the question of how to transmit effectively the Christian tradition they learned in India to the children raised in America to enable them to mature as Asian-Indian Christians. Three modes of communication of cultural messages are through written and oral language, the communicative aspects of customary behavior in gesture or ritual, and the modification of material culture into symbols. Word and ritual are two dominant elements of Christian tradition, and religious groups distinguish themselves by giving priority to one or the other. Some believe that the communication through verbal and written discourse is most effective, and therefore emphasize the Word of God, a preaching ministry, the Sunday School, and study groups. Others emphasize ritual, the symbolism of ancient liturgy in movement, color, and sound. Certainly, all Asian-Indian Christian groups employ both modes of transmission – like a person desperately trying to give a warning by shouting, raising a red flag, and waving hands in the air – but the various groups can be placed on a scale based on their relative emphasis, reaching from the Brethren emphasis upon the word at one end to the Syrian Orthodox reliance upon ritual at the other. One extreme is the fundamentalists' reliance upon the written book to the neglect of both the oral tradition and the rich symbolism of ritual, which one bishop compared to the Gnostic heretics because "they published books and engaged in false interpretation thereby dividing the church." At the other extreme, conservatives and evangelicals accuse those who rely upon "empty ritual" of being only nominal Christians without any personal knowledge of either the words or gesture language of the liturgy.

The ability to communicate in a common language creates both a significant boundary for a group and the strongest emotions of internal coherence leading to group bonding and commitment. The reason given by most first-generation immigrants for choosing to participate in an Asian-Indian congregation is the opportunity it provides to "worship in my native language," or "to meet and talk with my friends in Tamil/Malayalam/Gujarati." Hence, the words in the native language in both the liturgy and in social intercourse are conducive to loyalty. The second most common reason for participating is to help their children gain an appreciation of their cultural heritage. These two goals create a dialectic resulting in several types of speech acts in worship services and social occasions similar to experience in churches of earlier immigrants.

Older immigrants remember when the change took place in the verbal language of the liturgy, from Syriac or Latin to the Indian languages, and some Asian-Indian services still preserve snatches of Syriac as the sacred language of Jesus. Parents can remember worshiping in a liturgy that was considered a sacred language and recognize that their children face a situation where Malayalam, Tamil, or Telugu is becoming a sacred language. The difference is, however, that in the earlier situation the distinction was between the priests who understood the meaning of the sacred language and the laity who did not, but now the distinction is between the parents who understand and the children who do not. Parents remember that they did not understand the Syriac, but nevertheless grew to love Christian services, and hope that their children will come to love the services in Indian languages that they only partially understand. Some churches conduct all their meetings in Indian languages, while others make a distinction between liturgical speech (usually in an Indian language) and non-liturgical speech (often in English).

Other concessions are made to the decreasing fluency in Indian languages by both the elders and the youth. Leaders often overlook the fact that adults lose some of their native language fluency when it is used only for minimal communication within the family or that they grow increasingly less confident of themselves when they must speak to larger groups in more formal contexts. A bishop gives an example of a Keralite officer of a congregation in north India who was so embarrassed when forced to display his inability to read aloud a church notice in Malayalam that he left the congregation to join an English-speaking Anglican Church. One Telugu congregation has developed a kind of antiphonal style in which the leader starts in Telugu but changes back and forth into English depending upon the responses given by participants in Bible reading, prayers, or answers to questions. Extemporaneous prayers, testimonies, and reading of Bible verses are offered by the older participants in an Indian language and by the youth in English. A few pastors give a running English summary of points of their sermons, and some have translators who give a sentence-by-sentence translation. This latter style develops its own staccato rhythm and power that, when well-done, moves listeners of all ages. A common pattern is that services of worship are in Indian languages, whereas most programs of Christian education are in English. It is becoming more common for Asian-Indian churches to have services in English. One model is to have one or two services a month in English; another in larger congregations is to have an early service each Sunday in English – for the young people, it is said – and the second service in an Indian language.

Translation is a curious problem for this group of immigrants because they come from a country where a form of English is one of the two national legal languages. Hence, virtually all are reasonably fluent in the English language. They share English fluency with most of the other recent brain-drain immigrants who studied in English as well. A problem of translation remains, however, because English in India is British English modified as it developed independently over the past half-century. The assumption of similarity creates misunderstanding similar to that caused by French "false friends" – words that look like English words but have different meanings. Indian English is not American English, so materials prepared in English in India do not meet the needs of American-educated young people. It is more than a matter of words and syntax; it involves the entire context. It is worth noting that the points in an English conversation or a speech at which the speaker reverts into an Indian language occur when the speaker wishes to joke with the audience or to refer to a part of the liturgy. Joking and liturgical expression embody a complexity of hermeneutical ability that makes translation difficult. English lessons, liturgies, Sunday School materials, and stories prepared for people educated in English-medium village schools in India seem almost as foreign to youth in American cities as if they were in Malayalam or Gujarati. Material prepared by denominational and commercial presses in the United States are readily understood, but they do not convey the subtleties of Indian Christianity. Parents may be fluent in some specialized segments of English – for example, intricacies of medicine or engineering – but not have the facility to communicate the subtleties of Indian Christian theology and practice in a form of English familiar to their children. Several of the churches have appointed committees or instituted programs to prepare appropriate curriculum material, but it is difficult to know how to communicate across the cultural chasm. Immigrants and their children are caught between cultures and do not have a language adequate for that marginal state. They are forced to make do the best they can with communication in a mélange of languages.

Ritual is the communicative aspect of customary behavior, and its syntax is as rich and complex as that of a language of words. Asian-

Indian young people have as much difficulty appreciating and learning the elaborate symbolism of the Syrian Orthodox or Syro-Malabar Catholic rites as young people of other churches have with their own. They complain that the services are "too long," "too elaborate," or "too boring" because they understand neither the Indian languages nor the symbolic complexity of the liturgy. Not having alternate experience for comparison, most conclude that the difficulty of appropriation is an aspect of migration and stems from unfamiliar aspects of Indian culture. It is true that some ritual elements dealing with color, movement, shape, sound, and food are influenced by the centuries of Orthodox Christianity in India, but there is much else beside. The arrangement of physical space so that the mysteries of the Qurbana occur behind a screen, sometimes just a sheet strung across a stage, is part of the Eastern liturgy and not an Indian adaptation. The beauty and power of the ritual do prove effective for some even though they may not be able to explain details of interpretation; for example, the censer as the womb of Mary, the fire inside symbolic of Jesus, and the chains representing the Holy Trinity. Some leaders and parents argue that it is not necessary for people to be fluent in either the language or symbolism of the liturgy in order for it to be efficacious. They expect priests from India to perform the liturgy well with the same beauty and power they experienced growing up in India, but they hope that the priests or others will also be able to interpret the meaning to the young people so that they will share their allegiance to the ancient rites. They trust that a combination of "things said" over "things done" in the liturgy will provide a coherent message of the Christian faith.

Part of the attraction of the charismatic movement is the revaluation of both language and gesture in Pentecostal meetings. Ecstatic speaking in tongues involves a deconstruction of speech and its elevation to a level removed from domination by either Indian or American syntax. The formulaic speech patterns, involving much repetition of simple paradigmatic statements, do not require long training or great expertise to employ or appreciate. Pentecostals tend to devalue ritual as "empty gestures" even though the gestures in Pentecostal meetings are highly stylized and shared by the entire congregation, involving arm gestures, a holy movement in a type of sacred dance, physical manifestations of "slaying in the Spirit," and interjectory responses. The emotion embodied in these is complex, but the array of gesture acts is relatively small and simple and transcultural so as to permit easy appropriation by people with a wide range of interpretive skills. A hermeneutic of the heart and emotions, rather than of the head and the intellect, revises the standards of excellence in communication that certify persons for leadership. Immigrants and their children are on a more equal footing. Leaders of the high church traditions note that some of their members, especially the youth, seem to be attracted to the lively music, friendliness, and high emotion of charismatic gatherings. What may be a major attraction is the accessibility of the relatively simple languages of word and ritual they encounter in the meetings. The charismatic movement seems particularly strong among people who are moving between cultures, classes, and social settings, in short, among people at the margins who are uncomfortable in the set forms of communication in more stable settings. The attraction is the deconstruction of forms of syntax that places marginal people on an equal plane with others in the communication and appropriation of meaning through ecstatic speech and gestures.

Many of the youth are in near-rebellion against both the linguistic and cultural trappings of the religious services. One high-school student argued with the vehemence and self-righteousness of youth in a church magazine: "Youths do not want to hear that crap about the Malayalam language epitomizing our great Keralite Indian culture because the only culture that we youths accept is the norms, rules and regulations of Jesus Christ! The life and teachings of our Lord God Almighty is the only culture we need" (Ninian, 1993:31). While few would make such a stark distinction, the Asian-Indian Christian community is struggling to determine the essential core of the Christian faith and the cultural appurtenances, both Indian and American, that overlay and/or enhance the message.

Indigenization

The issue raised thus far is that of indigenization, but it is not clear exactly what that means in an immigrant group bearing a specific form of Eastern Christianity into a setting of Western Christianity, all the while creating a new form of Christianity within an ethnic group. Immigrants adapt their traditional genres to new settings and invent new forms for strategic incorporation. Such stability and change is a dynamic interplay of balancing available cultural and religious resources with demands for relevance. Creative flexibility in selecting symbols and in selecting strategies used to relate those symbols to current contexts is the manner in which ethnicity is shaped and transmitted. Stephen Stern summarizes, "Symbols of ethnicity are not merely static products of ethnic culture but are solutions to problematic situations" (Stern and Cicala, 1991:xi–xiii). Indigenization can be viewed as the concerted effort to reconcile age-old words and rituals with the distinctive symbols of different ethnic subcultures (Christiano, 1991:182). Three contexts of indigenization are relevant to the immigrants: in India, in American culture, and in an ethnic subculture.

Indigenization is an ancient reality in India captured in the oft-repeated saying that St. Thomas Christianity is Christian in religion, Oriental in worship, and Indian in culture. It is not always evident to one inside a culture how much of the cultural garb has become integral to religious thought and practice. When asked about Indian or Hindu customs that have become part of Christian practice, immigrants generally recall first some aspects of life-cycle rituals – a vegetarian meal to break a fast after death of a family member, a hair-cutting ritual for a small child, the tying of a *tali* ornament by the groom around the neck of the bride. Baths and fire have significant roles in the cultic life of the community, and the use of special flags, flag posts, decorated umbrellas, musical instruments, and other paraphernalia in processions make them almost indistinguishable from Hindu festivals. Nevertheless, a common attack on Christianity in India is that it is a foreign religion. A parallel attack on missionary practices made in liberal Christian circles in the West is that missionaries were involved in a cultural imperialism of importing a westernized form of Christianity into India.

A modern response has been a movement of indigenization that both severs ties with Western denominations and attempts to reclothe Christianity in Indian dress. Several churches, of which the Indian Pentecostal Church is the most prominent, claim that they are indigenous, founded by Indians and not reliant upon foreigners for either direction or support. An ashram movement attempts to plant deep roots in Indian soil by adopting indigenous dress, calendars, ritual objects and gestures, language, and customs. The most prominent leader of the ashram movement was Bede Griffiths, a British priest who went to India as a missionary in 1955 and joined the Saccidanand Ashram in Tamil Nadu. He summarized his life's work in an autobiographical note, "I have come, therefore, to see that the Indian Church, in the words of the founder of our ashram, Jules Monchanin, has to be neither Latin nor Greek nor Syrian but totally Indian and totally Christian" (Griffiths, 1984:8). Critics react negatively to the movement as advocating a dangerous syncretism, especially when it leads to reverence for Hindu texts, yogic meditation exercises, Hindu *bhajans*, elevation of Hindu and other Indian heroes (gods), and Hindu cultic practices. A Syrian priest argues that it does not make sense to impose Hindu elements onto Indian Christianity when it has a history of almost two millennia in India whereas classical Hinduism is a relatively modern construct of Western scholars. Thus, the ancient "rites controversy" about the propriety and limits of indigenization rages on in India.

Modern mobility raises new issues on the old theme, however. What does it mean for Indian Christianity to adapt to American Christianity? One strategy would be to excise all the Indian or Oriental elements and to replace them with American rituals, music, customs, and ethos. The result would be a complete assimilation. In India, liberals favor aspects of assimilation of Christianity into Indian culture, whereas in America liberals oppose the loss of ethnic identity through assimilation. Thus, the tables are turned. It certainly is the case that neither Christianity nor any other religion appears naked; it is always clothed in cultural garb in ways that make it difficult to distinguish the religious core from the cultural garb. Incarnation is always involved.

Foodways provide an analogy because the preparation of food is always a cultural act never divorced from social expectations. Foodways always send messages. In the 1970s and early 1980s, Asian-Indian Christian gatherings in the United States regularly included sumptuous Gujarati or Keralite meals prepared in as authentic a manner as local ingredients permitted. Currently, gatherings still conclude with a meal in the fellowship hall where one table of Indian food is surrounded by the immigrants and a second table holding submarine sandwiches and spaghetti attracts the young people. A few people move from table to table, selecting items according to personal taste developed by a wide array of associations in school, neighborhood, and at work. It is too soon to predict if Asian-Indian Christianity will eventually preserve its distinctive Indian characteristics or will assimilate fully into dominant forms of American Christianity, or even what such assimilation would mean.

It is erroneous to assume that one American Christianity or one Indian Christianity exists. Rather, a creative flexibility of cultural expression results in a variety of subgroups, and Stern advises that observers remain sensitive to fine shades of ethnic attachment, to the processes of tuning in and out, to the converts and the disenfranchised, and to numerous subethnic groups that influence adaptation (Stern and Cicala, 1991:xiii). Indigenization in its first stage means adapting Christian faith and practice to the needs of a newly developing set of ethnic groups in America, not yet Asian-Indian but rather still Tamil, Telugu, Gujarati, or Malayalee. The negotiation has both horizontal and vertical dimensions. Horizontal negotiations with other subethnic groups and with a dominant group that is rapidly shrinking into a minority status establish what is effective both in preserving personal and group identity and in establishing recognition and effective relations with other groups. Vertical disagreement and negotiations between the generations within the immigrant community lead to judgments about what promises to be most effective in maintaining some unity among the generations and preserving the young people within the church and the community. Each church bears in its life and work an array of strata of indigenization as it has adapted in each century and generation to new circumstances.

Music

Music in Asian-Indian churches is a potpourri of styles, both within an individual congregation and across churches from different traditions, that provide a measure of past and present cultural influences on the community. Music is a specialized form of communication as an eclectic union of word and ritual. It is common for a congregation in one service to move from a solo in Carnatic style, to an English hymn in Western notation accompanied by an organ, to a Tamil hymn accompanied by a harmonium and drums, to a Western chorus sung by the youth playing guitars. The strata of musical styles in language, tunes, and theological affirmation are somewhat bewildering and reveal a relatively unstable and undefined musical repertoire that characterizes most of the churches. Hearing the English revival hymn "Are you washed in the blood of the Lamb?" in a Saturday night prayer service in a Syrian Orthodox Church causes one to ask how that hymn and musical style found its way into that service. Likewise, hearing the chorus "We are one in the Spirit" taught by college students playing guitars and drums in a youth conference raises the same question. Churches are both conservative and eclectic regarding musical styles. The conservatism of earlier immigrants was noted by Marcus Lee Hansen in a note about a bookseller in Bergen who had too many copies of hymnals which had been superseded in the Norwegian churches and sent them for quick disposal to congregations in the United States (1942:83). A distinction is made in several traditions between liturgical music (on which conservative influences are strong) and non-liturgical music (more open to eclectic

development). For example, the Orthodox Qurbana has distinct traditional chants, but prayer services and youth meetings are non-liturgical;
Brethren Assemblies reject instrumental music in the Sunday service but
permit it on other occasions. The conservatism and eclecticism preserved in strata of musical styles and evident in the immigrant churches
traces a history of intercultural contacts that continue as immigrants
adapt to American society.

The history of church music reveals the diversity of cultural contacts
in India. Although the Syriac language has given way to Malayalam in
the churches of Kerala, both the East Syriac and West Syriac chant
modes are used in the Syro-Malabar Catholic and the Syrian Orthodox
Churches. The West Syriac form of liturgical music has eight modes that
are used in a prescribed rotation, and it is very difficult to translate the
music of the Qurbana into English. The churches also sing in the South
Indian Carnatic style and the North Indian Hindustani style that are
also common in the Hindu *bhajan* music. These styles are more commonly used for solo performance, and seem not so well adapted to
congregational singing. South Indians do not encourage Hindustani
singing, but it is used in some ecumenical gatherings. In some cases the
Indian musical style is used to set words composed in Indian languages,
and at other times it accompanies words translated from English.
Missionaries introduced Western notation, instruments, hymn tunes and
texts, and emphasized congregational singing. Thus, a store of Western
hymns, songs, and choruses were already part of the repertoire before
immigrants came to America, but an exact account of what was known
before immigration and what was added in America by each group is
not available. Contemporary church music in India is shaped by film
music, which is a popular distinct genre. Loudspeakers and radios
broadcast film music incessantly across Indian villages and cities, and
cassette tapes of both secular and religious music in that style are much
in demand. Relatively few Christians are familiar with musical notation
in either its Indian or its Western forms, so there are no standard ver-
sions of tunes, which vary considerably from church to church. These
immigrants face a greater challenge than did earlier immigrants from
European countries who shared the same musical notations and har-
monic systems even though the languages and styles were diverse. Traditional *talas* and *ragas* in India are different from Western rhythm and
tonal scales. Musical styles continue to change in India, change speeded
up by dramatic media developments in the past decade. The latest pop
styles are available on video tapes and through satellite transmission of

Western channels such as MTV. These add new strata of musical styles, such as rap music, which influence church music at first because of their popularity among the young people. Ravi Shankar collaborated with Yehudi Menuhin at the United Nations Human Rights Day concert in 1967 and with George Harrison at Woodstock in 1969, in gestures symbolic of the fact that cross-cultural transmission and amalgamation of musical styles is increasingly a result of modern mobility and telecommunication.

Immigrants bring all that music with them, choosing from that storehouse and borrowing from the storehouses of other American churches to create a new pattern. Church music requires a group of skilled people, generally outside the clergy, to preserve, transmit, and create a musical tradition. Instrumentalists adept with several Western and Indian instruments, composers of both tunes and texts, vocalists, and teachers who can instruct and inspire good congregational singing are needed for every church. In India the context supports music in both Indian and Western styles, but in America there is little cultural support of Indian-style music, so the churches face a difficult challenge in preserving that musical heritage and passing it on to their children, who may not be able to understand the words in Indian languages even if they can sing the tunes. Leaders recognize the need for assistance to bring an effective coherence to their musical programs. A professor of church music in the Old Seminary in Kerala spent several months of 1991 in the United States leading workshops on music in Malankara Orthodox congregations, but the churches carry on without a resident expert on Indian church music. Annual conferences are occasions for reviving Indian musical styles as well as invigorating the use of Indian languages. They also provide the locale for negotiation of the extent to which Western tunes and texts will be incorporated into the life of the churches.

Thus, a rich and sometimes bewildering mixture of musical styles is present in Asian-Indian churches. The question remains of what influences have created the particular constellation of musical styles in any congregation when it is clear that elements were brought from India and others were adapted in the United States. A two-tiered system is often observed when youth dressed in jeans and sports shirts, playing Western instruments, lead songs in English for the first part of the service and their fathers dressed in suits, playing Indian instruments, lead songs in an Indian language during the rest, or when parents sing and pray in Indian languages upstairs while their children sing and pray in English downstairs. Will they ever come to "sing the Lord's song" off the same page?

How are the various styles learned and transmitted? What are the agents of change? In what contexts do Christian immigrants and their children sing with other Christians in ways that influence their worship? Following those networks provides information about the process of adaptation and assimilation.

The following contexts provide networks where intercultural transmission of musical styles occurs. (1) Asian Indians attend worship services in established congregations of the dominant society and become increasingly competent in the verbal and musical vocabularies. It is common for a family to attend an established church regularly and attend an Indian church in the evenings or on one Sunday of a month. The family thus becomes a conduit of cultural exchange. (2) Asian-Indian parents send their children to daily Vacation Bible Schools in one or more churches and encourage their children to attend Christian youth gatherings. Here the children learn songs and choruses similar to those popular in camps and conferences. (3) Multiethnic congregations use a variety of musical styles in worship, including African-American and Caribbean. People who gather at annual conferences of the Brethren Assemblies and the New Testament Church (Ceylon Pentecostal Mission), teach one another new hymns and songs. (4) Ecumenical cooperation among Asian-Indian Christians provides occasions for sharing and learning from other ethnic groups. In the early days of immigration, people from various church groups gathered for Christian worship and taught each other a broader range of Christian music from India than any church possessed individually. When congregations gather for ecumenical services, such as the Keralite Christmas Programs, each congregation provides a choir or other special music for the program, and those gathered sing songs in several styles. (5) Youth develop as church musicians by participating in evangelical youth organizations such as the Campus Crusade for Christ and the Intervarsity Fellowship. One youth leader remarks that most of the youth who are fully involved in the life of the immigrant churches – like those playing guitars and drums and leading singing at annual conferences and youth conventions – have been influenced by their experience in evangelical campus organizations. Most of the other youth, he observes, have become inactive or left the churches. The immigrant churches tend to be conservative in both theological and social matters, and involvement of the youth in evangelical activities enhances that conservative tendency. (6) Television evangelists and the music in TV religious programs have a significant influence on immigrant Christians, both in inculcating the evangelists' condemnation of American mores and society and in assimilating elements of American evangelical Christianity, including its musical styles. One should not overlook the influence of television programming on the socialization of both immigrants and their children.

Music provides an illustration of the complexity of the transmission of religious tradition and of indigenization of religion among highly mobile communities. In an Evangelical and Reformed Church founded in Oklahoma by immigrants from Germany, the men's choir sang Christmas carols in German well into the 1960s, but that and an occasional greeting in German were the only occasions for the use of the native language of that immigrant church. A cultural and religious assimilation encouraged by the ethos of the times and the wars against Germany led to a gradual loss of ethnic identity. Indigenization in that context meant assimilation. Recent immigrants, at the end of the century, enter a society that seems currently to place a high value on ethnicity and to encourage preservation of elements of ethnic culture. Moreover, they are operating in a new context of communication that encourages development of transnational forms of music and ritual that have roots in the Indian community reaching from several regions of India. It is unclear what indigenization of Asian-Indian Christianity will come to mean in this context and what forms of word and ritual will be most effective and appropriate.

GENDER RELATIONS

A great divide separates women from men in most Asian-Indian churches. Men sit on the left side of the aisle facing the altar, the women on the right. Men and boys are at the front serving at the altar and pulpit, all the women are in the pews. Although a handful of Asian-Indian women are ordained in America, none serving as pastors of Asian-Indian congregations were identified in this study. The physical separation would seem to symbolize firm social boundaries and clearly defined gender roles, as indeed it did in India. India has a firmly hierarchical social structure in which the gender roles are clearly defined, and fathers and husbands assume dominance and authority. A head nurse who administers workers, including several men, in an American hospital, remembers that in India she would never sit in front of her father and speak. Husbands were responsible for providing for the family, and until well after Indian independence it was rare for upper-class women to work outside the home. When people in the community extol the family values that Indians offer as their contribution to American society, some have in mind the relatively calm social structure created by clearly defined and accepted roles. The seeming tranquility of the separation of women from men in congregations hides a turmoil of social change and gender role reversal that is inducing conflict and changes in both Asian-Indian families and churches.

Large-scale movements of people carry the potential for changing women's status within families and communities because migration transforms household structures, sex ratios, and marriage patterns in both sending and receiving communities. Women enter the work force to provide additional resources for immigrants to establish security. Families are divided and adopt a nuclear family residential pattern, and the absence of in-laws frees both men and women from restrictive expectations. Thus, migration across international boundaries involves a shift in socio-cultural systems in parallel with a change in gender strat-ification systems (United Nations Population Fund, 1993:29). (See Kibria, 1993:108–43, for analysis of gender relations among Vietnamese immigrants.) These changes take on a distinctive character in the Asian-Indian Christian community because, as detailed in chapter 1, so many of the women gained immigration permits as nurses. No other segment of the Asian-Indian community experienced a pattern of migration in which women took the lead. The nearest parallel is the Filipino Christian community, a large segment of which was created in the United States through the immigration of nurses (see Guillermo, 1991). More distant parallels are the current migration of Hispanic and Caribbean women to work in menial service jobs and the earlier migra-tion of African-American women to work as maids in northern cities. Nevertheless, the role of women in the Asian-Indian Christian commu-nity is distinctive.

Nurses occupy a dominant position in immigration. They entered as graduate students or were recruited to work in urban hospitals and gained the green card, the much-sought-after ticket to permanent resi-dence. They entered alone and, if married with family, worked for months or years to earn sufficient income and status to sponsor their hus-bands and children to join them. If unmarried, they generally returned to India for marriage negotiations in which their worth was greatly increased because their permanent resident status brought with it the almost immediate entry of the husband and eventual rights of immigra-tion for members of the extended families. Whereas previously nurses were not prime candidates for upward mobility through marriage, a secure job in the United States, incredibly high income viewed from an Indian perspective, and the opportunity for establishing the family in America enhanced their marriage prospects. Their daughters were and are much sought after by men in India searching for brides because they offer the opportunity to immigrate. Nurses sponsored siblings and other relatives for immigration, so that tracing the network of an extended family or congregation often leads to an "immigration matriarch" whose decision to immigrate ultimately led to a much larger community of family and friends being formed in the United States.

Asian-Indian Christian women enjoyed higher wages, greater job security, and higher prestige than the men. Although some of the men gained entry as professionals – of the 394 men in a survey of Asian-Indian Christians, 17 are physicians and 79 are engineers or in applied science – anecdotal evidence suggests that in most of the Christian families the women earn a higher income than the men. Some of the men had relatively prestigious but low-paying positions in India and are underemployed in the United States; hence, male underemployment is a significant problem. One man had a master's degree in history and taught in a college before he joined his wife, who is a nurse, but his degree was of very little value in finding a position. He took the only job open to him in a fast-food restaurant. In a hardy attempt at humor, he joked, "I fell from being a college professor to making french fries." He subsequently joined the Methodist Church and became a lay preacher. Low pay and insecurity came with their entry-level jobs. In the early 1980s many who had gained a foothold on the lower rungs of the ladder lost their jobs in the recession that hit the northern cities in the "rust belt" and the southern regions due both to the oil crisis and the recession in the aeronautical industry. A congregation in Houston began construction of a new church building, and six months later half of the congregation had lost their jobs, primarily the men. Such job insecurity was novel for men from India because, although India and especially Kerala has a high unemployment rate, those who have jobs keep them for life without lay-offs or dismissals. Many of the men are by now quite successful after starting businesses or retraining for occupations, many of them in the health care system, but they were supported through the tough times by the secure incomes of their wives.

A woman working as a management trainee makes astute observations about her difficulty adjusting to the expectations at the office. She points to what she calls "the nature of Malayalee corporate thinking" to explain that in India most important decisions were made – marriage, occupation, immigration, for example – as group decisions within the extended family. Rarely were important decisions made through individual initiative. That differs from the individualistic American model that she calls "a market mentality." Hence, she says that in the corporate world she takes longer to make a decision than others and is always found waiting for agreement and approval before taking initiative. Her tendency is generally to focus on the group rather than upon the individual in decision making. She sees values in each model of behavior and is torn between the two, pushed at home and church into joint decisions where others take the lead and urged at work to take individual initiative. She concludes, somewhat simplistically, that the West defines through individual initiative, but the East leaves mystery through the process of making joint decisions.

These Christians point with justifiable pride to their close family relations and to family values that they exemplify. Most of these families seem exemplary in the manner in which they are successful in combining the best of traditions regarding families they brought from India with the opportunities and freedom in America. They appear to be close, loving families who are doing a better job than most in coping with the pressures of American society. Nevertheless, leaders view with apprehension the growing tensions in the families. A bishop who visits his churches in America often speaks about "the inferiority complex" he runs into frequently among the men. They are not able to provide for their families as their tradition expects and they therefore feel that they are "living off their wives." Some moved to the United States with false expectations about what they would be able to accomplish for their families both in the United States and back in India and are bitterly disappointed and ashamed by their underachievement. Their wives move more freely among male co-workers and are perceived to share levels of intimacy that, while innocuous by American standards, would be unheard of in Indian society, creating apprehension and jealousy. Wives overwork themselves, often working a night shift in the hospital and taking on a second job, which means that husbands and wives have little time for themselves or together with their children. A pastor reported that a major difficulty is that members in his congregation have an understandable but unhealthy yearning for wealth. They have not learned to live with the "lure of affluence." The absence of a close extended family provides freedom for the couple to work out problems without interference, but it also means that they have little assistance in coping with child care and tensions that develop. While divorces are as yet relatively rare occurrences in this community, rumors of divorce appear as the dark cloud preceding a destructive deluge that will weaken the very foundation of their community. It is possible to view these as difficulties arising from systemic immigrant structures, and not simply as individual personal problems resulting from individual flaws.

Such tensions are not unique to Christians in the United States, but are developing in India as well. Women gain more freedom through educational and professional opportunities and some earn more than their husbands. Their children are stretching beyond the boundaries of traditional patterns. Indeed, bishops and other leaders in India are trying to marshal their resources to provide services to families in distress in the United States. Although many Asian-Indian pastors there have training and occupations outside the churches as counselors and undoubtedly do confidential counseling in their churches, little else has been done in a formal way to meet the challenges to families there. One bishop sent a person from India to conduct marriage and family seminars in his churches. Discussions about establishing counseling services, telephone hotlines, and special seminars for families occur in virtually every conference, but it proves difficult to establish structures and regular programs when the communities are so scattered. Such programs require ecumenical cooperation across urban areas, but the institutions are not in place to implement them.

Everyone complains about disputes and politics that seem omnipresent in Asian-Indian churches. Youths accuse their parents of teaching them more about group politics in the churches than about theology or devotion. Schism and conflicts are present in both local congregations and national organizations. One cause may be related to the same endemic systemic issues that create tensions in the families.

A bishop reflects upon the fact that the church is one institution in which immigrant men can seek to gain status and ego satisfaction denied them in other social contexts. As bishop, he was attempting to mediate a dispute in a local congregation and asked one of the protagonists to sit down and be quiet. The layman later remonstrates: "My wife is a nurse and is making a good salary, but I had to take a job paying less than what it takes to provide day care for my children. Nevertheless, I took the job so my friends will not make fun of me for being supported by my wife. Because my wife provides in the home, I have little authority or respect there. I have a small job and I cannot speak out where I work. And now, bishop, you are not letting me speak out at church." Governing-board

meetings and diocesan committees are arenas in which the men attempt
to gain recognition and status by using their Keralite, Tamil, or Gujarati
skills honed in India. One who has only passable public speaking skills in
English may be able to move a crowd in Malayalam; one who has little
opportunity to exercise leadership at work may aspire to election as president of a congregation or chair of a diocese. Whereas in churches in
India the exact definitions of leadership, and the structures for its validation, are fixed and well understood, in America no such fixed structures
exist, which encourages conflict over leadership. The bishop concludes
that many of the disputes have less to do with the substance of the matter
than with feelings of inferiority and the need of individuals to gain status
and ego satisfaction. He proposes that the churches discover ways to
provide creative avenues for positive status enhancement for all the
immigrants, both male and female, both youth and adults.

The split scene at a family conference was one of pandemonium.
Adults seated on one side of a partition with men and women separate
argued in Malayalam about the role of women in the churches, and on
the other side, college-aged young people seated in a circle discussed the
same topic in English – voices raised in anger, tears on the cheeks, inter-
ruptions, laughter, rudeness, conciliation, bishops caught in the middle
moving gingerly among two divided groups. Women in this church were
not arguing for the right to become priests, as few of these upwardly
mobile families have that as a goal for their children, male or female, but
the women were claiming their right to be members of governing boards
and committees, to have a greater say in church affairs, and to participate in the Holy Qurbana in ways laymen are permitted to do.

A great majority of the churches in India from which immigrants
come organize themselves by family units. Thus, the churches even in
America report their membership by families, not by individuals,
because each family has one vote in church decisions. (How a church
counts members is significant, and both of these differ from the calcula-
tion of financial support "by pledging units" so common among
American churches.) The old hymn would have to be sung as "Win them
one family by one family" rather than "one by one." It is customary in
India that the male head of the family serve as its representative on governing boards and other church bodies. Unmarried children and widows
have little legal status in society or in church except through fathers or
brothers. Collective membership in most of the Indian churches is
threatened by the pattern of individual conversion propagated by some
evangelical and Pentecostal churches. To be "born again" or "filled with

the Spirit" is an intensely individual experience based on propositions that call into question the membership basis of many of the immigrant churches. A bishop vehemently opposed rebaptism of individuals because that denied family solidarity and the efficacy of the parents' action at infant baptism. The principle of family solidarity in church organization may perpetuate a patriarchal pattern that underlies the nascent administration of Asian-Indian congregations and dioceses. It is driving a wedge between men and women, between adults and youth, and between the churches in the United States and the leadership in India.

Women are active supporters of the church – one pastor estimating that 80 percent of the money in the offerings comes from wages of women – and they are active in the educational and service work of the congregations, but they are increasingly uncomfortable with their second-class membership. They argue their case on both theological and practical grounds. The older women debate gently, saying that, if a man and a woman become one in holy marriage, it is just as appropriate for the woman to take leadership positions as for the man. Moreover, they argue that it is not wise to ignore half of either one's human resources or one's market. The younger women tend to be more blunt – as one said, "If you want to be more than a one-generation church, you must change." Changes are taking place – slowly. More women and young girls take positions of leadership near the altar, at the lectern, and in the pulpit in local congregations. Two of the dioceses invite women to join men in governing-body meetings, even though this practice is permitted *de facto* rather than being mandated *de jure*. No woman currently serves as pastor of any of the Asian-Indian churches in this study, even though thirty-six women are preparing for some form of church ministry (thirty-one in theological seminaries or divinity schools and five in Bible colleges). Only four are identifiable as permanent residents in the United States (two Lutheran, one Mar Thoma, and one IPC Pentecostal) and only one, a Lutheran student, plans to be pastor of a local congregation while one plans to become a missionary in India. Nevertheless, these women trained in American theological seminaries will precipitate changes in gender relations in the churches.

Women speak of their agitation for rights in the church by analogy to the civil rights struggle of African Americans. Some older women, they say, are willing to move slowly and urge cooperation within church structures in order to bring about change, following the model of the Revd. Martin Luther King, Jr. Some of the younger women are more restless and strident and quote the call of Minister Malcolm X for change "by any means necessary." Asian-Indian Christian immigrants began to enter the United States at a time of dramatic change of American thinking and action regarding ethnicity and assimilation. They are forced to reshape their personal and group identities in a context where what it means to be an ethnic and religious minority is evolving. The nurses and their families have begun to establish their families and their roles as wives and husbands at a time when gender identity and status is in flux. Hence, they face a double difficulty, like jumping without much of a parachute from a moving plane into the torrent of a river.

TRANSITION OF GENERATIONS

A major reason immigrants give for establishing churches and religious institutions is to assist them in socializing their children as Indian Christians in American society. The time when congregations begin to develop is when a sufficient number of the children of immigrants reach the age when they move out of the home to be influenced by peer pressures at school. That is the point when they come into meaningful contact with people "not like us" whose presence calls into question the plausibility structures that support identity developed within the Indian families. Asian-Indian Christians do not live in ghettos, so they have little assistance in their neighborhoods. Parents search for assistance and strategies to help their children know who they are in a larger world and, therefore, they congregate in churches. Young families of internal migrants moving to suburbs tend to do the same, and it seems likely that most new congregations come into existence to serve families at this stage of development. The number of children playing in a changing neighborhood or new suburb is probably the best index of the viability of a new congregation. Intense desire for effective Sunday Schools and youth ministries is present in the Asian-Indian Christian community because they have so few support agencies in the secular sphere.

Personal identity is a social construct molded from individual and corporate memories and current perceptions of reality and potentials. Memory, reality, and potentials often exist in creative tension in the definition of values in all communities, but especially in an immigrant community because of the greater discontinuity between the past and the present. The transmission of religious tradition is an attempt to preserve in a definable context with transcendent bases a unity of a past in memory, the present in reality, and a future potential, and the terms in which this process is couched are generational. The attempt to maintain a unity and continuity between the generations has three generational foci. (1) Parents in India are authority figures for a form of socialization and religious behavior that greatly influence immigrant parents in their attempts to raise their own children. When immigrants tell stories about India, their parents seem larger than life, wise in their judgments, devout in faith, and diligent in parish activities of devotion and worship. Their parents were active in making decisions about what careers they would enter and about who would emigrate and when. They are the past personified, and continue to exercise influence both direct and indirect on decisions of immigrants. (2) New immigrants arrive all the time and renew the integration of the Indian past and the American present that the immigrants who arrived twenty-five years earlier experienced. (3) The children are the future, and the greatest anxiety in the community is about whether the children will be able to maintain the continuity that will lead to a healthy personal and group identity. Most Asian-Indian churches are concerned with these issues internal to the community, and very few – perhaps an occasional Baptist or Pentecostal church – are evangelistic in reaching out to those who are not engaged in the same struggle for identity and generational continuity.

The concept of "generation" is a cultural construct created out of, and useful primarily in, analyzing the American experience. What would it mean, for instance, for an Englishman or German to say he or she is a member of the fifty-first generation? Werner Sollors points out that generational metaphors serve both to shape interpretations of consent and descent in American culture and to construct a sense of kinship and community upon the descendants of heterogeneous ancestors. He concludes that when Americans engage in generational rhetoric, they leave history and enter "the myth of America," which "perpetuates one cultural moment, freezes the historical process into ahistorical conceptions and into metaphors of timeless identity as sameness" (1986:210, 234). Generational rhetoric is widely used in transethnic discourse and in analyses of ethnic movements and is useful as an instrument of cultural criticism and as a rhetorical device that creates a sense of cohesion among a diverse population, but it should be noted that "generation" defies measurability when dealing with several dynamic communities. The numbered generations become ideal types, useful for metalevel discussions but rarely isolated in a pure form on the ground. Still, the tensions developing between immigrant parents and their children are discussed within the churches in generational terms.

The Cambridge University anthropologist, Meyer Fortes, spoke often about the "living present" that is the subject and boundary of a researcher's work, constituted by the grandparents, the parents, and the children found in any village. They provide the data, including the grandparents' living memories of the past, Fortes argued, that are the resources for an ahistorical analysis of the social structure and life of any small-scale community. The generational "living present" of the new immigrants admitted after 1965 is foreshortened. The first generation includes those who immigrated as adults over 18 years of age. (Note that the age is established in immigration law, but that the period of youth in the Indian community stretches to around 30 years of age. Indian youth conferences and meetings include people much older than in youth groups typical of other churches.) The experience of those who immigrated with their parents, as children already having their early socialization in India, is sufficiently different to require a separate designation as the "first and a half generation." They faced a wrenching separation and difficult adaption to new cultural patterns at a "pint-sized level" at the same time their parents struggled with monumental difficulties in establishing themselves and their families. It is often the case that the eldest in families, especially the eldest son, experiences extraordinary pressures to conform to social pressures and to excel, but pressures on the entire first-and-a-half generation were and continue to be intense. The second generation consists of the children born in America to immigrants from India. Their entire socialization occurs in America, and they are for all intents and purposes American children. If one is the eldest in the family, the pressures to succeed are great, but the brunt of that storm has already been borne by their elder cousins. The third generation is just being born and remains blissfully ignorant of the challenges facing it.

One reason the generational lines become blurred is that new first and first-and-a-half generations are entering all the time, so that the generations no longer age through the stages together, as was the case during the period of the lull in immigration. New immigrants renew contacts with Indian culture and churches and complicate relations between the parents and children who established themselves earlier. It appears that the United States is one of few countries that will allow continued large-scale legal migration and also offer citizenship, so that the pool of first-generation immigrants from India will be constantly renewed, and Christians will continue to be a significant minority of those immigrants. Each of the generations has its own personal development requirements and meets those needs in a variety of social contexts. Immigrant churches provide a primary location for meeting, and adjudicating among, those requirements.

The acronym "ABCDs" conveys in humorous discourse the confusion of American children of Indian immigrants and some of the tension between the generations. "American-Born Confused Desis" they are called, using the Hindi word "desi" referring to compatriots from a native area. The confusion is real and is displayed in dramatic fashion in the story of Dave.[1] He was born in the United States to parents who were in graduate school and was raised in an American environment. He was very bright, finishing high school at the age of 16, and his parents sent him to Bombay for college. He reports living a "double life" in Bombay, ceasing to be a Christian, falling in love with a Hindu, and having great difficulty adjusting to life in the "jungles of Bombay." He was unable to communicate easily in the midst of the language diversity of India because, he said, "my mother tongue is American English." He returned to a series of colleges in America, has attempted suicide three times, and brought a Christian from an ethnic group different from his own to be his wife. He summarized his experience with the confession, "I just didn't know who I was." The example is extreme because he returned to India for study, thereby moving physically between two cultures in ways that other children of immigrants move psychologically and socially between two worlds. His peers among ABCDs appear to be much better adjusted, psychologically and socially, but great stress is present. They jokingly throw a different acronym in the face of recent arrivals, calling them JOBs – Just Off the Boat – and tease them for still wearing Indian dress, not being able to speak colloquial American English, and not being able to fit in comfortably in American youth culture. They may or may not realize that they are making statements about the behavior of their parents a decade or two earlier.

A priest points to a conflict of values as endemic in the relations between the first and second generations. The parents have a memory of India now twenty years old, and they try to establish that set of values and customs. Their children are immersed for five days a week, at school and related activities, in American culture which promulgates a different and often conflicting set of values. The young people are very confused about values and about how they should live. It would be relatively simple if the young people were permitted to select one or the other set of values, but that is not the case. They are expected to excel according to standards and values established by both cultures. They should be willing to implement group decisions of the family, effectively employ Indian gestures of respect toward their elders, speak an Indian language with a facility that will permit meaningful conversation within the family and bring honor to the parents, and be able to follow and participate in the Indian-style worship service at church. At the same time, they should be at the top of their school class, popular with their peers, leaders in social activities, and able to represent the family well in community affairs. A great deal of secrecy and shame are involved as young people are afraid to let parents know what they do away from home and ashamed to reveal too much of their family life to their friends. In short, they have a double responsibility to bring honor to the family in both the Asian-Indian and the dominant societies. It is a heavy burden, and occasional stories of youths who crack under the pressure circulate within the community.

Each problem is general in character, but specific in experience. All parents and children experience similar tensions because of cultural changes through time. Can a child learn to play and explain both Mozart and Nirvana? Certainly, tensions between the generations have been common throughout American history, and the development of the generational rhetoric is a way of organizing and explaining them. Nevertheless, these immigrants and their children perceive their experiences as resulting from their unique situation, as being a particular experience of Asian-Indian Christians living in late twentieth-century American society. Indeed, at one level their experiences are unique to themselves, but, though it may be only bittersweet comfort to learn, the experience is shared by others as well.

Churches are the primary forum for naming and addressing these problems, so some of the joint meetings of parents and children in congregations or at family conferences are fraught with contentious debates that end with both parents and children weeping and, perhaps, praying. The reason is that the church is the only inter-generational association where serious discussion of values, goals, and problems takes place. Nowhere else outside the family does an organization provide the opportunity for inter-generational group discussion of these significant issues. Hence, although the church appears to be the locus of the conflict, it does in fact provide the primary locus of conflict resolution. One reason is that, viewed from one perspective, an appeal to transcendent authority undergirds the parents' authority to impose a set of values learned in India so that a detailed exploration of that transcendent authority is necessary if parents are to be comfortable changing their minds. Viewed from another perspective, loyalty and obedience to a transcendent authority is essential in bringing a common judgment against the unnecessary strictures of both cultures. The young man mentioned above was appealing to that type of transcendent authority in an argument with parents when he said that the only culture that the youth accept is the norms, rules, and regulations of Jesus Christ and that the life and teachings of our Lord God Almighty is the only culture they need. That appeal to transcendent authority is evident in intense and emotional discussions among Asian-Indian Christians and in the attention they give to fundamental theological issues such as biblical authority, the relation of scripture and tradition, doctrines of creation, anthropology, atonement, and ecclesiology. Here theology has practical effects in shaping the values that parents and youth are able to share. In the Syrian tradition, the wedding service installs the bride and bridegroom as priests for the family, but they have little training for that priestly function and the practical theological questions they face.

Beyond the theological grounding of values and lifestyles, several priests say that the specific contributions the church makes to the negotiation between the generations are in developing parenting skills and communications skills. Discussions by parents in the church revolve around how to raise their children and how to deal with disagreements and rebellions. A laywoman who is in one of three Asian-Indian families attending a mixed Brethren Assembly says that she values the opportunity to learn from experienced Christian women how to bring up children in America. Others appreciate the opportunity to discuss with other Asian Indians the specific problems they face. Invitations to seminars on parenting are both attractive because of their relevance and threatening because of the intensity of the problems involved and a reticence to reveal internal family affairs. A bishop quotes the title of a popular book on parenting as the challenge Asian-Indian Christians face: *How to raise PG kids in an X-rated society*. Both parents and children confess to needing assistance in communication. Both are so busy that little time or energy is available for careful discussion of conflicts and misunderstandings. Children are afraid to reveal honestly, and parents fear the worst and are afraid to hear it. Moreover, parents and children speak languages different in more ways than one. Children speak a little Malayalam or Gujarati, and parents speak a modest amount of English; neither is adequate to explain or to understand the subtlety of the issues before the families. Laughter and crying are universal messages, but innermost feelings, desires, and fears require great facility in a shared language for expression. In a recent survey, 90 percent of the Asian-Indian young people interviewed said that their parents were "extremely unaware of the pressures and dilemmas they face outside of the home" (Agarwal, 1991:57).

Four issues that create tensions and the potential for a clash of values are regular topics of conversation at church gatherings: (1) family and friendship, (2) dating and marriage, (3) career selection, and (4) respect for elderly and parents.

Family and friendship

It is simplistic to say that parents value family whereas children value friendship, but a dialectic between the two is one way of explaining a set of tensions between the generations. A survey of Asian-Indian parents (120 people) and their children (120 people) examined what they were most interested in retaining about Indian culture; in the first order of value, family was listed by 96 percent and religion by 75 percent (with some who were interviewed obviously giving more than one response), indicating considerable agreement about family values (Agarwal, 1991:41). In traditional Indian society, especially in Kerala, the family is the primary unit, and relationships with relatives dominate attention outside work. One immigrant illustrates the point by referring to his family in India: "I have fifty first cousins who live in close proximity; who has time for friends?" Energy is reserved for family. A result of that tradition is that parents in the first generation do not have friendship as a major operative category. Whereas in India they lived in the midst of an extended family, many of whom participated in the same parish, in America they feel isolated and live what one bishop calls "anonymous lives." They do not often visit socially in the homes of Asian Indians outside their extended families, except on formal ceremonial occasions, and they are rarely well acquainted and at ease socially with the parents of their children's friends. Even if researchers are eventually invited into closer personal associations, they enjoy a fictive family designation as "uncle" or "auntie." A youth noted, "My father doesn't talk on the telephone with anyone outside the family unless it is to arrange a prayer service." Hence, the immigrant parents have little contact with the wholesomeness of much of American family life; their attitudes are shaped by what they see presented in the media, which terrifies them and makes them even more protective of their children. A young woman laughs about her brother's frustration when trying to instruct his parents about how to develop friendships in America. One youth remarked that his parents' generation carry in their minds a mistaken view of Kerala from twenty years ago and a false view of American society derived from television, so they are doubly removed from reality in helping their children interact positively with their friends.

The children interact with other children who are also isolated from extended families and for whom friendship is the primary category of relationships, so the young people invest a tremendous amount of time and energy in establishing friendships. Parents are torn because they want their children to succeed and be popular at school, and, indeed, an inordinate number are leaders in their school, both academically and socially. When the young people display fondness for friends and monopolize the telephone for hours, however, it is incomprehensible to the parents. In angry exchanges they accuse their children of disloyalty: "You care more about your friends than about your family." The points at which the dialectic reaches a fever pitch are conflicts between parents and young people over the dual potential in dating: a common expression of friendship and a process of marriage selection, the foundation of family solidarity.

Dating and marriage

Two fathers standing near the pool of the hotel at a family conference observed boys and girls talking casually, touching, and "hanging out" and noted, somewhat wistfully, "When we were their age, we were not permitted even to talk alone with a girl; it was considered a sin." Dating is considered an alien and dangerous practice by most adults in the Asian-Indian Christian community. The traditional practice in India is for the two candidates for a marriage arranged by the parents to meet only briefly prior to the wedding. Even more progressive parents understand dating as a process in which parents select several girls whom the boy can meet, perhaps for a day, so the young people can make a marriage decision. The American practice of casual relationships and long-term dating is viewed with alarm and is prohibited by most parents and discouraged by all. Young people socialized in America see nothing wrong in dating and feel excluded from significant contexts for developing and maintaining friendships with both boys and girls by their parents' "old-fashioned ways." Secret dating of a sort is commonly admitted by young people, but the deceit tears at their relationships. Girls feel that they are more restricted and carefully guarded than their brothers, accusing their parents of discrimination and favoritism. Most American parents may approach Prom Nights with some trepidation because of accounts of drugs, alcohol, and sex, but approaching Proms create flashpoints of conflict about dating in Asian-Indian Christian families. A priest was called in as mediator after a young man dutifully asked his parents for permission to attend the school Prom and permission was denied. The son was so distraught that he ran away from home. Another priest recalls an example of what he termed "an arranged Prom." The parents reluctantly compromised by agreeing that their daughter could attend the Prom, but only if they could select the date and negotiate with his parents some appropriate guidelines for the evening. The model is, of course, that of an arranged marriage, which burdened the scene with more cultural baggage than either of the young people would have desired.

Priests report surprisingly few weddings in their churches, but the number is bound to increase. Most of those in the first generation who were not already married when they immigrated went back to India to arrange marriages and to bring their spouses to join them in the United States. A few found marriage partners among other immigrants, and fewer still married out with people from other racial, ethnic, and religious groups. Anecdotal evidence suggests that a significant number of the first-and-a-half generation go back to India for marriage and that the pressure is often put on the eldest son to do so. Members of the second generation are just reaching what has become the accepted age of marriage – the late twenties – so the marriage patterns for this group are nascent. One change in marriage practice, both in India and the United States, is that families are delaying weddings until young people finish their educational and professional training, which changes the dynamics between parents and children regarding marriage. A 29-year-old scientist is less malleable than a 17-year-old. Informal concentric circles of endogamy are always present in the minds of parents as they picture the ideal prospect for marriage to their children, but few have as much direct influence on actual choices as Asian-Indian parents expect to exert.

Three types of marriages are discussed in the churches. The first option is to return to India to arrange a marriage with someone in the same community. A young couple laughed in good humor about their fright during a first and definitive meeting arranged in India by an uncle. The man returned to India for two weeks during a vacation from work to meet a series of young women and was prepared to ask a series of questions that he and his friends had prepared. He walked in the room to meet this woman and was surprised that she was "so modern" because she wore her hair short. They talked for about an hour as he went down his list of questions in a formal manner; she remembered stumbling over the question, "Why do you want to live in America?" and he explained his reason for the question was because unrealistic expectations about life in America are common. Following that meeting he asked his uncle to arrange the marriage, extended his vacation by a week, married the girl, and arranged for her to follow him back home. Criteria of caste, education, profession, dowry, and income are significant to such negotiations. Several young men in an informal conversation indicated that their parents encouraged them to attend the Christian family conference so they could become acquainted with families of potential marriage partners, but said they would probably go back to India to arrange marriages because "girls in America are too outspoken and forward," "they have gone out on dates," and "girls in India are more traditional." When asked if the young women had put themselves at risk in the marriage process by demanding rights in the church, the young men answered, "No! They will find someone; perhaps they will go back to India for marriage." Many young women born and raised in America fear going back to India for marriage. If they have to stay in India, the adjustment to expectations there is overwhelmingly difficult for American girls; if the man wishes to come to America, the fear is that the reason for the marriage is simply to gain a passport to America. The differences in expectations regarding dominance and submission and relationships are so great between a man socialized in India and a woman socialized in America as to create great difficulties of adjustment.

Fewer of the ABCDs are in fact going back to India for marriage, so the second option is to arrange for marriage within the Asian-Indian community. The number of eligible and desirable marriage partners in America increases each year, and networks in India weaken as marriage contacts become dormant when more of their family members move to America. Although some parents attempt to use church networks in India, most search in America. Again, parents try to take the lead and desire marriage candidates from within the same ethnic and religious community. Marriages create relationships between families of which the relationship between the couple is only a part. Marriages are mechanisms by which families broaden their extended families and establish important working relationships. Finding appropriate marriage partners for the individuals and contacts for families is difficult both because the

Table 8 *Second-generation sample: fields of study*

	Male	Female
Medicine	38%	30%
Engineering & related fields	25%	16%
Business	32%	25%
Other fields	5%	29%

Source: Adapted from Agarwal, 1991:46

networks are new and ill-formed in America and because the standards of expectation regarding education, income, family status, and prospects are not yet fixed. What can a Syrian priestly family expect in return when they put forward a handsome or beautiful newly qualified MD with admission to a residency program in emergency medicine? No one knows what the market will bear in America. Some of the young people are relieved not to have to find a partner, but most desire that theirs will be "love marriages" rather than "arranged marriages." What comes as a relief for most parents and young people is a "semi-arranged marriage" in which a couple meet and decide that they want to get married and then ask the parents to make the arrangements – arranged love marriages. A few churches place primary emphasis on marrying within the church group; some place it on marrying within the Syrian community, so there is significant intermarriage among Jacobite, CSI, Mar Thoma, and Syrian Catholic young people. Next in preference is marriage with an Asian-Indian Christian from a different regional–linguistic group. Very few Christians marry Muslims or Hindus, and such marriages are strongly opposed by the parents.

Last on the preference list of parents are intercultural and interracial marriages. First-and-a-half-generation children of early immigrants in the late 1960s and early 1970s did not have many marriage options within the community, so if they did not go back to India they entered love marriages, primarily with Caucasians. Only the New Testament Church (CPM) encourages interracial marriages as examples of the Kingdom of God. Priests of other churches currently report occasional mixed marriages between Caucasian, Jewish, Hispanic, Korean, and African-American partners. Most of these couples leave the Asian-Indian congregations for other churches and are increasingly alienated from Asian-Indian affairs. Some churches allow priests to perform such weddings; others prohibit sacramental recognition. Parents have strong prejudices regarding their fears of intermarriage with the various ethnic groups that some children judge as an un-Christian imposition of casteism and racism from India. Parents counter with rumors that circulate in the churches of bad marriages and instances of divorce in cases of such marriages, stories that function to reinforce some level of endogamy.

Peter Berger notes that, when a young American couple on a date sit in a car in the moonlight and talk about marriage or living together, they think they are making free individual decisions, when in reality the whole scene is constructed by unseen social pressures too numerous and too strong to calculate (Berger, 1963:85–7). Similar, but more explicit, pressures influence Asian-Indian decisions, made clearer but perhaps more difficult because of the distinct patterns of marriage that are juxtaposed for the community. The Indian Christian summary is "You come to love the person you marry!" not "You marry the person you come to love." Indeed, one is hard pressed to demonstrate that the latter produces more wholesome or long-lasting marriages. Couples across the two and a half generations in Asian-Indian churches display a remarkable level of dedication to one another and to the well-being of their families.

Career selection

It is striking to be reminded that most societies, including that in India, are only a generation or two away from hereditary occupations in which sons were apprenticed to their fathers in crafts and daughters to their mothers at home. The ethos in the Indian community is that career decisions are family decisions and that the primary criteria are not personal status, enjoyment, or success, but family honor and security. It is a blessing when all these combine, but the latter are foremost for parents and they do not recognize a broad range of choices. Young people are encouraged to prepare for careers in medicine, engineering, and business. (See Table 8.) Children endure a great deal of pressure and, one must say, significant positive support from parents to excel in academic work as preparation for entry into lucrative and prestigious occupations. Young people who are comfortable with the career paths laid out for them enjoy the best possible encouragement and support from their parents, who spend a great amount of their wealth and energy on the education of their children. Those who desire to make individual decisions to follow less secure or less promising careers face significant opposition and discouragement.

Respect for elderly and parents

Parents wonder aloud in private conversations if their children "will care for us [in the multiple senses of the phrase] when we are old." Family values mean for Indians that the children are obedient to their parents and provide for them when they are old. A small portion of those currently immigrating under family reunification provisions are grandparents because the elder sons bear responsibility for them according to the traditional pattern. Their presence is felt as both a blessing and a problem for all concerned. They tend to take authoritarian positions in families that have become less authoritarian, exemplify aspects of Christian devotion and dedication to families that have become more secular even while being active in the churches, expect daughters-in-law who are working professionals to exemplify homely virtues, and tend to judge both their children and grandchildren by Indian standards. Parents often have to mediate between their own parents and their children, and they read responses of the children as judgments of themselves. They feel like "the sandwich generation" caught between their ageing parents and their maturing children. One describes the situation: "Dealing with the issues of three widely different generations is like handling a balancing act with two legs and a stilt, stretching into three worlds that do not easily coordinate with each other" (Meer, 1994).

That portion of the first generation that first took advantage of the open door when they were in their late twenties are now in their fifties and thinking more about retirement. They are uncertain about the future. Some of the elders talk about returning to India – the convertibility of US dollars and a very favorable exchange rate make retirement there financially attractive – but they realize that their children will never emigrate to India. Moreover, they cannot be sure what reception they will have in India because they have been out of touch for so long, and many of their extended family and neighbors are no longer there. Churches become significant as potential networks for facilitating either return to India or retirement in congenial surroundings in America. Church magazines are beginning to carry articles calling for the establishment of retirement centers and nursing homes for Asian-Indian Christians, which recognizes the fragile character of the relations between the generations in America. Still, the churches try to instill family values that will preserve a close relationship between parents and children that will survive into the new century.

These are the main issues that face the Asian-Indian Christians and which, therefore, precipitate fierce debate and deep theological discussions in church meetings. The primary justification for having distinctive Asian-Indian churches is that they are strategically located at this stage of community development to deal constructively with these issues, and the future viability of these churches depends to a large extent on their response to these troubling issues. The task is daunting because of what one priest called the "three Ds" of difficulty in their current situation. (1) First, most are displaced, not having their own building in which to conduct a program of Christian nurture. Many meet in inadequate converted rental space, and others are guests in the houses of others. Buildings evacuated by other churches and purchased by Asian-Indian churches do not provide the most up-to-date facilities. A few congregations have constructed new buildings, but those are rare. Some leaders discourage investing in buildings when the present need is for programs and the future is so uncertain. (2) A second related difficulty is that the church members are widely dispersed. One pastor spoke of the problems of arranging meetings for nurture and study in addition to the Sunday worship because several of his congregation travel more than a hundred miles to attend and most travel more than twenty-five miles. Most of the congregations in India, especially in the south, operate on a parish system in which members live in relatively close proximity. There they live "public lives" and the community provides strong support for Christian nurture, whereas in America they live "anonymous lives" far removed from such support. (3) The third difficulty is that everyone is distracted. Both parents are employed, some at more than one job each, in order to provide financial security for the family; children are active in a full range of academic and extracurricular activities, which makes life at home hectic; the family is rarely together in contexts where they can deal constructively with the issues raised. Priests and pastors experience some of the same issues in their own families, which both bewilders them and makes them more sympathetic with their parishioners. They too are distracted, however, because a good majority are either employed in secular occupations or are studying for advanced degrees. Moreover, the demands of establishing new congregations and inaugurating basic programs of worship and institutions leaves little time or energy for addressing effectively or in detail some of the most important issues. Hence, provision of adequate leadership is critical.

LEADERSHIP

Priests, pastors, and bishops, like other religious specialists, occupy marginal status as intimate strangers moving among their people. Ordination and consecration set them apart, and symbols that elevate the office, such as ecclesiastical robes, titles, crosses, caps, and gestures of deference, function as boundaries that mark them as strangers outside ordinary intercourse. Many priests in the Syrian tradition were from families with considerable status, and part of the ethos was for them to cultivate a somewhat reserved and remote image. Moreover, some bishops and priests acquire the marginal status of monks through vows of permanent celibacy, poverty, and obedience. It is precisely this designated status as strangers that permits religious specialists entry to community affairs as intimate participants. They are honored guests and participants in the most intimate family occasions, such as life-cycle rituals. They are valued counselors in times of family crises and disputes. It is sometimes a lonely, demanding, and frustrating experience to live as an intimate stranger moving from the margins to the center of community affairs. The religious specialists for the immigrant church become not only symbolic mediators between earth and heaven, but also practical mediators between India and the United States, between parents and children, between the religiosity of an Indian past and the secularity of the American present, and between Christian immigrants and other churches. Hence, they are caught between demands of two cultures in ways similar to members of the second generation, forced to meet two sets of expectations, one Indian and the other American. One priest indicated that his two daughters were his "gurus" teaching him what he needed to know about American youth culture in order to mediate disputes in his congregation.

Most of the Asian-Indian congregations result from the volunteer work of lay people who later arrange for specialized ministries. Hence, laymen have a greater role in church affairs than is the case in India, which creates problems for the pastors. Pastors claim that some of the lay people who knew very little about church doctrine or discipline in India put themselves forward as authorities in America to gain status. A constant tug of war between priestly authority and lay responsibility nags the churches and occasionally breaks out into a conflict or test of wills and strength. The ambiguous status of the clergy is seen in alternations between gestures of respect accorded them and evidences of anticlericalism found in criticisms that they attempt to apply old solutions from India to new problems experienced in America. The variety of types of interaction between religious leaders and the lay people is a most important feature of the evolution of Asian-Indian Christianity.

Leadership is defined by the particular sectarian ethos and the specific local context of the congregation. Each of five types of leadership common in the churches exhibits positive and negative aspects.

(1) The first are full-time priests dispatched from India to serve congregations. These are primarily in the Mar Thoma and Catholic Churches, although the Catholic priests often assist in diocesan parishes where they are located. The value of these priests is that they are generally well trained in India, fully authorized by ecclesiastical authorities, and conversant with the Indian Christian context that shaped first-generation immigrants. Most are temporary residents who expect to return to India after a tenure of three to five years, and they see their motives as pure in serving the church in contrast to immigrant priests and pastors who, as several commented, are using the church to establish themselves and their families in America. Bishops have been occasional visitors, but current growth of congregations is leading to the appointment of bishops to reside in America for a term. Their short tenure means, however, that they never become acquainted with either American culture or the long-term challenges of adjustment their parishioners face. They become remote authority figures for the children as strangers, but not intimately acquainted with their problems or involved in their lives.

(2) The second type are the immigrant priests who were trained, certified, and gained experience in India, but who took the opportunity to move to America. Most have families and secular occupations in America – a handful have become more prosperous than members of their congregations – and they face the challenges and tensions of other immigrants. Their part-time and, in some instances, volunteer service to the congregations is evidence of dedication to their vocation. Because they are serving only on weekends, they have time and energy for only the basic services necessary to define a congregation. Moreover, service in churches in India may not be the best preparation for leading the immigrant churches. Occasional outbreaks of authoritarianism, especially with respect to the youth, are not easily accepted. Arrival of new immigrant priests often results in division of congregations into segments too small to sustain an effective ministry or programs.

(3) A third type are those who entered the ministry as a second career after arriving in the United States. They may have been well educated in

India, but underemployed after they accompanied their wives to America. Their theological training after immigration may have been in undergraduate Bible colleges or in evening seminary classes, and only a few earned the Master of Divinity degree, generally required for full ordination. Nevertheless, they were ordained, often in churches other than those of which they were members in India. The changes resulted from an experience of being "born again," the influence of the school they were able to attend, the intervention of an influential relative, or an invitation from a congregation. Migration offers freedom for occupational change and for switching church loyalties.

(4) A fourth type are those ordained with standing in an Indian church but who are employed by other churches, agencies, educational institutions, or organizations. Many are pastoral counselors, a few serve in ecumenical or denominational bureaucracies, some teach in colleges and seminaries (seminaries in the United States report a total of ten Asian-Indian faculty members), and some in social-work agencies. It is common for these to assist congregations on the weekend, but many are only marginally related to the local activities of the Asian-Indian churches.

(5) The fifth type of leadership is the continuation of the early pattern of lay leadership. Local congregations certify elders and lay preachers and their ministry receives validation by charismatic gifts as defined by the ethos of the congregation. They do not constitute a financial drain on the congregations, but they are rarely recognized as community leaders beyond the confines of the congregation.

One aspect of the leaders' role as mediators between church leaders in India and the immigrants in America is to develop institutional structures that will facilitate positive interchange. Religious migration provides the opportunity for dissolving and reconstituting hierarchical structures, a process currently underway among Asian-Indian churches. Priests and leaders tend to be fairly conservative in doctrinal and moral matters, but are more liberal in organizational matters. The operative words in negotiations of constitutions, appointments, and regulations are "democratic procedures" and "local autonomy." The commonly accepted judgment is that the congregations in America must have freedom from policies, structures, and decisions imposed from India. Clergy and laity agree on this, but it is difficult to develop new patterns that will serve the Indian church well by maintaining in the organization structure itself the best of the Indian past and the American present. One frequent speaker at conferences of young people who tries to mediate the desires of parents to maintain strict Indian discipline and those of youth to demonstrate appropriate freedom described his tenuous position as like a soldier in the Civil War "dressed in the blue blouse of the North and the grey trousers of the South being shot at by both sides."

A key issue facing the churches is the location and type of training required for their religious specialists. South India is one of the rare locations that produces a surplus of pastors, priests, nuns, and monks, so no shortage exists of people prepared to accept a call to serve the church in America. United States immigration regulations and procedures restrict entry to those who have networks supporting their applications, so the churches are not able to make a free selection of religious specialists to serve them. The conjunction of factors of immigration law, existing networks, personal initiative, and opportunities in congregations may not produce the best corps of clergy for the immigrant church, and their leadership is a source of much frustration in the churches. At some point in the development of the churches in America, some think sooner rather than later, training and pastoral experience in India will be viewed as a hindrance rather than a necessity for ministry in America.

The volume of calls for young people in the second generation to enter the Christian ministry increases steadily. Parents desire religious leaders who can understand and influence their children, and some argue that the problem will be solved only when ABCDs are trained in the United States and become pastors and priests. Few parents, however, are willing to encourage their sons or daughters to enter a church vocation rather than medicine, business, or engineering. Thus, the young people receive conflicting messages of institutional encouragement and familial discouragement. Even if young people step forward, relations with American seminaries are tenuous, and schools are ill-equipped to prepare clergy for the churches of new immigrants. Candidates cannot study effectively in India because they are not fluent in Indian languages or familiar with the culture, and immersion in both may not be the best preparation for ministry in their home churches. Nor are procedures in place that will permit certification of ordination and standing that will be valid in both India and the United States. The result for these churches may unfortunately be the situation found in other transnational churches in which the clergy is divided into two or three segments by education, income, social standing, language, and commitments. Future leadership for Asian-Indian churches will depend to a great extent on American church colleges and seminaries and on the willingness and ability of these institutions not simply to train students in existing programs but to redirect their programs to meet the needs of these immigrant churches. (See the section on seminaries in chapter 7.) The requirement is for a fuller array of well-trained religious specialists in addition to priests and pastors: specialists in youth work, music (both Eastern and Western styles), Christian education, counseling, and translation from Indian languages, both liturgical and general, into American English.

Outside the family, priests, pastors, and bishops are central figures in the transmission of tradition and in shaping the personal and group identities insofar as these are influenced by both Indian and Christian elements. They must speak the language of all the diverse membership of immigrant churches – newly arrived grandparents who do not speak English very well, parents who move back and forth between an Indian language and English with some fluency, and children who speak American English with increasing fluency but little of any Indian language with decreasing fluency. Their work is to maintain the unity of the memory of the past, present realities, and future potentials that will preserve the integrity and coherence in Asian-Indian Christian experience in America. If successful, they will be recognized as faithful servants able to lead their people through the trials interpreted as Exodus and Exile and through what may be an even greater challenge, that of entering a Promised Land.

CHAPTER 6

Going home: bridges to India

The Lord watch between you and me when we are absent one from
the other.

Genesis 31:49

A television ad showing a young Asian Indian in Chicago chatting over
the telephone with her brother in Bombay is part of elaborate advert-
ising campaigns by communications companies to tap the growing telecommunications market between India and the United States. Full-page
ads in Asian-Indian newspapers promise discounts and direct connections to cities and villages in India for voice, fax, and e-mail communications. Connections on the new information highways take only a few
moments, and most Christian immigrants talk frequently with relatives
and occasionally with religious leaders in India. One immigrant notes
that when he first arrived twenty years ago, a cable to India took up to
three days and often arrived at an incorrect address, but now he dials
directly on the telephone and speaks immediately to his parents anytime
he wishes. Satellite television reception is in an estimated 8 million
Indian homes, and one immigrant reports discussing on the telephone
with his sister back home scenes of a disaster they both were seeing on
television. Asian Indians also make periodic visits to India; planes carry
families loaded down with American-made gifts, both as evidence of
their American success and as concrete symbols of ties to their homeland and kin. A nurse at a family conference explains that she tries to
take her family back to India about every three years, and in the intervening years they attend the family conferences because they are "a little
like going back to Kerala." Hence, this group of immigrants is able to
maintain closer relations and more rapid communication with people
and institutions in their homeland than was possible for earlier immigrants.

227

COMMUNICATION AND MOBILITY

Three factors make the relations of these immigrants with their families and churches in India significantly different from the relations of those who arrived before the lull of immigration. (1) Modern transportation and communications are easy and very rapid along the modern form of a dual highway so that visitors come from India bringing video and audio cassettes at the same time that expatriates return to India also carrying cassettes of religious services, marriages, and funerals conducted in the United States. Bishops and other religious leaders travel back and forth, thereby influencing both communities and, to some degree, moderating the exchange. Events in India appear almost immediately on ethnic television programs and in ethnic newspapers in America. Thus, a tremendous amount of information moves along the new information highway with ever-increasing speed. (2) Communication is relatively cheap. A short telephone call to India costs less than $10, and a round-trip air ticket for the 15-hour journey costs around $1000. Asian-Indian immigrants, especially the professionals who came in the 1970s, almost immediately gained financial success, enabling them to communicate easily with people they left behind in India. One reason for frequent communication is to demonstrate that success. No great delay causes separation from family and church affairs. Indian political stability preserves networks for communication, and both messages and people fly over disturbed areas between India and America. (3) Family reunification continuously brings new immigrants who revitalize contacts and nurture them even when members of the second generation might slacken off in efforts to preserve contacts. It is increasingly the case that entire families are relocated in the United States – parents, siblings, and parts of the extended family – but entry of affines opens up new networks for contacts. Now those dynamic networks reach into every town and village of south India and to many villages beyond that are the native places for Asian-Indian Christian immigrants.

The experience of European immigrants between 1875 and 1925 was very different. Steamship travel reduced the time required for transatlantic crossing from around two months on sailing ships earlier in the nineteenth century to around two weeks from Chicago to London or Munich (Smith, 1892:45–6). The travel time remained relatively constant until the introduction of an aerial service in 1925, which came, however, toward the end of the immigration cycle and was in any case too expensive for any but the most wealthy. Few of those who came as "your tired, your poor, your huddled masses" had the time or the resources for return to their homelands to renew contacts with relatives and friends. The picture of people arriving from Europe at Ellis Island is dramatically different from that of the physicians, engineers, or nurses arriving from India at O'Hare airport. Prospects for their first decade in America differ as well. Poverty of earlier immigrants greatly weakened the myth of return. Moreover, the First World War in Europe brought severe dislocation which made communication with portions of Europe virtually impossible. Letters went back and forth slowly, typically with invitations and money to support the immigration of a relative or a pastor, but these contacts were relatively formal and infrequent. Memory was more vital than personal contacts. Ethnic churches and newspapers published in America were primary media for preserving the memory, establishing forms of adaptation, and disseminating information about the homeland. Reunions, one in the United States and others in a European country, between siblings who had been long separated because of barriers that existed between the sending community and the immigrant community in America, have been common in recent decades.

Asian-Indian Christians constitute a specific example of the new relations established between the country of origin and country or countries of settlement made possible by rapid communications and mobility. These immigrants bring several societies into a single social field that relates India to the Gulf states, Great Britain, Canada, the United States, and other countries as well. These relations emerging among migrants at the close of the twentieth century generate a new transnational approach to the study of migration, which studies migrants "who develop and maintain multiple relations – familial, economic, social, organizational, religious, and political that span borders...and take actions, make decisions, feel concerns, and develop identities within social networks that connect them to two or more societies simultaneously" (Glick Schiller, Basch, and Blanc-Szanton, 1992:1–24). These transnational movements often bypass governmental authority patterns and encompass multiple levels of analysis (Stack, 1981:6). Immigrants with transnational relations are able to maintain several identities and to express these at times and in ways that are most advantageous to them in adapting to current circumstance and in preserving options for the future. Immigrants are inherently insecure, and uncertainties in the global economy force them to cultivate options in more than one setting. One way to do this is to use the wealth, social ties, and status gained in one location to develop status and capital in another (Glick Schiller, Basch, and Blanc-Szanton, 1992:112). One result is the necessity of remapping the social and religious fields of the new immigrants to America.

A new conceptualization of the migration process is necessary to analyze the manner in which current immigrants are holding together, in their experience and social fields, more than one social context, thereby reducing the relevance of earlier perspectives on migration and breaking away from the two competing paradigms heretofore dominant within migration studies: assimilation and ethnic pluralism. Palmira Rios calls for "a more dynamic and humanistic approach to the migration phenomenon, one that can capture the complexity of the experiences lived by individuals, families and groups straddling in two worlds,...whose actions are opening new spaces for social exchanges" (Rios, 1992:226).

Although religion has not received much attention in transnational studies, religion is a major aspect of creating and maintaining identities across geographical and national boundaries. It is increasingly evident that immigrants are maintaining transnational ties in ways different from the earlier immigrants, demanding new perspectives on the transnational vitality of religions and religious life. (See Williams, 1984:ch. 7, for a transnational view of a Hindu group.) The so-called "Sikh nationalism" in support of a separate state of Khalistan in India is, in fact, a transnational movement developing out of the emotional and political needs of Sikhs in Britain, Canada, and the United States, as well as out of dynamics in the Punjab. Christians among new immigrants to America maintain transnational ties that reform the ecumenical understanding of the church and the nature of interaction across previously impermeable barriers or ones that facilitated only one-way traffic of influence. They are adding a new strategy of adaptation to the migration experience and context, one that holds several societies together in a transnational nexus. The study of contemporary religion and Christianity must develop a new conceptualization to describe and analyze adequately the new religious situation. Both the practice and the study of religion, and especially Christianity, have developed methods and agencies reflecting the migration and ecumenical character of religious groups, but the experience and study of earlier immigrants did not reveal the same transnational character of religion experienced by the new immigrants. Both ecclesiastical concepts and academic studies must now take account of the transnational aspect of religious groups. The situation calls for a new sociological description of the lived reality and social fields of Christian immigrants and of the vitality of their relationships within and between several societies, and it demands a new conceptualization of ecclesiology that will take into account new forms of church interactions.

Two results of the new immigration and the constant rapid communication and movement back and forth are new forms of transnationalization of religion and the reverse effects that Christian immigrants have on the sending society in India.

TRANSNATIONAL FAMILIES AND CHURCHES

Tamil Christians gather for a Christmas celebration and offer up a special prayer "for our brothers and sisters in India, Sri Lanka, Malaysia, Singapore, the Gulf states, England, and America." The phrase "brothers and sisters" has a double meaning because family members of many of those present are living and working in other countries and because Tamil Christians are establishing churches and prayer groups in all the areas mentioned. Moreover, the networks coming into existence between these communities are being transformed by contemporary mobility and communication. Popular media present discussions on effects of multinational corporations, and a new academic subfield of transnational studies is developing, but little is said about the new shape of transnational families and the new transnational churches. Indeed, what is new here is not the fact that people and churches are established in new lands, but the quality of the relationship that exists between those in the sending society and those residing in the receiving societies.

The presence of Indian Christians in various countries results from several distinct patterns of immigration. In the earlier decades of the twentieth century when British colonial control linked many countries, emigration from south India was primarily by unskilled laborers to other south Asian countries: Malaysia, Singapore, Burma, and Sri Lanka. Independence of these nations following the Second World War led to restrictions on immigration, but a number of British Commonwealth countries opened their doors, including Britain, Australia, and Canada. Most of the Indian Christian congregations in Canada join with those from the United States in annual conferences and diocesan affairs, but Canadian members participated in a different migration pattern. Immigration to Britain and Canada has become much more difficult, so the congregations there are growing primarily through natural growth of families. The United States is the preferred goal for immigration. A small number of Indian Christians become permanent residents in the United States after a period of residence in Canada.

Large-scale migration to west Asia (commonly referred to by Indians simply as "the Gulf") is a recent phenomenon, increasing dramatically after the steep rise of oil prices in 1973. Hence, the Gulf War of 1990–91 created a great deal of anxiety among Asian Indians regarding the welfare of "brothers and sisters" facing adversity in west Asia, and some reduction in the numbers of Indians in the Gulf states resulted. Nevertheless, a large number of South Indian Christians work in the Gulf states. An estimate of Indian immigrants in west Asia in 1981 was 599,500 at a time when the number in the United States was approximately 400,000. The main difference between the two groups is the high level of "professional, technical, and kindred workers" in the United States (75 percent) when compared to those in west Asia (9 percent) (Clarke, Peach, and Vertovec, 1990:193).[1] Their immigration status in the Gulf differs from that of their compatriots in the United States because they are temporary workers and cannot become permanent residents in any of the Gulf states. Workers are on fixed-term contracts and must return to India at least for a furlough at the end of the contract. Unskilled workers below a certain salary are not permitted to keep their families with them, but professional workers, such as nurses and physicians, may live with their families during their tenure. Many elect to go as singles to work and send money back to support their families in south India. Hence, the goal of these immigrants is not to establish long-lasting institutions in the Gulf states, but to stay as long as permitted and to earn as much as possible to secure their families' financial future in India. Hence, frequent going and coming and a great deal of interchange takes place between the Gulf states and south India, especially Kerala, which sends many nurses, teachers, and other professionals to the Gulf.

Christians make up a significant portion of the guest workers in the Gulf. They face many restrictions on expressions of their religion, more stringent in Saudi Arabia than in the other states where church gatherings are permitted, but not proselytizing. In some places meetings are restricted to specified buildings. Nevertheless, most of the church groups now established in the United States also have congregations in the Gulf states which are administered through dioceses or headquarters in south India. The CSI has seven congregations in the Gulf states, each larger than those in the United States because local regulations do not permit many separate meetings. A detailed study of Christians from India in the

Gulf states remains to be carried out, but such a study promises to be more difficult than in the United States because leaders may be reticent to call public attention to an active Christian presence. Pastors are commissioned from India to work in the Gulf states, but they are admitted as teachers to work in secular jobs and not as Christian pastors. The congregations serve a constantly evolving cadre of temporary workers who never create a permanent second generation and, therefore, have a different perspective on their future and their associations with relatives and institutions in India than do immigrants to America. Moreover, Indians in the Gulf states are more isolated from the host culture than those in the United States. Hence, they may preserve an Indian ethos more easily and may be less influenced by their stay abroad. Churches and institutions in India developed a *modus operandi* with the churches in the Gulf states that affects the relationships that Christians in India have with their sister churches in America. A significant number of the nurses and medical technicians in the United States report having worked in the Gulf states before emigrating to America, and some of their children were born there. They report higher incomes and no taxes in the Gulf, which provided a great deal of wealth, but fixed-term contracts and the unavailability of permanent residence or citizenship made their future precarious. Long-term opportunities are greater in America. Hence, many move to America with prior experience in forming and sustaining immigrant churches. Some of the immigrants in America complain that the ecclesiastical leaders treat these permanent residents who will never return to India in the same manner they treat those in the Gulf, expecting them to return their tithes and support to India in the same manner even though they face the necessity of establishing permanent religious institutions in America.

The Gulf states and the United States represent two contexts into which Christians from developing countries are moving and where they must adapt to differing political, social, and religious realities. Christians from India must adapt their Indian Christianity and culture to the different contexts in the countries to which they emigrate. In the Gulf states Christians live, work, and worship under Islamic governments and adapt to the Islamic culture and ethos. They operate under various restrictions to their freedom and adapt to cultural expectations regarding the conduct of women and expressions of their faith. Those in the United States live under a secular democratic government and must adapt to modern secularism and to living among Christians who are shaped by that context. They perceive excesses in the exercise of freedoms as threats to the preservation of their ethnic and religious identities. They become almost immediately observers of, and tentative, unwilling participants in, the culture wars that divide American society. These two contexts of Islamic society and secular democracy promise to dominate the migratory patterns of Christians and other people from developing countries into the twenty-first century, so developing strategies for maintaining Christian identity and witness in both is critical.

Families in Kerala communicate with relatives establishing outposts in the cities of India and in several other countries and can accurately be described as "transnational families." Those locations provide escape routes from poverty, lack of opportunity, and any perception of oppression. Families invest members and sometimes funds abroad to enhance opportunities for the entire family, so, as one observer comments, "many families have an escape hatch to the United States and keep their eyes focused on Chicago or Muscat." People move from one location to the other for both short visits and long-term immigration. Elinor Kelly uncovered this network of transnational families (she calls them "transcontinental families") while working in a village in Gujarat:

Gradually, as they told their stories and discussed the pros and cons of the different countries where they worked, I realized that...my country was only one of a number of options which they would consider in order to earn the cash which should flow as remittances into their villages...I soon realized that I was experiencing something else which all the literature on Asian communities in [the West] had somehow failed to convey. (1990:252)

New forms of transnational churches are also developing through modern migration. The phrase "global village" or reference to "globalization" are faulty descriptions of the situation because the major locations for transnational families and churches are determined by specific patterns of migration and social contexts. Thus, the three primary locations for the expression of Indian churches are India, the Gulf states, and North America. Each of the churches in India is adjusting to its current situation as a developing transnational church. Structures developed to administer congregations in a small area or region are expanding, sometimes enduring great stress, to reach around the world. Disciplines developed to lead farmers in villages of Kerala toward Christian maturity are made available to (or imposed upon, depending upon one's perspective) young professionals and second-generation children in Houston and New York. Symbols shaped by centuries of use in India are truncated and reinterpreted to be meaningful throughout a transnational church. Much of the anguish and conflict evident between the churches reflects these developments resulting from immigrants and churches breaking loose from the cocoon of Kerala to fly free and exposed in several countries as transnational churches. It is increasingly necessary to develop a genuinely comparative perspective in the study of Indian Christianity, one that will take account of both the diverse contexts of the churches in India, the Gulf, and North America and the new complex relationships that these churches establish between East and West.

The presence of Christians from India in the United States is part of a new pattern of relationship between Asian Christianity and American Christianity within a new transnational Christianity which is exemplified also among immigrants from Korea, China and Taiwan, and southeast Asia. The old pattern that was dominant prior to Indian independence involving Western missionaries going to evangelize Indians is no longer viable, both because of the weakening and redirection of energies of most American mainline churches and because of Indian governmental restrictions on granting visas to missionaries. Christian immigrants to America generally hold positive views of missionaries and their accomplishments, coming as they do from segments of society less influenced by liberation theology, even while recognizing that the Indian church can no longer rely on Western missionaries. A second pattern of relationship has developed in the second half of the twentieth century in relationships between American denominations, especially through denominational world mission boards, and their "partner churches" in India. The communication and assistance moves between West and East at the level of ecclesiastical bureaucrats and institutions, with little contact between congregations or individuals. A third pattern is aborning, a new relationship established by immigrants in several countries with the congregations and ecclesiastical structures back in India. Underneath the church bureaucracies that help keep international lines of communication open, networks develop between Christian immigrants and their Christian "brothers and sisters" that are as yet largely unnoticed or unappreciated by those involved in missions or ecumenical affairs. An Asian-Indian professor in a conservative seminary notes, for example, that at the same time his American denomination is using its resources to send American fraternal workers to visit Indian churches, he can name fifty well-trained immigrants with Indian visas, fluent in Indian languages, who would be willing to return to India for a period as missionaries at a third of the cost and with much greater effect. The new pattern of relationship is between Indians abroad and

Indians, and, although the Asian Indians are influenced by Western secularism and values, the relationship they establish is not along the old East–West divide. The relationship becomes much more complex, as must the structures developing out of the relationship, a complexity more congruent with the new transnational character of the churches. It seems likely that the networks established by immigrants will be the most important for sustaining relationships between American churches and Indian Christians – and with Christians in other parts of Asia as well. At present, however, the lines are crossed and mixed messages are being sent and received because the patterns established in earlier decades remain and have not been transformed or replaced by new patterns of transnational Christian relations. That transformation remains an important task for the churches as they prepare for a new century.

The potential that Christian immigrants possess to affect the shape and future of American Christianity is a primary focus of this work, but an equally important revision of the patterns of relationship between Christians in the East and the West and the reverse impact immigrants have upon the countries that send them will affect international ecumenical relations in the twenty-first century.

REVERSE EFFECTS IN TRANSNATIONAL CHURCHES

The immediate answer leaders of churches in India give to the question "What effects are the Christian immigrants in America having on your churches?" is that they are having no effect whatever. Their wont is to discuss the potential contributions their churches have to make to American Christianity: family values, spirituality, discipline, and ancient symbols. The numbers from each church are relatively small, they say, and the immigrants are too involved in establishing themselves and their families in their new homes to affect church affairs in India. Then, however, they begin to mention in anecdotal fashion the contributions, financial and otherwise, that the immigrants make to their churches and institutions. As examples mount up, it becomes obvious that the immigrants are more involved and are having a greater impact on Christianity in India than anyone has calculated.

The minimal attention that Christians among the new immigrants do receive from scholars focuses on their growth and development in the United States and tangentially on their effect on American Christianity. The reverse effects on churches in Asia are virtually ignored, in part because studies of earlier immigrants reflected the period when communication was difficult and reverse effects were slow in appearing. Moreover, an antipathy exists in many circles against the imperialistic impact of Western societies on countries in Asia. Although the influence of immigrant Christians in America on Asian societies is of a different order, it does constitute part of the larger revolution brought about by the new world-order of telecommunications and capitalism that evokes opprobrium in both church and academic circles. Indeed, it is difficult to separate the reverse effects that immigrants have upon their families and churches in India from the general social and cultural impact that, for example, international television networks have in every part of India and that multinational companies exert on national and regional economies and development. Nevertheless, the reverse impact of immigrants is substantial and will, it seems likely, become the most important aspect of relations between the churches in India and America. Several reverse effects are already evident in finances, family and marriage, leadership transfer, missions, theology and practice, and transnationalism as church ethos.

Finances

Transnational movements of money by both temporary and permanent migrants are so important that governments aggressively pursue them, pass laws to make transfers easier, and calculate such hard-currency income into their long-range plans. Remittances from workers overseas worldwide are worth some US$66 billion annually, second only to oil in value in world trade (United Nations Population Fund, 1993:ii). Non-resident Indians (NRIs) contribute liberally to their families and communities in India, with the result that those areas sending workers abroad experience a significant stimulus to their local economies, increase in land values, a building boom, and increased family security. The World Bank reports that in 1988 India received US$2,850 million from the Gulf, the United Kingdom, and the United States (Segal, 1993:152). Recent governmental decisions leading to a dramatic rise of the exchange rate to over 30 rupees to US$1 greatly increased the amount and impact of remittances. Effects of these hard-currency remittances are most noted in Gujarat and Kerala, but spread more widely. A new suburb in Bangalore is popularly known as "The Dollar Colony" because the land development was reserved by the government for people who could invest hard currencies in the project. Hence, physicians, engineers, employees of international companies and agencies, and other NRIs build splendid homes for their parents or for their own retirement, many of which are sitting empty. The Dollar Colony is only an isolated visible evidence of the tremendous reverse impact that financial remittances by immigrants have in India, of which the ripple effects on society are so wide-reaching and subtle that they are almost incalculable.

Religious institutions share in this wealth in random and unexpected ways that affect the vitality of religious organizations, status of religious leaders, and the balance of influence of religious groups in areas of India. In earlier decades, Islamic institutions received support from wealthy individuals in the Middle East, and Christian institutions through missionary organizations in the West. Now, the primary sources of external income for all the religious organizations throughout India are from immigrant participants from those religions in the Gulf states and North America. Hinduism has emerged as a growing transnational religion, and a great deal of support for neo-Hindu organizations and for political movements of Hindu solidarity comes from abroad. Many networks are being developed for religious fund-raising reaching out from India to the expatriate communities. Regular tours by Indian religious specialists and administrators of institutions to visit contacts in North America are personal extensions of these networks. Asian-Indian newspapers contain regular announcements and large advertisements about visits of religious specialists of many groups every summer. Remittances to parents and other family members affect religious institutions indirectly in a diffuse manner because part of the general family wealth is donated toward religious activities. Major remittances go directly from religious institutions in America to those in India (which is the most efficient conduit because such gifts may be tax-exempt in the United States) or from individuals directly to the institutions or individuals of their choice. No reliable estimate of the total remittances to religious organizations in India from the United States is possible because no central accounting exists. Few of the records are available to outsiders so most evidence is anecdotal, and immigrants themselves complain about the increasing number of requests and the lack of accountability and reporting regarding some of these funds. A stimulus for establishing firm organizational structures is the desire to regulate the requests for funds and assistance and to maintain discipline regarding their proper expenditure in India. Of course, leaders in India have an interest in maintaining some control over those contributions that, used in the wrong ways, could prove to be ill-advised and enormously disruptive. On occasion they must feel like parents dealing with generous but unruly children. A major issue of institution building is who will be the gate-keepers for these exchanges, a position bringing with it great power for exerting influence on the religions in India.

Christian immigrants contribute to Christian institutions and activities in India. A notice-board in the entrance of a Pentecostal church in Houston contains a list of members of the congregation with the amounts they contributed in the past month to projects in India. A leader of another congregation reported that in a two-month period the church sent over US$25,000 to India. Several of the annual family conferences provide booths at which organizations inform participants about, and encourage support for, Christian work in India. Tithes of these immigrant Christians are available for substantial gifts to India for two reasons: first, the community as a whole is relatively wealthy by American standards and extremely wealthy by Indian standards; second, they do not yet have substantial expenses in their own congregations. Few have to support full-time pastors, most do not maintain their own church building or institutions, nor do they have extensive ecclesiastical bureaucracies in America. They are like many American adolescents who have more expendable personal income during that period of their lives than they will for a long time thereafter because they are not responsible for any fixed expenses. The appearance of dioceses, headquarters, church buildings, and other institutions will certainly reduce the amount of tithes sent back to India, and such institutions will also exert more control and redirect the money that is sent.

Types of contributions and the networks through which they are given are diverse. Congregations of hierarchically organized churches have an obligation to pay the same regular subscriptions to the headquarters as congregations in India, a modest amount assessed per family. Moreover, the congregations collect offerings to support the synods, dioceses, or headquarters in India on special Sundays, analogous to the annual Catholicos Day Offering in the Malankara Orthodox Church. In addition, Sundays are designated for special-day offerings to support authorized agencies of the church, such as the Sunday School association, evangelistic association, women's fellowship, youth work, seminaries, and bishop's relief fund. Fourteen Mar Thoma Church agencies have rights to designated Sunday offerings in all the congregations. Congregations and individuals respond to formal requests from church leaders and institutions to support a large number of special projects of the church in India; among those listed, for example, are: construction of a diocesan retreat center, a housing scheme for low-income people to cel-

ebrate a bishop's jubilee, a retirement home for the elderly, marriage
assistance fund for poor women, job training for poor people, a seminary
endowment, and an earthquake disaster relief fund. Knanaya Catholics
in Chicago and New York sent $10,000 as an unsolicited gift to the
bishop for relief of earthquake victims in Maharashtra. A faculty
member raised the equivalent of 2.3 million Indian rupees for his seminary endowment during one fund-raising trip. A bishop estimated that a
letter requesting funds for a special project will garner a $10 contribu-
tion, a letter from parents requesting a gift for the same project gets $25,
and a visit from the bishop raises $100. Another bishop said that mar-
riage assistance schemes for poor women are very popular among
women's groups. It takes about 15,000 rupees to make a young woman
marriageable – 3,000 for expenses of the wedding and 12,000 as a
deposit for the couple. Dowry is now illegal in India, so the contribution
is made to the couple and is called a deposit to undergird their marriage.
Although many of these special offerings support welfare activities
among people who are not Christians, the offerings accrue to the wealth
and strength of the Christian community.

Individual initiatives in both India and America result in a flow of
funds to India. Wealthy immigrant Christians establish personal foundations or institutions in India. A pastor built a retirement home for priests
in his hometown in India as an individual project. Others contribute to
local congregations, schools, and individuals as part of their Christian
stewardship. Individuals in India send personal requests to their
acquaintances in America for assistance for themselves or for their projects. Immigrants and congregations are inundated by such requests.
The competition for gifts causes some conflict among individuals and
institutions in India. Some individual projects are perceived as being
threatening to already established institutions and projects.

Many of the colleges, universities, and medical schools, both governmental and private, have alumni organizations in America that provide a
great deal of support. A few Christian institutions maintain support
groups or alumni organizations in America. Madras Christian College
maintains a list of 700 alumni in the United States, and the alumni director estimates that 1,000 live there, only a portion of whom are Christian.
Vellore Christian Hospital has long had an office in New York to maintain contact with Christian denominations and other granting agencies,
but now graduates among physicians and nurses living in the United
States provide a wealthy resource for Vellore and other Christian teaching hospitals in India. Vellore has some 250 physicians among its alumni

in the United States who hold an annual conference attended by almost 100 families. Approximately 3 out of 4 are Christians. Many nurses and allied health professionals among graduates are also in America. Alumni are taking over as the major funding source for the Vellore board as their traditional sources dry up. A majority of people in a Tamil congregation in Queens, New York, have ties to Vellore. The United Theological Seminary in Bangalore maintains a list of 27 Asian-Indian alumni and attempts to cultivate support by visits from the principal and faculty members. Transnational fund-raising from Asian Indians and their institutions in America is a growth industry, but the potential is just being tapped and the networks are in the process of being developed.

If Christian women had not entered the nursing profession in large numbers, thereby becoming eligible for work permits in the Gulf states and for immigration to America, the church in Kerala would have a great deal less wealth. Remittances from Keralite Christian immigrants and those from other areas of India are having significant reverse effects upon Christian institutions. It is a matter of some discussion whether financial support from NRIs is salutary or disruptive of Christian development in India. The Church of North India discourages contributions to institutions, dioceses, or individuals and prefers that all foreign contributions be given directly to the synod for distribution. That may be one reason a CNI bishop said that when members go to America they are lost: "They are lost in their world, and we are lost in ours." Others argue that the immigrants have a moral responsibility to support Christian works in the land that provided them with both Christian faith and special educational opportunities. Money talks, and remittances of money provide a firm foundation for other ways immigrants affect Indian society.

Family and marriage

The Indian marriage market is now transnational, affected by decisions made and opportunities available in several locations abroad. The influx of money to support the marriage of poor women and to provide an economic foundation for their families affects marriage patterns in India, especially in those areas where Christians are a significant portion of the population. In the 1970s and 1980s, nurses were elevated to preferred marriage partners because they brought with them opportunities for immigration. Now that nurses are in less demand in America, some young people make career decisions on the basis of what occupations will make them more attractive marriage partners for NRIs. Some who fail to gain admission to medical school enter counseling because there is a rumor in India that counseling jobs are available in America. Thus, opportunities abroad affect career decisions and educational goals in India. Increasingly, an important consideration for parents in both educational decisions and marriage negotiations is whether they wish their son or daughter to reside in India or abroad. The pattern seems to be developing that men return to India for brides, but women prefer to marry Asian-Indian men in the United States, creating a minor gender imbalance in the marriage networks for the well-educated elites in central Kerala and a few other areas that send many immigrants. Viewed in crass terms, market values are changed. The market value of a well-educated professional bridegroom in Kerala is affected by the value placed on him in the transnational market – that is, what his family can expect in a bride and accompanying gifts.

New transnational networks are just developing for arranged marriages with people abroad. Because marriage negotiations are conducted in private, it is difficult to quantify the effects that churches have on the negotiations, but churches do constitute one aspect of the developing networks. They are the transnational institution with the closest contact to the personal and family lives of its members. According to the order of discipline in some churches, the leaders in India must authenticate marriage arrangements before the union will be recognized by the church or, among Knanaya, by the ethnic group. Bishops and pastors on occasion take a more active role in recommending partners and negotiating terms. Church festivals and conferences attract people from several countries and become occasions for transnational marriage negotiations.

Such transnational marriages remove sons and daughters-in-law from the traditional extended family living arrangements in Kerala. Many more Christian parents are living alone in their old age than was the case in the past because their children and grandchildren are living abroad. If the entire family emigrates abroad, the issue is where the parents will live in retirement. A number of Christian pastors retire early in India to join children in America, where they continue to serve immigrant churches. It is common for one son to remain in India to care for the parents, oversee family resources, and inherit the property, while siblings living abroad send funds to provide for the parents. The family structure is changed irrevocably. The general wealth, standard of living, and status of Christian parents who have children abroad is greatly enhanced. They become migrants themselves as they occasionally travel abroad in their old age for visits to their children and grandchildren. Hence, expectations for activities for the elderly and social patterns for a significant portion of the population are dramatically changed. Old eyes see new things and return to India with new insights regarding both church and society.

Leadership transfer

A speaker at a Christian family conference compliments his audience by saying that they are "export quality brains," noting that "the very good graduates in Kerala go to North India, the excellent go to the Gulf states, and the very best come to the United States." Many of the best young people of all the churches, those with high professional qualifications, are permanently lost to the churches in Kerala and other parts of India when they emigrate. Some of the most progressive and best-known church leaders receive assignments in America. Who does that leave to lead and support the churches in India? One can argue that the financial assistance that immigrants return to the churches in India is not able to replace the financial support and leadership that the immigrants would have made available had they remained to live and work in India. If the claim, made by several priests, that more Indian psychiatrists and counselors work in America than in India is correct, that would have a dramatic effect on Indian society. A historian of the church in Gujarat noted the loss: "The loss of such talented people to the Church in [India] is great; yet this was the urge which first populated America and Australia from Europe, and its future effect on the Indian Christian community will be interesting to watch" (Boyd, 1981:226).

A counter-argument is that availability of jobs in America and the Gulf provides an incentive for young people to study hard and prepare well for occupations that will advance the Christian community and society in India. Such incentive is important in areas of high unemployment and low wages. Skills developed in the hope that they will lead to opportunity in America will also serve the young person well in the developing Indian economy. For example, children in Kerala and Gujarat study English with great intensity. Kerala continues to produce more highly trained professionals than its economy can yet support, and it could be argued that would not be the case if no opportunities existed outside the state. It also produces more priests and pastors than are needed to staff the Christian churches and institutions in the state. As long as such overproduction of specialists continues, it can be argued that the loss of "export quality brains" is not a great detriment to India but rather creates a healthy focus on and optimism about education.

As Asian economies become stronger, some Asian Americans are returning to take positions in the countries of their birth, including India. The Census Bureau now estimates that 195,000 foreign-born Americans each year are part of a growing emigration movement – the highest number since the First World War. They are part of the transnational mobility between countries. Many of those returning to Asia retain their American citizenship or their green cards as a way of keeping their global options open. As Ashley Dunn notes, they are, for all intents and purposes, "neither here nor there forever" (1995:A1, A5).

Some temporary immigrants develop specialized skills that are contributed to India when they return. While they are on assignment in America, many of the priests and pastors undertake specialized training that they subsequently take back to India. One pastor received his pastoral training in India but earned a master's degree in missiology from an American seminary and graduate credit at a university before he returned to teach at Serampore and is now principal of a church mission school in Orissa. Another earned a graduate degree in social work with the hearing-impaired so he could return with greater skills to the school for the hearing-impaired where he was principal before he moved to the United States. A group of physicians and nurses discussed the possibility of returning to India to provide medical camps and special seminars. The stimulus and leadership for the Catholic charismatic renewal movement in India comes from students who first were attracted to and became leaders in the charismatic movement at American universities. A women's study course at Serampore College was prepared by a woman faculty member from Madras after she had completed a degree in women's studies at Claremont. These are samples of diverse skills that return to Indian churches with migrants. It is often said that priests and pastors have a difficult time adjusting when they return to India after service in America, but some of that difficulty may be due to their attempts to contribute some of what they learned to their communities in India.

The production of information on and interpretations of American and Indian culture and Christianity will certainly be a transnational enterprise in the future. In earlier decades before rapid communication, many American Christians learned much of what they knew about India, China, and Africa from missionaries on furlough who traveled around the United States to tell Christians about their "brothers and sisters" abroad and from newsletters sent by living-link missionaries to their supporting congregations. The information flow is now reversed as a great deal of what Christians in India know about American religion comes from reports by immigrants, who have become latter-day "missionaries" to the West. Some evangelical immigrants refer to themselves as such. It is remarkable how much of the research into and teaching about Indian religions is carried out in American universities by children of missionaries, who grew up in India and now occupy major chairs in Asian studies. Until now very few of the children of immigrants have engaged in academic work in social studies or the humanities – parents still direct them toward scientific and technical professions – but it will be interesting to chart the future impact of scholars arising in the community on the academic study of transnational Indian culture and religion. That study would inevitably have considerable influence on the self-understanding of people in India.

Missions

Missions are now truly transnational, both here and there at the same time. Immigrants support specific mission projects of their churches in India. Indian Christians as a whole tend to be more conservative and evangelical than their American counterparts, but a division exists among the Orthodox, Catholic, and Protestant churches in the types of mission activity supported in India. The Orthodox and Catholic congregations support primarily social service work in India, whereas the Protestants and the Mar Thoma churches support evangelistic work to establish churches and gain converts as well. Some of the speakers at conferences in America remark on the fact that Christianity has been in India for almost 2,000 years and yet has not "won the subcontinent for Christ." Indeed, the Syrian churches in Kerala evolved an informal, unstated peace accord with their neighbors that ruled out aggressive evangelism. Many calls for mission support involve sending evangelistic workers into north India both to serve migrants from the South Indian Christian communities and to gain converts from other communities. Each year, Asian-Indian Christians in America are sending a great deal more to India to support missions than the American denominations collectively have sent annually during the past fifty years.

Support for evangelistic work in parts of India includes support for individual evangelists, provision of bicycles and motorcycles for village Bible teachers, scholarships for evangelists at Bible Training Institutes, correspondence courses, construction of church buildings, production and translation of evangelistic literature, Christian advertisements in the Indian edition of *Reader's Digest*, and production of audio and video cassettes. One observer attributes the Pentecostal revival in areas of India largely to support, both financial and in personnel, coming from Pentecostal immigrants in America. Indian citizens living abroad have the legal right to return to India to conduct all types of religious activities, whereas religious activity by non-citizens is greatly restricted. No reports exist of coordination of mission activity between the Asian-Indian churches and other churches or denominational mission agencies in the United States. It is clear that the shape of mission activity in India is not being decided primarily by mission executives of the mainline churches in America but by the voluntary contributions and encouragement of Indians themselves who are residents in America. Such evangelistic activity is noted and opposed by leaders of other religious communities, and, while it contributes to the growth and strength of Christianity in India, it may also exacerbate communal tensions. Hindu leaders and politicians complain about such outside influences from Islamic and Western countries that they perceive as threats to the ancient traditions of India.

Theology and practice

A newly assigned priest enters the sanctuary in Dallas to conduct the first service in his new parish, and it is the first liturgy in English he has ever conducted. The second service of the morning is in Malayalam. Now the English translation of the liturgy made for the benefit of young people in America is also used in cities of India where English is the common language. That is one example of hundreds of ways adaptations and contributions made in America find their way back into the Indian churches. Bishops assigned to America are mediators of influence going both ways; they attempt to preserve the unity of the church by representing Indian Christianity in the United States, but when they go back to the councils and synods of India, they speak about church affairs with an "Americanized accent." For example, one bishop promised people at a family conference that he would try to get the by-laws of the church in India changed to permit women to vote in general body meetings and to hold offices in the church. The call for a shorter, more streamlined liturgy for the American churches results in studies of the liturgy and some adaptations in India as well.

Congregations in America play a minor but growing role in church politics in India. Success in America enhances the career and status of a church official; failure is a great setback. New organizational structures provide for representatives of congregations in America on general councils and boards. One layman now living in the United States reports with pride that he received the largest number of votes in an election to a significant post on a council in India, indicating, he concludes, the prominence church members in India give to the powerful and growing Asian-Indian church in America. Congregations and individuals in America take sides in disputes in India, as when immigrant members of the Church of the Brethren seek to influence the decision whether congregations would continue as a part of the Church of North India. They are in frequent communication with both leaders in India and those at the international headquarters in Elgin, Illinois. Their influence in the matter is applauded by some but decried by others.

Theology changes even more slowly than aspects of church order and ministry. Western influence on theology has long been present in the Indian church, first through the influence of missionaries and then through pastors and seminary professors who studied in the West. The number of missionaries is greatly reduced, although several teach in seminaries, but the number of Western-educated faculty members in Indian seminaries is relatively large. Several Indian Christians are prominent in the World Council of Churches and its theological conferences. Transnational movement of scholars, theologians, and ideas is more rapid now than ever before. Moreover, a new pathway at the grassroots opens the possibility of theological cross-fertilization from the United States to India. The contemporary attempt to contextualize Indian theology faces the new situation of including the context in the United States and other countries as well as India. For example, lay people in India are surprised to learn that liberation theology is popular in some American churches, and that it is possible to develop a liberation theology not based on Marxism. Scholars developing out of the Asian-Indian churches may serve to moderate that Marxist influence while developing a basis for liberation theology that will survive the weakening of Marxist influence resulting from recent political changes in communist countries.

Transnationalism as church ethos

One could argue that the church has from the first century been part of a transnational movement – the claims of Indian Christians regarding the origin of their church being a prime illustration. Various forms of world-wide communion on Sundays call attention to the ecumenical character of the church. That focus on the wholeness of the church is somewhat abstract compared to the immediate awareness of the transnational nature of the church that comes from having young people and relatives from one's own congregation establishing congregations in several locations abroad. Keralite and other Indian Christians seem to have a greater international consciousness than others of their same social and economic class because of these close contacts in several countries of the world. Pastors and leaders travel regularly to many countries to conduct services and visit their members. Metropolitans, bishops, and church councils increasingly have to take account of the fact that they sit at the top of church hierarchies that reach around the world. They now oversee sending churches, not receiving churches.

Structural changes that come with the establishment of new dioceses, or new procedures permitting ordination and assignment of priests and pastors abroad, create tensions within the churches in India. Negotiations with denominations and church leaders abroad place the interests of the Indian churches beside those of the churches abroad, especially those in the United States. Some of the Indian religious groups are becoming truly transnational for the first time – Hindu, Sikh, and Jain groups come to mind – but the Christian groups are becoming transnational in a manner different from the old missionary relationship. It is difficult for both Indian and Western churches and their leaders to adjust to the new transnational character of the church and the different networks that carry influence back and forth across old boundaries. Old structures developed in previous decades appear to be unsatisfactory in monitoring and mediating the new relationship. New structures are developing slowly and on an *ad hoc* basis. Notice, for example, that one portion of the Malankara Orthodox Church in America is attempting to establish a new and relatively independent connection with the council and Catholicos in Kerala. Churches face a challenge similar to that faced by the church in the first century as it moved across the Mediterranean world and beyond, even as far as India.

Conclusion

Christians sing a favorite hymn that boldly states, "in Christ there is no East or West." A vision of one world linked together by almost instantaneous communication is rapidly being realized by modern technologies, but a consciousness of the spiritual unity that might lessen the threats of destruction brought about by other powers of modern technology lags behind. Nevertheless, the movement of Indian Christian immigrants to the United States is part of a worldwide pattern of migration that brings Christians and those of other religions together in transnational groupings that must be calculated in any accurate estimate of future potential. Ironically, Indian immigrants in the United States affect churches and institutions in their homeland in ways they do not recognize and, perhaps, in ways they do not intend.

The thesis of this chapter is that Asian-Indian churches in America are establishing new channels of communication and influence that cause them to have significant reverse effects upon the churches in India. These effects are part of the larger impact that transnational agencies, corporations, and institutions are having throughout the world, which some call transnationalism. The potential for reverse effects on the churches in India – and, indeed, in Korea, China, Africa, and other countries sending Christian immigrants to America – is much greater than that of earlier immigrants from Europe because of the speed of contemporary travel and communication. Hence, a new field is open for the study of reverse effects of immigrants on the sending societies and religious organizations analogous to the study of the effects of earlier missionary movements. The thesis of the previous chapter is that Asian-Indian Christians face significant challenges as they attempt to adapt to American Christianity and culture. Together the two chapters demonstrate the artificiality of separating the challenges in America (in chapter 5) from the reverse effects on India (in chapter 6). In fact, they are two sides of the one coin, and any study of the new transnational character of the church requires a comprehensive integration of the challenges and opportunities of the churches, moving in a dialectic manner between the United States and India; indeed, moving in a more complicated pattern among manifestations of the church in several contexts that are becoming more and more alike because of modern migration and the rapid travel and communications that make migration possible.

CHAPTER 7

Adding rooms to the house

In my Father's house are many rooms

John 14:2

By happenstance of scheduling in 1986, Malankara Orthodox families met for their annual conference on the same college campus as Methodist women gathered to prepare for their mission study on south Asia. As part of their study, Methodist women dressed in saris, discussed Hindu texts and deities, and watched a classical Indian dance; meanwhile, Keralite Christian women in beautiful saris passed by on the way to discussions about how to maintain their faith and raise their children as Christians in America. It would be pleasant to note that the scheduling error was providential and led to intercultural harmony and understanding, but, alas, that was not so. A misunderstanding about rooms arose because the Methodists had better dorm rooms and air-conditioned meeting halls on days when the temperature reached almost 100 degrees. Those who were there first and had better accommodations could not understand why the others thought there was some discrimination. The Methodist pastor in charge of the conference dressed in modish Western sports clothes and never attempted to talk to the Malankara bishops dressed in their Orthodox gowns and caps. Confusion regarding protocols in the dining room led to hard feelings and accusations of rudeness. Schedules of both groups were too full and rigid to allow for serious conversations, which might have resulted in understanding and Christian fellowship. The groups shared some common space but had little contact until the Malankara women finally offered, "If you insist on wearing the saris, let us show you how to put them on correctly." (See Williams, 1986.) This series of incidents – parabolic in import – illustrates the difficulty of adding rooms to the house of faith and achieving intercultural understanding in the church.

American society is multiplying social categories used to describe, analyze, and understand itself because the make-up of society is changing so rapidly. Since 1965 new ethnic groups, new religions, new nationalities, new forms of Christianity are all appearing in the neighborhood, necessitating new social constructions analogous to adding new rooms and creating a new architectural design for the house. It is a complicated process because each of these new entities is being reformulated in the United States in an evolving process that is difficult to capture except in a series of snap shots and the potential of which is difficult to measure and project. How do you add on rooms to a house for a growing family? The tendency is to force both the experience and interpretation of new immigrants into the established patterns of the older immigrants without taking into account either the new worldwide migration of which the new immigrants are a part or the new American contexts which they enter. Indeed, the new transnationalism and other developments call for revisions of earlier definitions of ethnicity, nationality, and religious affiliation that affect not only ways of constructing but also ways of analyzing and evaluating the results. The new social categories involve establishing new networks (doorways) and new boundaries (walls) that regulate the interaction between the new immigrants and established American institutions and agencies.

E. Allen Richardson discusses the responses to diversity in the United States and illustrates the role of mediating institutions: schools, hospitals, and interfaith organizations (Richardson, 1988:200–18). He suggests that one effect of the combination of increased ethnic and religious diversity is a homogeneity of public life that leads to a reduction of public interaction, and to estrangement, and isolation. His thesis is that unless institutions are available and competent to mediate among diverse groups, the experience of isolation and estrangement will continue with detrimental effects. Although Richardson's focus is upon contemporary Hindu, Muslim, and Jewish immigrants, his emphasis upon the need for mediating institutions that can provide a middle ground between public and private life and between values of homogeneity and diversity applies equally well to Christians among the new immigrants.

Methodist and Malankara Christians and others like them will continue to pass each other in the darkness in the absence of effective mediation of institutions. This chapter deals with the responses of Christian groups and leaders to Asian-Indian Christians in their midst and with the need for more competent mediating institutions to facilitate the development and adaptation of the new Christian immigrants from many churches and lands now in America. Asian Indians constitute only a small portion of the new Christian immigrants. Christians from Korea, China, the Philippines, and other Asian countries share with new immigrants from Africa, Eastern Europe, and other sending countries the task of building new rooms on the house of American Christianity. What is learned from Asian Indians about their experience, and potentials for new initiatives of mediating institutions relevant to them, are also applicable to other contemporary Christian immigrants. The primary mediating institutions for these new immigrants are seminaries, local congregations, ecclesiastical judicatories, ecumenical agencies, interfaith organizations, and ethnic churches.

SEMINARIES AND THEOLOGICAL SCHOOLS

Graduate theological institutions have long had important roles in maintaining connections between American churches and the churches in India. Three periods reflect different impacts that the schools had on Indian Christians: (1) the period of mission emphasis prior to renewed immigration; (2) the period of assisting the new immigrant churches; (3) the current period of training Indian pastors for transnational churches.

(1) It was common for priests and pastors to travel to the United States for graduate study after the Second World War and Indian independence. During the 1950s and early 1960s seminaries and graduate schools provided scholarships for Indian Christian leaders, and the elite graduates from Indian seminaries traveled westward. Councils of churches and denominational missions boards also provided financial assistance. As the West rebuilt and became prosperous after the war, Indian Christians traveled to British and European universities. The goal was to encourage and train the leadership for the churches then enjoying political independence and increasing ecclesiastical independence from Western nations and churches. The expectation of all parties was that the students would return to lead the churches in India, and that indeed happened. Now it is common to meet bishops and other ecclesiastical administrators, both Catholic and Protestant, who recall their student days at American seminaries and universities. Their memories of American churches and seminaries are of the expansionist days of American Christianity. Several bishops who studied in America find themselves returning to become leaders for the Asian-Indian churches because some leaders in India feel that they will better understand the experience of the immigrants. Two bishops now consecrated for Asian-Indian churches studied at Princeton Theological Seminary and Boston

University. A large number of faculty members in Indian seminaries also received their graduate education in the West because Serampore is the only Protestant institution in India authorized to grant doctoral degrees in theology. American seminaries were influential in the preparation of leadership for the Indian church in the immediate post-war, post-independence period.

(2) Seminaries have been the most important mediating institutions during the growth of Asian-Indian churches following the changes in the immigration law in 1965, even though the seminaries are largely unaware of what they have accomplished and are only indirectly related to the Asian-Indian churches. Many students who came on student visas in the early 1960s stayed on to become permanent residents and to serve as organizing pastors of Asian-Indian churches. The churches were too small to support full-time pastors, so many who changed their visas from student status to permanent resident status entered secular occupations in order to remain in the United States. That created some misunderstanding with seminary officials who thought that they had been training leaders for the church in India and not subsidizing immigration to America. As a result, some seminaries placed restrictions on their scholarships requiring that recipients return to India following their studies or face repayment of the scholarship grants. Some of those restrictions are still in place. Seminaries also provided visa certification, scholarships, apartments, and medical insurance for some students and their families, who were sent by churches in India to serve Asian-Indian congregations while completing graduate degrees. Urban institutions where large numbers of Indians arrived in New York, Chicago, and Dallas were especially helpful to immigrants. Without these elements of support it would have been impossible for Indian churches to provide leadership for their members in America in the 1970s and 1980s. These student pastors were among the most over-worked of all church workers as they completed graduate degrees, served growing congregations, ministered to families facing stresses of adjusting to American society, and, in some cases, supervised the construction or renovation of church buildings. After the immigrant churches grew, lay leaders asked ecclesiastical officials in India not to send pastors for advanced studies while serving the churches because the demands were too great. Theological schools were also helpful in training a different clientele, men coming with their wives who had gained permanent resident status as nurses. A number of these men gained some certification for ministry after their immigration by attending night classes, continuing education seminars,

and through correspondence courses. Studies were diverse – from doctoral programs to Bible college correspondence courses, liberal and fundamentalist, full-time and part-time – but without the unwitting assistance of seminaries and theological schools, the Asian-Indian churches would have had a much more difficult time establishing themselves in America. Much of a whole immigrant generation could have been lost to the churches.

(3) The number of Asian or Pacific Islander students is increasing in American theological schools, up from 2,065 in 1989 to 3,119 in 1992 (2,425 men and 694 women), and current trends of Chinese, Indian, Korean, and Filipino immigration leads to the expectation that the numbers will continue to grow (King,1993:45). The Association of Theological Schools reports that there were 52 Asian faculty members in 1991 and 16 Asian administrators in 1992 (from personal correspondence). The new context for education of these students is shaped both by the variety of residency status they exhibit and by the new transnational character of the churches they are preparing to serve. Students continue to come on temporary student visas, and when they first arrive they share with seminary officials the expectation that they will return to their country of origin after completing studies. Increasingly, however, Asian students are coming from the ranks of permanent residents and citizens. Many serve new congregations established by the immigrants, and their options regarding future ministry are expanded by the transnational character of their churches. Few seminaries are aware of these changes in the character of their student bodies, the differences in the churches they serve, and the expanded range of options that they face. A reason for this ignorance is that the students are widely scattered so that few institutions have a large number of any Asian minority.[1] Another reason is that educational institutions are reticent to gather and share data regarding many aspects of their students' personal affairs for fear of transgressing civil rights statutes, even at the same time as they are required by the government to keep some data to prove affirmative actions and non-discrimination. Institutions are overwhelmed by governmental requirements to preserve an array of official statistics regarding their students but are not geared up to gather and preserve what would be necessary to describe fully their student bodies. Staffs are inadequate, computers not sufficiently powerful, and other demands for time and funds too great. Fuller Theological Seminary may well be strategically located to have the greatest potential for educating the future leaders of Asian transnational churches because it already has stu-

dents from over sixty countries and a large percentage of "ethnic students" (39 percent), but the director of academic information systems and research reports that they do not keep data about their students' status beyond that required by the government. Boston University has a long history of Christian students from India, but statistics regarding the current students are not available. Indeed, most institutions record and preserve data only in the categories required by the government, showing Asian, Black, Hispanic, and Native American data, but not gathering information about sub-groups of Koreans, Asian Indians, Chinese, or Filipinos. A few institutions are belatedly in the process of trying to catch up with the changes in their student bodies. Unfortunately, neither the Association of Theological Schools nor the American Association of Bible Colleges maintains records regarding students with family backgrounds in India.

A survey conducted as part of this research reveals a total of 195 students (158 male and 37 female) with family backgrounds in India (here referred to as Asian Indians) in 84 theological schools and Bible colleges in the United States during the 1993–94 academic year. The survey of these institutions, and a second survey completed by 77 of the students identified by the seminaries (with 63 students) and Bible colleges (with 14 students), provide the best profile of these students currently available.[2] There are 10 theological seminaries which have Asian Indians on their faculties, but no Bible college in the survey reports having an Asian-Indian faculty member. Anecdotal evidence suggests that many Asian-Indian Christian laymen and several pastors are faculty members in colleges and universities, but no exact data is available.

The family origin of the students reflects the strength of Christianity in the four states of South India, with almost three out of four students coming from those states (Kerala, 31 percent; Tamil Nadu, 17 percent; Karnataka and Andhra Pradesh, 10 percent each). The northeast region of India where the numbers of Christians are growing very rapidly (Assam, Meghalaya, Manipur, and Nagaland) provides 8 percent of the students. A few are from Gujarat, Goa, Chandighar, Maharatshra, and Uttar Pradesh. Four out of five of the students are male, and two out of three are married. Their median age is 37 years; the eldest is 58 years old and the youngest is 18. Prior to 1965, all the students from India entered the United States on temporary student visas, but now less than two-thirds (62 percent) of the students enter as temporary residents. The rest have the legal status of Asian Indians as United States citizens (15 percent) or as permanent resident aliens with green cards (23 percent).

This increase of Asian-Indian citizens and permanent residents in the theological and Bible schools has significant implications for the future of Asian-Indian churches.

Twenty-three different church affiliations are claimed by the students. The Church of South India is most often mentioned (by 17 percent), and the Baptist Churches (13 percent) and the Pentecostal Churches – Assemblies of God, India Pentecostal Church, Four Square, and independent Pentecostal – follow close behind (13 percent total). Catholic students from all three rites study in the United States (12 percent), but now all but two persons identify themselves as Latin-rite Catholics. The Lutheran Churches (8 percent), the Church of North India (4 percent), and the Presbyterian Churches (4 percent) are mentioned by several. A surprising one out of four students is now affiliated with a church different from their church affiliation in India, having changed membership from fourteen different churches, but no identifiable patterns exist in this movement between churches. Over a third of these students are serving congregations while they are in school, and a third of these church placements are with Asian-Indian congregations.

These students pursue the full range of degree programs as reported by school officials for 193 of them. Most in the Bible colleges pursue bachelor's degrees in religion (19 percent of the total). A large number in graduate schools pursue the basic ministerial degree, Master of Divinity (28 percent), and an equal number are enrolled in another master's or doctoral program (Doctor of Philosophy or Doctor of Theology). A smaller number are enrolled in a Doctor of Ministry program or seeking another advanced degree (7 percent). The rest are scattered among an array of degree programs (18 percent). The median number of years they have lived in the United States is three, and the median number of years in school is two. Most who responded to the survey identify more than one career goal in the church. A majority are preparing for either seminary and college teaching (27 percent) or for the local ministry (26 percent). Pastoral counseling is mentioned by a significant number (14 percent) confirming the reports among Asian-Indian Christians of the need for counselors in India and the attractiveness of counseling as a career path in the United States. Many indicate a desire to be evangelists (14 percent), and a slightly larger number are preparing to be missionaries (20 percent). Other career goals mentioned are chaplaincy, Christian education, health administration, youth work, and social work. Each student was asked the question, "Where do you plan to engage in ministry when you complete the degree?" Several elaborate their responses with the remark that they are willing to serve "wherever the Lord leads." Half of the students plan to return to India to serve the church. Almost one in five plans to remain in the United States, and another one in five indicates a desire to minister in either the United States or India. A majority of both the United States citizens (60 percent) and green card holders (52 percent) indicate their willingness to serve in India, but a larger number of the latter indicate a strong preference for a ministry in the United States. The other locations for ministry mentioned by students are Canada, Asia, Australia, Singapore, and Fiji.

Data is lacking regarding students from India in earlier decades that would permit a careful comparison and contrast with current students. Comments of church leaders in both India and the United States suggest that the context and goals of the current students are different. A larger number are now citizens or permanent residents in America, and that number is sure to grow. The number coming directly from India on scholarship from ecumenical agencies or from seminaries affiliated with mainline denominations is dropping because of the decline in financial support for these agencies and institutions. More of these students will decide to remain in the United States and accept calls from congregations, both Asian-Indian churches and others serving the majority population. The students are already conscious of their potential roles in transnational churches and of the variety of options they enjoy regarding the location of their ministries. Their careers may well be divided into periods of service in several areas of the world, but not according to the old model of Western missionaries sent to serve in foreign lands. Those in charge of planning and curricula in theological schools and Bible colleges seem little aware of these changes and of how to best prepare their students for the new world-order of theological education.

Christians are unique among immigrants from India because many of them bring their well-trained religious specialists with them when they immigrate and discover seminaries and schools readily at hand to assist with the training of leaders for their newly formed congregations. Hindu, Muslim, Sikh, and Jain communities were established by lay people without the assistance of resident religious specialists in the early days and no relevant American educational institutions existed to assist them. Seminaries, divinity schools, and Bible colleges are continuing to assist the immigrant and transnational churches as they move into new stages in their development.

Several suggestions for potential initiatives emerge from conversations with Asian-Indian Christians. (1) Seminaries can create both formal and informal links with seminaries and schools in India. The Mar Thoma Seminary in Kottayam enjoys associations with Princeton Theological Seminary and Pittsburgh Theological Seminary that in the past provided opportunities for faculty members and graduates to study in the United States. Although established at a time when the expectation was that all the students would return to India, future links between institutions could facilitate preparation of leaders for Indian churches that now cross national boundaries. (2) Schools could work with bishops and other ecclesiastical executives who are responsible for priests from India assigned to serve Asian-Indian churches to help prepare them to minister to immigrants and their children living in American society. A period of adjustment in the context of a Christian seminary community with opportunities for study of American society and the experience of immigrants would enable newly arrived pastors to be effective more quickly and help them bridge the chasm that divides the cultures and the generations. (3) In-service continuing education programs designed specifically for Asian-Indian pastors and lay leaders would reduce the isolation of those removed from the regular support structures of their churches. Studies and discussions of youth ministries, liturgies, church and society, American church history, and contemporary theology would provide opportunities for cross-cultural exchange and mutual enrichment. (4) Seminaries need to pay attention to the difficulties emerging churches face in training pastors and other specialists. It is becoming obvious that theological training, knowledge of an Indian language, and pastoral experience in India are not necessarily the best preparation for serving the immigrant churches. Moreover, it is becoming clear that sending young people back to Kerala or Gujarat for theological education is not a viable option. What is not clear is where these young people will receive their theological education, because none of the churches can support a seminary in America. Perhaps a few seminaries could establish an affiliated relationship with Asian-Indian churches. A few strategically located seminaries or associations of schools could gather the bishops and ecclesiastical executives of Asian-Indian churches to discuss the best strategies and locations for educating their future clergy. A pre-seminary national conference of Asian-Indian youth considering Christian ministry as a vocation could explore options before the churches and the seminaries. (5) All seminaries and Bible colleges, whether they expect to educate Asian-Indian students or not, should review their curricula in an effort to better prepare all their students to become effective ministers in the midst of a changing religious landscape. The presence of Asian-

Indian Christians inside and on the doorsteps of many American seminaries constitutes part of the dramatic changes in American Christianity and these new immigrants in seminaries are best situated to help seminary colleagues and their teachers to understand these new contexts and opportunities.

The educational institutions that serve Asian-Indian Christians are liberal and conservative, Protestant and Catholic (only one student is enrolled at an Orthodox seminary), ecumenical and sectarian and represent the wide array of American Christianity. It is difficult to foresee what arrangements with diverse Asian-Indian groups will be salutary. Cooperation among seminaries in creating understanding and cooperation between new and old immigrants and among the newly emerging Christian churches would be a major step in creating a vital and harmonious future for American Christianity. They face a marvelous opportunity.

LOCAL CONGREGATIONS

A circuitous route in search of nascent Asian-Indian Christian groups in Dallas in the early 1980s eventually led to a pastor of a large church, who remembered that a group of some 200 Christians from India had rented the church gymnasium for worship services always followed by Indian dinners that wafted an aroma of curry throughout the rest of the complex. He never knew what region or church in India the people came from nor much about the pastor, thinking that perhaps he had been a student in a local seminary. Nor did he know what happened to the group; they just moved on. Benign neglect! Local congregations often are the first point of contact with immigrant Christians, and the effectiveness and depth of those contacts determine to a large extent the shape of the development of churches and institutions and strategies of adaptation new immigrants follow.

Several models of cooperation are currently experienced by Asian-Indian Christians.

(1) Individual Asian Indians join already existing congregations and participate in worship, study, and administration in ways common to other members. A strategy of assimilation rather than separation is actively undertaken by some families, thinking that is the best way to adjust to their new homeland and to encourage the Christian commitment of their children. Others who live where few Indian Christians are present have few options but to participate in churches that welcome

them. It is also common for immigrants to worship regularly in a church with the majority population and also worship in the evening or once a month with an Asian-Indian congregation, enjoying the best of both worlds. It would seem wise for congregational leaders to encourage such dual membership and participation and to attempt thereby to meet the special needs of both the immigrants and their children. Families regularly direct tithes and offerings to Christian projects in India, and at least one congregation takes a special offering to support a project sponsored by one of their Asian-Indian families. Individuals report that most congregations readily accept them as long as few other Asian Indians are present or until they participate long enough to assume leadership responsibilities. Then several report facing some resentment and subtle discrimination. Moreover, the ethos of some congregations runs counter to the commitments of Asian-Indian Christians and is perceived as a threat to their children, which leads them to gravitate to churches of more conservative denominations.

(2) Congregations rent out space and provide times for immigrant churches to meet in sanctuaries, chapels, or fellowship halls. These are contractual arrangements in which the immigrants are guests in the house and can be viewed as primarily providing a financial benefit to the established congregation or as part of the Christian service to provide low-cost or free facilities for the immigrants. Such arrangements are essential for nascent groups that have part-time ministerial services and cannot afford their own building. The pastor and leaders of the host church will benefit from learning as much as possible about their guests, because unnecessary tensions often accompany such arrangements and intercultural negotiation and understanding are always necessary. One arrangement broke down because members objected to the odor of the Indian fellowship meals served in the church hall. Tension arose over timing of services because the only times offered to Asian Indians were mid-afternoon and evening, which created a real problem for them because their discipline required fasting from Saturday evening until they received communion on Sunday. Existence of a separate chapel simplifies such arrangements. A Church of South India has been meeting in the chapel of a large Methodist Church in Dallas for many years. The Mar Thoma congregation in the Chicago area met in the chapel of the First Methodist Church in Evanston in the early years of development. The hospitality of the church enabled them to grow rapidly so that on at least one Sunday more Mar Thoma Christians (375 persons) were worshiping in the chapel than Methodists (295 persons) in

the main sanctuary. The Mar Thoma congregation by 1995 occupied its own large building in Des Plaines, with a weekly attendance of almost 700. A second parish of 20 families was commissioned on the south side of Chicago in January 1995.

(3) More formal agreements are reached by some congregations, referred to as "nesting," by which two congregations jointly manage buildings and schedules, but maintain separate services and programs. The congregation of immigrants maintains full control over its identity and commitments. Cost savings for underutilized facilities are great, and opportunities for learning about each other are enhanced by joint boards and committees. Sharing facilities often leads to joint programs in Sunday Schools, youth activities, social outreach, and summer programs.

(4) Asian Indians form units within multi-ethnic congregations in which they preserve their linguistic and ethnic distinctiveness. A congregation in Chicago has three "fellowships" and three services each Sunday in English, Gujarati, and Hindi. A congregation in Flushing, New York, has services in English, Tamil, and Korean. The arrangements regarding Christian education and youth programs depend upon the relative size of the fellowships and the stage of development. In many cases, separate language programs continue for adults, and joint programs are created for the children and youth. In one Methodist Church the English-speaking congregation numbers 30 members, and the immigrant congregation some 450 members. The *New York Times* reports: "They have been the salvation of First Methodist. Immigrants may see America as a land of opportunity, but for hundreds of churches like First Methodist, the immigrants themselves have been an opportunity" (July 30, 1986: B1). Unfortunately, in too many cases, the arrangement provides for the older English fellowship to support the newly emerging immigrant fellowships until it dies away. Yet some may look upon it as resurrection – life coming forth from death.

(5) Opportunities exist for cooperation between congregations that have their own buildings but intentionally develop programs that bring their members together for work, study, fellowship, and worship. Such cooperation is still rare. Asian-Indian congregations could benefit from adopting a congregation serving a different ethnic group so the two could share common challenges and successes. Very little contact exists between Asian-Indian congregations and those serving the Korean, Filipino, Chinese, African, or Caribbean Christians, even though these churches of new immigrants face many of the same problems. They

share the challenge of "singing the Lord's song in a foreign land" in ways not understood by the majority population. Together they constitute a major shift in American Christianity, but they do not recognize or provide mutual support to each other. The young people of immigrant congregations face special difficulties that could be alleviated through participation in sensitive and supportive groups. Established congregations of the majority population would benefit from cooperative arrangements with immigrant churches, learning thereby both the ecumenical character of Christianity and novel elements that will help shape American Christianity in the next century.

Each of these models represents an array of opportunities and challenges. The basic challenge is the creation of a context which provides opportunities for maintaining linguistic and ethnic identity, preserves freedom to evolve multiple options of adaptation, and encourages intercommunal harmony within the fellowship of faith that will be a leaven and example for the larger community. A motivation sure to lead to disaster is that of simply gaining members and additional financial support for established churches. Immigrants are distressed if they feel the established churches aim to win them away from their Indian church affiliations and fearful if they sense that the churches tend to create a deeper gulf between their Indian Christian identities and the American Christianity of their children. Church leaders need to be knowledgeable about Indian Christianity and sensitive to the special difficulties experienced by immigrants in order to welcome them truly as "brothers and sisters in Christ." Mutual learning and sharing is essential. Christian education programs and youth activities shared with immigrant Christians must take into account the particular customs, beliefs, and culture they bring to the encounters. Churches should encourage visits and periods of fellowship between families across cultural lines, which will provide insights for immigrants into American family life that they do not obtain through other social contacts and for others into the distinctiveness of Indian Christian family life and worship. Everyone needs to be sensitive to the understandable but peculiar dilemma of immigrant parents: they want their children to be successful as American Christians, but they fear that they will become like American Christians. Perhaps the arrival of Christian immigrants from many parts of the world will bring about a new and better vision of what it means to be American Christians. That will only happen, however, when salutary relations are established at the local level among Christians of many types.

ECCLESIASTICAL JUDICATORIES

Mar Thoma Christians met at their national conference in an American city and invited the local Episcopal bishop to be chief guest at the sesqui-centennial celebration of the "Protestant reformation of the Orthodox church in India." He sent as his representative a young priest from his office who meekly confessed that he knew nothing about the church in India or the reformation in Kerala. In those early days of new immigration, it seemed that only local politicians carefully identified, attempted to understand, and cultivated the new ethnics. A few years later the Mar Thoma national conference was in Washington, DC, and again another local Episcopal bishop was chief guest. The Mar Thoma bishop presented to the Episcopal bishop a plaque of thanksgiving showing the symbols of both churches side by side to symbolize the close partnership between the two churches. The two scenes illustrate the wide range of knowledge about and responses to immigrant churches, even within the same denomination, and the difficulty synods, conferences, and ecclesiastical chancelleries face in relating to newly formed churches in America. A denominational executive sensitive to many issues involved pondered aloud whether and how he should make contact with the American outposts of churches with which his denomination and several others were partners abroad. Would his initiative seem like a proselytizing move to have them join his denomination? Should he first contact local congregations in the United States or his ecclesiastical counterparts in India? Would his churches have anything to contribute to the immigrants? Would it seem like a new form of imperial interference? For the time being he did nothing, lest he make a mis-step. It may well be that the immigrant churches need a period of independence from too much outside influence and control before they can take their places; as one priest remarked, "First let us stand up and then we will be able to join in the dance." Nevertheless, isolation is hurtful.

Three models are dominant in judicatory relationships between Christians: denominational partnerships and intercommunion, minority caucuses within church structures, and mission churches. Judicatories attempt to provide for relationships with new immigrant congregations along lines of all three models with varying success. Those churches that maintain some contact are moving toward new models of association that will take account of the diversity of groups now within most of the church bodies in America.

Denominational partnerships and formal agreements of intercommunion are in place for some Asian-Indian churches, but until recently that meant, as a bishop noted, "full communion, but from afar." Now it is no longer from afar. The Episcopal Church enjoys a partnership relationship with both the Mar Thoma Church and the Church of South India and is strategically positioned to provide most assistance to the Episcopal churches of India. (See chapter 3.) Winston Ching, the chief officer of the Asian-American Ministries in the national office of the Episcopal Church, has been the most knowledgeable, sensitive, and influential person in establishing relationships with several of the Asian-Indian churches. He attends their conferences in both India and the United States, negotiates official agreements with ecclesiastical leaders, and marshals the resources of the Episcopal Church to assist with the certification of priests, negotiations regarding visa clearance, and provision of medical insurance. His personal initiative and service to the immigrant churches have been exemplary. A few Episcopal dioceses have made redundant buildings available to Mar Thoma congregations at reduced cost. Agreements reached when the immigrant churches were first formed are not adequate, however, when they establish dioceses and other institutions in America, but they did provide greater stability and essential nurture in the early days. New agreements are being contemplated that will reflect the new status.

Roman Catholic dioceses and officials are trying to adjust to new requirements of the Indian Eastern-Rite churches – Syro-Malabar and Syro-Malankara – that require a new model of relationship somewhere between partnership of separate churches and minority relationships within a single church. The Roman Catholic Church in America has experience dealing with nationality-based churches and language-based churches, and the first inclination was to treat the Indian churches in the same manner as a distinct ethnic group within the Latin rite. Although several dioceses still organize their ministry to Asian-Indians under ethnic or language ministries, Asian-Indian Catholics are slowly winning the battle to be recognized as a distinct church with a recognized rite. Ethnicity is preeminent in the American church; rite is preeminent in the Indian Catholic Church. American bishops are now entering into agreements with Indian bishops that allow priests from India to serve in the Oriental rites in America, and oversight is shared by the bishops – liturgical order coming from India and discipline being exercised in the United States. If the Catholic Church is able to fashion a model of relationship attentive to distinct rites, both in India and in the United States, it will have the value of combining the strength of unity and the beauty of diversity. Moreover, it could provide theological understanding of particularity within the church.

The mission model of relationship with new congregations creates confusion between overseas mission boards and home mission boards of some churches. Some Baptist conventions and Pentecostal organizations view the immigrant populations as "the mission field that moved next door" even though there seems to be little communication between executives in overseas missions, who seem most likely to know about the churches in India and other locations from which immigrants come, and those in home missions, who assume responsibility for reaching the "new ethnics." A blurred focus results from uncertainty about whether the mission is to gather the newly arrived Christians into ethnic churches or to convert nominal Christians and those who are not Christians into the missionary church. Individual Asian Indians and Asian-Indian congregations are somewhat apprehensive when they are approached as objects of mission. Billy Sunday is said to have once met with pastors of liberal churches in a city where he held an evangelistic mission only to be told that they did not like the way he evangelized. He responded, "Well, I don't like it much either, but I like it better than your way of not evangelizing." That could be the response of church executives who are trying to reach and provide some assistance to newly arriving Christians; it is better than ignoring them or treating them as interlopers. The Southern Baptist Church supports national consultants in the Language Division of the Home Missions Board to work with ethnic groups. Although they currently do not have a national consultant for Asian Indians, they do support catalytic ministers to work in the immigrant community. Although problematic for some immigrants, the mission model is effective in the early stages of immigration, but it requires some revision or a replacement with new modes of cooperation when the immigrant community becomes well-established.

Most American denominations house minority caucuses modeled after the black caucuses that developed out of the Civil Rights Movement. The existence of that structural category encourages immigrant churches and pastors to adapt their relationship along those lines. The structure is gently, but firmly, coercive in shaping judicatory adaptation to new immigrant churches and provides one of the few ways that immigrants can exercise political influence in the established churches. The Methodist Commission on Religion and Race sponsors several ethnic, regional, and national caucuses, including the National Federation of Asian American United Methodists. The Southern Asian

National Caucus of the United Methodists (SANCUM) is a recognized organization that brings pressure to bear upon denominational agencies and leaders, primarily on behalf of the clergy. Joining in caucuses provides some minimal political power, but it also serves to isolate the Asian Indians. Caucus structures at the conference and synod level are even less effective although they are better placed to provide assistance to struggling immigrant churches and pastors.

The tension between unity and particularity within the church places minority groups in an ambiguous position, and new immigrants share that uncomfortable position. Sang Hyun Lee provides a poignant description of the position as experienced by Korean Presbyterians:

The fundamental issue is this: In the present situation, the Presbyterian Church and its Korean American members are caught in a dilemma. On the one hand, the Korean immigrant churches' predicament of having to be ethnically particular for their constituency's all-essential communal needs is fully legitimated and recognized by the denomination. Yet, on the other hand, the ethnically particular communal needs of the Korean American Presbyterians are not allowed to be fulfilled in other aspects of the denominational life. The heightened ethnic role of Korean American churches is affirmed on the local congregational level and then denied on other levels of the church's life and work. What is expected of the Korean American churches beyond the congregational level is what goes against the very essence of their social function. That, in a nutshell, is the problem. And this problem will undoubtedly demand a resolution of some sort. (1991:326)

In 1994 the Presbyterian Church (USA) established a new Midwest Korean American Presbytery as a non-geographic presbytery of fifteen churches. Asian-Indian Christians are not as concentrated in one church body as the Korean Presbyterians, but their dilemma is similar, not only inside a single denomination, but within the larger Christian community as well. What role will ethnic churches have within ethnic communities through the passing of generations? What role will they have within the Christian community? How can the requirements and expectations of both communities be maintained within a coherent structure and program?

A major challenge facing ecclesiastical judicatories is to find the will and wisdom first to relate positively to the presence of newly arrived Christian immigrants and then to adjust their structures to respond effectively to the new diversity of peoples and churches in America. The two foci for these agencies at every level of the churches should be the religious initiatives of the newly arrived Christian immigrants and the new transnational character of the church (see chapter six). Current judicatory structures seem unable to sustain a unified mission, so a restructuring of what in some churches are called overseas ministries and homeland ministries could lead to a more efficient program. Cooperation with immigrants and their churches is not distinct from cooperation with the churches in their homelands. Moreover, each judicatory should structure itself so that it is attentive to the new Christians within its jurisdiction, both territorial and spiritual. Just as the territorial barriers that previously divided transnational churches are weakening, so too should the bureaucratic divisions that fragment the ministry and focus of the churches.

ECUMENICAL AGENCIES

Asian Indians have been engaged in the grassroots tasks of forming congregations, joining in local Indian or Malayalee Christian fellowship groups, and more recently designing dioceses and zonal councils, so that they have not had time or energy to pay much attention to ecumenical agencies. When viewed from the ground, little evidence suggests that the ecumenical agencies have recognized the presence of Asian-Indian Christians. Ecumenical groups at local and national levels engage in projects under the rubric of "Immigration and Refugees" – as do some ecclesiastical judicatories – but these are directed mainly at resettlement of refugees and affect Asian Indians only indirectly.

Councils of churches and ministerial associations in local areas would seem to be natural points of contact between immigrant Christians and churches and other leaders and churches. However, no pastor or lay person interviewed in this research mentions participation in any program of local councils or associations. None of the lay people among these immigrants comes with experience of participation in local ecumenical organizations, so they do not seek them out. Moreover, most of the Asian-Indian Christians live in large metropolitan areas, and their congregations are not neighborhood based. Rather, members drive from across the city and suburbs to attend services and have little knowledge of, or contact with, any organizations in districts where they meet. Urban councils have difficulty maintaining networks even among long-established churches and have little expertise, energy, or enthusiasm left over to reach out to new immigrants.

Indian Christians have substantial contacts with the World Council of Churches, and the recently appointed bishop of the Mar Thoma

Church in North America, Zacharias Mar Theophilus Episcopa, is a member of the Central and Executive Committee of the World Council of Churches. Another member of an Asian immigrant group has served as president of the National Council of Churches of Christ in the United States. Nevertheless, no substantial contact exists between the National Council of Churches and Asian-Indian churches. The council is based on denominational membership of a certain minimum size, forcing the immigrant churches to view themselves in denominational terms and to confirm the size of their membership before they are eligible to participate. That requirement seriously diminishes the impact that the ecumenical agency can have on immigrant Christians and their relatively small churches in the tenuous early period of migration or upon relatively large national groups of immigrants that are divided into several church groups. The period of growth of Asian-Indian churches and dioceses coincided with a period of retrenchment of the National Council of Churches, when serious cutbacks of staff, programs, and initiatives were required by the decline of support from the churches and other financial sources. Survival itself is in question. A Federal Council of Churches existed in the first part of the twentieth century to be replaced by the National Council of Churches in the second. Perhaps a new council or a totally revamped one will be necessary to face the opportunities and new contexts of American Christianity in the twenty-first century.

One group of ecumenical agencies that do have early and effective contact with the immigrants and their children are those engaged in campus ministries. A large portion of the immigrants become students in colleges and universities soon after immigration, and virtually all of their children attend or are headed for college and graduate schools. Indications are that conservative ecumenical campus ministries are reaching and serving Asian-Indian students. The Campus Crusade for Christ and the Intervarsity Christian Fellowship are important to some immigrants. One observer remarked that many of the young people between the ages of 20 years and 30 years remain active in the Asian-Indian congregations because of the influence of such campus organizations. Influences of these contacts are evident in the music, prayers, theology, and speeches at youth conferences, family conferences, and local services of the churches. A small number of young men are considering Christian ministry as a vocation, a career choice which is encouraged by their participation in campus groups, and leaders of these organizations typically direct them to conservative Bible colleges and seminaries. One young man changed his college major and dedicated himself for ministry while attending the Urbana conference of the Campus Crusade for Christ in 1987. Several Asian-Indian Catholics and Protestants remember as very important their participation in charismatic groups on university campuses; indeed, some indicate that they joined the Catholic renewal movement or Pentecostal churches as a result. The years at college or university are when young people reaffirm, revise, or discard the religious traditions transmitted to them by parents and church, and ecumenical campus ministries affect that process. Ecumenical campus ministries of liberal churches are on most large campuses and may serve some Asian-Indian Christians, but no mention was made of those organizations by immigrants in the course of this research.

The reality is that except on campus a majority of Asian-Indian Christians have little contact with Christians of other national, ethnic, or denominational groups. That contributes to a sense of isolation in the new churches, which reinforces tensions and misunderstandings that are often based on stereotypes derived from representations of American families and young people in the media, unchecked by personal interaction. The separation deprives established churches of primary opportunities to learn about the wider Christian world and to experience the growing religious diversity in their cities and nation. That diversity is largely Christian, even though much of the emphasis, both in the public media and in the churches, has been upon new immigrants from other religious traditions.

INTERFAITH ORGANIZATIONS

Interfaith organizations and programs are a "growth industry" in the United States as religious leaders respond to the new immigration and the push toward pluralism and multiculturalism that permeates academic and ecclesiastical discussions. The scope of interfaith organizations has expanded in stages throughout the century. In the early days discussions were primarily intracommunal among various branches of liberal Protestantism as expressions of or outgrowths from ministerial associations and alliances. Interfaith organizations still emerge primarily out of such associations as they change their focus and character. Following the Holocaust and the Second World War, Jewish leaders expanded their participation in interfaith dialogues and projects. Catholics became full participants in large numbers as a result of initiatives inspired by the

Second Vatican Council. Now another stage of development is reached resulting from demographic changes influenced by the immigration act of 1965 in which Protestants, Catholics, Jews, Muslims, and others join in the conversation. Evangelical Christian leaders generally do not participate in the meetings or programs of these interfaith organizations, nor would they receive warm welcomes.

How widely the net is cast for participants depends upon local circumstances and the specific occasion that generates interfaith action. Often it is a crisis in the community precipitated by misunderstandings regarding civil and religious rights of new immigrant religions: Muslim children are denied excused absences for religious observances; a Hindu group has extraordinary difficulty obtaining a building permit for a new temple; or Sikhs request permission to wear turbans as part of their military or municipal uniforms. The primary focus of interfaith organizations seems to be on facilitating the adaptation of new religions in America and removing both mutual ignorance and misunderstandings of other religions and cultures. The focus on the great world religions, as they are called, could reinforce the old misconception that East Asians are Buddhists, South Asians are Hindus, and West Asians are Muslim. A greater complexity of world religions is revealed in the new immigration to the United States, and that complexity includes Christians from all parts of the world.

Asian Indians are not yet participants in American interfaith organizations, even though some Christian theologians from India participate in programs of the Office on Inter-Religious Relations of the World Council of Churches. One reason for absence from American discussions is that the new immigrants are so busy trying to adapt and to learn how to live with other Christians in America that their eyes have not adjusted to another level of interfaith dialogue. Moreover, interfaith organizations seem more interested in dialogue and cooperation with Hindus from India, who are novel, rather than with Christians from India, who are similar to people already known in America. The absence from the table of these new immigrants is regrettable because they have experience of living as minorities among other religions. Hence, they have valuable contributions to make to analyses on the local level of both the theoretical and practical aspects of the relation of Christianity to other religions, which the Secretary General of the Office on Inter-Religious Relations of the World Council of Churches urges on local pastors and ecclesiastical leaders (Ucko, 1994:5).

The United States contains the broadest collection of religions ever found in one country; all the religions are here in the lives of immigrants and their descendants. The challenge is to develop modes of thought and behavior that are adequate to this new context. Within the Christian community, two models – of dialogue and mission – dominate discussions of interfaith relations, but those involved in interfaith conversations are moving slowly toward new models of relationship. If the new context in America successfully engenders new salutary modes of thought and behavior that can help sustain religious freedom and civic order, those could become the major contribution of America to humanity. Asian-Indian Christians and other Christians among the new immigrants should be invited to contribute their voices to these important conversations.

These mediating institutions are engaged to some degree in adding rooms to the house of American Christianity that will house both old immigrants and new immigrants. Should one build for permanent or temporary residence? A bishop in charge of one of the Asian-Indian dioceses suggests that the Asian-Indian churches will not continue long after the generation of first immigrants disappears. Youth in the churches face problems dealing with Indian languages and cultures and ask the pointed question, "Will ours be a one-generation church?" The experiences of earlier immigrants suggest that ethnic churches survive and transform themselves to meet new challenges to the community, so that rooms in the house are continuously remodeled, sometimes to the discomfiture of its residents. It is certainly the case that Asian-Indian churches now have a mission to shepherd immigrants and their children as they attempt to maintain their identities, faith, and culture in America. Mediating institutions are important agents both in helping to preserve the older generations in the faith of their fathers and, if their descendants decide to assimilate into other Christian communities, in assuring that vital and welcoming faith communities will be there to receive them.

Leadership is the key, but it is unclear where the leadership is being developed to respond effectively to these new challenges. Analysis of leadership roles within the Asian-Indian community (in chapter 5) suggested that religious specialists occupy a marginal position between India and the United States, between old and new immigrants and their descendants, between the generations, and between the past and the future. If in that challenge "India" is changed to "the world," the proposition holds good for all the leaders of established Christian congregations, agencies, and institutions in the United States. The danger is that leaders will think that new immigrants can be squeezed into already existing rooms or that new rooms or temporary lean-tos can be added without changing the basic structure of the house. New visions of the future of American Christianity are demanded from those who would lead into the new millennium, and without a vision, or at least without a carefully thought-out set of plans, the people will perish.

Conclusion: immigration and the many faces of Christ

An immigrant from India enters an American church and views a picture of Warner Sallman's portrait of Christ in a prominent place beside the pulpit and wonders what that picture means. Sallman's portrait of Christ is the most popular representation of Jesus in America, prominently displayed in many churches and homes. It captures the devotion of generations of immigrants to America. Yet it is also the case that Christians picture Jesus in their own image – Africans see Jesus as African, Chinese people as Chinese, and South Asians as Asian – so Jesus has many faces around the world. How is Jesus to appear in the eyes of Americans in the twenty-first century? One can imagine a computer-generated Jesus image evolving through a process called "morphing" generated for a popular music video in the mid-1990s, the sequence beginning with a single image and evolving through facial features of men, women, and children of all races and nationalities – a moving composite of the whole human family. Only such a complex picture adequately captures the reality of the many faces of Christ that attract the devotion of the growing diversity of Christians who now live in America. In no other country does such a rich diversity of colors, nationalities, races, ethnic and language groups, and church affiliations enrich the Christian community. Only computer-generated morphing images can capture the reality of American Christianity.

The shaping of American Christianity results from a long and complicated history of immigration and responses to patterns of migration developing across the past two centuries. The nation enters a new millennium in the midst of a new transnational reality and a distinctive pattern of immigration created by the immigration act of 1965. Christian immigrants from India are a small minority of these immigrants, but the reality is that every religious group entering the country is a small minority; that is part of the experience of being new immigrants. They join descendants of earlier immigrants and carry on the task of shaping

273

the face and future of America. An immigrant Indian pastor said, "The United States is a country of immigrants, so the people understand us." He expressed the sense that he and his congregation are writing a new chapter in the history of Christianity in America and that his new chapter rests beside those being written by Hindus, Muslims, Buddhists, and others in the contemporary story of religion in America. Hence, Christians are telling an old tale with new twists, one that reveals some of the continuities and discontinuities of the religious experience of coming to America.

AN OLD TALE WITH NEW TWISTS: CONTINUITIES WITH AN OLD TALE

(1) The strategies of adaptation followed by Asian-Indian Christians – individual, national, ecumenical, hierarchical, ethnic, and denominational, as described in chapter 3 – are strategies adopted by earlier immigrants as well. They are evident in secular spheres as well as religious: creating social clubs, newspapers, political parties, neighborhoods, burial societies, and a wide range of social service organizations. Religious organizations are a major component in the adaptation of immigrant groups. This work argues that it is the most important component both because it is often the first stage of association beyond the family and because religion anchors both personal and group identity in a transcendent realm.

Interactions among voluntary associations shaped by these strategies in America create much of the dynamism of American society because they constitute the mediating institutions through which groups of immigrants negotiate their new identities in relation to other social and religious groups of similar types. A thesis of this work is that religious and social groups do not constitute themselves and create boundaries for the purpose of remaining isolated from the larger society, but, rather, for the purpose of providing a secure social location from which they can negotiate with greater success their identities and relations with others. Conflict and conflict resolution, both internal to groups and external among groups, is a fundamental aspect of such negotiation, and that is what fuels the dynamism in social relations. Without the mediation of associations formed by these strategies of adaptation, the civic order would revert to an individual state of nature, "tooth and claw."

In a free society, an individual is able to sustain elements of a variety of social identities, align with several more or less coherent voluntary associations, and move with alacrity between strategies of adaptation that best meet needs in a given situation or social location. One must be aware of a complexity of strategies of adaptation in different contexts. They permit a specialized form of social mobility stemming from personal freedom that enables the conflict and conflict resolution to take place over time and within individuals as well as among groups, thereby reducing the risk of destructive conflict between unyielding social groups that imprison individuals. The American contract extending to immigrants both religious freedom and freedom of association continues to provide, as it has in the past, the best hope for the relatively peaceful integration of new social and religious groups into the fabric of the nation. That is the defining characteristic of the American experiment.

(2) Asian-Indian Christians assimilate easily with American society in some ways but are blocked from full assimilation in other ways just as were previous immigrants, such as the German Jews in the nineteenth century. A majority of Asian-Indian Christians are highly educated, technologically proficient, and professionally successful; therefore, they move without much assistance or disturbance into jobs, adequate housing, and many social groups. As Christians, some individuals find a welcome in congregations and, when they have desired to have separate meetings as denominational or ethnic groups, find assistance in using church buildings and facilities. Young people are successful in schools and colleges, and some are entering seminaries and graduate programs. As a whole, they are writing another American success story, modeled on those of earlier immigrants.

Asian Indians are people of color, as are a majority of new immigrants admitted since 1965, so prejudices in American society based on race and color erect barriers, both psychological and structural, to full participation. Race has been an ambiguous legal category for immigrants from India since early in the twentieth century when immigrants from the Punjab were granted citizenship as Caucasians. That claim to be legally considered Caucasian was denied by the United States Supreme Court in the case of *United States v. Bhagat Singh Thind* (261, US 204) on February 19, 1923. Justice Sutherland declared that an immigrant from India was not "a free white person" within the meaning of the existing law and hence not eligible for American citizenship or for land ownership. *De jure* racial restrictions to civil rights no longer pertain, but Asian Indians suspect that they do *de facto*. A frustrating aspect of their experience is that they cannot be sure how much of the difficulty in assimilating is due to color or to some other characteristic they share with other immigrants (e.g. language difficulty) or with the general population (e.g. deficiency of interpersonal skills). Generally, Asian Indians are reluctant to complain of racial or color discrimination because that involves a self-defined alliance with minorities rather than with the majority.

Asian-Indian Christians find themselves in the arena of negotiations in American society based on color. One option is to seek the most advantageous social location based on color, which may result in establishing a color hierarchy in which Asian Indians occupy a location next to Caucasians, the strategy of the Asians in East Africa, and to distance themselves from other Asian Americans, Latin Americans, and African Americans. One portion of Will Herberg's thesis that has some relevance here is that marriage patterns, only just now developing among Asian Indians, may indicate the role that race, color, and religion have in the assimilation of new immigrants. Conversations and sermons in the Asian-Indian Christian churches that link American racism with Indian casteism indicate that the issue is a potent one in the community. As in India, so in America, the issue becomes critical in marriage arrangements. It is no accident that marriage ads in Asian-Indian newspapers regularly list "fair" as a requisite for marriage partners. Another option is that Asian-Indian Christians will occupy a mediating position in the color conflicts in America, softening the dualistic conflict between white and black, and will lead the way to more harmonious relations. That is a great deal to ask of a new immigrant group, but some Asian-Indian Christian leaders see that as their special calling.

(3) The realities of life in Christian America do not meet the expectations of new Christian immigrants, just as they did not for earlier Danish or Swedish Lutherans. "Gates of pearl and streets of gold" are metaphors for both secular economic prosperity and the religious kingdom of God. New immigrants generally earn more than would be possible for them in India and, by many measures, are far better off. Still, people do not live by bread alone, and some worry that they have gained a world and lost their souls. Material prosperity does not result in a greater sense of security, more leisure time, or even the services they took for granted in India. Moreover, they are disappointed in the general spiritual condition of Christian America. They arrive thinking of it as "the righteous empire" and "a Christian nation," but soon develop a sense of alienation from the reality they discover. A Christian leader confesses that, when meeting visitors from India at the airport, he drives them the long way

around to his house to avoid exposing them to evidences of urban blight, personal suffering, and social disorder they would otherwise encounter. "I don't want them to see the dark side of America," he says.

The tension between the anticipated ideal and the lived reality forces new immigrants to redefine the relationship of individuals and groups to American "Christian" society. They cannot recreate the relationship that existed in India, nor can they comfortably adopt elements of the concordat that shapes the social contract of church and society relations in America. Hence, Asian-Indian Christians are in the process of redefining what it means to be a Christian in contemporary America. If the role of immigration is as important in defining American culture as this research suggests, the continual redefinition by immigrants in their negotiation with churches and society is a major source of the vitality of religion in America, temporarily redirected by the lull in immigration at mid-century, but now again in full force, not only among immigrant groups but throughout society as well. Asian-Indian Christians may have a small voice in defining religion in America in the twenty-first century, but they and other new immigrants constitute a cacophony of voices that will in no small measure shape the debate.

(4) Tensions exist within and among Asian-Indian Christian groups about how Americanized the religious community should become. These tensions are similar to those existing among Roman Catholic immigrants arriving during periods of Anglo-Protestant hegemony. Some Asian-Indian churches attempt to preserve ancient forms of Oriental orthodoxy in doctrine, ritual, and custom. They face many of the same difficulties as did the earlier Catholic immigrants in trying to preserve the "sacred" language of both word and ritual in alien settings. Ethnic customs and cuisine are under attack, especially by young people, and it is difficult for the elders to distinguish clearly between relatively insignificant aspects of cultural heritage and those fundamental beliefs and practices that are part of their basic Christian commitments. For example, marriage has been experienced as a Christian rite involving specific commitments by the couple's extended families prior to the marriage. How much of that is Christian? How much can be jettisoned without loss of the family's Christian identity? In addition to strong pressures to conform exerted by secular society and experienced by all Christians, most Christians among the new ethnics are compelled by their ecumenical vision of the universal church to work out accommodations with their Christian brothers and sisters, which always involves some compromises, made all the more difficult because other Christians

are not aware of the price new immigrants are paying for being cooperative. A few sectarian groups maintain their strict separation and lambast the "nominal Christians" living at peace in the kingdom of the devil. Each individual and group is trying to decide where to "draw a line in the sand" that will set limits to their compromises with what they perceive to be the evils of American society.

(5) One expression of these tensions is an overwhelming concern for the young people and for the transmission of both ethnic and religious traditions to the second generation. Immigrants are separated from their extended families, which traditionally have been loci of cultural transmission. They also lose contact with mediating structures at the same time that alternative mediating structures in American society are perceived to be weakening. An entire genre of literature developed in narratives of children growing up in families of earlier immigrants. Tensions within families, sometimes destructive but often enormously creative, document the difficulties immigrant families have in transmitting their traditions and maintaining unity and harmony between the generations. Similar stories of the new ethnics are not yet written; they are being lived. Outside the home, religious communities are the most significant ethnic associations in which these tensions are acknowledged, discussed, and worked out, because of the transcendent basis of their authority. Religious communities also serve as fictive extended families for immigrants. One hypothesis resulting from this research, as yet undocumented from the experience of earlier immigrants, is that churches, temples, synagogues, and other religious organizations begin to develop at the time when children in the second generation come under the sway of social groups and influences outside their homes and nuclear families. During earlier periods of immigration, as now, parents expressed their concern for the well-being and religious identity of their children by turning to the church. It is too early in this immigration cycle to predict whether the developing second generation of Asian-Indian Christians will remain more faithful to the ways of their parents than descendants of previous immigrants.

(6) Asian-Indian Christians are experiencing internal splits in their churches over the authority of the clergy. Hence, they follow the example of earlier immigrants in dividing into many separate small congregations and establishing schismatic church organizations. Divisions relative to two types of religious authority are present. First, disputes occur regarding the religious and constitutional rights of the church in India to extend its authority over clergy living and working in

the United States. A tendency exists for new churches to uphold legal independence and the constitutional separation of religious authority, especially because many of the earliest churches were established by lay-people. Hence, it is thought that the congregations in the United States have the right to select their own clergy. Second, disputes occur regarding the charismatic authority of pastors and their personal characteristics and abilities for ministry to both parents and young people in the United States. Because few of the churches have a regularized clergy in America, few mechanisms exist for the training and placement of clergy to serve the immigrant communities. Moreover, splits occur based on family loyalties, as, for example, when a pastor arrives and leads members of his extended family and friends in the formation of a new congregation. Personality conflicts and competitions for status often result in division in the church.

More is involved, however, than personality conflicts or strong egos. The structure of religious freedom in the United States and the ethos of voluntary organization encourages a group- and status-specific division of religious groups, especially among recent immigrants. Divisions in both religious and secular organizations result from the redefinition of personal and group identity that immigration requires and that residence in America encourages.

AN OLD TALE WITH NEW TWISTS: DISCONTINUITIES AND NEW TWISTS

New immigrants are not the same as the earlier ones; that is the dramatic effect of the changes in the US Immigration and Nationality Act of 1965. Nor are the experiences of the Asian-Indian Christians the same as those of Christians who came from England or Europe in the nineteenth century. Their stories have new twists that reflect the changed circumstances of immigration and changes in American society.

(1) They are the first Christians from India to come to the United States as part of the brain-drain from developing countries. They join other Asian Christians in America in establishing forms of Christianity new to the nation. Hence, they come from, and arrive in, a different cultural context from earlier immigrants. These Christians predominantly have in common specific occupations in health-care, not common to earlier immigrants. They come from a single modern nation shaped by the dynamics of nation-building, but it is not clear that they represent one ethnic group because they come from diverse Christian groups

separated by language, ethnicity, and church identities. They represent a complex internal diversity joining a larger diversity.

Their migration is part of a new transnational reality that changes the nature of their relationships with relatives and churches in India from that experienced by previous immigrants. The period after 1965 saw a renewed valuation of ethnicity, extending the pride of "black is beautiful" to the new ethnics. Now the concept of ethnicity is being reconsidered because of the effects of transnational mobility and communication. Asian-Indian Christians experience church life caught between two cultures through transnational associations of church leaders. Increasingly, however, they are buffeted by the division between two church cultures, liberal and conservative, that are becoming more important than denominational identity. The dichotomy between liberal and conservative Christians is itself becoming transnational, creating reverse effects on the churches of India. Hence, the new immigrants represent new configurations of forces loose in a new world order.

(2) Christian immigrants from India join other new ethnics who come from what some still think of as "the mission field" even though they claim an ancient heritage. The fruits of mission activity are now being harvested in America, which is a novel experience. These new immigrants and their churches already have pre-existing relationships with the receiving culture through denominational mission boards and churches. A group of Gujarati Christians joined the church that sent the first missionary to their hometown of Bulsar. Immigrants tell of traveling to retirement homes to visit missionaries they had known in India. Before they immigrated, some Indian bishops and pastors were well acquainted with American church leaders through denominational boards and ecumenical agencies. Such pre-existing relationships change the dynamics of negotiations between immigrants and American churches.

The vision and the structures of the churches are, however, generally not adequate to take account of these changes. The goal of mission activity of American churches was to establish and strengthen Christian churches and institutions abroad, not to train people to immigrate to America, so the arrival of Christian immigrants is not perceived to be a positive or desired result of mission activity. Moreover, mission activity of the churches is still geographically specific and directed "over the heads" of the arriving immigrants to their churches in India and other developing countries. American denominational and judicatory structures have not adjusted to the new transnational reality of families and churches, but are still divided into separate foreign mission and home mission boards. Hence, neither the emerging churches nor the already existing churches are generally able to benefit from the pre-existing relationships. Only the Roman Catholic Church and the Episcopal Church, the latter with the guidance of Winston Ching, have been marginally successful in responding to the responsibilities of the pre-existing relationships.

(3) The mission field has come to America in more ways than one. A striking reversal of the location of the mission field has occurred. American churches currently send out few missionaries, a situation resulting from theological developments in formerly mainline churches and from financial restrictions that direct a larger portion of reduced church income to local and national bureaucratic structures. America itself seems to need new types of missionaries in the form of nurses to work in urban hospitals and priests to serve the Asian-Indian Christian community. Pastors are moving slowly out of the immigrant churches to serve other congregations, a development more pronounced in the Roman Catholic Church in which priests and nuns from India and other developing countries are meeting the crisis caused by the dramatic decline in numbers of people choosing religious vocations in the United States.

The new transnational context requires both the restructuring of denominational and mission boards and the redefinition of "missionary." A few boards have revised their nomenclature to refer to "fraternal workers" to avoid negative, imperialistic connotations of "missionary." Churches in every country are likely to become both sending and receiving churches requiring new ways of relating to immigrants who work in the helping professions and who see themselves following a Christian vocation even though not paid by the churches. Priests, pastors, and others also immigrate to serve churches of new immigrants, join ecumenical agencies, and serve multiethnic churches. Church structures to recognize, validate, encourage, and support these new "missionaries" from the mission field are nascent, inefficient, and relatively powerless. Much has been said about the adaptation of new immigrants; a great deal of adaptation is required in American churches and church agencies to take account of the new situation.

(4) Indian immigrants introduce new strands of Christianity in the United States that were developed and tested in the crucible of Indian history and culture. Other new immigrants contribute different strands from Korea, China, Viet Nam, Africa, and the Caribbean. The question immediately arises: what is the newness of Indian Christianity other than ethnicity? Enjoyment of the new dress, cuisine, accent, and sounds of

ethnic religions may well lead to greater appreciation and even tolerance of difference, but a more fundamental issue is the contribution Asian-Indian Christian neighbors can make to American Christian understanding of itself and to contemporary faith and commitments. The St. Thomas Christians bring an ancient tradition shaped by long association with Syrian Orthodox theology and practice. Others represent generations of Christian experience, both fending off and adapting to Indian cultural influences. How have these experiences influenced theology and ritual in ways that can enrich American Christianity? The answer requires more disciplined attention than has yet been devoted to the question and more knowledge of the life of Christians from India, Korea, China, and other countries than is currently available even among theologians and pastors, much less among laypeople. Perhaps the question will reopen and redirect theological and ecumenical discussions that have become moribund. Perhaps the contributions of these new strands of Christianity will be ignored and lost in the process of adaptation. The issue is undecided, but is already included in the subtle negotiations among Asian-Indian Christian groups and with those already established in America. Such negotiations involve both expressions of power and a search for truth, and it is too early to predict how they will evolve.

(5) Asian-Indian Christians experience the move from a minority position in a modern secular state to alliance with a Christian majority in the receiving nation. Other minorities elect to remain minorities of one sort or another – one thinks of Jews and Amish. Indeed, every religious group is a minority in some social contexts. Nevertheless, Asian Indians and other recent Christian immigrants come from experiences of living in states dominated by Hindus, Muslims, Buddhists, or others. American Christians have spoken a great deal about religious pluralism but without the experience of living as a minority, or, indeed, where many religions are present.

Minority status seems to result in a stronger inclination to maintain boundaries and to establish clear identity than is currently exhibited by much of the speculation about interreligious dialogue appearing in the United States. Some of these new immigrants had success in their native places in developing close working relationships, if not of affirmation, at least of tolerance with other religious groups. New immigrants bring with them all the religions of the world, which will make more urgent, and surely change the character of, interreligious dialogue and cooperation in America. Asian-Indian Christians add new perspectives and new voices to that conversation.

(6) Thus far, Asian-Indian Christians enjoy a positive, or at least indifferent, reception in the receiving society. India and Indians rank relatively high on the positive scales of public opinion in relation to other new ethnics. Christians among them enjoy the generally positive evaluation accorded to Christianity in public opinion. Their experience is significantly different from that of Muslims and Hindus from India, because both Islam and Hinduism are judged harshly by some in the society. Negative reaction has been relatively mild, despite some color bars that occasionally appear. Most earlier immigrant groups aroused negative, nativist reactions.

Initiatives to limit immigration, primarily of illegal aliens who arrive through holes in the southern border, may gain strength and wash over Asian-Indian Christians. That could complicate negotiations among religious groups in the short term. Still, it is impossible to be a little bit pregnant, and it is unlikely that the doors to the United States will again be closed to people from India. New ethnic and religious groups will continue to grow, establish churches and other religious institutions, and plant their roots in American soil. There is no turning back.

LAST WORDS

The question of whether Jesus appears with one face or with many faces is a parable for the dual interpretations and models of immigrant experience in America: assimilation and pluralism. The issue is usually couched in Christian terms as being between ecumenical unity of the body of Christ and the continuation of denominational, ethnic, economic, or color-based divisions. The new situation of Christian immigration breaks some old patterns and demands new, more dynamic models of stating the relation of identity, self-understanding, and community. Perhaps in this time of rapid communication, created in large measure by telecommunications systems, the best symbol of the new Christian reality is the computer-generated morphing of the human face as the evolving face of Christ. More varieties of colors, national origins, races, ethnic groups, and church affiliations are present in American Christianity than in any other location in the world, and many of them have been added since 1965. That is a remarkable fact, one that cannot be overlooked in any analysis of contemporary American Christianity. Only something like an evolving image could be an appropriate symbol.

An essential purpose of these Christian groups, in common with other social groups, is to create and maintain boundaries within which individuals can fabricate their identities and preserve continuities with the past. These groups can form either workshops or prisons. The challenge for the Christian church in America is to provide materials, perhaps newly conceived and newly worked, with which groups can build porous boundaries, ones strong enough to sustain personal and group identity but sufficiently permeable to allow easy, natural, non-threatening movement among groups that will promote cooperation and goodwill.

If the church succeeds, the civic and religious conversation will involve new voices that will enable all to hear ancient truths and modern voices of liberation from around the world. The conversation will enlarge to encompass a lively interreligious dialogue based on regular, familiar, and honest interchange among neighbors from a world community now a part of the American experiment. If not, the glorious American experiment may be closer to its end than any are wont to think.

Notes

1 "Asian Indian" is the official government designation established in the US Census of 1980 for people with family origins in India. "Indian Americans," "Indian/Americans," "Indians," "East Indians," and "Indo-Americans" are designations informally used in some contexts. The official designation is used in this work even though a minority of immigrants from India are uncomfortable with it.

2 At issue in the case of a nurse trained in the Philippines was whether "Registered Professional Nurses" without a baccalaureate degree were included in the professional category. The ruling was: "On the basis of these considerations it is concluded that a nurse may be considered as a member of the professions if she has been awarded a diploma or certificate signifying successful completion of a program for professional nurses conducted by an accredited hospital or independent school, or has attained a baccalaureate degree or an associate degree in nursing, as described in the Occupational Outlook Handbook" (*Administrative Decisions under Immigration and Nationality Laws of the United States*, XII:420). This opened the door for nurses from India who were trained in approved mission or government hospitals.

3 Note that the Immigration Act of 1990 dramatically changed the preference classifications for both family-based and employment-based immigration (letter of January 31, 1994 [HQ 203.8–C] from Edward H. Skerrett, Chief, Immigrant Branch, Adjudications, Immigration and Naturalization Service, US Department of Justice).

4 In 1980 the ethnic identity of Registered Nurses in the United States was: White 1,521,752 (91.5 percent), Black 60,845 (3.7 percent), and Asian & Pacific Islanders 33,600 (2 percent). (*The Registered Nurse Population: An Overview from the National Sample Survey of Registered Nurses*. Nov. 1980, rev. 1982 HRS-P-OD, January 1983).

5 Of the 2,720 persons of Indian origin who became naturalized citizens in 1975, 1,687 were listed as professionals and technicians and 141 as managers. Another 520 were housewives and children. These new immigrants were predominantly young. Of the arrivals in 1970, 1 out of 7 was under 10 years of age and more than 3 out of 5 were under 30 years (Hess, 1976:176). Only 1 in 50 Asian Indians was over 65 years of age in 1980.

6 The variation is great between Asian Indians who entered before 1980 (mean family income of $84,119 and per capita income of $36,653) and those who entered between 1980 and 1990 (mean family income of $42,665 and per capita income of $12,916).

7 Of the 450,406 foreign-born Asian Indians in the 1990 census, 157,210 were naturalized citizens and 293,196 were not citizens (65.1 percent). A larger percentage eventually are naturalized. Of the immigrants of Indian origin admitted in the calendar years 1970–79 some 51.9 percent became citizens by 1991 (*INS Statistical Yearbook*:121, Chart).

8 The gender percentages of the 45,064 immigrants from India in 1991 are: males 60.7 percent and females 39.3 percent (INS, 1991:52, Table 12).

9 The estimate is the author's, based on calculations of participants in all the established Asian-Indian churches, an estimate of those participating in other congregations, and an estimate of "unchurched" Asian-Indian Christians. Hence, Christians are a distinct minority among the more than 1 million Asian Indians in the United States.

10 The first communist government was ousted in 1959. In June 1991 the latest communist-led government was removed in the general election.

11 Percentages of adult literacy for India in 1990 were 62 for males and 34 for females (United Nations Population Fund, 1993:52).

12 Those surveyed do not represent a scientific sample, because questionnaires were distributed widely to adults at annual family conferences and at two congregational gatherings: Mar Thoma Family Conference in McLean, VA, on July 2–4, 1993 (217 responses); Syrian Orthodox Family Conference in Dallas, TX, on July 9–11, 1993 (42 responses); Church of South India Family Conference in Fort Worth, TX, on July 8–11, 1993 (25 responses); Malankara Orthodox Family Conference in Los Angeles on July 15–18, 1993 (99 responses); Indian Brethren Conference in Mt. Vernon, OH, on July 21–25, 1993 (80 responses); Church of the Brethren congregational meeting in Naperville, IL, on January 30, 1994 (15 responses); Malankara Orthodox congregation luncheon in St. Louis, MO, on March 20, 1994 (27 responses); and Indian Pentecostal Conference in Chicago, IL, on July 1–3, 1994 (161 responses). The request was made that only adults fill out the questionnaires even though many children and youths were present, so very few people under 18 years of age are included in the sample. The questionnaires are anonymous, but many questions were left unanswered by a significant number; the item regarding family income completed by only 615 people is one example. Of those who indicated gender 256 were female and 394 male. A higher percentage of the sample is Keralite than is the case for the immigrant community as a whole. Most of the questionnaires came from people with sufficient financial resources and religious commitment to attend family conferences, which last several days and involve considerable expense.

The survey indicates that very few of the people attending the conferences have changed churches. No pattern exists regarding which churches lose members, but several churches lost members in small numbers (Syrian Orthodox 16; Catholic 10; Pentecostal 9; Brethren Assemblies 6; CSI 6; and Mar Thoma 5).

2 CHRISTIAN STORIES ABOUT INDIA

1 The most helpful general works on the history of Christianity in India for reformulating and checking the stories told by immigrants are: Neill, 1984, 1985; G. Menachery, 1973, 1982; Moffett, 1992; Brown, 1956; and Pothan, 1963. These works were used regularly in the preparation of this chapter to check dates, interpretations, and details and for guidance in relating parts of the stories.

2 The Byzantine, Alexandrian, Antiochene, Armenian, and Chaldean are the five principal rites used in their entirety or in modified form by the various eastern churches.

3 Unofficial estimates in the mid-1980s put the number of Catholics belonging to the Syro-Malabar rite in the largest cities in India as follows: 60,000 in Bombay, 35,000 in Madras, 36,000 in Bangalore, 10,000 in Delhi, 10,000 in Pune, and 8,000 in Calcutta (Mundadan, 1984:105).

4 For the complete text of the decree, see n.a., 1966: 165–78.

5 The 1981 Census of India recorded for Kerala a Christian population of 5,233,865 (Hindus, 14,801,347; Muslims 5,409,687), the greatest concentrations in districts from Cochin to the east and south: Ernakulam 1,019,249 (Hindus 1,173,596; Muslims 339,737); Kottayam 805,953 (Hindus 807,014; Muslims 84,217); Alleppey 635,193 (Hindus 1,539,534; Muslims 175,021); Idukki 419,288; Quilon 637,516; Trivandrum 459,396. Concentrations are smaller as one moves north from Cochin: Trichūr 612,438; Palghat 76,690; Malappuram 57,217; Kozhikode 107,711; Wayanad 135,504; Cranganore 267,710. Christians were identified as rural (4,294,063) and urban (939,802).The total number of Christians in India was recorded as 16,174,498. For comparative purposes, one may note that the number of Christians given for Gujarat was 132,703 (*1981 Census of India Household of Population by Religion of Head of Household, 1985*). The Christian community in Tamil Nadu grew from 1,763,000 (5.23 percent of the population) in 1961 to 2,798,000 (5.78 percent) in 1981. The Kanya Kumari district at the southern tip of India had the highest concentration of Christians with 551,908 among a population of 1,423,399, comprising 38.8 percent (Grafe, 1990:135, 137).

6 Plymouth Brethren and the Brethren Assemblies are not affiliated with the Church of the Brethren found in Gujarat. They are different denominations.

7 Eight main centers are in Kerala, with many branches: Kottayam, 40; Trivandrum, 28; Kottarakara, 50; Tiruvalla, 45; Munnar, 11; Trichur, 10; Ernakulam, 13; Calicut, 23. Outside Kerala representative centers are: Madras, 65; Bangalore, 20; Bombay, 21.

8 Personal conversation with Fr. Fio Mascaranhas, SJ, in Bombay on March 1, 1994.
9 The North Kerala Diocese is more diverse than the other two and is divided for administrative purposes into three districts: the Basel Mission area, the CMS area, and the Wynaad area made up primarily of new settlers.
10 Contemporary terms now designate untouchables (*dalits*) and tribal peoples (*adivasis*), but use of these terms to describe earlier social relations involves an anachronism.
11 When the Latin diocese of Cochin was divided in 1950–53 to make the new diocese of Alleppey, the churches of the Agnuttikar existing within the territory of the diocese of Cochin were put under the bishop of Alleppey (who was of the Agnuttikar community), and the churches of the Ezhunnuttikar existing within the territory of the diocese of Alleppey were put under the bishop of Cochin (who was of the Ezhunnuttikar community). As an eminent Catholic scholar concluded, "Thus it is clear that it is not difference of rite that divides the Christians of Malabar into different water-tight communities" (Podipara, 1986:116).
12 Notice the difference in numbers between the social service institutions owned by the Syrian Catholic Christians and the Latin Catholics:

colleges: Syrian 30; Latin 12; total 42
high and middle schools: Syrian 500; Latin 212; total 712
hospitals: Syrian 116; Latin 20; total 136 (Koiparampil, 1982:205)

3   BECOMING WHAT YOU ARE: ST. THOMAS CHRISTIANS FROM KERALA

1 The constitution of 1950 established certain affirmative action initiatives on behalf of the scheduled castes and tribes. A Presidential Order in 1950 denied to Christians belonging to those groups most of the benefits of compensatory discrimination. That order resulted in a long struggle by *dalit* Christians for equal rights, most recently manifested in a protest march in New Delhi in August, 1990.
2 For an earlier description of strategies of adaptation focused primarily on Hindu organizations, please see Williams, 1992:228–57.
3 These two branches of the Syrian Orthodox Church were united between 1960 and 1971, but divided when a new law suit was filed in India. The case is still before the Indian Supreme Court.
4 Christology is an important topic in these ecumenical discussions because of early controversies regarding Nestorian doctrines attributed to the churches of the East.
5 These decisions and instructions are in a letter No. 84/95 from Baselios Marthoma Mathews II, Catholicos of the Apostolic Throne of St. Thomas and Malankara Metropolitan, dated April 28, 1995, to the vicars, managing committees, and parishes in the diocese of America.
6 The title "metropolitan" is reserved in the Mar Thoma Church for the most

senior bishop of the church in terms of years since ordination, and that bishop is the titular head of the church. The suffragan is the second most senior bishop and is metropolitan-elect. Other Syrian churches use the term "metropolitan" to refer to any bishop.

7 The 1992 directory lists active membership in parishes by families: Chicago, 236; Dallas, 193; Houston, 271; Ozone Park, NY, 218; Merrick, NY, 130; Philadelphia with two churches, 196 and 103; and several churches with around 100 families.

4 BECOMING WHAT YOU ARE: CATHOLICS AND PROTESTANTS FROM INDIA

1 Supreme Court of the State of New York, County of Queens. "India Catholic Association of America against The India Catholic Association of America, Inc., and John Panicker" decided by Judge Calabretta on January 28, 1982, in favor of the defendants' motion for a dismissal (Index No. 17664/81).

2 The first Malankara Catholic Church Mass was celebrated in the United States in 1947 by Archbishop Metropolitan Mar Ivanios Panickeruveetil. Benedict Mar Gregorius visited and celebrated the Mass in 1953.

5 WILDERNESS, EXILE OR PROMISED LAND: EXPERIENCE AND INTERPRETATIONS OF MIGRATION

1 The name and some of the details of the story have been changed so the individual will not be identifiable.

6 GOING HOME: BRIDGES TO INDIA

1 The number of South Asians in west Asia in 1987 was 1,217,141 (United Arab Emirates, 382,302; Oman, 190,000; Kuwait, 355,947; Saudi Arabia, 79,987; Qatar, 51,500; Bahrain, 48,050) (Clarke, Peach, and Vertovec, 1990:2).

7 ADDING ROOMS TO THE HOUSE

1 The exception may be Korean Presbyterians, who are present in significant numbers. McCormick Theological Seminary in Chicago now conducts some classes in the Korean language.

2 The survey was conducted in two stages. The first was to send institutional survey forms to presidents, deans, or registrars of 185 seminaries, divinity schools, and theological schools in the United States listed in the American Theological Schools Bulletin #40 for 1993–94 and to 76 Bible colleges in the United States listed in the Directory of the American Association of Bible Colleges, for a total of 261 institutions. A second request was made to those

institutions that did not respond to the initial request within three months. Responses were received from 155 seminaries and 61 Bible colleges, for a total of 216 institutions. School officials were the best source for information about total numbers, gender, resident status, and degree programs, but generally lacked detailed information regarding regional–linguistic background, denominations affiliation, or career goals.

A student survey form was sent to each student identified by the institutional official. When names of students were provided, the survey form was sent to each with a personal letter. In those cases where institutions refused to provide names on the grounds of confidentiality, survey forms were sent to the officials with the request that they forward the forms to the students. The pool does not represent a scientifically defined sample. Surveys were anonymous, and no names were recorded. The promise was given that data would be reported only in aggregate form. Of the 195 survey forms distributed, 13 were returned as undelivered, and 77 completed forms were returned, many with additional information written on the back of the page. These forms confirm the detailed information from the first survey mentioned above and give more reliable data regarding place of origin, marital status, church affiliation, and career goals.

Bibliography

1969. *Kretzmann Commission Report: Theological Education in Andhra Pradesh*. Hyderabad, India: Andhra Christian Theological College.

1993. *Statistical Abstract of the United States 1993*. 113th edn., US Bureau of the Census.

Agarwal, Priya. 1991. *Passage from India: Post-1965 Indian Immigrants and Their Children*. Palos Verdes, CA: Yuvati Publications.

Alexander, K. C. 1972. "The neo-Christians of Kerala." In *The Untouchables in Contemporary India*, ed. J. Michael Mahar, pp. 153–64. Tucson: University of Arizona.

1977. "The problem of caste in the Christian churches of Kerala." In *Caste among Non-Hindus in India*, ed. Harjinder Singh, pp. 50–65. New Delhi: National Publishing House.

Anthony, K. S. 1988. "Development of the Syro-Malabar Mission of Chicago." In the *Souvenir for the Syro-Malabar Catholic Mission Inauguration of the Mar Thoma Shlecha Church in Belwood, Illinois on September 10, 1988*. N.p.

Apopassery, George, and Thomas Arukalil, eds. 1986. *Catholic Directory of Kerala 1986*. Angamaly, India.

Badhwar, Inderjit. 1980. "Indians in America – at the crossroads." *India Tribune*, August 16, 1980, pp. 16–17.

Banks, Marcus. 1992. *Organizing Jainism in India and England*. Oxford: Clarendon Press.

Basch, Linda, Nina Glick Schiller, and Christina Blanc-Szanton. 1994. *Nations Unbound: Transnational Projects, Postcolonial Predicaments, and Deterritorialized Nation-states*. Langhorne, PA: Gordon and Breach.

Bayly, Susan. 1989. *Saints, Goddesses and Kings: Muslims and Christians in South Indian Society 1700–1900*. Cambridge University Press.

Beach, Harlan Page, and Charles Harvey Fahs, eds. 1925. *World Missionary Atlas*. New York: Institute of Social and Religious Research.

Beaver, R. Pierce. 1971. "Comity." In *Concise Dictionary of the Christian World Mission*, ed. Stephen Neill, Gerald H. Anderson, and John Goodwin, p. 123. Nashville: Abingdon Press.

Bellah, Robert N., Richard Madsen, William M. Sullivan, Ann Swidler, and Steven M. Tipton. 1985. *Habits of the Heart: Individualism and Commitment in American Life*. New York: Harper and Row.

Berger, Peter L. 1963. *Invitation to Sociology: A Humanistic Perspective.* New York: Doubleday.

Bernard, William S. 1980. "Immigration: history of US policy." In *Harvard Encyclopedia of American Ethnic Groups*, ed. Stephan Thernstrom, pp. 486–95. Cambridge, MA: Belknap Press.

Boyd, R. H. S. 1981. *A Church History of Gujarat.* Madras: Christian Literature Society.

Brown, L. W. 1956. *The Indian Christians of St Thomas: An Account of the Ancient Syrian Church of Malabar.* Cambridge University Press.

Chandramohan, P. 1981. "Christian middle class and their fight for civic rights in Travancore." In *Christian Heritage of Kerala*, ed. K. J. John, pp. 263–83. Cochin, India: George Veliparampil.

Chang, Jonah. 1991. "Movement of self-empowerment: history of the national federation of Asian American United Methodists." In *Churches Aflame: Asian Americans and United Methodism*, ed. Artemio R. Guillermo, pp. 135–53. Nashville: Abingdon Press.

Christiano, Kevin J. 1991. "The church and the new immigrants." In *Religion and the Social Order: Vatican II and US Catholicism*, ed. Helen Rose Ebaugh, vol. II, 169–86. Grenwich, CT: Jai Press, Inc.

Clarke, Colin, Ceri Peach, and Steven Vertovec, eds. 1990. *South Asians Overseas: Migration and Ethnicity.* Cambridge University Press.

Cose, Ellis. 1992. *A Nation of Strangers: Prejudice, Politics, and the Populating of America.* New York: William Morrow and Company, Inc.

Cyril, 1973. "Introduction to the Antiochene rite." In Menachery, 1973: 79–88.

Daniel, David. 1986. *The Orthodox Church of India.* New Delhi: private publisher.

Daniels, Roger. 1989. *History of Indian Immigration to the United States: An Interpretive Essay.* New York: The Asia Society.

1990. *Coming to America: A History of Immigration and Ethnicity in American Life.* New York: Harper Collins Publishers.

Das, Man Singh. 1991. "Sojourners in the land of the free: history of Southern Asian United Methodist Churches." In *Churches Aflame: Asian Americans and United Methodism*, ed. Artemio R. Guillermo, pp. 19–34. Nashville: Abingdon Press.

DeMelo, Carlos Merces. 1982. "The Portuguese padroado in India." In Menachery, 1973: 21–88.

DeSilva, Ranjit. 1980. *Disciplining the Cities in Sri Lanka: A Challenge to the Church Today.* Peradeniya, Sri Lanka: Church Growth Research Center.

Dickinson, Richard D. N. 1971. *The Christian College in Developing India: A Sociological Inquiry.* Oxford University Press.

Downs, Frederick S. 1982. "The Baptists in India." In Menachery,1982: 69.

Dunn, Ashley. 1995. "Skilled Asians leaving US for high-tech jobs at home." *The New York Times*, February 21: A1, A5.

Eriksen, Thomas Hylland. 1993. *Ethnicity and Nationalism: Anthropological Perspectives.* London: Pluto Press.

Fentress, James, and Chris Wickham. 1992. *Social Memory: New Perspectives on the Past*, ed. R. I. Moore. Oxford: Blackwell.

Firth, C. B. 1960. *An Introduction to Indian Church History*. Bangalore: Christian Literature Society.

Glick Schiller, Nina, Linda Basch, and Christina Blanc-Szanton, eds. 1992. *Towards a Transnational Perspective on Migration: Race, Class, Ethnicity, and Nationalism Reconsidered*. Annals of the New York Academy of Sciences, 645. The New York Academy of Sciences.

Goel, Sita Ram, ed. 1988. *Catholic Ashrams: Adopting and Adapting Hindu Dharma*. New Delhi: Voice of India.

Goldberg, Barry. 1992. "Historical reflections on transnationalism, race, and the American immigrant saga." In Glick Schiller *et al.*, 1992: 201–15.

Gordon, Charles, and Stanley Mailman. 1991. *Immigration Law and Procedure: Special Alert, The Immigration Act of 1990*. New York: Matthew Bender.

Gough, Kathleen. 1961. "Nayar: Kerala." In *Matrilineal Kinship*, ed. David Schneider and Kathleen Gough, pp. 298–444. Berkeley: University of California Press.

Grafe, Hugald. 1990. *History of Christianity in India*, vol. iv, part 2: *Tamilnadu in the Nineteenth and Twentieth Centuries*. Bangalore: Church History Association of India.

Griffiths, Bede. 1984. *Christian in India*. Springfield, IL: Templegate.

Guillermo, Artemio R. 1991. "Gathering of the scattered: history of Filipino American United Methodist churches." In *Churches Aflame: Asian Americans and United Methodism*, ed. Artemio R. Guillermo, pp. 91–112. Nashville: Abingdon Press.

Halbwachs, Maurice. 1992. *On Collective Memory*. Translated by Lewis A. Coser. The Heritage of Sociology, ed. Donald N. Levine. University of Chicago Press.

Hansen, Marcus Lee. 1942. *The Immigrant in American History*. Cambridge, MA: Harvard University Press.

Herberg, Will. 1960. *Protestant, Catholic, Jew*. New York: Anchor Books.

Hess, G. R. 1976. "The forgotten Asian Americans: the East Indian community in the United States." In *The Asian Americans: The Historical Experience*, ed. Norris Hundley, pp. 157–88. Santa Barbara, CA: Clio Press.

Higham, John. 1955. *Strangers in the Land: Patterns of American Nativism. 1860-1925*. New Brunswick, NJ: Rutgers University Press.

Hobsbawm, Eric. 1983. "Introduction: inventing traditions." In Hobsbawm and Ranger, 1983: 1–14.

Hobsbawm, Eric, and Terence Ranger, eds. 1983. *The Invention of Tradition*. Cambridge University Press.

Hudson, Winthrop S. 1987. "Denominationalism." In *Encyclopedia of Religion*, ed. Mircea Eliade, vol. iv, 292–8. New York: Macmillan.

Ignatius, Zakka I Iwas, Mar. 1983. *The Syrian Orthodox Church of Antioch at a Glance*. Translated by Emmanuel H. Bismarji. Aleppo: Gregorios Yohannan Ibrahim.

INS (United States Immigration and Naturalization Service) 1991. *Statistical Yearbook of the Immigration and Naturalization Service*.

Jacoby, Harold S. 1979. "Some demographic and social aspects of early East Indian life in the United States." In *Sikh Studies*, ed. Mark Juergensmeyer and N. Gerald Barrier, pp. 159–71. Berkeley: Graduate Theological Union.

Jayasingham, W. L. 1963. "Inter-caste relations in the church of Kerala." *Religion and Society*, 10, 4: 58–78.

Jeffrey, Robert. 1890. *The Indian Mission of the Irish Presbyterian Church: A History of Fifty Years of Work in Kathiawar and Gujarat.* London: Nisbet and Co.

John, K. J., ed. 1981. *Christian Heritage of Kerala.* Cochin, India: George Veliparampil.

Jones, Delmos. 1992. "Which migrants? temporary or permanent?" In Glick Schiller *et al.*, 1992:217–29.

Kelly, Elinor. 1990. "Transcontinental families - Gujarat and Lancashire: a comparative study of social policy." In Clarke *et al.*, 1990:251–67.

Kibria, Nazli. 1993. *Family Tightrope: The Changing Lives of Vietnamese Americans.* Princeton University Press.

King, Gail Buchwalter, ed. 1993. *Fact Book on Theological Education.* Pittsburgh: The Association of Theological Schools.

Kivisto, Peter. 1993. "Religion and the new immigrants." In *A Future for Religion? New Paradigms for Social Analysis,* ed. William H. Swatos, pp. 92–108. Newbury Park, CA: Sage Publications, Inc.

Koiparampil, George. 1982. *Caste in the Catholic Community in Kerala: A Study of Caste Elements in the Inter Rite Relationships of Syrians and Latins.* Cochin, India: St. Francis De Sales Press.

Kollaparambil, Jacob. 1992. *The Babylonian Origin of the Southists among the St. Thomas Christians.* Orientalia Christiana Analecta, 241, ed. Robert F. Taft. Rome: Pontifical Institutum Studiorum Orientalium.

Koshy, Ninan. 1968. *Caste in the Kerala Churches.* Bangalore, India: The Christian Institute for the Study of Religion and Society.

Kosmin, Barry A., and Seymour P. Lachman. 1993. *One Nation under God: Religion in Contemporary American Society.* New York: Harmony Books.

Kurian, Raju. 1979. "Patterns of emigration from Kerala." *Social Scientist*, 78 (January 1979): 32–53.

Kuriedath, Jose. 1989. *Authority in the Catholic Community in Kerala: A Sociological Study of the Changes in the Authority Structure of the Syro-Malabar Church.* Bangalore, India: Dharmaram Publications.

Lee, Sang Hyun. 1980. "Called to be pilgrim: toward a theology within a Korean immigrant context." In *The Korean Immigrant in America*, ed. Byong-suh Kim and Sang Hyun Lee, pp. 76–98. Montclair, NJ: Association of Korean Christian Scholars in North America.

—— 1991. "Korean American Presbyterians: a need for ethnic particularity and the challenge of Christian pilgrimage." In *The Diversity of Discipleship: Presbyterians and Twentieth-century Christian Witness,* ed. Milton J. Coalter, John M. Mulder, and Louis B. Weeks, pp. 312–30. Louisville: Westminster/John Knox Press.

LeRoy, Douglas. n.d. *T. M. Varughese: Without Counting the Cost.* Missionary Hero

Series. Cleveland, TN: Pathway Press.

Lessinger, Johanna. 1992. "Investing or going home? a transnational strategy among Indian immigrants in the United States." In Glick Schiller *et al.*, 1992:53–80.

Mahar, J. Michael, ed. 1972. *The Untouchables in Contemporary India.* Tucson: University of Arizona Press.

Manickam, S. 1988. *Studies in Missionary History: Reflections on a Culture-contact.* Madras: The Christian Literature Society.

Mathew, K. V. 1985. *Faith and Practice of the Mar Thoma Church.* Kottayam, India: Mar Thoma Theological Seminary.

Mattackal, Abraham, ed. 1993. *Mar Thoma Messenger: A Publication of the Diocese of North America and UK,* 12, 4.

McAnally, Thomas S. 1993. "Southern Asian United Methodists gather for second annual convocation." United Methodist News Service. Report no. 356, 10–33–71 (16 August).

McGavran, Donald A. 1971. "People movement." In *Concise Dictionary of the Christian World Mission,* ed. Stephen Neill, Gerald H. Anderson, and John Goodwin, pp. 479–80. Nashville: Abingdon Press.

Meer, Aziza K. 1994. "Immigrants caught between two generations." *News India–Times,* 14 January, p. 49.

Menachery, George, ed. 1973. *The St. Thomas Christian Encyclopaedia of India,* vol. II. Trichūr, India: The St. Thomas Christian Encyclopaedia of India.

  ed. 1982. *The St. Thomas Christian Encyclopaedia of India,* vol. I. Trichūr, India: The St. Thomas Christian Encyclopaedia of India.

Menachery, Maggy G. 1983. "From Tranquebar to the Sepoy mutiny." In Menachery, 1982:41–7.

Moffett, Samuel H. 1992. *History of Christianity in Asia,* vol. I: *Beginnings to 1500.* San Francisco: Harpers.

Mundadan, A. Mathias. 1984. *Indian Christians: Search for Identity and Struggle for Autonomy.* Bangalore: Dharmaram Publications.

  1989. *History of Christianity in India,* vol. I: *From the Beginning up to the Middle of the Sixteenth Century (up to 1542).* Bangalore: Church History Association of India.

n.a. 1966. *The Teachings of the Second Vatican Council: Complete Texts of the Constitutions, Decrees and Declarations.* Westminster, MD: The Newman Press.

n.a. 1984. *Mar Thoma Syrian Church of Malabar Constitution.* Tiruvalla: Mar Thoma Church.

n.a. 1986. *Malankara Orthodox Church: The Catholicate of the East: A Brief Account.* Kottayam, India: Church Publication Department.

n.a. 1993. *Time:* "Special issue: the new face of America." (Fall): 87.

n.a. 1994. *News India–Times,* March 11, p. 3.

Naff, Alixa. 1980. "Arabs." In *Harvard Encyclopedia of American Ethnic Groups,* ed. Stephan Thernstrom, pp. 128–36. Cambridge, MA: Harvard University Press.

Nedumpurath, William. 1984. *Glimpse of Bethany: A Brief History of Bethany Ashram and Bio-data of Bethanians.* Kottayam, India: Bethany Publications.

Nedungatt, George. 1989. "A new era for the church in India." *Vidyajyoti Journal of Theological Reflection*, 53 (January): 15.

Neill, Stephen. 1984. *A History of Christianity in India: The Beginnings to 1707.* Cambridge University Press.

———. 1985. *A History of Christianity in India: 1707–1858.* Cambridge University Press.

Niebuhr, H. Richard. 1929. *Social Sources of Denominationalism.* Camden, CT: Scarecrow Press.

———. 1975. *Christ and Culture.* New York: Harper.

Ninian, Simon. 1993. "Meeting the challenges of the 21st century head on." *Mar Thoma Messenger*, 12 (4): 31.

Nossiter, T. J. 1982. *Communism in Kerala: A Study in Political Adaptation.* Berkeley: University of California Press.

Oosthuizen, G. C. 1975. *Pentecostal Penetration into the Indian Community in Metropolitan Durban, South Africa.* Durban: Human Sciences Research Council.

Petty, Robert. 1985. "The margins of knowledge." In *The Margins of the Humanities*, ed. Eric Dean, pp. 17–34. Crawfordsville, IN: Wabash College.

Podipara, Placid J. 1986. *The Latin Rite Christians of Malabar.* Kottayam, India: Denha Services.

Pothacamury, Thomas. 1958. *The Church in Independent India.* World Horizon Reports, 22. New York: Maryknoll Publications.

Pothan, S. J. 1963. *The Syrian Christians of Kerala.* New York: Asia Publishing House.

Ranaghan, Kevin and Dorothy Ranaghan. 1969. *Catholic Pentecostals.* Paramus, NJ: Paulist Press Deus Books.

Raval, R. L. 1987. *Socio-religious Reform Movements in Gujarat during the Nineteenth Century.* New Delhi: Ess Ess Publications.

Richardson, E. Allen. 1988. *Strangers in this Land: Pluralism and the Response to Diversity in the United States.* New York: The Pilgrim Press.

Rios, Palmira. 1992. "Comments on rethinking migration: a transnational perspective." In Glick Schiller *et al.*, 1992:225–29.

Robinson, Vaughan. 1990. "Boom and gloom: the success and failure of South Asians in Britain." In Clarke *et al.*, 1990:269–96.

Salins, Peter D. 1993. "Take a ticket." *The New Republic: The Immigrants*, 27 December, pp. 13–14.

Samuel, V. T. 1993. "Ordained ministry: traditional patterns and new realities in the Mar Thoma Diocese of North America and UK." *Mar Thoma Messenger* (October). 7–89.

Sandeen, Ernest R. 1970. *The Roots of Fundamentalism: British and American Millenarianism 1800–1930.* University of Chicago Press.

Saran, Parmatma. 1979. "New ethnics: the case of the East Indians in New York City." In *Sourcebook on the New Immigration*, ed. Roy Simon Bryce-Laporte, pp. 303–12. New Brunswick, NJ: Transaction Books.

Segal, Aaron. 1993. *An Atlas of International Migration.* London: Hans Zell Publishers.

Sharma, O. P., and Robert D. Retherford. 1990. *Effect of Female Literacy on Fertility in India.* Delhi: Office of the Registrar General and Census Commissioner, Government of India.

Shin, Eui Hang, and Hyung Park. 1988. "An analysis of causes of schisms in ethnic churches: the case of Korean-American churches." *Sociological Analysis,* 49, 3: 234–48.

Shiri, Godwin, ed. 1985. *Wholeness in Christ: The Legacy of the Basel Mission in India.* Mangalore: The Karnataka Theological Research Institute.

Smith, Timothy L. 1978. "Religion and ethnicity in America." *American Historical Review,* 83 (December): 1155–85.

Sollors, Werner. 1986. *Beyond Ethnicity: Consent and Descent in American Culture.* New York: Oxford University Press.

Stack, John F., ed. 1981. *Ethnic Identities in a Transnational World.* Contributions in Political Science. Westport, CT: Greenwood Press.

Steel, Richard D. 1993. "Immigration category definitions and preference status." In *1993–94 Handbook for Asian Indians in the USA,* n.e., pp. 2–5. Pittsburgh: Spindle Publishing Company.

Stern, Stephen, and John Allan Cicala, eds. 1991. *Creative Ethnicity: Symbols and Strategies of Contemporary Ethnic Life.* Logan: Utah State University Press.

Suria, Carlos. 1990. *History of the Catholic Church in Gujarat.* Anand, India: Gujarat Sahitya Prakash.

Swiderski, Richard Michael. 1988. *Blood Weddings: The Knanaya Christians of Kerala.* Madras: New Era Publications.

Tatford, F. A. 1983. *That the World May Know,* vol. III: *The Challenge of India.* Bath: Echoes of Service.

Thekkedath, Joseph. 1988. *History of Christianity in India,* vol. II: *From the Middle of the Sixteenth to the End of the Seventeenth Century (1542–1700).* Bangalore: Church History Association of India.

Thekkel, John Mathew. 1992. "A brief outline of Kerala history." In *Kerala Directory,* eds. John Mathew and T. A. Mathew, pp. 27–9. Houston: private printing.

Thoma, Alexander Mar. 1986. *The Mar Thoma Church Heritage and Mission.* Houston: T & T Copy and Printing.

Thomas, Annamma, and T. M. Thomas. 1984. *Kerala Immigrants in America: A Sociological Study of the St. Thomas Christians.* Cochin, India: Simons Printers.

Thomas, Anthony Korah. 1993. *The Christians of Kerala: A Brief Profile of All Major Churches.* Kottayam, India: D. C. Offset Printers.

Thomas, M. A. 1977. *An Outline History of Christian Churches and Denominations in Kerala.* Trivandrum, India: n. p.

Thomas, T. J. 1978. "The shepherding perspective of Seward Hiltner on pastoral care and its application in the organizing of a congregation in Dallas of East Indian immigrants from the Mar Thoma Syrian Church of India." Doctor of the Ministry Thesis, Dallas: Southern Methodist University.

Tomlinson, B. R. 1993. *The Economy of Modern India, 1860–1970*, vol. iii.3. The New Cambridge History of India, ed. Gordon Johnson. Cambridge University Press.

Ucko, Hans. 1994. "Expectations from BAAR I to BAAR II." *Current Dialogue* (June): 3–9.

United Nations Population Fund. 1993. *The Individual and the World: Population, Migration and Development in the 1990s: The State of World Population 1993*. New York: United Nations.

US Bureau of the Census. 1991. "Census Bureau press release." June 12, 1991, Table 1.

Verghese, Hebel G. 1974. *K. E. Abraham: An Apostle from Modern India*. Kadambanad: Christian Literature Service of India.

Verghese, Paul. 1973. "The Syrian Orthodox Church." In Menachery, 1973:79f.

Vijayanunni, V., ed. 1985. *Census of India*, Series 10, paper 1: "Household population by religion of head of household." Delhi: Government of India.

Warner, R. Stephen. 1993. "Work in progress toward a new paradigm for the sociological study of religion in the United States." *American Journal of Sociology*, 98, 5, (March): 1044–93.

Wattenburg, Ben. 1991. *The First Universal Nation: Leading Indicators and Ideas about the Surge of America in the 1990s*. New York: Free Press.

Webster, John C. B. 1992. *A History of the Dalit Christians in India*. San Francisco: Mellen Research University Press.

Wiebe, Paul. 1970. "Protestant missions in India: a sociological review." *Journal of Asian and African Studies*, 5: 293–301.

Wiebe, Paul D, and S. John-Peter. 1977. "The Catholic church and caste in rural Tamil Nadu." In *Caste among Non-Hindus in India*, ed. Harjinder Singh, pp. 37–49. New Delhi: National Publishing House.

Willetts, Peter, ed. 1982. *Pressure Groups in the Global System: The Transnational Relations of Issue-orientated Non-governmental Organizations*. New York: St. Martin's Press.

Williams, Raymond Brady. 1984. *A New Face of Hinduism: The Swarninarayam Religion*. Cambridge University Press.

1986. "Translating Indian Christianity to the United States." *The Christian Century*, October 19: 927–8.

1988. *Religions of Immigrants from India and Pakistan*. Cambridge University Press.

1992. "Sacred threads of several textures: strategies of adaptation in the United States." In *A Sacred Thread: Modern Transmission of Hindu in India and Abroad*, ed. Raymond Brady Williams, pp. 228–57. Chambersburg, PA: Anima Publications.

Index

Abdulla, Patriarch, 67
Abraham, K. E., 52
Abraham, Mar, 64–5
adivasi, *see* caste
Ahatalla, 65
Ahmedabad, 35, 81, 111
Alabama, 31
Alma College, 123
American Association of Bible Colleges, 255
Andhra Pradesh, 14, 82, 84, 87, 157, 255
Anglo-Indians, 69,
Antioch, Patriarch of, 52, 62, 65–8, 71–2, 112, 115
Antiochene liturgy, 66, 71
archdeacon of the St. Thomas Christians, 65
Arcot Mission of the Reformed Church, 80
Ashland University, Ohio, 162
Asiatic Barred Zone, 22
Assam, 255
Assemblies of God, in India, 84;
    in North America, 161, 163, 166, 169, 256
Assemblies of God Fellowship in the Northeast, 169
Association of Theological Schools in North America, 254–5
Athanasius, Geevarghese Mar, 133, 135
Atlanta, 176–7
Australia, 231

Babylon, Patriarch of, 62, 65
Baptist churches, 6;
    in India, 75, 79, 82–3, 87;
    in North America, 99, 108, 172, 176–8, 256
Baptist Convention of the State of Georgia of
    the Southern Baptist Convention, 176
Barnabas, Mathews Mar, 122–32
Basel Mission, 52, 76, 79, 87
Baselius, Cyril Mar, 148
Basilica of Bom Jesus, 60
Bellah, Robert, 97,
Bellerose, New York, 129

Bellwood, Illinois, 145
Berger, Peter, 219
Bernardin, Joseph Cardinal, 145
Bethany Ashram, *see* Order of the Imitation of
    Christ
Bible colleges, 8
Bihar, 88
Bombay, 78, 123
Boston, 119, 121
Boston, University, 121, 140, 252–3, 255
Brahmins, Nambudiri, 54–5, 89
brain-drain, 8, 9, 13, 31, 90, 131
Brethren Assemblies (Plymouth Brethren), 5,
    in India, 52–3, 82–3;
    in North America, 135, 155–61, 172, 200, 213
British Columbia, 30
British East India Company, 73, 78, 82
Brooklyn, New York, 129, 146, 162, 164
Buffalo, New York, 123, 128
Bulsar, Gujarat, 52, 81, 175

Cabral, Pedro Alvares, 59
Calcutta, 78–9
Calicut (Kozhikode), 58–9, 79
California, 25, 26, 32
Cambridge University, 210
Campus Crusade for Christ, 200, 268–9
Canada, 118, 128, 230–1
career selection, 219–20
Carey, William, 51, 82
Carmelite Order, 65
caste, 54–5, 69, 72, 74–5, 87–90, 119–21, 149;
    Nambudiri Brahmins, 54–5, 89;
    adivasi, 184–5;
    dalit, 101, 154, 184–5
Catholic Bishops' Conference of India, 70
Catholic Charismatic Movement, 53, 86, 150;
    see also National Service Team for Catholic
    Charismatic Renewal in India
Catholicos of the East, 55–6, 67–8;
    in Kerala, 124–5, 130, 248

299